Dictionary of
English Phrasal Verbs
and their Idioms

Dictionary of English Phrasal Verbs and their Idioms

Tom McArthur and Beryl Atkins

Collins: London and Glasgow

Also available from Collins in the Patterns of English series
Building English Words
Using English Prefixes and Suffixes
Using Compound Words
*Using Phrasal Verbs
Learning Rhythm and Stress
Using Modal Verbs
Times, Tenses and Conditions

First published in 1974
Fourth Impression 1978
© Tom McArthur and Beryl Atkins
ISBN 0 00 325267 1
Printed in Great Britain
Collins Clear-Type Press

Introduction

1 The Problem

Phrasal verbs look simple enough. They are, usually, combinations of simple, monosyllabic verbs (put, take, get etc.) and members of a set of particles (on, up, out etc.). The combination is nowadays called phrasal because, on paper, it presents the appearance of a two-word phrase rather than a single item. Although it looks like a phrase, it functions in many respects like a single word, although under certain conditions other items (direct objects, adverbs) can come between verb and particle.

It is probably true that the children of English-speaking people learn phrasal verbs earlier than any other kind of verb, and that foreign learners seldom master them under current teaching conditions. The problem is four-fold:

a   A verb of this type may have a meaning which is simply the sum of its parts, but may also have a meaning which bears little apparent relation to those parts.
b   The particle may indicate some kind of direction but may just as easily have a meaning little related to direction.
c   The same particle can serve as a preposition or adverb and a student can easily confuse these functions.
d   There are so many phrasal verbs in modern English (and the number is constantly growing), they are so important in the spoken language, and they have so many shades of meaning that the student may despair of ever mastering this area of language. This situation has been aggravated by the lack of a good description of the phrasal verb, and by a shortage of useful teaching material.

This dictionary, with its companion workbook, is based on a systematic study of the phrasal verb undertaken by Tom McArthur for Collins in 1970, in connection with the preparation of the Collins bilingual dictionaries. It reflects the belief of the authors that these verbs are far more consistent in their behaviour and far more teachable than is generally supposed.

2 Phrasal Verbs

Phrasal verbs are mainly colloquial. They are used casually, in everyday speech, or in order to express vivid, emotional and frequently slangy points, to conjure up special metaphoric relationships and jokes and to label actions in such everyday areas as cooking, gardening, maintaining the car, repairing things and shopping. Similarly, they occur widely in the technical languages of artisans and technicians, and are beginning to make inroads into sciences which have until recently depended upon Latin and Greek for their terminologies. Computer science, economics and statistics are cases in point. Being mainly Anglo-Saxon in origin, phrasal verbs still function as part of the familiar, informal stream of English vocabulary. They are frequently used in preference to verbs of Classical origin which have similar meanings but unsuitable overtones of formality, pomposity or difficulty. You would expect someone to tell you that they climbed down (a ladder etc.) rather than descended; that they have learnt to put up with their mother-in-law rather than to tolerate her.

At least 6 types of verb can be phrasalised:

a   verbs of movement (usually monosyllabic and of Anglo-Saxon origin): **go, come, run, walk, hop, skip** etc.

b   verbs of invitation and ordering etc.: **invite, order, summon, let** etc.

c   the so-called 'empty verbs' or verbs of indefinite meaning: **get, put, take, make, do** etc.

d   verbs formed with or without the suffix -en, from simple monosyllabic adjectives: **brighten, slacken, flatten, dry, cool** etc.

e   verbs formed unchanged from simple, usually monosyllabic nouns with such paraphrase patterns as:
    chalk up = mark up with chalk
    brick up = seal up with brick

f   a random scattering of two-syllable verbs of Latin origin, with which some kind of direction or emphasis is required: **contract** (out), **measure** (up), **level** (off) etc.

3 The Dictionary

This dictionary has been compiled to assist foreign learners of English who have reached at least an Intermediate level of competence in English. That is to say, they have mastered the basic sentence patterns of the language and have an active vocabulary of 3,000 words plus. The student will find this book most valuable when used in conjunction with its companion workbook in Collins 'Patterns of English' series – 'Using Phrasal Verbs'. However it is also suitable for use as a general reference book in the classroom and library.

The body of entries in the dictionary is based on a study of the previous relevant work in this field, supplemented by the results of discussion with both foreign and native speakers of English. Because of the many meanings and uses for such compositions as **put up** and **take down,** some commentators have argued that each sense should be treated as a distinct verb: that it is better to regard **put up,** for example, as a set of homonyms rather than as one varied item. The compilers of this dictionary do not adopt this view, but argue that differences of meaning occur within a continuum of meaning, beginning with the simple verb + particle and ranging through to the more opaque idioms. Such verbs are unique blends of syntax, semantics and idiom, and are dealt with here as so many themes and variations. No claims are made to exhaustiveness either in the number of the verbs covered or in the number of senses identified for any verb.

Since a large number of phrasal forms are simply the grammatical operation of verbs of movement plus particles of direction, the dictionary lists such verbs as special entries, each marked with an asterisk, and followed by a gloss and one or more illustrative sentences, e.g.:

*move+particle (*move, with direction*) 1 vi They bought a new house and moved in immediately. Our neighbours have begun to move out. The people moved aside to allow the procession past ...

The gloss is not meant to be a 'definition' of the verb in the ordinary dictionary sense. The gloss for a particular entry is meant to be read together with the illustrative sentences to show the area of meaning occupied by the verb. Apart from the common words which are assumed to be known at this stage e.g. move, take, put etc., the gloss supplies, as far as possible, grammatical equivalents which can replace the phrasal verb in the sentence. Occasionally the equivalent is not a perfect match, because the verb may be unique in that sense. It should also be noted that in most instances when a phrasal verb such as **move up** is glossed by a more latinate verb *promote*, the latter does not possess the same features of informality, familiarity, and vividness as the phrasal verb.

Each entry provides the following information about the verb:
- a classification of the verb type
- an indication of the fields and/or style of language in which certain verbs may be used
- a gloss
- one or more illustrative sentences
- a reference to derived verbs, adjectives, nouns and idioms where relevant.

A Classification

All verbs are initially classified as transitive (*vt*) or intransitive (*vi*); that is, as to whether they take a direct object or not.

Transitive verbs are next divided into separable verbs (*sep*) and fused verbs (*fus*).

Separable Verbs

Verbs which are separable are those which, under certain conditions, may have an item inserted between the verb and particle. These conditions are as follows:

If the object of a separable phrasal verb is a noun, the particle may precede or follow the noun.
e.g. He picked the book up.   OR   He picked up the book.

If, however, the object is a pronoun, the particle must follow it:
e.g. He picked it up.
The vast majority of phrasal verbs are in this category.

Fused Verbs

A fused verb is not normally separated by an item or items coming between the verb and the particle. The particle in a fused phrasal verb has in effect been 'stolen' from another phrase. The result is a special idiom and the fused structure should be spoken and thought of as a unit.

e.g. The man came across//his friend.
     contrast with
     The man came//across the street.

Fused phrasal verbs are more difficult to isolate for inclusion in a dictionary than separable phrasal verbs. There appear to be varying degrees of 'fusedness' between certain verbs and certain particles. This is particularly true when an intransitive phrasal verb (such as **keep on** in the sense of *continue*) is followed by such a preposition as **at**. In some instances it makes more sense to treat these as phrasal verbs followed by an unattached preposition, while in other metaphoric instances it is best to take them as a fused whole. We have done this for the expression **keep on at** when it is taken to mean *nag*.

Placing Adverbs with Phrasal Verbs The rules for using adverbs with phrasal verbs relate to whether the phrasal verb is intransitive or transitive.

a Intransitive rule: place the adverb either BETWEEN the verb and the particle, or AFTER the particle.
    e.g. He ran away.
         He ran happily away.
         OR He ran away happily.
b Transitive rule: place the adverb either BEFORE the verb, or AFTER the object or particle, whichever comes last.
    e.g. She picked the letter up.
         She eagerly picked the letter up.
         OR She picked the letter up eagerly.
         OR She picked up the letter eagerly.

B Field and Style Labels

In the gloss of verbs whose use tends to be restricted there are indicators of these restrictions. For example, the entry **add up** 1 *vi* (*a*) (*Math: total*) shows that the verb can be used when talking about mathematics where it has the meaning *total*. Similarly **billow out** *vi* (*a*) (*Naut: swell or belly out*) shows that this verb is used in talking about nautical matters, i.e. sailing. *Math* or *Naut* are **Field Labels.**

Equally important are the indicators which show the style or tone of the language situation in which the verb is used. For example **buck up** 1 *vi* (*a*) (*Sl: be or become more cheerful*) makes clear that this verb is slang usage and therefore not suitable for use in writing an academic essay or for formal speech. The abbreviation *Sl* is therefore a **Style Label.**

A complete list of the Field and Style Labels used in the dictionary can be found in the list of abbreviations following this introduction.

4 Acknowledgements

The list of verbs and the classification adopted here have also served as the basis for entering phrasal verbs and their translation equivalents in the Collins bilingual dictionaries (English to French, German, Italian and Swahili).

Additionally, the material was developed for teaching purposes in the 1970–72 classes of English for foreigners conducted by the Department of Educational Studies, the University of Edinburgh. We would like to thank Dr John Lowe, head of that department, for his co-operation.

The typing of the fair copy was a remarkable achievement on the part of Alwyn Cooper.

It is customary to mention long-suffering spouses at this point. We should like to congratulate both an indoctrinated wife and a faintly sceptical husband for coming through 3,000 phrasal verbs almost unscathed.

Abbreviations used in this book

The special labels used with the glosses are guides to how and in what situations a particular phrasal verb is used.

a Field Labels

Arith	arithmetic
Aut	automobile, driving
Aviat	aviation
Biol	biology
Chem	chemistry
Cine	cinema
Comm	commerce
Elec	electricity, electronics
Fin	finance
Geol	geology
Ind	industry
Math	mathematics
Med	medicine
Met	meteorology, the weather
Mil	military
Mus	music
Naut	nautical matters, the sea, sailing
Parl	parliamentary usage
Phot	photography
Pol	politics
Tec	technology, crafts
Tel	telecommunications
TV	television
Stat	statistics
Theat	the theatre

b Style Labels

Euph	euphemistic
Fam	familiar, informal, very colloquial
Lit	literal, basic, physical, observable
Pej	pejorative, debasing, insulting
Sl	slang
Vulg	vulgar

c Grammatical Terms

adj	adjective
fus	fused, not separable (see Introduction p. 7)
imper	imperative
n	noun
neg	negative
n cpd	noun compound. For the purposes of this dictionary this is a combination of two nouns. e.g., **a cattle round-up, a getaway car, a takeover bid**
n phr	noun phrase. For the purpose of this dictionary this is a combination of adjective + noun, e.g., **a nervous breakdown, a medical check-up, a funny setup**
pass	passive
sep	separable, *may* be separated (see Introduction, p. 7)
vi	intransitive verb
vt	transitive verb

d Other Abbreviations

Brit	British usage
Dial	dialect usage
emph	emphatic
impers	impersonal
orig	originally
partic	particularly
Scot	Scottish usage
US	American usage
usu	usually

Dictionary of English Phrasal Verbs and their Idioms

abide by *vt fus* *(keep to, adhere to)* I expect him to abide by his decision to help us. She will abide by her promise.

act out *vt sep* *(act in full, present in a theatrical way)* He acted out all that had happened to him. In group therapy, patients can act out their problems.

act (up)on *vt fus* *(do something definite about)* You should act upon this letter at once, or it will be too late.

act up *vi* *(a)* *(Fam: behave badly)* The children have been acting up all day, and I'm exhausted. *(b)* *(Fam: perform erratically)* My car has started acting up and badly needs servicing.

add in *vt sep* *(insert)* Would you add in these items, please, in order to complete the list?

add on *vt sep* *(add as an extra or extras)* Would you please add these names on (to your list)? Add the other items on at the bottom of the page.

add together *vt sep* *(intensive of* **add***)* He added the numbers together.

add up 1 *vi* *(a)* *(Math: total)* These figures don't add up right. *(b)* *(Fig Fam: make sense)* It all adds up, I can see now why he left so suddenly. Nothing he does seems to add up. 2 *vt sep* *(a)* *(Lit: total)* They added up several columns of figures. *(b)* *(Fig: assess)* They added up all the advantages and disadvantages and tried to come to a decision.

add up to *vt fus* *(a)* *(Math: amount to)* The money he spent added up to more than £1,000. *(b)* *(Fig: signify, indicate)* The evidence all adds up to a case of murder.

admit of *vt fus* *(leave room for)* This work admits of no delay.

agree with *vt fus* *(a)* *(have same opinion as)* I can't agree with you in this matter. *(b)* *(coincide with)* His explanation agrees with the facts of the situation. *(c)* *(suit the health of)* The climate of southern France agrees with me. Rich food doesn't agree with her. (*d*) (*Fam: approve of*) I don't agree with people drinking brandy all day long. (*e*) (*Gram: of verb, adjective etc.*) A verb always agrees with its subject.

*allow + particle *vt sep* (*permit, with direction*) The doorman allowed the people in one by one. They allowed me out in order to make a telephone call. The doctor allows her up for two hours each day, because she has made such excellent progress.

allow for *vt fus* (*take account of, make concession for*) You should allow for his poor eyesight. The company will allow for extra expenditure next year. When making up this kind of material, you should allow for shrinkage (in the wash).

allow of=admit of.

*amble + particle *vi* (*walk slowly and gently, with direction*) The cows ambled along, chewing gently. He ambled up to me and asked what time it was.

answer back 1 *vi* (*reply insolently*) Don't answer back like that! The little boy answered back cheekily to his father. 2 *vt sep* (*reply insolently to*) The little boy answered his father back several times.

answer for *vt fus* (*a*) (*be responsible for*) You must answer for any missing articles after the party. They have a lot to answer for and must have uneasy consciences. (*b*) (*guarantee*) I will answer for the truth of his statements. He can answer for his son's behaviour.

answer to *vt fus* (*correspond to, be in accord with*) A man answering to the police description was arrested in London last night.

ante up (*Fam: from poker*) 1 *vi* (*a*) (*Lit: make an initial stake*) They anted up and started to play. (*b*) (*Fig: contribute a sum of money*) The government anted up to the tune of 20 million pounds. 2 *vt fus* (*a*) (*Lit: stake, in order to start a game*) They each anted up ten dollars. (*b*) (*Fig: contribute*) The government anted up £20 million as its share in the project. (*c*) (*Fig: pay*) They finally anted up 400 dollars for the use of the premises.

argue away 1 *vi* (*argue continuously*) They sometimes argue away for hours. 2 *vt sep* (*dismiss with a plausible argument*) He tried to argue the matter away. You can't argue away this problem.

argue down *vt sep* (*silence through argument*) They argued him down fiercely.

argue out *vt sep* (*argue to a satisfactory result*) They intend to argue the whole problem out tomorrow night.

*ask + particle (*invite, with direction*) We asked them in for coffee.   They asked us over for dinner.   I'll never ask her out again, her tastes are too expensive!

ask after   *vt fus*   *(seek information about, in a sympathetic way)* They were asking after you, and I told them you were very well. She asked after the children.

ask for   *vt fus*   (a) *(request)* He asked for the money.   (b)=**ask after**.   (c) *Idioms:*   (i) to ask for trouble=to invite trouble unnecessarily.   (ii) He asked for it!=This is the trouble he invited!   *Example:* She had been teasing the dog for weeks, and I'm not surprised it bit her—she certainly asked for it.

*assist + particle   *(help, with direction)* They assisted him in from the street and laid him on the bed.   She assisted the old man out.

attend (up)on   *vt fus*   *(Old: serve)* The courtiers attended upon the king.

auction off   *vt sep*   *(sell by auction)* They auctioned off all the paintings last week.

average out   1 *vi*   *(reach an average)* His taxes should average out at about one quarter of his income.   2 *vt sep*   *(make or calculate the average of)* They averaged out the numbers and got the result 7·5.

average out at   *vt fus*   *(be averaged at)* Their working hours average out at 40 per week.   His weekly earnings average out at £35.

average up   *vt sep*   *(raise to meet the average)* They averaged up the wages of the lower-paid workers.

babble away   *vi*   *(babble, chatter continuously)* The children sometimes babble away for hours.   He babbled away about his problems.

babble on   *vi*   *(continue babbling, usu unpleasantly)* She babbled on about her problems.   He was babbling on about his golf score.

babble out   *vt sep*   *(say or emit in a babble of words)* In his fear, he babbled out the names of his accomplices.   She babbled out something I couldn't understand.

back away   1 *vi*   *(retreat)* The frightened horse backed away from the snake.   2 *vt sep*   *(reverse away)* He backed the lorry away, so that we could get into the garage.

back down   *vi*   (a) *(descend backwards)* He backed down carefully, while I held the ladder for him.   The car at the top of the slope backed slowly down.   (b) *(Fig Fam: give way, yield)* He backed down and accepted our proposals.   The trade union expects the management to back down.   They are too proud to back down and admit mistakes.

back on to   *vt fus*   *(be neighbour to, at the back)* The house backs on to a market garden.

back out 1 *vi* (*a*) (*go out backwards*) The courtiers backed out (of the royal presence). He backed out when the dog came towards him. The truck backed out of the narrow lane. (*b*) (*Fig: withdraw*) He has decided to back out (of the scheme). I think they will back out when they see how much it will cost. 2 *vt sep* (*bring out backwards*) He backed the car out (of the garage).

back up 1 *vi* (*move up backwards*) The trucks backed up as far as possible to make room for the others. 2 *vt sep* (*a*) (*move up backwards*) They backed the trucks up as much as possible, to make room for the others. (*b*) (*Fig Fam: support*) I hope you will back me up in this argument. He always backs up his friends. Nobody backed her up when she protested against the decision. I'll back your story up, if they ask me about it.

bail out *vt sep* (*a*) (*Law: pay money as a surety for*) His brother bailed him out (of prison). He was bailed out. (*b*) (*Fig: help in an emergency*) I hope someone will bail me out of this.

bale out 1 *vi* (*a*) (*Aviat: leave by parachute*) The crew baled out (of the blazing plane). We shall have to bale out soon. (*b*) (*Sailing: expel incoming water*) They baled out desperately, to stop the boat sinking. 2 *vt sep* (*empty out*) You must bale out the water in the bottom of the boat or we will sink.

ball up *vt sep* (*a*) (*make round*) He balled up the clay in his hand. (*b*) (*Sl: spoil, ruin*) It was his fault that the scheme failed, he balled up the whole thing.

band together *vi* (*join together in a band or group*) They banded together to defend themselves.

bandage up *vt sep* (*bandage, bind as fully as possible*) She bandaged up the wound. In the hospital they bandaged up his arm.

bandy about/around/round *vt sep* (*Fam: pass about, spread around, usu in an unsatisfactory way*) I don't like my name being bandied about by all the gossips in town. The story is being bandied about that you are going to leave.

*bang + particle 1 *vi* (*Fam: move with a banging noise, with direction*) The boys banged about upstairs. She banged off angrily to her room. The old car was banging along. 2 *vt sep* (*put or fix with banging noise, with direction*) He banged the book down on the table. She banged it back on the shelf and walked out angrily. He banged the box away and closed the drawer. He banged in the nail with a hammer.

bang away 1 *vi* (*a*) *see* ***bang** (*b*) (*Fam: shoot continuously*) The soldiers were banging away at the target. 2 *vt sep* *see* ***bang**.

bang into *vt fus* (*a*) (*collide with*) He banged into a bus on the high street. The car banged into a wall. (*b*) (*Fig Fam: meet by* *chance*) I didn't expect to bang into him again.   You never know who you're going to bang into in this place.

bang out 1 *vi* *see* *****bang** 2 *vt sep* (*a*) *see* *****bang** (*b*) (*produce noisily*) He banged out an article on the typewriter.   She banged out a tune on the piano.

bank up *vt sep* (*support, usu with banks*) They are banking up the whole terrace, to prevent it collapsing.   The sides of the canal have been banked up with concrete.   He banked up the fire before he went to bed.

bank (up)on *vt fus* (*Fam: count on, depend on*) I'm banking on you to help us.   Can we bank upon this promise?   Don't bank upon any money from me.

bar in *vt sep* (*lock in with bars*) She barred herself in so no one could get at her.

bar out *vt sep* (*lock out or exclude with bars*) He barred the men out by bolting both doors and windows.

bar up *vt sep* (*block with bars*) The basement windows were barred up against burglars.

bargain away 1 *vi* (*bargain or haggle continuously*) The men in the bazaar often bargain away for hours. 2 *vt sep* (*lose through bargaining*) He bargained away the property.   They have bargained away all hope of success.

bargain for *vt fus* (*Fam: expect*) I didn't bargain for what happened.   This is not what I bargained for at all.   When he challenged them, he didn't bargain for such a humiliating defeat.

*****barge + particle** *vi* (*Fam: blunder or charge clumsily, with direction*) They barged off to find a pub.   The boys barged about, making a lot of noise.   I wish you would stop barging in without knocking.

barge in *vi* (*a*) *see* *****barge** (*b*) (*Fig Fam: interrupt*) I hope you don't mind me barging in like this.   He always barges in on other people's conversations.

bark out *vt sep* (*shout out in a sharp or barking voice*) The sergeant barked out his orders.

barricade in *vt sep* (*enclose with barriers*) They have barricaded the whole area in.   The street was barricaded in.   He has barricaded himself in with a shotgun and two hostages.

bash about/around *vt sep* (*Fam: beat physically*) He bashes his wife about.   The child has been badly bashed about.

bash in *vt sep* (*a*) (*dent, usu severely*) The top of the box has been bashed in.   (*b*) (*Fam: batter, beat in*) The gang bashed in his head.

bash up *vt sep* (*smash badly*) He has bashed up his car. The gang bashed up his face. They said they would bash me up if I went to the police.

batter about/around=**bash about.**

batter down *vt sep* (*knock down with heavy blows*) The men have battered down the door.

batter in *vt sep* (*knock in by battering*) The men have battered in the door. The murderer battered in his victim's head.

battle on *vi* (*fight on, continue to do battle*) (*a*) (*Lit*) The army must battle on. (*b*) (*Fig*) We must battle on against all opposition. The ship battled on against the gale.

bawl out 1 *vi* (*shout out loudly and raucously*) The steer bawled out in pain. 2 *vt sep* (*a*) (*shout out loudly and raucously*) The man bawled out his commands. He bawled out the news. (*b*) (*Fig Fam: reprimand*) The colonel bawled us all out·for inefficiency. *Idiom:*— a bawling-out=a severe reprimand.

*be + particle *vi* (*be, with location*) Oh, if you're looking for her, she's about somewhere. If you want to see him, he's always in at six p.m. They are up in the attic, looking at some old pictures. He's down in the cellar, getting some coal. She's away in London at the moment. I'm afraid he's out, and won't be back till about midnight.

be about *vi* (*a*) *see* ***be** (*b*) (*tense use + infinitive*=*be going to do in the near future*) He is about to go to work. She was about to phone you when you came in. (*c*) (*be doing*) What is he about now? I wish I knew just what they were about.

be above *vi* (*a*) *see* ***be** (*b*) (*Fig: be superior to*) He is above such petty things. She thinks she is above criticism. He is not above stealing to get what he wants.

be after *vt fus* (*want, seek*) He is after promotion. I think she's after him, and not his friend. What are they after?

be along *vi* (*a*) *see* ***be** (*b*) (*Fam: appear, arrive*) He'll be along in a moment. Please have a seat, someone will be along soon.

be at *vt fus* (*a*) (*Fig Fam: nag*) She's at him all the time about his behaviour. (*b*) (*Fig Fam: be occupied with, be doing*) He's at it again. They're hard at it, trying to get finished before nightfall. She's at this job day and night. (*c*) (*US Sl: be happening*) This is where it's at, man.

be away *vi* (*a*) *see* ***be** (*b*) (*exclamation on departure of vehicle or aeroplane etc*) It's away! They're away! (*c*) *Idiom:* to be away with the fairies=to be slightly mad, to be rather eccentric. (*d*) (*Fig: be detached or transported mentally*) She's away in a world of her own. He's away somewhere.

be back *vi* (*a*) *see* ***be** (*b*) (*Fam: return*) I'll be back in a few minutes.

be behind 1 *vi* (*a*) *see* ***be** (*b*) (*be late or delayed*) I'm rather behind today (with my work/with the schedule). They are behind with their rent/payments. (*c*) (*be slow or retarded*) He's rather behind in his work at school. I'm afraid she's behind in her arithmetic. 2 *vt fus* (*Fig: be slow in relation to, be less capable than*) He's behind the others in his work.

be below *vi* (*a*) *see* ***be** (*b*) (*Naut: be below deck*) The captain is below.

be beneath *vt fus* (*be too undignified/vulgar for*) He thinks it is beneath him to speak to ordinary workers.

be by *vi* (*a*) *see* ***be** (*b*) (*come near or past, pass by*) He'll be by in a moment and you can ask him yourself.

be down *vi* (*a*) *see* ***be** (*b*) (*specifically, be down from a bedroom*) She'll be down in a moment. (*c*) (*Fig: be depressed, ill*) He's a bit down just now. She's down with 'flu.

be down for *vt fus* (*have one's name down in a register for*) We are down for a new council house. He's down for promotion.

be down on *vt fus* (*be critical of, be antagonistic towards*) I'm afraid they are rather down on him at the moment. She has always been down on them since they complained about her.

be for *vt fus* (*a*) (*be in favour of*) I'm for the Conservatives, but she's for the Socialists. (*b*) (*be going to, be heading for*) I'm for the hills this vacation! (*c*) (*be used for*) It is for eating. This gadget is for opening letters. (*d*) (*Fam: be due for trouble or a reprimand*) Hey, you're for it, mate! You'll be for it if they catch you. *Idiom:* to be for the high jump (if found out or caught) = (*i*) *Orig*, to be condemned to death by hanging. (*ii*) *Now*, to be due for a severe punishment or reprimand.

be in *vi* (*a*) *see* ***be** (*b*) (*specifically, to be at home or in one's office, etc*) She's in. He's in, but he's busy. (*c*) (*come in, arrive*) He'll be in shortly. The train will be in any minute now. (*d*) (*be elected or assigned to a post*) Their candidate is in. He's in now, and can get on with the job. (*e*) (*be in place or position*) The nails are in, so we can finish the work. The furniture's in, and the new house is beginning to look like home. (*f*) *Idiom:* to be all in = to be exhausted.

be in for *vt fus* (*be due for, be in line for*) They are in for promotion. She is in for a surprise/shock. He'll be in for trouble if he goes on like this.

be in on *vt fus* (*be party to, be fully involved in*) He is in on the whole sordid business. They were definitely in on the conspiracy. I'm sure she's in on their plans.

be in with *vt fus* (*be in favour with, be friendly with*) He is in with her at the moment. She's (well) in with those people.

be off 1 *vi* (*a*) *see* ***be** (*b*) (*specifically, to leave*) He's off now. Well, I'm off! They are off to London tomorrow. (*c*) (*be cancelled*) I'm afraid the meeting's off. The whole scheme is off. (*d*) (*be unavailable*) The waitress told them that chicken was off. (*e*) (*to have gone bad*) The meat's off, don't eat it. (*f*) (*cry at race meeting*) They're off! 2 *vt fus* (*a*) (*be prevented from eating etc*) He's been off alcohol since his illness. (*b*) (*dislike*) I'm off eggs just now, I ate so many last week. She's off Bill now, she likes John better.

be on *vi* (*a*) *see* ***be** (*b*) (*be fixed for a specific time*) The meeting is on. The party is on again, in spite of the problems. (*c*) (*Fam, in betting: I accept your wager or challenge*) Okay, you're on! (*d*) (*Neg: be impossible, unacceptable*) Your suggestion is just not on, it's too expensive.

be on at *vt fus* = **be at** (*a*).

be on to *vt fus* (*be on the track of, be aware of*) I think the police are on to his little game. The tax authorities will soon be on to your trick.

be out *vi* (*a*) *see* ***be** (*b*) (*specifically, be out of the house or office etc*) She's out, and I don't know when she'll be back. I'm afraid he's out. (*c*) (*be impossible*) What you suggest is quite out (of the question). It's out, I'm afraid. (*d*) (*be revealed, made public*) The news is out now. The scandal is out for all to see. (*e*) (*be published*) His book is out. (*f*) (*be blossoming*) The flowers are out. (*g*) (*be on strike*) All the workers are out.

be out for *vt fus* (*be seeking*) He's just out for his personal gain. Those boys are out for trouble. He's out for everything he can get.

be out of *vt fus* (*a*) (*have no*) The shops are out of bread. They are completely out of milk. I'm afraid I'm quite out of money. (*b*) (*be safely away from*) She is out of that place now. They are out of danger. *Idioms:* (*i*) to be out of harm's way = to be safely away from danger. (*ii*) to be well out of something = to be safely uninvolved. *Example:* He's well out of that friendship, they had a bad influence on one another. (*iii*) to be out of reach = to be beyond the reach of someone, to be beyond the influence of someone. (*iv*) to be out of luck = to have no luck at all.

be over *vi* (*a*) *see* ***be** (*b*) (*specifically, to be flying or moving over*) The bombers will be over soon, so we had better make for the shelters. (*c*) (*specifically, to come over or across*) He'll be over in a few minutes. The doctor will be over as soon as he can.

(d) (*Fam: be finished, be at an end*) The play's over. Well, it's all over now. I can hardly believe it's all over. It's over and done with. (e) (*Sport: beyond the barrier, above the barrier etc*) The ball's over! The horse is over and still going strong.

be through *vi* (*be finished*) She said they were through, and she'd give him back his ring.

be through with *vt fus* (*be finished with*) She says she's through with men forever. I think he is through with that particular job.

be up *vi* (a) *see* *be (b) (*specifically, to be out of bed*) He's up now. They are usually up by this time. (c) (*specifically, be up from a lower level*) He's down in the cellar, but he'll be up in a few minutes. (d) (*Fam, of period of time: be finished*) Time's up, I'm afraid. Your half-hour is up, you must bring in the boat now. When three days were up he returned to town. *Idioms:* (i) The game's up=you cannot pretend any longer, you can't succeed now (ii) It's all up with him=there is no hope for him.

be up against *vt fus* (*be faced with, be confronted with, be afflicted with*) He is up against very tough opposition in his work. She is up against it, now that her husband has died.

be up and about *vi* (a) (*be active*) He's up and about every morning at dawn. (b) (*specifically, be active after an illness*) Yes, she's up and about again.

be up to *vt fus* (a) (*be engaged, usu secretly, in*) I wonder what they are up to. I expect he's up to something (mischievous). Those boys are always up to something. (b) (*be able to, feel well enough to*) He has done that work very badly, I'm afraid he's just not up to it. She is getting better but still isn't up to going out yet.

be well up in *vt fus* (*be expert in, be well versed in*) She's well up in her subject.

*bear + particle *vt sep* (*Old: bear or carry, with direction*) They bore in his body. The ambassadors to the emperor bore away great gifts. The envoy bore back to us tidings of war.

bear down (up)on *vt fus* (a) (*Naut: steer dangerously towards*) The great ship bore down upon our helpless dinghy. (b) (*Fig: approach ominously*) The policeman bore down upon the small boys. The matron bore down upon the terrified nurses. (c) (*weigh heavily on*) This responsibility bears down on me. (d) (*reprimand or punish*) They will bear down heavily on you if you fail.

bear in (up)on *vt fus* (*Formal, usu pass: bring to the attention of*) It was slowly borne in on me that he would never return. It must be borne in upon you all that such behaviour will not be tolerated.

bear off *vt sep* (*a*) *see* ***bear*** (*b*) (*Old: carry off, steal*) The raiders bore off many of the local girls. (*c*) (*win*) He bore off all the prizes.

bear out *vt sep* (*a*) *see* ***bear*** (*b*) (*support, confirm*) I hope you will bear out what I tell them. He will bear me out. I'm afraid that the results bear out my earlier suspicions.

bear up 1 *vi* (*Fam: carry on, continue to do the necessary things of life, survive*) He bore up well under/against his father's death. How is she bearing up after her illness? Come on, bear up! 2 *vt sep see* ***bear***.

*beat + particle *vt sep* (*force by beating or striking, with direction*) We managed to beat the enemy back. They beat the birds out (of their cover). She tried to beat the mosquitoes away/off.

beat back 1 *vi* (*Naut: go back, under sail*) The yacht beat back towards the shore. 2 *vt sep* (*a*) see ****beat*** (*b*) (*stop from advancing*) The men tried to beat the flames back.

beat about 1 *vi* (*Old Naut: turn about, under sail*) The galleon beat about, and headed for the Caribbean. 2 *vt fus* (*search*) They were beating about for him. *Idioms:* to beat about the bush =to prevaricate, stall, waste time. Don't beat about the bush=Don't stall.

beat down 1 *vi* (*fall hard, pour down*) The monsoon rains were beating down. 2 *vt sep* (*a*) *see* ****beat*** (*b*) (*Fig: reduce by haggling or outbidding*) They tried to beat the price down. That's my price and I'm sticking to it—you can't beat me down any further/any more. (*c*) (*flatten*) The wind has beaten the corn down.

beat in *vt sep* (*a*) *see* ****beat*** (*b*) (*batter or break in*) The police beat in the door. The gang beat his brains in.

beat out 1 *vi* (*Naut: sail into the wind*) The sailing ship beat out to sea. 2 *vt sep* (*a*) *see* ****beat*** (*b*) (*sound by beating*) The drummers beat out a steady rhythm. (*c*) (*extinguish by beating*) The men succeeded in beating out the fire.

beat up 1 *vi* (*Naut: go up, under sail*) The dinghy beat up to windward. 2 *vt sep* (*a*) *see* ****beat*** (*b*) (*mix to a paste by beating*) She beat up the eggs/cream. (*c*) (*beat savagely*) The gang beat him up and left him for dead. *n* **a beating-up.** (*d*) (*Old Mil: summon*) The army is beating up recruits for the campaign. (*e*) (*Fig: seek strenuously*) The manager himself has gone out to beat up custom for the shop. She tried to beat up some support for the campaign she was leading. (*f*) (*Sl, usu pass: exhausted*) I'm all beat up.

*beckon + particle *vt sep* (*beckon, or summon with direction*) She beckoned me in. The man stood there, beckoning us out.

He beckoned her over, and showed her the books.

become of *vt fus* (*impers: happen to*) What will become of those refugees? What is to become of me if you go away? I don't know what will become of her.

bed down 1 *vi* (*go to bed*) We bedded down for the night in a small inn near the mountains. I'm afraid we haven't a spare room but you can bed down on the settee. 2 *vt sep* (*a*) (*put to bed*) She bedded the children down without much trouble. He was bedded down with his brother. (*b*) (*settle for the night*) They bedded the horses down comfortably.

bed out *vt sep* (*Gardening: transfer to special flower beds in the open air*) The bulbs should now be bedded out.

beef up *vt sep* (*US Fam: reinforce, strengthen*) The army is to be beefed up by several divisions. The general has decided to beef up the garrison.

*beetle + particle *vi* (*move like a beetle or with quick scuttling actions, with direction*) The little car beetles along quite well at 50 mph. The man beetled off to attend to the work. She beetled about, cleaning the house energetically.

belch out 1 *vi* (*pour or billow out*) Smoke belched out from the volcano. Blue smoke belched out from the car's exhaust pipe. 2 *vt sep* (*emit*) The volcano belched out smoke and cinders. The car's exhaust belched out blue smoke.

belch up *vt sep* (*emit by belching, regurgitate*) The volcano began belching up hot ash and cinders.

bellow out (*roar out*) 1 *vi* The bull bellowed out in pain. 2 *vt sep* The sergeant bellowed his orders out.

belly out *vi* (*usu Naut: swell out like a belly, billow out*) The sails bellied out in the strong breeze.

*belt + particle *vi* (*Fam: move rapidly, with direction*) The car was belting along at 90 mph. The motorbike belted past. The boys belted in, looking for something to eat.

belt out 1 *vi* *see* ***belt** 2 *vt sep* (*Sl: sing or pound out loudly*) The blues singer belted out the number. They belted it out for all they were worth.

belt up 1 *vi* (*a*) *see* ***belt** (*b*) (*put belts on*) The soldiers belted up and went out. (*c*) (*Sl: be quiet*) I wish he would belt up. Oh, belt up, would you? Belt up! 2 *vt sep* (*fit up with or by means of a belt*) They belted the mechanism up.

*bend + particle (*bend, lean with direction*) 1 *vi* He bent down to pick it up. He bent over. The road bends away at that point. She bent back to escape being kissed. 2 *vt sep* He bent it back. She bent the corners over. Can you bend it in?

He bent it backwards and forwards till it broke.

bend over 1 *vi* (*a*) *see* ***bend** (*b*) (*bend over to receive strokes, usu of a cane, on the buttocks*) The master told the boy to bend over. 2 *vt sep see* (*a*) ***bend**. (*b*) *Idiom:* to bend over backwards (*to do something*) = to make every possible effort (*to do it*).

billow out, *vi* (*a*) (*Naut: swell or belly out*) The sails billowed out as the breeze filled them. (*b*) (*pour out, usu in circling gusts*) The smoke billowed out of the wrecked tanker.

bind down *vt sep* (*keep down by binding or tying*) They bound their prisoner down. He was bound down with cords. The surgical patient had to be bound down tightly before the operation, because movement was dangerous.

bind on *vt sep* (*put on by binding*) She bound the pad on (to his arm) with a roll of bandage. He bound it on with tape.

bind over *vt sep* (*Fig Law: enjoin, warn*) The magistrate bound him over to keep the peace. He has been bound over by the judge.

bind up *vt sep* (*a*) (*Lit: seal or enclose tightly by binding*) She expertly bound up the wound. He bound the package up with tape. (*b*) (*Fig: completely enclose or wrap up*) My life is bound up in yours now. She is bound up in him, and won't listen to advice. (*c*) (*Fig, pass only: be absorbed*) He is completely bound up in the book he is writing. (*d*) (*Fig, usu pass: connected*) One question is intimately bound up with another.

bite back 1 *vi* (*a*) (*bite in return*) The cat bit back. 2 *vt sep* (*a*) (*bite in return*) The little boy bit his friend, and got bitten back. (*b*) (*restrain*) She wanted to tell him her real feelings, but she bit the words back. 3 *Idiomatic vi* **to backbite** = to gossip maliciously, to slander and carp.

blab out *vt sep* (*Sl: reveal carelessly in speech*) He blabbed out our secret. She always blabs out confidences.

black out 1 *vi* (*become unconscious, faint*) I'm sorry, I just blacked out for a few minutes. 2 *vt sep* (*a*) (*make completely black or dark*) The city has been blacked out because enemy bombers are expected. *n* a **blackout** (*b*) (*delete by making black*) He blacked out the words he didn't want.

blacken out = **black out** 2 *vt sep* (*b*).

blare forth = **blare out.**

blare out (*sound out brassily*) 1 *vi* The trumpets blared out. The car horns blared out. 2 *vt sep* The car horns blared out their warnings. The trumpets blared out a fanfare. The radio loudspeakers blared the news out.

blast off 1 *vi* (*Aviat: take off with the power of jets or rockets*) The spaceship blasted off. The jet fighters blasted off from the deck of the aircraft carrier. 2 *vt sep* (*displace, remove or destroy by blasting*) The explosion blasted the roof off.

blaze abroad=blaze out (*a*).

blaze away *vi* (*a*) (*blaze or burn continuously*) The fire blazed away for a long time, without needing more fuel. (*b*) (*Mil: fire continuously*) The soldiers blazed away at the enemy positions.

blaze down *vi* (*a*) (*send down great heat*) The sun blazed down pitilessly from a white sky. (*b*) (*come down blazing*) Cinders and ash blazed down from the erupting volcano. A bomber blazed down, out of control.

blaze forth=blaze out (*a*).

blaze out *vi* (*burn out violently or intensely*) (*a*) (*Lit*) A light blazed out from the window. Flames blazed out from the crater of the volcano. (*b*) (*Fig*) Anger blazed out of her eyes.

blaze up *vi* (*burn up violently or intensely*) (*a*) (*Lit*) The fire blazed up when he poured petrol on it. (*b*) (*Fig*) Her anger blazed up when she was told what he wanted.

bleach out *vt sep* (*a*) (*remove by using bleach*) She bleached the stains out (of the cloth). (*b*) (*fade*) The sunlight has bleached the colours out. The dress is old and has a bleached-out look.

blend in 1 *vi* (*come together as a blend, harmonize*) The colours blend in nicely. The house blends in with its surroundings. 2 *vt sep* (*bring in as part of a blend, mix in*) He hopes to blend the substance in with the others. The architect wants to blend the house in with its surroundings.

blink away 1 *vi* (*blink, wink continuously*) That fellow just sits there, blinking away. 2 *vt sep* (*remove by blinking*) She said nothing, and tried to blink away her tears.

blink back=blink away 2 *vt sep*.

block in *vt sep* (*a*) (*enclose with blocks*) The space has been blocked in. (*b*) (*trap, surround*) The car has been blocked in by all those lorries.

block out *vt sep* (*a*) (*mark out in blocks*) The area has been blocked out, and building will begin soon. (*b*) *stop from getting through*) That wall blocks out all the light.

block up *vt sep* (*fill up, close up*) The traffic is very heavy, and has begun to block up the streets. The drains are blocked up.

blossom forth=blossom out.

blossom out *vi* (*come out in blossom, develop fully*) (*a*) (*Lit*) The fruit trees have blossomed out beautifully. (*b*) (*Fig*) She has blossomed out into a lovely young woman. His hopes seem to be blossoming out.

blot out *vt sep* *(erase by blotting)* *(a)* *(Lit)* He blotted out his mistakes. *(b)* *(Fig: kill, destroy)* The whole city has been blotted out by saturation bombing. He intends to blot out all opposition. *(c)* *(Fig: erase)* He tried to blot out the memory of that embarrassing moment.

*blow + particle *(blow, with direction)* 1 *vi* The papers blew out. The leaves blew in. The smoke blew away. 2 *vt sep* The wind blew the papers out of the window. The breeze blew the leaves in. He blew away the cigar smoke.

blow down 1 *vi* *see* ***blow** 2 *vt sep* *(a)* *see* ***blow** *(b)* *(fell, knock down, demolish, by blowing)* The storm blew down many trees. The explosion blew several buildings down. *(c)* *(dislodge downward)* The wind has blown apples down. Soot has been blown down into the fireplace.

blow in 1 *vi* *(a)* *see* ***blow** *(b)* *(implode, burst in)* The walls have blown in because of the pressure from outside. *(c)* *(Fig Fam: arrive casually or unexpectedly)* Say, look who's just blown in! *Idiom:* look what the wind's blown in=see who has just arrived. 2 *vt sep* *(a)* *see* ***blow** *(b)* *(cause to implode)* The pressure has blown the walls in.

blow off 1 *vi* *see* ***blow** 2 *vt sep* *(a)* *see* ***blow** *(b)* *(remove or displace by an explosion)* They blew the door off with a small charge of gelignite. The shell had blown his head off.

blow out 1 *vi* *(a)* *see* ***blow** *(b)* *(billow out)* The curtains blew out as the wind caught them. *(c)* *(explode and stop functioning)* The electric fire seems to have blown out. *n* **a blow-out** *(d)* *(explode outward)* The walls have blown out under the pressure from within. 2 *vt sep* *(a)* *see* ***blow** *(b)* *(extinguish by blowing)* She blew out the candle. He blew the oil lamp out. *(c)* *(blast out)* The bombs should blow them out (of that bunker). 3 *n* **a blow-out**=*(Sl)* an expensive celebration. *Example:* They spent £10 on drink and had a real blow-out.

blow over 1 *vi* *(a)* *see* ***blow** *(b)* *(Fig: pass, vanish)* It's a problem now, but I expect it will all blow over. It has blown over, and everything is back to normal. 2 *vt sep* *see* ***blow**.

blow up 1 *vi* *(a)* *see* ***blow** *(b)* *(Lit Met: develop)* A storm seems to be blowing up. It began to blow up cold. *(c)* *(Fig: develop suddenly and probably ominously)* Trouble has blown up at the factory. Something is blowing up and I don't like it. *(d)* *(Lit: explode, erupt)* The bomb blew up. The chemical plant has blown up. The volcano unexpectedly blew up. *(e)* *(Fig: explode, begin violently)* The whole dispute has blown up again. I expect this affair to blow up any minute now. *Idiom:* To blow up in one's face=to fail suddenly and publicly, with embarrassing consequences. *Example:* His scheme blew up in his face after all, despite his optimism. (*f*) (*collapse, especially under investigation*) The case blew up when they examined it more closely. (*g*) (*Fam: become suddenly angry*) He blew up (at me) when I told him I couldn't do it. I wish she wouldn't blow up like that whenever you mention the subject. (*h*) (*swell, inflate*) The balloons blew up easily. This tyre won't blow up. 2 *vt sep* (*a*) *see* ***blow** (*b*) (*Lit: inflate*) He blew up the balloons/tyres. (*c*) (*Fig: exaggerate, inflate*) This whole affair has been blown up (out of all proportion to its importance). Don't blow this thing up more than necessary. (*d*) (*Lit: destroy by exploding, detonate*) The terrorists blew up the police station. The army is blowing the bridges up as it retreats. (*e*) (*Fig: destroy, as if by explosion*) His reputation has been blown up completely. (*f*) (*Phot: increase in size, enlarge*) He has blown the print up as large as it'll go. *n* **a blowup**=an enlargement. (*g*) (*Fam: reprimand angrily*) The headmaster blew the boys up about the broken window. 3 *vt fus* (*Met with subject 'it': start*) It may well blow up a storm tonight.

***blunder + particle** *vi* (*move clumsily or foolishly, with direction*) They blundered about in the dark. He blundered in; drunk. I suppose he'll blunder through in his own inimitable way.

blunder (up)on *vt fus* (*come upon by chance, stumble upon*) They have blundered upon the trail of a gang of criminals. She just blundered upon the evidence of his dishonesty.

blurt out *vt sep* (*thoughtlessly tell*) He has blurted out everything we wanted to keep secret. Trust you to blurt it all out.

bluster out *vt sep* (*defend by bluster or noisy assertion*) He will try to bluster it out, but we all know he was responsible for the loss.

board in *vt sep* (*enclose or seal with boards*) The entrance has been boarded in.

board out *vt sep* (*send out to a separate place for bed and board=daily requirements*) The institution boards the children out to neighbouring families. The boys are boarded out when their parents are abroad.

board up *vt sep* (*seal up with boards*) The shop is boarded up. They boarded the door up and went away.

***bob + particle** *vi* (*move with bobbing actions, with direction*) The cork bobbed along in the water. Some debris was bobbing along on the tide. Some pieces of wood bobbed past. The children bobbed in and out among the trees.

bog down 1 *vi* (*get caught, as if in a marsh*) (*a*) (*Lit*) Your car will bog down in that mud. (*b*) (*Fig*) The negotiations bogged down over the question of repatriating the prisoners of war. 2 *vt sep* (*catch in a bog or in mud*) (*a*) (*Lit*) This rain will bog all the cars down in the field. (*b*) (*Fig*) The question of the prisoners will bog the negotiations down.

boil away 1 *vi* (*a*) (*boil continuously*) The water was boiling away in the kettle. (*b*) (*boil until none left*) All the water boiled away and the kettle was ruined. 2 *vt sep* (*remove or eliminate by boiling*) They boiled the excess liquid away.

boil down *vt sep* (*render down or decompose by boiling*) They boil down horses' hoofs to get glue.

boil down to *vt fus* (*can be reduced to*) It all boils down to whether you want to go or not. The whole question boils down to the old debate about free will and determinism.

boil off＝**boil away** 2 *vt sep*.

boil over *vi* (*spill over after boiling*) (*a*) (*Lit*) The milk in the pan boiled over onto the cooker. (*b*) (*Fig*) Tempers have begun to boil over and there will be trouble.

boil up 1 *vi* (*come up boiling*) (*a*) (*Lit*) Lava boiled up from the crater of the volcano. (*b*) (*Fig*) Trouble is boiling up in the ghettos. 2 *vt sep* (*bring to boiling point*) The stew must be boiled up before serving.

bolster up *vt sep* (*Fig: support, prop up*) The government needs bolstering up. He expects us to bolster up his reputation. She takes gin to bolster up her courage/to bolster her up.

***bolt + particle** *vi* (*move suddenly and quickly, with direction*) The hare bolted off, with the hounds on its tail. He bolted away to find them. The cat bolted out when it saw the dog.

bolt back 1 *vi* *see* ***bolt** 2 *vt sep* (*hold or fix back with bolts*) They bolted the shutters back.

bolt on 1 *vi* *see* ***bolt** 2 *vt sep* (*fix on with bolts*) They bolted the handles on.

bolt down 1 *vi* *see* ***bolt** 2 *vt sep* (*a*) (*fix down with bolts*) He bolted the hatch down. (*b*) (*Fam: swallow quickly*) He just bolts his food down.

bolt up 1 *vi* *see* ***bolt** 2 *vt sep* (*close completely by means of bolts*) They bolted up the doors.

bomb out *vt sep* (*a*) (*bomb thoroughly*) The city has been bombed out. It is an old bombed-out building. (*b*) (*force to leave by bombing*) We shall bomb them out of that place. They were bombed out of three houses during the war.

bone up on *vt fus* (*Old Fam: learn, swot up*) I'll have to bone up on my German.

book down *vt sep* (*put down in a book; register*) He booked us down for the next ship.

book in 1 *vi* (*give name or information for a register*) Where do we book in? Those people haven't booked in yet. 2 *vt sep* (*a*) (*receive or accept by putting name or information in a book*) They haven't been booked in, I don't think the receptionist has noticed them. (*b*) (*reserve or obtain a place for*) Let's book him in at the Grand Hotel.

book out 1 *vi* (*state departure by entering name in a book*) I'll book out for both of us. 2 *vt sep* (*confirm departure by entering name in a book*) He booked me out. We didn't know that she books people out.

book up 1 *vi* (*make reservations*) You'd better book up if you want to go. 2 *vt sep* (*a*) (*reserve*) They have booked the whole place up for weeks. The performance is booked up. All the hotels are booked up for the season, you will never find anywhere to book in at now. (*b*) (*Fam, pass only: be engaged*) I'm afraid I can't come, I'm booked up all next week.

boom out 1 *vi* (*sound out with a booming noise*) The ship's foghorn boomed out. 2 *vt sep* (*say in loud booming tone*) He boomed out his greetings.

boost up *vt sep* (*a*) (*raise by pushing upwards*) He boosted his friend up to look over the wall. *n* **a boost-up**. *Example:* Give me a boost-up please, I can't reach it. (*b*) (*reinforce, strengthen*) The prestige of the government has been boosted up by this victory. The engine has been boosted up considerably. I hope you will be able to boost up the morale of the soldiers.

*boot + particle *vt sep* (*a*) (*Fam: move by kicking with a boot, with direction*) He booted the ball over. They were booting an old can about. The centre-forward booted the ball in. (*b*) (*Fig Fam*) The troublemakers were booted out.

border (up)on *vt fus* (*a*) (*Lit: lie on the border of*) The new housing estate borders upon the playing-fields. (*b*) (*Fig: verge on, touch on, come near to*) His action borders upon insubordination. The soldiers' behaviour borders on mutiny. This kind of risk borders upon insanity.

boss about/around *vt sep* (*Fam: order about*) I don't like being bossed about by you or anyone else. Stop bossing me about! He thinks he can come in and boss everybody about.

botch up *vt sep* (*Fam: spoil completely*) He has botched up our plans. I wish you wouldn't come along and botch everything up. Don't botch it up this time.

bottle up *vt sep* (*a*) (*Lit: seal in a bottle*) She bottled up all the gooseberries for the winter. (*b*) (*Fig: seal as if in a bottle*) She bottles up her emotions. The tension in the family is caused by everyone bottling up their feelings. Don't bottle it up, speak out!

*bounce + particle   (*bounce, rebound, with direction*)   1 *vi* The ball bounced back.   It bounced up and down.   (*Fig Fam*) She bounced in with the good news.   He bounced out excitedly. 2 *vt sep*   She bounced the ball along.   He bounced it up and down.

bounce out   1 *vi*   *see* *bounce   2 *vt sep*   (*a*) *see* *bounce   (*b*) (*Fam: eject by force*) They bounced the troublemakers out of the hall.   He has been bounced out of every bar in town.

*bound + particle   *vi*   (*bound or leap, with direction*) He bounded past.   The kangaroos bounded along.   The boys bounded about.

bow down   *vi*   (*a*) (*Lit: intensive of* bow) The envoy bowed down low.   (*b*) (*Fig: submit*) We shall not bow down to this disgrace.

*bowl + particle   *vi*   (*roll steadily, with direction*) The car bowled along smoothly.   They bowled up in a new car.   They bowled back to town in his Rolls-Royce.

bowl out   1 *vi*   *see* *bowl   2 *vt sep*   (*Cricket: make to leave the game through the ball striking the wicket*) The batsman was bowled out.

bowl over   1 *vi*   *see* *bowl   2 *vt sep*   (*a*) (*Lit: knock over with a bowl*) He bowled the skittles over.   (*b*) (*Fig: knock over*) The car bowled the gatepost over.   He came running round the corner too quickly and bowled the old lady over.   (*c*) (*Fig: astonish*) I was completely bowled over by his proposal.

box in   *vt sep*   (*enclose with a box or something like a box*) They boxed the garden in with fences.   I feel boxed in here, because of the design of the houses.

box off   *vt sep*   (*mark off or separate in a box or box-like plan*) They have boxed the area off into separate sections.

box up   *vt sep*   (*put in boxes, package*) The goods have been boxed up and are ready to go.

brace up   1 *vi*   (*prepare or steady oneself*) He braced up for the bad news.   Come on, old chap, brace up!   2 *vt sep*   (*make steady or more secure*) They braced up the old building with baulks of timber.   A whisky will brace you up a bit.   Brace yourself up!

branch off   *vi*   (*diverge, take a separate route*) The road to the coast branches off from the main road in about a mile.   We'll have to branch off shortly to get to the village.

branch out   *vi*   (*diversify, develop a new line*) They are branching out into textiles.   She began as an artist but she has branched out and is making toys now as well.

brave out   *vt sep*   (*endure*) She has braved out the gossip and rumours. You'll just have to brave it out for a time.

brazen out   *vt sep*   (*resist and dismiss insolently*) She brazened out the scandal. Trust him to brazen it out, as if nothing had happened.

break away 1 *vi* (*a*) (*come away in pieces*) The surface is rotten and breaks away when you touch it. (*b*) (*rebel*) I imagine he will try to break away. The state has broken away from the union. *n* **breakaway**=secession. *n cpd* **a breakaway state** =a state which rebels or secedes. 2 *vt sep* (*remove by breaking*) They broke away the veneer with a chisel.

break down 1 *vi* (*a*) (*stop functioning*) The car has broken down. This machine will break down if you don't take care of it. *n* **a breakdown**=a failure to function. *n cpd* **breakdown service**=service offered by a garage to assist in car breakdowns. **a breakdown van/lorry**=a van/lorry which can be used to tow broken-down cars. (*b*) (*stop, come to nothing*) Talks have broken down over the disputed territory. I expect the negotiations to break down soon. (*c*) (*burst into tears, lose control of one's emotions*) She broke down when she heard of her husband's death. *Idiomatic n phr:* **a (nervous) breakdown**=a critical nervous condition, a crisis in someone's emotional life. 2 *vt sep* (*destroy, reduce to pieces, demolish*) They broke the door down. The cars have been broken down for scrap. (*b*) (*reduce to constituent parts, analyse*) I want you to break this data down. *n* **a breakdown**=an analysis.

break in 1 *vi* (*enter illegally*) A burglar broke in during the night. *n* **a break-in**=a burglary. 2 *vt sep* (*a*) (*knock in, smash in*) The men broke the door in with axes. He broke in the top of the box. (*b*) (*tame*) It will be difficult to break that horse in. (*c*) (*Fam: help adjust*) I shall give you an easy job just to break you in to the work.

break into *vt fus* (*a*) (*enter illegally, enter by stealth*) The burglar broke into the house. (*b*) (*Fam: burst into, begin to exude*) He broke into a cold sweat. (*c*) (*Fig: suddenly*) They broke into song. (*d*) (*interrupt*) He broke into our argument/discussion.

break off 1 *vi* (*a*) (*break or sever an engagement to marry*) They've broken off. *see* **break (off) with** (*b*) (*stop for a rest or break*) Let's break off for ten minutes. (*c*) (*interrupt oneself*) He broke off and didn't start again. 2 *vt sep* (*a*) (*knock off by breaking*) He broke the handle off. She broke the top off by accident. (*b*) (*sever, discontinue*) They have broken off the negotiations/ talk. She has broken off the engagement.

break (off) with *vt fus* (*have no further relations with*) I intend to break with these people. She broke off with him long ago.

break out 1 *vi* (*a*) (*escape from a place*) The prisoners have broken out. *n* **a breakout**=an escape. *n cpd* **a prison breakout**. (*b*) (*appear, start suddenly*) War broke out in 1914. Cholera has broken out in Bengal. *n* **an outbreak** 2 *vt sep* (*a*) (*get out by breaking*) He broke the panels out. (*b*) (*take out of store*) I'll break out some of that 1954 vintage, to celebrate.

break out in *vt fus* (*Med: exhibit suddenly*) The child has broken out in spots. He has broken out in a rash. *n* **an outbreak**= a sudden epidemic. *Example:* There was an outbreak of measles in the school.

break through 1 *vi* (*a*) (*Lit: force a way through*) The soldiers have managed to break through. (*b*) (*Fig: achieve something new, make a major advance*) The biologists claim to have broken through in a new area of genetics. *n* **a breakthrough**=a major new success. 2 *vt fus* (*force a way through*) The soldiers broke through the enemy lines.

break up 1 *vi* (*Fam: disintegrate*) The formation has broken up. Their partnership has broken up. *n* **breakup**=disintegration. (*b*) (*Fam: disband*) School has broken up for the holidays. 2 *vt sep* (*a*) (*reduce by breaking*) He broke up the soil. The prisoners were breaking up rocks. (*b*) (*Fig: stop*) He broke up the fight between the two gangs. Come on, break it up! (*c*) (*Fam: destroy, upset completely*) This trouble has really broken him up.

break with=**break (off) with.**

breathe away *vi* (*breathe continuously and freely*) He breathed away deeply for a few minutes, to recover from the effort.

breathe forth *vt sep* (*Old: breathe out, emit*) The dragon breathed forth fire.

breathe in 1 *vi* (*inhale*) Breathe in deeply and hold your breath please. 2 *vt sep* (*take in by breathing*) The workers inevitably breathe in poisonous fumes.

breathe out 1 *vi* (*exhale*) He breathed out. 2 *vt sep* (*a*) (*emit by breathing*) He breathed out whisky fumes. (*b*) (*whisper*) He breathed out their names just before he died.

*****breeze + particle** *vi* (*Fam: go like a breeze, with direction*) He breezed in to see her. They breezed off somewhere. He breezes about in a little sports car.

brick in *vt sep* (*enclose with bricks*) The area has been bricked in.

brick over *vt sep* (*cover over with bricks*) The surface has been bricked over.

brick up *vt sep* (*seal up with bricks*) They bricked up the windows to keep children out of the derelict house. It looks like an old bricked-up doorway.

bridge over *vt sep* (*link with a bridge*) The gorge has been bridged over. They will bridge it over with planks.

brighten up 1 vi (a) (*Lit: become bright or brighter*) The sky brightened up after the storm. (b) (*Fig: become more lively*) The party brightened up when the pop group arrived. 2 vt sep (a) (*Lit: make bright or brighter*) She brightened up the room with some colourful curtains. (b) (*Fig: make more lively, liven up*) They brightened the party up with some music and dancing.

*bring + particle vt sep (*bring, with direction*) He brought the box in. She brought her mother out to the car. They will bring some friends over. I want to bring her along to see you.

bring about vt sep (a) (*Naut: turn completely*) He brought the ship about and headed for safety. (b) (*cause to happen*) This accident has been brought about by your recklessness.

bring down vt sep (a) see *bring (b) (*cause to be reduced*) Their demands have brought the prices down. After much hard bargaining he brought the trader down to £100 for the carpet. (c) (*cause to be defeated, defeat*) Their action may yet bring the government down. This scandal could well bring him down.

bring forth vt sep (a) see *bring (b) (*produce*) He brought forth a new plan, just as unworkable as the old one. (c) (*Old: give birth to*) She brought forth twins.

bring forward vt sep (a) see *bring (b) (*advance, propose*) She brought forward a new proposal. (c) (*advance in time*) They have brought the meeting forward to next Monday. (d) (*Bookkeeping: bring into next column etc*) Have you remembered to bring forward the profit from last month?

bring in vt sep (a) see *bring (b) (*introduce*) He intends to bring in some reforms. The government is bringing in new legislation on this matter. You will have to bring in some outside help or you will never get the job finished in time. (c) *Idiom:* to bring in the New Year=to stay up till midnight on December 31st, to celebrate the New Year.

bring off vt sep (a) see *bring (b) (*rescue, take off successfully*) The coastguards have brought all the crew off, and the ship is sinking by the bows. (c) (*complete successfully*) He brought the deal off in a spectacular way. Trust her to bring it off.

bring on vt sep (a) see *bring (b) (*introduce, usu on a stage*) He brought on the guest speaker, amid applause. (c) (*usu Med: cause*) This kind of weather often brings on hay fever. The trouble might bring on her headaches again. I hope your experience doesn't bring on anything nasty.

bring out vt sep (a) see *bring (b) (*develop*) Her teacher wants to bring out her talent. (c) (*Fam: evoke*) This kind of work brings out the best in him. (d) (*coax to be less shy*) She may be able to bring him out a bit, but it won't be easy. (e) (*publish*) The company intends to bring out a new series of educational books.   (*f*) (*Comm: introduce into the market*) They are bringing out a new brand of soap powder next month.

bring round   *vt sep*   (*a*) *see* ***bring**   (*b*) (*bring casually on a visit*) She brought her friends round to see us.   Why don't you bring her round sometime?   (*c*)=**bring about** (*a*).   (*d*) (*Fam: revive, restore to consciousness*) The doctor brought the man round quite quickly after the accident.   (*e*) (*convert, persuade*) We should have very little difficulty bringing him round to our way of thinking.   They'll bring her round, don't worry.   (*f*) (*steer in a desired direction*) He keeps trying to bring the conversation round to politics.

bring through   *vt sep*   (*a*) *see* ***bring**   (*b*) (*conduct safely through*) He brought his party through without accidents.

bring together   *vt sep*   (*a*) *see* ***bring**   (*b*) (*Fam: bring into contact*) He likes bringing young people together.   (*c*) (*unite*) Fate has brought them together.   Emergencies often serve to bring people together.   (*d*) (*re-unite*) I'll do what I can to bring them together, but it won't be easy.

bring up   *vt sep*   (*a*) *see* ***bring**   (*b*) (*raise, educate*) They have brought their children up well. That child is very badly brought up.   *n* **upbringing**=rearing and education (of a child).   (*c*) (*Fam: raise, mention*) He brought up the subject of money again last night. I feel I ought to bring up this matter. I hope you won't mind me bringing this up again.   (*d*) (*vomit*) He brought up his food. She keeps bringing up everything we give her.   *Idiom vi:* It's enough to make you bring up= it's enough to make you vomit.

bristle out   *vi*   (*stick out or protrude with or like bristles*) His beard bristled out aggressively. The porcupine's quills bristled out.

bristle up   *vi*   (*a*) (*stick up with or like bristles*) His hair bristled up· The hair on the dog's neck bristled up.   (*b*) (*Fig Fam: become angry*) She bristled up when I suggested that the job wasn't suitable for her. He bristles up very easily.

broaden out   1 *vi*   (*become broad or broader*)   (*a*) (*Lit*) The road broadens out here. The view will broaden out shortly. He was quite thin when I last saw him, but he has broadened out a lot.   (*b*) (*Fig*) The scope of the programme broadened out towards the end of the series.   2 *vt sep*   (*make broad or broader*) They have broadened out the avenue considerably. He intends to broaden out the general policies of the company.

brown off   *vt sep*   (*Sl: bore, frustrate*) This kind of job really browns me off. I'm browned off with working so hard for so little money.

***brush + particle**   *vt sep*   (*move with a brush, sweep, with direction*) She brushed the dirt out. He brushed the hairs off.   They brushed the leaves away.

brush against=brush up against.

brush aside *vt sep* (*a*) *see* ***brush** (*b*) (*Fig: discard, wave aside, treat as unimportant*) He brushed aside all our objections. I don't like being brushed aside like this.

brush away *vt sep* (*a*) *see* ***brush** (*b*) (*Fig: treat as neither important nor desirable*) He brushed the whole business away. You can't just brush it away like this!

brush off *vt sep* (*a*) *see* ***brush** (*b*) (*Fig: reject*) He brushed off all our suggestions. I didn't expect her to brush us off like this. *n* a **brush-off**. *Idiom:* to give someone the brush-off=to reject someone/someone's advances or suggestions.

brush over 1 *vt sep* (*a*) *see* ***brush** (*b*) (*brush fully*) He brushed the coat over. 2 *vt fus* (*treat lightly, almost ignore*) He brushed over the details of policy.

brush up *vt sep* (*a*) *see* ***brush** (*b*) (*brush thoroughly, clean thoroughly with a brush*) You should brush the place up a bit. (*c*) (*Fig: improve*) I want to brush up my Italian. He wants to brush up his knowledge of electronics.

brush up against *vt fus* (*a*) (*touch lightly*) I brushed up against her unintentionally. (*b*) (*Fig: encounter*) He has brushed up against trouble.

brush up on *vt fus* (*revise, improve*) I must brush up on my French before I go to France.

*bubble + particle *vi* (*move, in, with or like bubbles, with direction*) Water began to bubble up. The stream bubbled away down the hill. We watched the hot liquid bubbling out. The boiling milk rose up and bubbled over.

buck off *vt sep* (*throw off by bucking*) The horse bucked its rider off.

buck up 1 *vi* (*a*) (*Sl: be or become more cheerful*) This news will make him buck up a bit. Oh, buck up, things could be worse. (*b*) (*Sl: hurry up*) Buck up or we'll be late! 2 *vt sep* (*Sl: make more cheerful*) This news should buck you up. Your help has bucked me up a lot.

buckle down 1 *vi* (*Fam: get to work*) You'll just have to buckle down and show that you can do it if you want. He expects you to buckle down to the job whether you like it or not. 2 *vt sep* (*fix down with a buckle or buckles*) He buckled the harness down. The equipment was firmly buckled down.

buckle on *vt sep* (*fix or put on with buckles*) The soldiers buckled their equipment on. He buckled the horse's harness on.

buckle to *vi* (*get busy*) They buckled to and got the work done.

cf **buckle down**.

buckle up   *vt sep*   (*put on with the buckles tight or secure*) The soldiers buckled up their equipment. Everything is buckled up.

build in   *vt sep*   (*fix in, in a permanent way*) The cupboards are built in to the walls of the house. It will not be difficult to build wardrobes in if you want them.   *n cpd* **built-in cupboards**. *Idiomatic:* He's been so long with that firm you'd think he was built in with the bricks.

build on   *vt sep*   (*add on as a new part*) We can build an extension on later if you want one. The annexe has been built on to the main building.

build up   1 *vi*   (*a*) (*Mil: become stronger, concentrated*) Enemy forces are building up in the hills.   *n* **a build-up** (of troops, materials, forces etc).   (*b*) (*Met: become concentrated*) Clouds are building up over the sea.   (*c*) (*Fig: grow*) Tension is building up in the old part of the city.   2 *vt sep*   (*a*) (*raise by building*) He built up the wall in several stages until it was the height he wanted. (*b*) (*develop*) He has built up a remarkable physique by following these exercises.   (*c*) (*amass*) They have built up quite a fortune in that business.   (*d*) (*acquire, consolidate*) He hopes to build up a reputation for honesty and craftsmanship.   (*e*) (*Mil: increase in power and numbers, strengthen*) The enemy are building up their offensive capacity along the border.   (*f*) (*increase in prestige or fame*) They have built that boy up into a leading singer.   (*g*) *n* **a build-up**=prepared and concentrated publicity before an event.

bulge out   *vi*   (*intensive of* **bulge**) Her swollen abdomen bulged out. The contents of the bag began to bulge out.

bum along/about/around   *vi*   (*Sl: go about like a tramp or bum*) He just bums along, living from day to day.

*bumble + particle   *vi*   (*go in a particularly clumsy, incompetent way, with direction*) He bumbles about, doing everything wrong. They bumble in without warning from time to time. He will bumble through somehow.

*bump + particle   *vi*   (*move with a bumping noise, with direction*) The body bumped along as they pulled it. You could hear something bumping about upstairs. The car bumped down on to the road from the pavement.

bump off   1 *vi see* ***bump**   2 *vt sep*   (*Sl: kill, murder*) A gang of thugs bumped him off. Be careful they don't try to bump you off next.

bunch up   1 *vi*   (*come close together in a bunch*) The sergeant shouted at the men not to bunch up.   2 *vt sep* (*put together in a bunch*) Don't bunch up all the candlesticks in one corner of the shelf.

***bundle + particle** *vt sep* *(Fam: move in, or as if in, a bundle, with direction)* She bundled the children up to bed. She decided to bundle them off to the seaside. If you get tired of them, just bundle them over to us. She bundled the clothes up and took them to the laundrette.

***bung + particle** *vt sep* *(a)* *(Sl: throw, with direction)* Bung that book over, please! Bung them in here! He bunged the boxes down to his pal.

bung up *vt sep* *(fill or block with, or as if with, a bung)* The potato peelings have bunged up the sink   The pipe is all bunged up.

bunk down *vi* *(Fam: find a bed)* We might as well bunk down in that hotel. Can you bunk down on the floor for the night?

burble on *vi* *(Fam: talk on incessantly and rather inanely)* He burbled on and on about this and that, but no one listened to him.

burn away 1 *vi* *(continue to burn)* The forest fire burned away for days. This fire is burning away beautifully. 2 *vt sep* *(remove by burning)* They burned the paint away.

burn down 1 *vi* *(a)* *(burn completely, until destroyed)* The house burned down. *(b)* *(burn low, until in need of more fuel)* The fire has burned down, get some more coal please. 2 *vt sep* *(set alight and so destroy)* The terrorists burned the embassy down.

burn off *vt sep* *(remove completely, by burning)*   The farmers burned off the heavy vegetation before ploughing. The paint has been burned off.

burn out 1 *vi* *(a)* *(burn visibly)* The lamp burned out in the darkness of the night. *(b)* *(burn until without fuel)* The oil lamp has burned out. *(c)* *(Fig: die, burn to an end)* Their anger seems to have burned out. Her enthusiasm has burned out. *Idiom:* to burn oneself out=to work until one is no longer capable of any further effort. 2 *vt sep* *(a)* *(remove or excise by burning)* He tried to burn the flaw out, but couldn't. *(b)* *(force out by burning)* The gang decided to burn their opponents out (of the house). *(c)* *(usu pass: burned utterly)* The town is completely burned (or burnt) out. The airfield was littered with burned-out planes.

burn up 1 *vi* *(burn quickly and brightly)* The fire burned up when he added some kerosene. 2 *vt sep* *(a)* *(burn thoroughly, destroy by burning)* The fire burned up a number of valuable manu-scripts. A huge area was burned up in the forest fire. *(b)* *Sl Idiom:* to burn up the road=to move very fast in a car (as if burning the road with friction). *(c)* *(Sl: anger)* This kind of thing really burns me up. He was all burned up about it. *(d)* *(Sl: reprimand)* He burned them up when he found out what they'd done.

*burst + particle *vi* (*move in a bursting, explosive manner, with direction*) The men burst out from prison. The water burst in through the thin walls. The soldiers burst past into the room. The car burst away from the starting line.

burst forth *vi* (*a*) *see* ***burst** (*b*) (*blossom forth*) The leaves have burst forth in a riot of green. (*c*) (*Fig: break out*) The birds have burst forth in song.

burst in 1 *vi* (*a*) *see* ***burst** (*b*) (*break in*) The police burst in and told everyone to stand still. 2 *vt sep* (*break or smash in*) They had to burst the door in because they had lost the key.

burst into *vt fus* (*a*) *see* ***burst** (*b*) (*break or smash into*) The men burst into the room. (*c*) (*Fig: suddenly break into*) The people burst into frantic applause. The choir burst into song. She burst into peals of laughter. *Idiom:* to burst into tears= to start to weep.

burst out *vi* (*a*) *see* ***burst** (*b*) (*Fam: start violently*) He burst out laughing. She burst out in perspiration. They burst out into a storm of abuse. *n* **an outburst** (of anger, emotion, cheering etc).

bust up *vt sep* (*US Fam: burst or break up, wreck, destroy*) They have bust the whole place up. Their holiday arrangements are all bust up (or busted up). He bust(ed) up a good business. *n* **a bust-up**=a wreck, a complete failure or collapse, a violent quarrel

*bustle + particle *vi* (*move busily, with direction*) The people were bustling along towards the shopping centre. She bustled up to attend to things. He bustled about officiously. They bustled back and forward, looking important.

buoy up *vt sep* (*a*) (*raise, as if with a buoy*) The gas buoys up the whole framework, while the engine propels it. (*b*) (*Fig: raise, maintain at a high level*) This news certainly buoys me up. Success buoys up one's morale.

*butt + particle *vt sep* (*butt or impel with head or horns, with direction*) The bull butted its opponent back. The stag butted the doe aside. The footballer butted the ball in (to the goal).

butt in 1 *vi* (*Fam: interrupt*) Excuse me butting in. Excuse my butting in. He always butts in when we are talking. You shouldn't butt in to people's conversations. 2 *vt sep see* ***butt**.

butter up *vt sep* (*Fig Fam: flatter, treat with great but probably exaggerated and hypocritical respect*) She always butters up the boss. Look at him buttering up the director.

button up 1 *vi* (*a*) (*do up with buttons, have buttons as the means of closing or fixing into position*) This dress buttons up. (*b*) (*Sl: be quiet*) Just button up! He buttoned up and listened. 2 *vt sep* (*close or fix by doing up the buttons*) She buttoned up her coat before going out.

buy in 1 *vi* (*pay money to obtain a connection or membership*) When he heard about the success of the company, he tried to buy in. 2 *vt sep* (*a*) (*get in by buying*) We have bought in large stocks of this material. They bought in as much food as would last the winter. (*b*) (*often reflexive: pay money to become connected with something, or a member of something*) He bought himself in. He bought his way in.

buy back *vt sep* (*get back by buying*) We did not intend to sell that table, and had to buy it back from the dealer. The brokers were willing to buy back stock from their clients. The company is usually prepared to buy the house back when you leave.

buy off *vt sep* (*Fam: pay money to eliminate as a danger*) The black-mailer hopes you will buy him off. I don't like the way they are trying to buy me off—there must be something suspicious going on.

buy out *vt sep* (*obtain control by buying all shares in*) The bigger company has bought out all the shareholders of the smaller one. We have enough money to buy you out any time we want.

buy over *vt sep* (*win over by paying money*) The enemy may try to buy you over. He seems to think he can buy us over very cheaply.

buy up *vt sep* (*obtain by buying as widely as possible*) They have been buying up all available land. Speculators are trying to buy up supplies of raw materials.

buzz away *vi* (*a*) (*fly away with a buzzing noise*) The bee buzzed away. (*b*) (*buzz continuously*) The bees were buzzing away among the clover. The machine buzzed away for more than an hour.

buzz off *vi* (*a*)=**buzz away** (*a*). (*b*) (*Sl: go away*) I told them to buzz off. Buzz off, can't you see I'm busy!

*call + particle 1 *vi* (*call, with direction*) He called out when he saw her. She called across to me. He called down from the top of the ladder. 2 *vt sep* (*summon by calling, with direction*) I called him over to tell him the story. She called me aside to tell me the bad news. He was called away by his friends.

call back 1 *vi* (*a*) *see* ***call** (*b*) (*Tel: re-contact*) Thanks for the news, I'll call back in half an hour. 2 *vt sep* (*a*) (*Lit*) *see* ***call** (*b*) (*Fig: summon*) He was called back from his holiday to handle the problem. (*c*) (*Tel: re-contact*) I'll call you back when I get more information.

call down 1 *vi* *see* ***call** 2 *vt sep* (*a*) (*summon from below*) They called her down from upstairs to answer the telephone. (*b*) (*summon, as from God*) The old man called down curses on the heads of those who disbelieved.   (*c*) (*US: reprimand*) They really called me down for doing that.

call for   *vt fus*   (*a*) (*Lit: summon, demand*) The customers called for more beer.   (*b*) (*collect*) I'll call for you at seven o'clock and we can go there together.   She called for the books she had lent me.   (*c*) (*Fig: demand, require*) This job calls for a man of considerable initiative.   The work calls for endurance and patience. The present situation calls for entirely new measures.

call forth   *vt sep*   (*demand, bring into play*) The emergency called forth reserves of energy which she did not know she possessed.

call in   1 *vi*   *see* *call   2 *vt sep*   (*a*) *see* *call   (*b*) (*summon to a place*) They decided to call in a doctor, because the child was no better.   (*c*) (*require to be brought in*) The library is calling in all outstanding books.   The bank has begun to call its money in.

call off   *vt sep*   (*a*) (*abandon, cancel*) The workers have decided to call off their strike action.   The businessmen suddenly called the deal off.   He phoned me and called the appointment off. (*b*) (*prevent from attacking*) The dog frightened me until its master called it off.

call out   1 *vi*   *see* *call   2 *vt sep*   (*a*) *see* *call   (*b*) (*summon from a place*) They called out the guard to investigate the noises. Someone called out the fire brigade on a false alarm.   We hope it will not be necessary to call out the army.   Doctors are often called out in the middle of the night.   (*c*) (*summon to a duel*) He has called out his rival, and they are meeting at dawn tomorrow.   (*d*) (*summon to strike*) The trade union officials have called their members out (on strike).

call over   1 *vi*   (*visit casually*) He called over to see us yesterday. 2 *vt sep*   (*a*) *see* *call   (*b*) (*call in sequence*) They called over all the names on the list.

call round   *vi*   (*Fam: visit casually*) He says he'll call round at about eight.

call up   1 *vi*   *see* *call   2 *vt sep*   (*a*) *see* *call   (*b*) (*Mil: summon' bring in*) The general called up reinforcements.   (*c*) (*Mil: mobilize*) The army is calling up reservists in case of emergency. *n* **call-up**=legal summons to join the armed forces.   *n cpd* **call-up papers**.   *Example:* He got his call-up papers yesterday =he received notice that he must report for military service. (*d*) (*Tel: contact*) I'll call you up if I need your help.

call (up)on   *vt fus*   (*a*) (*visit*) They called on me yesterday for about an hour.   (*b*) (*visit for a special purpose*) The deputation called upon the mayor to invite his co-operation in their work. (*c*) (*invite, exhort*) We called upon him to speak at the meeting.

(*d*) (*invoke*) The men called upon God to help them. The government hopes that it will not be necessary to call upon emergency powers.

calm down   1 *vi*   (*become calm, quiet*) I expect she'll calm down in a few minutes, when she gets over the shock.   2 *vt sep*   (*make calm*) I tried to calm him down after the bad news.

camp out   1 *vi*   (*live in a camp or tent*) The boys like camping out in good weather. The battalion camped out on the plain. 2 *vt sep*   (*Mil usu pass: to house in tents or a camp*) The men were camped out near the town.

cancel out   *vt sep*   (*a*) (*Math: delete*) Next, you should cancel out all the noughts.   (*b*) (*Fig: annul, eliminate, neutralize*) I'm afraid your present behaviour cancels out any past help you gave us. The two things are so opposed that they just cancel each other out.

*****canter** + **particle**   (*move at the speed of a horse, between trot and gallop, with direction*)   1 *vi* The horses cantered along. The rider cantered away. The troopers cantered up to the house. 2 *vt sep* The troopers cantered their horses up to the house.

*****caper** + **particle**   *vi*   (*leap and jump in a light-hearted manner, with direction*) The children were capering about in the garden. The clowns capered up to us laughing and joking.

care for   *vt fus*   (*a*) (*look after, attend*) She has been caring for her invalid mother for many years.   (*b*) (*Fam: like*) I don't really care for that sort of thing. I don't much care for sweets. Would you care for a cup of tea? She doesn't care for him any more.

*****career** + **particle**   *vi*   (*move very rapidly, often dangerously, with direction*) The car was careering along at a terrific speed. The huge machine came careering down on us.

*****carry** + **particle**   *vt sep*   (*carry, with direction*) She carried the box up to the attic. He carried the tray in. The butler carried the empty bottles away.

carry away   *vt sep*   (*a*) *see* *****carry**   (*b*) (*Fig: transport, enchant*) He was carried away with childish enthusiasm. Take your time and think carefully—don't get carried away! I'm afraid he got carried away and forgot what he was doing.

carry back   *vt sep*   (*a*) *see* *****carry**   (*b*) (*Fig: transport to an earlier time*) Ah, that music carries me back. The sight of the place carried her back to her childhood.

carry forward   *vt sep*   (*a*) *see* *****carry**   (*b*) (*Fig usu pass: be* *advanced*) He was carried forward on a wave of popular feeling. (*c*) (*Comm: pass forward to a new balance sheet*) The money was carried forward to the next month.

carry off *vt sep* (*a*) *see* *carry (*b*) (*Fig: gain, obtain*) He was a great success at school, and carried off all the prizes. I think he will manage to carry off the honours. (*c*) (*manage*) I think she carries off her act well, considering her age. (*d*) (*Euph Fam: kill*) Pneumonia carried him off last winter. She was carried off by a heart attack.

carry on 1 *vi* (*a*) (*continue*) Carry on with your work. Please carry on! (*b*) (*Fam: have an affair*) They have been carrying on for some months now. He is carrying on with the grocer's wife. (*c*) (*Fam: make a fuss*) The children have been carrying on a bit. *n* **a carry on**=a fuss, a burst of noisy excitement. *Example:* There was such a carry-on when she found she'd lost her purse. *n* **carryings-on** (*pl*)=doubtful behaviour. *Example:* There were a lot of carryings-on in that house before he left his wife. 2 *vt sep* (*a*) *see* *carry (*b*) (*continue, maintain*) He carries on a drapery business. I expect my son to carry on the family tradition.

carry out *vt sep* (*a*) *see* *carry (*b*) (*Fig: execute*) He carried out the plan without difficulty. I expect her to carry out her obligations/promises. The scientist was carrying out some interesting experiments. The police carried out an extensive search for the body.

carry over 1 *vi* (*continue*) The writing carries over on to the next page. 2 *vt sep* (*a*) *see* *carry (*b*) (*continue*) Would you please carry the report over on to another page? (*c*) (*Book-keeping: pass forward to the next balance sheet*) He carried the money over to the next month.

carry through *vt sep* (*a*) *see* *carry (*b*) (*help survive*) Her courage carried her through. (*c*) (*execute completely*) They carried the plan through to the last letter. He began the scheme but his wife carried it through.

*cart + particle *vt sep* (*transport or carry, with direction*) (*a*) (*Lit*) The farmer carted his potatoes along to the wholesaler. The men carted the earth out into the fields. (*b*) (*Fig Fam*) Surely you don't expect me to cart all my things up to the attic? Cart your belongings out of here immediately. These children keep carting their toys through into the living-room.

carve out *vt sep* (*a*) (*Lit: cut out by carving*) He carved out a beautiful little boat from that old piece of wood. (*b*) (*Fig: settle, colonize*) The pioneers carved out great areas of land from the virgin forest. (*c*) (*develop vigorously*) He has carved out a successful career for himself.

carve up *vt sep* (a) (*Lit: cut up by carving*) She carved up the roast beef and gave us each a portion. (b) (*Fig: divide*) The men decided to carve up the land between them. The companies carved up the market to suit themselves. *n* **a carve-up** (c) (*Fig Sl: slash with a knife*) The gang attacked him and carved him up a bit.

cash in *vt sep* (*hand in for money*) She needed money so she cashed in her shares. It's time to cash in those saving bonds.

cash in on *vt fus* (*Fig Fam: exploit for profit*) We ought to cash in on our business success while there is time. You shouldn't try to cash in on the fact that he likes you.

*cast + particle *vt sep* (*Formal: throw, with direction*) They were cast out into the desert. He cast down the sword in disgust. She cast aside the old clothes.

cast about/around/round *vi* (*search in an immediate area*) (a) (*Lit*) The hound cast about, seeking the scent. The dogs cast about for the scent. (b) (*Fig*) He has been casting about for a new job for some time. She looked as though she was casting about for something to say.

cast aside *vt sep* (*throw away, discard*) (a) see ***cast** (b) (*Fig*) I refuse to be cast aside in this manner. You can't just cast people aside like old clothes.

cast away *vt sep* (a) see ***cast** (b) (*jettison*) The men cast away the equipment they would not need. (c) (*Fig usu pass: abandon, maroon*) The people had been cast away on a desert island for ten years. *n* **a castaway**=a marooned person.

cast back 1 *vi* (*Fig: look back*) He cast back in his mind to the last war, trying to remember exact dates. 2 *vt sep* (a) see ***cast** (b) (*Fig: direct to the past*) He cast back his mind to earlier days. She cast her thoughts back to happier times.

cast down *vt sep* (a) see ***cast** (b) (*lower, throw down quickly*) She cast her eyes down shyly. *adj* **downcast** (*lowered*) She sat with downcast eyes. (c) (*Fig, usu pass: demoralize, discourage*) I feel rather cast down at the moment. *adj* **downcast**=(*sad*) Don't look so downcast, it might not be so bad! He was very downcast when he got the exam results.

cast off 1 *vi* (a) (*Naut: release a boat from its moorings*) The men cast off and began rowing out to sea. (b) (*Knitting: end a piece of knitting*) She cast off and put her needles down. 2 *vt sep* (a) (*Naut: release from moorings*) The sailors cast the boat off and allowed it to drift away on the tide. (b) (*Lit: completely discard*) Snakes cast off their old skins once a year. Some people cast off clothing long before it is worn out. *n* **cast-offs**=clothes no longer wanted. (c) (*Fig: leave, discard, abandon*) It's not nice to feel that you have been cast off by your friends. She quite happily cast off three boy friends in one week. (*d*) (*Knitting: finish*) Cast off three stitches at the beginning of the next two rows. Haven't you cast off that scarf yet?

cast on 1 *vi* (*Knitting: begin a piece of knitting*) She had cast on before she realized that the needles were the wrong size. 2 *vt sep* (*Knitting: make, begin*) Cast on three stitches at each end of the next four rows. I cast on the jumper yesterday but have not knitted much yet.

cast out *vt sep* (*a*) *see* ***cast** (*b*) (*Fig: expel*) The members of the association did not like his behaviour, so they cast him out. The prophet was said to be able to cast out demons. (*c*) *n* **an outcast**=a person who is cast out by society. *Examples:* In the past, lepers were outcasts. People refused to talk to him after the scandal and he became a social outcast.

cast up 1 *vi* (*vomit*) The drunk man began casting up. 2 *vt sep* (*a*) *see* ***cast** (*b*) (*Fig: direct upwards*) She cast her eyes up to heaven and asked for patience. (*c*) (*Math: calculate*) He tried to cast up the whole complicated thing. (*d*) (*refer to constantly, in reproach*) She goes on casting up his old infidelities. He always casts up at her the fact that she crashed the car. Don't cast that up at me the whole time!

catch in *vt sep* (*Fam Sewing: take in closer*) She caught the dress in at the waist.

catch on *vi* (*a*) (*Lit: catch, grab*) The child kept catching on to his mother's skirt. (*b*) (*Fig: become popular*) This is a nice tune and I think it'll catch on quickly. (*c*) (*understand*) He's no fool, he'll catch on soon enough to what you are doing.

catch out *vt sep* (*a*) (*Fam: discover, trap*) Be careful, or they'll catch you out telling lies. He was caught out cheating in the exam. (*b*) (*Cricket: be eliminated from the game through the ball being caught in the air*) The batsman was caught out after only one run.

catch up 1 *vi* (*succeed in pursuing*) (*a*) (*Lit*) You'd better drive faster, because the others are catching up quickly. (*b*) (*Fig*) I expect he'll catch up on lost time by working harder. She says she just can't catch up with her work. 2 *vt sep* (*a*) (*lift and keep in position*) She caught up her hair into a bun. (*b*) (*pick up quickly*) He caught up the ball as it rolled along and threw it back.

cater for *vt fus* (*a*) (*supply food to or for*) That café caters mainly for the workers from the factory across the road. We catered for forty but only twenty came. (*b*) (*serve*) This kind of place caters for all tastes. I expect he will be able to cater for your particular needs. (*c*) (*Fam: expect*) I didn't cater for all these problems when I bought this shop. She said she hadn't catered for the interference of colleagues when she took the job.

cave in   *vi*   (*a*) (*Lit: collapse*) The roof of the old mine is dangerous and could cave in at any time.   *n* **a cave-in**=a collapse. (*b*) (*Fig: yield abjectly*) The opposition expect the government to cave in on this issue, but I don't think they will.   He caved in under the weight of her complaints.   Enemy resistance soon caved in.

*cavort + particle   *vi*   (*move in a playful, skipping manner, with direction*) The young horses cavorted along.   I saw the kids cavorting about in the garden.

chain down   *vt sep*   (*hold or keep down with chains*) They decided to chain the prisoners down.   You should chain that dog down.

chain up   *vt sep*   (*restrain by means of a chain*) The guard dogs are kept chained up until evening, when they are released.

chalk out   *vt sep*   (*a*) (*Lit: mark out or delineate with chalk*) He chalked out a design on the blackboard.   The girl chalked out a game on the ground.   (*b*) (*Fig: outline clearly*) The general began to chalk out a plan of campaign.

chalk up   *vt sep*   (*a*) (*Lit: mark up with chalk*) He chalked up their names on a board.   (*b*) (*Fig: mark a score*) The numbers were chalked up as the results came in.   (*c*) (*Fig: gain, win*) The team chalked up another victory last week.   (*d*) (*mark up as credit*) They willingly chalked up £10 worth of sales to him. Just chalk it up and I'll pay next week.

chance (up)on   *vt fus*   (*meet by accident*) I chanced upon him last week for the first time in years.

change down   *vi*   (*Aut: go down one gear while driving*) The driver changed down from third to second (gear).   The driver changed down quickly.

change into   *vt fus*   (*a*) (*transform oneself into*) The witch changed into a frog.   (*b*) (*put on*) Just let me change into something less formal.   You must change into a clean dress before we go out.

change over   *vi*   (*make a conversion*) We have just changed over from gas to electricity.   The mechanism changes over automatically.   *n* **a change-over**.   *Example:* The change-over to decimal currency went very smoothly.

change up   *vi*   (*Aut: go up one gear while driving*) The driver changed up from third to top (gear).   The driver changed up too soon and the car stalled.

channel off   *vt sep*   (*divert by means of or through a channel*)   (*a*) (*Lit*) The engineers channelled the water off without difficulty.   (*b*) (*Fig: divert*) They tried to channel off some of the revenue earmarked for armaments and use it to alleviate poverty.

*charge + particle *vi* (*attack at a run or a gallop; move suddenly and forcefully, with direction*) The cavalrymen charged down on the defenceless villagers. The boy charged up and asked for an ice cream. The bull charged out into the sunlight of the arena.

charge up 1 *vi* *see* ***charge** 2 *vt sep* (*a*) (*credit*) Please charge the meal up to the company. I'll charge the expenses up. (*b*) (*Elec: provide an electrical charge for*) The man in the garage said he would charge up my car battery.

*charm + particle *vt sep* (*impel to move or do, by using charm, with direction*) He could charm the birds out of the trees. She managed to charm the little boy down from the top of the ladder.

charm up *vt sep* (*a*) *see* ***charm** (*b*) (*Fam: use charm on*) If you charm him up a bit, I'm sure he'll do what you want.

chart out *vt sep* (*a*) (*Lit: mark out on a chart or map*) The navigators charted this area out and it's quite safe to sail in it. (*b*) (*Fig: explore*) They hope to chart out that particular area of the Amazon.

*chase + particle *vt sep* (*pursue, with direction*) She chased the cat out into the garden. The boy chased his sister in and out among the bushes.

chase down *vt sep* (*a*) *see* ***chase** (*b*) (*Fig Fam: follow one drink with another*) He chased the whisky down with a pint of beer.

chase up *vt sep* (*a*) *see* ***chase** (*b*) (*Fig: pursue for a purpose*) I hope to chase the editor up and get a decision from him. They have been chasing the electricity people up for weeks but nothing has been done about the dangerous wiring.

chat away *vi* (*continue chatting; talk or converse casually*) They sometimes chat away for hours. They were chatting away about old times.

chat up *vt sep* (*Sl: get to know by talking to, used of men and women*) He likes chatting up the girls. Stop trying to chat me up!

chatter away *vi* (*talk rapidly and continuously*) The children are just like monkeys, and chatter away all the time.

chatter on *vi* (*talk rapidly without showing any signs of stopping*) That woman chatters on till I could scream.

check back *vi* (*a*) (*look back in records*) She checked back to 1930, trying to get at the facts. (*b*) (*re-contact*) I'll check back in half an hour and let you know what's been decided.

check in 1 *vi* (*Fam: arrive*) He checked in at the hotel on time last night. *n* **check-in**. *n cpd* **check-in point**. 2 *vt* (*Fam: arrange a place for*) I'll check you in at one of the best hotels.

check out 1 *vi* (a) (*Fam: leave*) He checked out last night, and left no forwarding address. *n cpd* **check-out**. *n cpd* **check-out point, check-out desk**. (b) (*Euph Fam: die*) I'm afraid he's just checked out. 2 *vt sep* (a) (*assist departure of*) We checked them out this morning. The airline has checked their luggage out. (b) (*confirm by carefully checking*) Would you check out these names and numbers, please? Ask him to check the information out for us.

check off 1 *vi* (*go off duty*) He checked off at eight o'clock. 2 *vt sep* (*mark off on a list*) He checked their names off as they went aboard the plane.

check over *vt sep* (*inspect carefully*) He checked over the names on the list to ensure that everything was correct. I would like you to check over the proofs of this book.

check up *vi* (*make a check, examine*) I'll just check up and find out if he is still here. The company will check up on the estimates for next year. I think the doctor wants to check up on how things are going with him. *n phr* a (**medical**) **check-up**.

check (up) on *vt fus* (*investigate, test*) We had better check on this story before we print it.

cheek up *vt sep* (*Sl: give cheek or insolence to*) That little fellow was cheeking up his mother again. I don't like kids who cheek you up.

cheer on *vt sep* (*encourage with cheers*) The spectators cheered the team on.

cheer up 1 *vi* (*become happier*) I expect he'll cheer up when he sees the new car. Oh, come on, cheer up! 2 *vt sep* (*make more cheerful*) He tried to cheer them up with funny stories.

chew away 1 *vi* (a) (*chew continuously*) He's been chewing away on that gum for hours. (b) (*chew destructively*) The rats have been chewing away at the woodwork. 2 *vt sep* (*chew destructively*) The rats have chewed the woodwork away.

chew over *vt sep* (a) (*Fig Fam: consider*) I've been chewing this matter over in my mind for some time. (b) (*discuss at length*) They have chewed the problem over for hours and hope to reach a decision soon.

chew up *vt sep* (a) (*Lit: chew fully*) The dog chewed up the meat. (b) (*Fig: spoil*) The machine chewed up the paper. (c) (*Sl: reprimand*) The chief really chewed us up yesterday because of what we did.

chew (up) on *vt fus* (*Fig: meditate on*) This is a problem for you to chew on.

chicken out *vi* (*Sl: dodge or escape, like a frightened chicken*) He's a coward, and he'll chicken out if he can.

chime in *vi* (*a*) (*Lit: sound in sequence*) The bells chimed in one
by one. (*b*) (*Fig Fam: interrupt*) He chimed in with some ideas
of his own.

chip away 1 *vi* (*a*) (*chip continuously*) The sculptor chipped away
steadily at the stone. (*b*) (*break off in chips*) I'm afraid this part
of the wall is chipping away rather badly. 2 *vt sep* (*remove in
chips, or piece by piece*) He began by chipping away the broken
surface.

chip in *vi* (*a*) (*Sl: interrupt*) He chipped in with several complaints
of his own. (*b*) (*Sl: contribute*) We decided to chip in with a
fiver (£5).

chip off 1 *vi* (*come or fall off in chips*) The surface has chipped off.
2 *vt sep* (*remove in chips, or piece by piece*) He began by chipping off
the broken surface. She chipped the old paint off.

chisel out *vt sep* (*cut out with a chisel or sharp tool*) He chiselled out
a number of holes in the stone. He began to chisel a face
out of the material.

*chivvy + particle *vt sep* (*Sl: urge or prod into movement, bully,
with direction*) We really ought to go and chivvy the builders up
a bit. He chivvied the children along as fast as he could.

choke back *vt sep* (*restrain, virtually by choking*) He choked back a
sharp reply. She choked back a sob.

choke down *vt sep* (*a*) (*Lit: swallow, virtually while choking*) He
didn't like the food but he managed to choke it down. (*b*)
(*Fig: accept, with humiliation*) He choked down the insult.

choke off *vt sep* (*a*) (*Lit: cut off or prevent by choking*) The burglar
choked off her scream. (*b*) (*Fig: cut off or sever by some violent
action*) The army has choked off the enemy's supplies.

choke up *vt sep* (*close by choking or filling very full*) The entrance
was choked up with weeds. The petrol lead appears to be
choked up with dirt.

chop back 1 *vi* (*Fig: cut back sharply, economize*) I'm afraid we'll
have to chop back on expenditure this month. 2 *vt sep* (*Lit:
cut back sharply*) The settlers chopped back the vegetation.

chop down *vt sep* (*cut down with sharp strokes*) The men chopped
the trees down.

chop off *vt sep* (*cut off with sharp strokes or a single sharp stroke*) He
chopped the branches off. The executioner chopped his head
off.

chop up *vt sep* (*cut up with sharp strokes*) (*a*) (*Lit*) He chopped
up some wood for the fire. (*b*) (*Fig: divide*) They have appar-

ently decided to chop the company up into smaller units.

*chuck + particle *vt sep* (*throw casually, with direction*) He chucked away the empty tin. They chucked out a lot of old furniture. She chucked the materials up to him.

chuck in *vt sep* (*a*) *see* ***chuck** (*b*)=**chuck up** (*b*).

chuck out *vt sep* (*a*) *see* ***chuck** (*b*) (*Sl: eject forcibly, expel*) They chucked him out of the college for being a bad influence.

chuck up *vt sep* (*a*) *see* ***chuck** (*b*) (*Sl Fig: abandon, resign from*) He has decided to chuck the whole thing up. He chucked up the work and went to another town.

*chug + particle *vi* (*move, accompanied by the noise of an engine, with direction*) The ship chugged along. As we neared the harbour, a small boat came chugging out. A steam train chugged past.

chum up *vi* (*Sl: become friends, cf* **pal up**) Those two seem to have chummed up pretty quickly. She chummed up with another new girl.

churn away *vi* (*continue to churn, shake*) The wheels of the paddle-steamer churned away, causing the water to swirl up.

churn out *vt sep* (*a*) (*Lit: produce by shaking in churns*) Those farmers churn out a lot of butter. (*b*) (*Fig: produce quickly in great quantities*) They were churning out consumer goods faster than the market could absorb them. That author has churned out a lot of rubbish in his time.

churn up *vt sep* (*agitate by churning*) The wheels of the trucks have churned up a lot of mud.

circle round *vi* (*move around in circles*) The hawk slowly circled round in the sky, watching its prey. Wolves circled around, waiting.

clam up *vi* (*Fig Sl: close one's mouth tight, like a clam; become silent*) They are afraid he's going to clam up on them. Don't clam up just when the story is getting interesting.

*clamber + particle *vi* (*climb heavily or clumsily, with direction*) The boy clambered slowly up onto the roof. The men clambered carefully along the mountainside. I hope you don't expect me to clamber down there.

clamp down *vt sep* (*close down tightly into position*) He clamped the metal lid firmly down.

clamp down on *vt fus* (*suppress, restrain*) The government may find it necessary to clamp down on such activities. *n* **a clampdown**=a severe restriction. *Example:* During the emergency there was a clamp-down on news from abroad.

clap on *vt sep* (*a*) (*encourage to come on, by clapping*) The audience clapped her on.   (*b*) (*put on firmly*) He clapped his hat on angrily and walked out.   (*c*) (*Naut: add*) The men clapped on more sail, to take advantage of the fresh wind.   (*d*) (*Aut: apply*) The driver clapped on his brakes when he saw the child.

clap out   *vt sep*   (*Sl: usu past p: exhausted or finished*) He was driving a clapped-out old car.   I feel really clapped out today.

clap to   1 *vi*   (*close noisily*) The door clapped to.   2 *vt sep* (*close noisily*) He clapped the door to.

clean down   *vt sep*   (*clean thoroughly, in a downward direction*) He cleaned the lorry down last night.

clean out   *vt sep*   (*a*) (*Lit: clean thoroughly*) He cleaned out his room.   (*b*) (*Fig: strip, empty*) The robbers cleaned the bank out, and got away with £100,000.   (*c*) (*Sl: leave with no money*) We played cards and he cleaned me out.

clean up   1 *vi*   (*a*) (*Lit: clean the place*) She had to clean up after the children's party.   *n a* **clean-up**   (*b*) (*Fig Fam: be successful, make a great profit*) He certainly cleaned up on that deal.   *n a* **clean-up**.   2 *vt*   (*a*) (*Lit: clean thoroughly*) She cleaned the place up after the children's party.   (*b*) (*Fig: reform*) The new mayor said he would clean the city up.   *n a* **clean-up**.

cleanse away   *vt sep*   (*completely clean or purify*) They cleansed away all the filth.   The preacher promised that God would cleanse away all their sins.

clear away   1 *vi*   (*a*) (*vanish*) The mist cleared away as the sun came out.   (*b*) (*clear the table*) Mother always clears away quickly when we have finished eating.   2 *vt sep* (*remove*) The engineers began by clearing away the debris.   Mother cleared the dirty dishes away when we had finished eating.   Clear away your toys now, children!

clear off   1 *vi*   (*Fam Emph: go away*) I told them to clear off.   Clear off!   2 *vt sep*   (*a*) (*settle*) He has at last cleared off all his debts.   (*b*) (*redeem*) I hope to clear off my mortgage in a few months' time.   (*c*) (*dispose of*) The manager wants to clear off all the old stock in the warehouse.

clear out   1 *vi*=**clear off**.   2 *vt sep*   (*a*) (*clean by clearing thoroughly*) He cleared out the cupboards.   *n a* **clear-out**.   (*b*) (*remove, evict*) He cleared the people out of the room.   They have cleared all the tenants out of those houses.

clear up   1 *vi*   (*improve*) I think the weather will soon clear up, don't you?   2 *vt sep*   (*a*) (*clean by clearing thoroughly*) I hope you don't expect us to clear up that mess you are making.   *n a* **clear-up**.   (*b*) (*solve*) The police hope to clear the matter up quickly.   It's a mystery that has never been cleared up.

*climb + particle   *vi*   (*move by hands and feet, with direction*) I

watched the men below climbing up. He said he would climb
down and help them. I opened the window and he climbed
through.

climb down *vi* (a) *see* *climb (b) (*Fig: compromise*) I expect
they'll climb down if you show them you are determined.
(c) (*admit defeat*) They had to climb down when they saw the
evidence.

clock in/on *vi* (*Industry: indicate time of one's arrival at work by
putting a card in a machine with a clock*) The men clock in at this
time every day.

clock off/out *vi* (*Industry: indicate time of departure from work by
putting a card in a machine which stamps the time on the card.*) The
men clock off at this time every day.

clock up *vt sep* (a) (*Lit: indicate time, speed etc by using a clock*) He
clocked up 150 km/h on the straight in that car. He has now
clocked up more overtime than any other man in the factory.
(b) (*Fig: gain, achieve*) I expect he'll clock up quite a few successes
in the next year or two.

clog up 1 *vi* (*become closed through clogging or filling with soft material*)
The water pipe has clogged up again. 2 *vt* (*close through
clogging*) The mud has clogged up the pipe. The sewers are all
clogged up.

close down (*close without intention of re-opening*) 1 *vi* That little
shop on the corner has closed down. The radio station closed
down for the night. *n* **a close-down**. 2 *vt sep* He has closed
down his business in London. They have decided to close that
branch down.

close in *vi* (a) (*approach*) The evening is closing in. The puma
closed in as its prey grew weaker. (b) (*of days: get shorter*)
The days are closing in now that winter is nearly here.

close in (up)on *vt fus* (*Mil etc: encircle, tighten the circle round*)
The army is now closing in upon the enemy positions.

close up 1 *vi* (a) (*come closer together*) The sergeant told the men
to close up. (b) (*close as the beginning of healing*) The wound in
his arm has begun to close up. 2 *vt sep* (a) (*bring close together*)
The sergeant told the men to close up their ranks. (b) (*close for
an indefinite period*) They have decided to close up the house while
they are abroad. (c) (*seal*) They closed up the mouth of the
pipe. That opening in the wall has now been closed up.

close with *vt fus* (*engage, grapple with*) The wrestler closed with
his opponent.

cloud over 1 *vi* (a) (*Met: become cloudy*) The sky has clouded
over. (b) =**cloud up**.

cloud up   1 *vi*   (*become cloudy*) The window has clouded up, because of the steam.   2 *vt sep*   (*make cloudy*) The steam from the kettle has clouded up the windows.

club together   *vi*   (*join together, as if in a club, to do something*) The men have clubbed together to help him with his debts.

clue in   *vt sep*   (*Sl: provide with necessary information*) Please clue me in on what you are doing, so that I can help.

clue up   *vt sep*   (*Sl: provide with necessary information, usually for professional purposes*) They really clue you up on things at that place.   He's pretty clued up on electronics.   They've got clued up on maths.

cluster round   *vi*   (*gather round in clusters or small tight groups*) We clustered round to listen.

clutter up   *vt sep*   (*Fam: make untidy by cluttering or crowding with many things*) The children clutter the place up with toys.   His writing style is cluttered up with fancy expressions.

colour in   *vt sep*   (*fill in with colour*) The child was colouring in a series of outline drawings.

colour up   1 *vi*   (*Fam: blush*) When I complimented her, she coloured up a bit and said it was nothing really.   2 *vt sep* (*a*) (*improve by using colour*) I'd like you to colour the place up a bit.   (*b*) (*Fig: exaggerate*) Some journalists like to colour their stories up with lurid details of people's private lives.

comb out   *vt sep*   (*a*) (*Lit: comb completely*) She combed out her long hair.   (*b*) (*Lit: remove by a combing action*) She combed the lice out of the child's hair.

*****come + particle**   *vi*   (*come, with direction*) He opened the door and came out.   She opened the door and came in.   He told the children to come along.   He said he would come back in half an hour.

come about   *vi*   (*a*) (*Naut: change direction*) The wind has come about in the last hour.   The ship came about and headed back for safety.   (*b*) (*Impers: happen*) How does it come about that you are here, and not in London?

come across   1 *vi*   (*a*) (*cross*) He came across to where we were standing.   (*b*) (*be received, make an impression*) His speech came across well/badly.   2 *vt fus*   (*find or meet by chance*) If you come across my book, will you send me it?   I came across him by chance one day last week.

come across with   *vt fus*   (*Fam: provide*) He came across with £10 just when I needed it.   The informer came across with the names of his accomplices in the bank robbery.

come along   *vi*   (*a*) *see* *****come   (*b*) (*hurry up*) Come along, girls!

(c) (*Fam: attend*) May my sister come along to the meeting as well? (d) (*accompany*) Would you come along with me, please? (e) (*develop, progress*) How is your broken arm coming along? It is coming along quite well now. His work is coming along well. My roses are coming along nicely.

come apart *vi* (*Fam: disintegrate*) The machine came apart when he started it up. I'm afraid the thing just came apart in my hands.

come at *vt fus* (a) (*find, get hold of*) I've been looking for that article, but can't come at it anywhere. (b) (*determine, discover*) It's difficult to come at the exact facts. (c) (*attack, approach in a threatening way*) The man came at me with a knife.

come away *vi* (a) (*leave*) She had to come away before the end of the play. Come away from that window! (b) (*become detached*) My heel has come away from the rest of the shoe. The woodwork has come away.

come back *vi* (a) (*return*) He came back two hours later. Now, to come back to what I was saying a moment ago. (b) (*return to one's memory*) His face is coming back to me now. (c) (*of fashion, to be popular again*) Short skirts are coming back. (d) (*reply vehemently*) When charged with the crime, he came back at us furiously. When accused of theft, he came back with a stinging counter-accusation.

come between *vt fus* (a) (*interpose oneself*) He tried to come between the quarrelling men. (b) (*cause trouble between*) I wouldn't like to come between two lovers, you know.

come by *vt fus* (*obtain*) How did you come by this painting? I don't know how she came by such an idea.

come down *vi* (a) (*descend*) I watched the climbers come down into the valley. The aeroplane came down in that field. Come down from there at once! (b) (*be demolished*) That old building is coming down next year. (c) (*Fig: drop, fall*) The price of beer is coming down soon. Her weight is slowly coming down. The child's temperature came down in the morning. (d) (*Fig: lose social rank*) I'm afraid the family has come down in the world lately. (e) (*be reduced to*) She has come down to begging for work. *n* a **comedown**=a humiliation. (f) (*extend downward*) Her hair comes down to her shoulders. (g) (*be passed on, be transmitted in a tradition*) This house has come down from father to son for eight generations.

come down with *vt fus* (a) (*become ill from*) He has come down with influenza. (b) (*pay out*) She has come down with £15 at last.

come down (up)on *vt fus* (a) (*Fam: punish, rebuke*) The government intends to come down heavily on tax evaders. He came down on me like a ton of bricks. (*b*) (*Fig: pounce on*) They came down on me for a subscription to their association.

come forward *vi* (*present oneself*) He has come forward with an offer of help. She has come forward as a candidate in the local elections.

come from *vt fus* (*originate from*) He comes from Turkey. This word comes from Latin.

come in *vi* (*a*) (*enter*) She opened the door and came in (*b*) (*arrive*) When does your train come in? (*c*) (*become seasonable*) When do strawberries come in? (*d*) (*come to be fashionable*) I expect long skirts will come in again soon. (*e*) (*flow in*) The tide comes in a long way at this point. (*f*) (*cricket: join the game*) The batsmen came in. (*g*) (*take position in a race or competition*) He came in fourth. (*h*) (*Pol: be elected to power*) The socialists came in at the last election. (*i*) (*be received as income*) He has £5,000 coming in every year. (*j*) (*have one's place or work*) Where do I come in, in your scheme? (*k*) *Idiom:* to come in handy = to prove useful.

come in for *vt fus* (*Fam: receive, suffer*) I'm afraid they come in for a lot of abuse from some people. She came in for a lot of criticism.

come into *vt fus* (*a*) (*Fig: inherit*) He has come into a lot of money from his old uncle's estate. (*b*) *Idiom:* to come into one's own = to achieve independence. *Example:* She has at last come into her own since her domineering sister left home.

come near to/come close to *vt fus* (*get close to*) I came near to telling him just what I thought of the whole business. I came close to screaming because of the din. He came close to committing suicide.

come of *vt fus* (*a*) (*result from*) Nothing came of it, I'm afraid. That's what comes of disobeying the instructions. (*b*) (*be descended from*) He comes of a good family. These racehorses come of excellent stock.

come off 1 *vi* (*a*) (*separate from something*) This button has just come off. (*b*) (*disappear*) I don't think these stains will come off. The marks came off after some rubbing. (*c*) (*take place*) Her wedding never came off. (*d*) (*prosper, succeed*) His plans haven't come off. The attempt isn't likely to come off. (*e*) (*acquit oneself*) He came off well by comparison with the others. 2 *vt fus* (*a*) (*separate from*) This button must have come off her coat. (*b*) (*fall from*) He has come off his bicycle and is lying in the street. (*c*) (*abandon*) The country came off the gold standard long ago. (*d*) *Idiom:* to come off it = to stop pretending. *Examples:* I told him to come off it. Oh, come off it.

come on 1 *vi* (*a*) *see* ***come** (*b*) (*continue to advance*) The soldiers came on in the face of heavy fire. (*c*) (*imper, for encouragement*) Come on, try it again! (*d*) (*progress, develop*) How are your potatoes coming on? I hope his plans are coming on all right. (*e*) (*begin*) Night is coming on. It came on to rain. I feel a cold coming on. (*f*) (*Law: arise for discussion and judgement*) His case comes on this afternoon. (*g*) (*Cricket: come into the game*) Their best man came on to bowl. (*h*) (*Theatre: appear*) The great man came on and gave a marvellous performance. 'Hamlet' is coming on next week. 2 *vt fus* = **come upon**.

come out *vi* (*a*) *see* ***come** (*b*) (*emerge, appear*) The sun came out later in the afternoon. The stars come out at night. Some flowers have begun to come out. (*c*) (*become known*) The truth has come out at last. This secret will finally come out. (*d*) (*appear as a publication*) The book will come out in September. That magazine comes out once a week. (*e*) (*Phot: be developed*) The photographs haven't come out very well. (*f*) (*look*) You always come out well in photographs. (*g*) (*Industry: strike*) The men have come out (on strike) for more pay. (*h*) (*emerge, show*) His kindness comes out when he speaks. (*i*) (*fade, vanish, go away*) I don't think these stains are going to come out after all. The dye won't come out, you know. (*j*) (*Math: resolve itself satisfactorily*) This equation just won't come out. (*k*) (*make a debut, of a girl*) She came out last season. (*l*) *n* **outcome** = (*result*). The outcome of their economic policy was more unemployment.

come out in *vt fus* (*Med: exhibit, of symptoms*) He came out in a rash last night. She has begun to come out in spots. I came out in a cold sweat.

come out of *vt fus* (*emerge from, survive*) He has come out of the ordeal well.

come out with *vt fus* (*Fam: say*) He comes out with some funny ideas. When I asked her where she had been, she came out with some story about visiting her aunt. You never know what that child will come out with next.

come over *vi* (*a*) *see* ***come** (*b*) (*cross over to visit*) You really must come over sometime and have dinner with us. (*c*) (*come from a distance, usually across a sea*) He came over from France last week, just to see us. They come over from New York every spring. (*d*) (*Sl: become, suddenly feel*) I came over all dizzy just for a moment, but I'm all right now. She came over queer.

come round *vi* (*a*) *see* ***come** (*b*) (*visit casually*) He came round (to see us) last night. (*c*) (*regain consciousness*) The unconscious man slowly began to come round. (*d*) (*begin to accept or appreciate something*) I think he'll come round eventually.

come round to *vt fus* (*begin to accept or appreciate*) She is slowly coming round to our point of view.

come through *vi* (*a*) *see* ***come** (*b*) (*survive*) I hope he will come through all right, despite the danger. Not many men in that regiment came through.

come to *vi*=**come round** (*c*).

come together *vi* (*converge*) The two lines come together at that point.

come under 1 *vi* *see* ***come** 2 *vt fus* (*a*) (*be entered in a list etc under*) This article comes under a different heading. Articles on farming come under 'agriculture'. (*b*) (*be subject to*) I think this shop will shortly come under new management. I think this kind of thing comes under the jurisdiction of the Foreign Office.

come up *vi* (*a*) *see* ***come** (*b*) (*occur, happen*) It's just one of those things that comes up. I expect something to come up soon. (*c*) (*be selected*) Maybe his number will come up soon. (*d*) (*present oneself*) He came up for interview but did not get the job. (*e*) (*develop a lustre, begin to shine*) The silver has come up beautifully. (*f*) *Idiom:* to come up trumps=to win.

come up against *vt fus* (*confront, be faced with*) I don't expect to come up against any monsters when I get there. You may come up against a bit of opposition. He came up against the head-master, and eventually had to leave.

come up to *vt fus* (*a*) (*reach the height of*) He's getting big, and comes up to my shoulder now. (*b*) (*attain, fulfil*) Do you think he will come up to expectations in that new job of his? This work hardly comes up to the required standard.

come up with *vt fus* (*produce*) He came up with a good idea for getting the lawnmower working again. She has come up with some fine suggestions.

conceive of *vt fus* (*a*) (*imagine*) I can't conceive of anything funnier than that. (*b*) (*consider*) He wouldn't conceive of her going to London at her age. I refuse to conceive of such a solution to our problem.

***conduct** + **particle** *vt sep* (*convey or escort, with direction*) He asked the guard to conduct us out. The receptionist conducted us in to meet the great man.

conjure away *vt sep* (*remove by conjuring or magic, make disappear*) (*a*) (*Lit*) The magician conjured the rabbit away. (*b*) (*Fig*) I don't trust him, and feel as though he's going to conjure all the money away. She thinks that the doctor can just conjure headaches away.

conjure up *vt sep* (*make appear by conjuring or magic*) (*a*) (*Lit*) The magician conjured up a white rabbit. (b) (*Fig*) The situation was desperate, but the general could hardly conjure up fresh reinforcements from nowhere. (c) (*cause to appear*) Some people claim to be able to conjure up the spirits of the dead. (d) (*evoke*) This scent conjures up many pleasant memories.

conk out *vi* (*Sl: stop functioning*) I'm afraid the engine has conked out.

contract in *vi* (*enter by contract or arrangement*) I'd like to contract in on this project, if I may.

contract out *vi* (*leave by contract or agreement*) I'd like to contract out of this project, if you don't mind.

cook-out *n usu no verb* (*a barbecue or similar outdoor cooking*) We had a cook-out in the garden yesterday.

cook up *vt sep* (a) (*Lit: prepare by cooking quickly*) She cooked up an omelette and chips when he arrived unexpectedly. (b) (*Fig Fam: invent, fabricate, concoct*) To avoid going to the meeting he cooked up an excuse about being ill. I don't like cooking up stories just to help you out of a difficult situation.

cool down 1 *vi* (*become cool*) (a) (*Lit*) The soup has cooled down. She let the dish cool down before touching it. (b) (*Fig*) The situation has cooled down a lot since yesterday. I shall let him cool down before discussing the subject again. 2 *vt sep* (*make cool*) (a) (*Lit*) She cooled the soup down by putting it in a cold dish. (b) (*Fig*) He cooled the situation down by offering to mediate between the disputing parties.

cool off 1 *vi* (*become cool*) (a) (*Lit*) They took time to cool off after the game. (b) (*Fig*) I hope the two countries will cool off a bit, or there will be war. *n cpd* a **cooling-off period**=a period of time in which a situation can cool off. (c) (*lose enthusiasm*) She has cooled off about him, I think. (d) (*lose one's affections*) He has cooled off a lot towards those people. 2 *vt sep* (*make cool*) (a) (*Lit*) He had a shower to cool himself off. Some rain would cool us off. (b) (*Fig*) His quiet advice cooled them off a little.

coop up *vt sep* (a) (*Lit: confine in a coop or cage*) The hens have been cooped up for the night. (b) (*Fig: confine*) She has been cooped up in her room for days. I sometimes feel really cooped up in this place.

cop out *vi* (*Sl: withdraw*) He doesn't like normal society, so he has copped out. He has copped out of his responsibilities.

copy out *vt sep* (*copy carefully, thoroughly*) The teacher asked him to copy out the letters from that book. He has copied the whole essay out again.

cordon off *vt sep* (*isolate by means of a barrier*) The police cordoned

off the area while the demolition work continued.   This part
of the city has been cordoned off.

cork up   *vt sep*   (a) (*seal completely with a cork*) The bottles have all
been corked up.   (b) (*Fig: repress, as if using a cork*) She has
corked up her feelings for years.

cotton on   *vi*   (a) (*Sl: understand*) He won't cotton on, he's much
too involved with his own affairs.

cotton on to   *vt fus*   (*Sl: understand, grasp, perceive*) I hope they
haven't cottoned on to what we are doing.

cotton to   *vt fus*   (*Sl: find sympathetic, like*) I'm afraid I just don't
cotton to him.   They don't cotton to your suggestion at all.

cough out   *vt sep*   (*eject violently, while coughing*) He coughed out
blood.

cough up   1 *vi*   (*Fig Sl: provide money or information*) I don't think
he'll cough up unless you put pressure on him.   2 *vt sep*   (a)
(*Lit: emit while coughing*) He began to cough up blood.   (b)
(*Fig Sl: provide*) He wouldn't cough up the cash when we asked
for it.

count down   *vi*   (*count backwards to zero, to reach a required time*)
The controllers counted down to blast-off.   *n* **a countdown**.

count for   *vt fus*   (*signify*) That doesn't count for much in this
country.   He seems to count for quite a lot in his firm.

count in   *vt sep*   (a) (*Lit: include by counting*) He has counted all
the guests in.   (b) (*Fig Fam: include*) Please count me in on this
project.   You can count me in.   We have counted you all in.

count on   1 *vi*   (*continue to count*) He counted on monotonously
until he reached 100.   2 *vt fus* = **count (up)on**.

count out   *vt sep*   (a) (*count on departure*) The doorman counted
the visitors out.   (b) (*provide while counting*) The bank teller
counted out the money in five-pound notes.   (c) (*Fam: exclude*)
You can count me out of this little plan of yours.   (d) (*Boxing:
pronounce to be the loser, after counting to ten*) The boxer was down
on the mat and the referee counted him out.   (e) (*Parl: adjourn
by counting to prove that there is not a quorum*) The House was
counted out at eleven pm.

count up   1 *vi*   (*intensive of* **count**) Count up to ten before you
open your eyes.   2 *vt sep*   (a) (*enumerate*) They began to count
up their losses after the battle.   (b) (*total*) The men counted
the money up carefully.

count (up)on   *vt fus*   (*depend on, rely on*) We are counting on you
to help.   I had counted upon having it completed by March.

couple up   *vt sep*   (*join by linking*) The railwaymen coupled up the wagons.

cover in *vt sep* (*enclose by means of a cover or roof*) They have covered in the whole market.

cover over *vt sep* (*a*)=**cover in**. (*b*) (*protect with a cover*) Would you cover the vegetables over, please?

cover up 1 *vi* (*cover oneself thoroughly*) It's cold and you should cover up warmly. 2 *vt sep* (*cover completely*) He covered the child up with a blanket.

cover up for *vt fus* (*Sl: shield, usu by lying or misrepresenting something*) The police think he is covering up for someone else. I tried to cover up for him, but without success.

cow down *vt sep* (*cow completely, intimidate*) He was quite cowed down by the other man's threats.

cower away *vi* (*crouch away from something, usually in fear*) The child cowered away from the angry man.

cower down *vi* (*crouch very low, huddle near the ground*) The animals cowered down in the hole, watching us approach.

crack down *vi* (*come down or descend with a cracking noise*) The whip cracked down on the horse's rump.

crack down on *vt fus* (*Fam: suppress*) The general cracked down on any sign of mutiny. You should crack down on these people before real trouble starts. *n* **a crackdown.**

crack up 1 *vi* (*break into pieces*) (*a*) (*Lit*) The soil is cracking up because of the drought. (*b*) (*Fig Fam*) I must be cracking up, because I'm beginning to forget everything I should be doing. 2 *vt sep* (*Fam usu pass: consider, claim*) This material isn't all it is cracked up to be.

*cram + particle 1 *vi* (*crowd or push violently or with some effort, with direction*) The boys crammed in to see the television. He opened the gate and we all crammed through. We ate as much as we could cram in. 2 *vt sep* (*push or stuff violently or with some effort, with direction*) They crammed as much equipment in as they could. He opened the hatch and we crammed the boxes through. They crammed the boxes together in a corner.

crank up *vt sep* (*operate by means of a cranking handle*) They cranked up the wrecked bus into a better position for rescuing the trapped passengers. Some field telephones need to be cranked up before you can contact anyone.

*crash + particle *vi* (*a*) (*make a crashing noise, with direction*) The cymbals crashed out. The brass section crashed in at the perfect moment. (*b*) (*move with a crashing noise, with direction*) The bull crashed out through the flimsy fence. The tanks crashed past in a haze of dust.

***crawl + particle** *vi* (*crawl, with direction*) The baby crawled along. A spider was crawling up into the pipe. They crawled down to rescue the injured miners.

cream off *vt sep* (*a*) (*Lit: remove the cream from*) She creamed off the milk. (*b*) (*Fig: remove as the best*) This educational system creams off the most promising pupils (from all the others).

***creep + particle** *vi* (*move in a furtive manner, with direction*) The hunter crept along, eyes alert. He opened the door quietly and we crept through. I don't like people who creep up on you without warning.

crop out *vi* (*Geol: emerge, protrude*) A seam of igneous rock crops out at that point. *n phr* **a rocky outcrop.**

crop up *vi* (*a*) (*Geol*)=**crop out.** (*b*) (*Fig: emerge, arise*) Some difficult questions crop up at this point. The same problems keep cropping up all the time. Something has cropped up and I won't be home tonight till late.

cross off *vt sep* (*eliminate from a list*) He crossed their names off as they answered him.

cross out *vt sep* (*delete from a sheet of paper*) He crossed the word out and wrote in another. Don't cross it out until you are sure you don't want it.

cross over *vi* (*cross to the other side*) (*a*) (*Lit*) He waited till the street was empty, then crossed over. (*b*) (*Lit: go over as a traitor*) He crossed over to the enemy last night. (*c*) (*Fig: change one's allegiance*) He has crossed over to the opposition.

crow over *vt fus* (*exult or triumph over*) They have won the fight, but they are not crowing over their defeated opponents. I wish you would stop crowing over his disappointment.

***crowd + particle** 1 *vi* (*come in crowds, with direction*) The people crowded in to see him.   They crowded out to look at the rocket. He watched the animals crowd together for security. We asked the children to crowd round and listen to the story. 2 *vt sep* (*a*) (*make come in a crowd, with direction*) The ushers crowded too many people in. The dogs crowded the animals along. (*b*) (*push to form a crowd, usu against one's will, with direction*) The horseman crowded the people aside, to make room for the king's party. The ushers crowded the people out into the street.

crowd out 1 *vi* *see* ***crowd.** 2 *vt fus* (*a*) *see* ***crowd.** (*b*) (*Fig: push aside, as if by a crowd*) This article was crowded out of yesterday's edition. I think we have been deliberately crowded out (of the scheme).

***cruise + particle** *vi* (*a*) (*move steadily, originally of ships, with direction*) The ship cruised along at a steady speed.   The police cruised around in their patrol cars. You should cruise down to the Canary Islands sometime. (*b*) (*Sl: move in a nonchalant way*) He cruised up to us and asked who we wanted to see. She cruised off with another fellow.

crumple up 1 *vi* (*collapse*) He just crumpled up when the bullet hit him. 2 *vt sep* (*crease up*) He crumpled the letter up and threw it away. The bedclothes are all crumpled up.

*crunch + particle *vi* (*move with a crunching noise, with direction*) The soldiers crunched along through the fallen masonry. The climbers crunched up through the scree.

crunch down 1 *vi see* ***crunch.** 2 *vt sep* (*a*) (*break down by grinding or with a crunching noise*) He crunched the rock down into a fine powder. (*b*) (*swallow after crunching with the teeth*) The boy crunched the crisps down.

crunch up 1 *vi see* ***crunch.** 2 *vt sep* (*break completely by crunching or with a crunching noise*) He crunched up the dry powder in his hand. The machine crunched up everything you put into it.

*crush + particle *vt sep* (*compress, squeeze*) The machine crushes up old cars. The juice is crushed out of the grapes. The gap was narrow but we managed to crush the materials through.

cry down *vt sep* (*Old: decry, criticize*) I wish he wouldn't cry everyone down.

cry off 1 *vi* (*withdraw one's support*) He cried off at the last moment. 2 *vt fus* (*withdraw from*) He cried off the project and left his friends in great difficulty.

cry out *vi* (*a*) (*Lit: shout aloud*) He cried out in pain. She cried out with delight when she saw him. They cried out to attract our attention. (*b*) (*Fig: demand, be in great need of*) This floor is crying out to be scrubbed. The business is just crying out for some capital.

cry out against *vt fus* (*reject loudly*) The people are crying out against this injustice.

cry up *vt sep* (*Fam, usu pass: praise, consider*) He is not all he is cried up to be.

curl up 1 *vi* (*a*) (*curl into a tight mass*) The cat had curled up near the fire. The child curled up in bed. (*b*) (*rise or ascend in curling movements*) The smoke curled up from the chimney. 2 *vt sep* (*make into a huddle or tight mass*) She curled herself up in the big armchair.

*curve + particle *vi* (*move or appear to move in a curve, with direction*) The bay curves away as far as the eye can see. The

headland curves out to sea. The design curves in and then
out. The rocket curved up into the stratosphere.

cut across   *vt fus*   (*interrupt*) The wall cuts across our line of vision.
His decision will cut across our basic plan.

cut along   *vi*   (*Sl: go quickly*) Cut along and ask him if he needs
our help.

cut away   *vt sep*   (*a*) (*remove by cutting*) He cut away the material
which he didn't need.   (*b*) (*shape by cutting*) He cut the collar
away.   *n cpd* **a cutaway collar.**

cut back   1 *vi*   (*return quickly*) He cut back through the woods to
where he had been standing before.   2 *vt sep*   (*reduce by cutting*)
The tailor cut the cloth back.   He decided to cut the plants
back, in order to improve their growth later in the season.

cut back on   *vt fus*   (*lower the rate of*) We must cut back on expenditure in order to remain solvent.   They cut back on
production during the power cuts.   *n* **a cutback** (in expenditure, production).

cut down   *vt sep*   (*a*) (*Lit: fell*) He cut the tree down.   The
bullets cut the soldiers down like corn.   (*b*) (*Fig: reduce*) We
must cut down expenses.   He ought to cut down the volume of
work.   The tailor cut the dress down.   (*c*) (*Euph, usu pass:
kill*) He was cut down in his prime by pneumonia.

cut down on   *vt fus*   (*a*)=**cut back on.**   (*b*) (*reduce*) You must
cut down on the amount of carbohydrates you eat if you want
to get slim.   He has been told to cut down on the work that he
takes home.

cut in   1 *vi*   (*a*) (*cut towards the centre*) The saw quickly cut in
through the veneer.   (*b*) (*intervene*) I think I ought to cut in on
what they are doing.   (*c*) (*interrupt*) She always cuts in when
other people are talking.   (*d*) (*move to intercept*) The police car
cut in ahead of the escaping robbers.   2 *vt sep*   (*a*) (*Lit: deal in
at cards*) Can you cut me in please?   (*b*) (*Fig: include*) I would
like to be cut in on this project.

cut into   *vt fus*   (*a*) (*Lit*) The knife easily cut into the cake.   (*b*)
(*Fig: consume valuable time from*) This plan of yours cuts into our
schedule rather badly.   (*c*) (*Fig: interrupt*) She cut into our
conversation several times.

cut off   1 *vi*   (*go away quickly*) He cut off down a side street.   2 *vt
sep*   (*a*) (*remove by cutting*) He cut the top off.   The rebels cut
off the heads of their captives.   (*b*) (*disconnect*) We were talking
on the telephone, and got cut off.   Our water supply has been
cut off again.   (*c*) (*isolate*) The enemy soldiers were cut off
from their regiment.   The floods cut us off from our homes.
(*d*) (*sever*) The platoon has managed to cut off the enemy's line

of retreat. The floods have cut off our supplies. (*e*) (*disinherit*) He has cut his son off without a penny.

cut out 1 *vi* (*stall, stop functioning*) The engine has cut out again. 2 *vt sep* (*a*) (*extract or obtain by cutting*) He cut out the photograph from the paper. They cut out a path through the jungle. (*b*) (*eliminate*) He has managed to cut out his rival and marry the girl. (*c*) (*Sl: stop*) Why don't you cut out all this nonsense? Just cut it out, will you? (*d*) (*refrain from*) He has decided to cut out smoking and drinking. (*e*) (*usu pass: intend*) He isn't really cut out for this kind of work. I think she's cut out to be a nurse. (*f*) (*usu pass: make worse*) He has had his work cut out for him by all this bad weather. *Idiom:* We'll have our work cut out to catch up = It will be very difficult to catch up.

cut up 1 *vi* *Sl Idiom:* to cut up rough = to become angry. 2 *vt sep* (*a*) (*Lit: slice, divide by cutting*) He cut up the meat. The machine guns cut up the enemy like knives. (*b*) (*Fam, usu pass: upset*) This news had cut him up. She is very cut up about her father's death. (*c*) (*Fig: attack*) His book was severely cut up by the critics.

*cycle + particle *vi* (*move on a bicycle, with direction*) The women cycled along. The workmen cycled off home. The boy cycled away, whistling.

dab on *vt sep* (*apply in small quantities*) She dabbed on the ointment with cotton wool. The child dabbed on the paint with her finger.

dam up *vt sep* (*a*) (*seal with a dam*) They have dammed that river up. (*b*) (*Fig: contain, restrain*) He dammed up his fury until he could no longer remain silent.

damp down *vt sep* (*reduce in strength by making damp*) She damped the fire down for the night.

dampen down = damp down.

*dance + particle (*dance, with direction*) 1 *vi* She felt she could dance on forever. The people were dancing about in the village square. The girl danced up to us and gave us some flowers. They danced out in a kind of procession. 2 *vt sep* He danced her out on to the verandah.

*dart + particle *vi* (*move suddenly and quickly, with direction*) The snake darted forward. The thief darted back into the shadows. Some figures darted past. Men were darting in and out among the trees.

*dash + particle *vi* (*run quickly or recklessly, with direction*) He dashed in breathlessly. She dashed out without telling us where she was going. He has dashed off somewhere. The boy dashed away to meet his friends.

dash down   1 *vi   see* ***dash**.   2 *vt sep   (throw down violently)* He dashed the cup down in his anger.

dash off   1 *vi   see* ***dash**.   2 *vt sep   (Fam: write or produce quickly or casually)* He just dashed the poem off.   She dashed off two articles before dinner.   I'll just dash off a letter to him.

date back   *vi   (go back in time to a particular date)* This manuscript dates back to the 8th century.

daub on   *vt sep   (dab on heavily, smear on)* The witchdoctor daubed on thick blotches of paint.   She certainly daubs her make-up on.   Some artists like to daub their colours on with a palette knife.

daub over   *vt sep   (cover over heavily)* He daubed the canvas over with paint.

*dawdle + particle   *vi   (walk slowly and aimlessly, with direction)* He dawdled up with his hands in his pockets.   I watched them dawdle off towards the shops.   He dawdles in for a drink sometimes.   They often dawdle about here.

dawdle away   1 *vi   see* ***dawdle**.   2 *vt sep   (waste)* He has been dawdling his time away.   We dawdled away three hours playing poker.

dawn (up)on   *vt fus   (Fig impers: come as a realization to)* It has slowly dawned upon us that he will not help.   It dawned on him that he was no longer as young as he used to be.

deck out   *vt sep   (decorate, dress)* They are decked out in their Sunday best.   He is decked out for some kind of party.   She's all decked out and ready to go.   The ship was decked out with flags and bunting.

deliver up   *vt sep   (Old: surrender)* The captain has delivered up himself and his men to the enemy.   They have delivered up the city.

dice away   *vt sep   (lose by dicing or gambling)* He diced his fortune away at the casino.

die away   *vi   (diminish or dwindle)* The sound of the car died away in the distance.   The echoes died away.

die down   *vi   (a)   (decrease, lose force)* The wind has died down a bit.   The fire has died down.   Towards evening the noise dies down.   *(b)   (Fig: decrease, diminish)* The protests of the students are beginning to die down.   His anger has died down a bit.

die off   *vi   (become extinct)* The species is dying off.   It would be a pity if these birds are allowed just to die off.

die out   *vi   (a)*=**die off**.   *(b)   (cease to be)* The fire died out.

dig away   1 *vi   (dig continuously)* He has been digging away for hours. 2 *vt sep* (*detach, loosen or displace by digging*) Animals have dug away the whole bank at this point. The workmen have dug away the foundations.

dig in 1 *vi* (*a*) (*Mil: dig trenches and similar defences*) The soldiers have dug in along the river. (*b*) (*Sl: start eating*) Okay, dig in! The boys dug in ravenously. 2 *vt sep* (*a*) (*Gardening: introduce into the earth by digging*) The gardener dug the compost in.

dig into *vt fus* (*a*) (*Sl: eat heartily*) They dug into the meal. (*b*) (*investigate thoroughly*) The detectives are digging into this whole business.

dig out *vt sep* (*a*) (*remove by digging*) The gardener dug out the weeds. (*b*) (*excavate*) The workmen dug out a deep channel for the water. They have dug out the foundations of the new houses. (*c*) (*release by digging*) The rescuers managed to dig out the trapped miners. The injured men have been dug out of the snow. Some people are still being dug out of the ruins of the building. (*d*) (*Fig Fam: find*) Where on earth did you dig out that old jacket? (*e*) (*Fig: obtain*) He has dug out a lot of information which they prefer not to be made public.

dig up *vt sep* (*a*)=**dig out** (*a*). (*b*) (*find or reveal by digging*) The archaeologists have dug up some interesting Neolithic remains. (*c*) (*prepare by digging*) He has dug up the garden. (*d*)=**dig out** (*e*).

dim out *vt sep* (*cause to fade out, make dim*) The lights of the city have been dimmed out because of the power cuts. *n* a **dim-out**=a time when lights are dimmed out.

din in *vt sep* (*Fig: force or push in*) We have been trying to din some sense in to him. Given time with him, his teachers may din something in.

dine in *vi* (*eat dinner at home*) They are not going out, but intend to dine in tonight. The students always dine in at their college on Thursdays.

dine out *vi* (*eat dinner in a restaurant*) We sometimes dine out at one of our favourite places.

dip in *vt sep* (*immerse briefly or lightly*) He dipped his finger in, to test the heat of the water.

dip into *vt fus* (*Fig: read small parts of, for pleasure*) I dip into this book whenever I can.

*direct + participle *vt sep* (*order, recommend or guide, with direction*) The policeman directed us across to the information office. He was directed up to the waiting-room by a receptionist.

dish out *vt sep* (*a*) (*Lit: serve out in a dish or dishes*) She dished out the food. (*b*) (*Fam: Fig supply*) They enjoy dishing out advice to everyone. He can dish out as much criticism as he gets.

dish up *vt sep* (a) (*serve up in a dish*) She dished up the stew. (b) (*serve up, with or without dishes*) She can dish up a lovely meal when she wants to. (c) (*Fig: provide*) He dished up a lot of useful facts and figures.

dispense with *vt fus* (*do without*) We can dispense with his help.

dispose of *vt fus* (*remove, get rid of*) They disposed of the rubbish.

dither about/around *vi* (*move about, trying ineffectually to do something*) She dithers about half the time, getting in everyone's way. Oh, stop dithering about!

*dive + particle *vi* (*dive, with direction*) The boy dived in off the high board. He dived out of the window to escape the fire. The thief dived away through the hole in the hedge.

dive in *vi* (a) *see* ***dive**. (b) (*Sl: start eating*) Dive in, folks!

divide off *vt sep* (*separate, partition*) The rooms have been divided off by means of thin pre-fabricated sheets.

divide out *vt sep* (*apportion*) The food was divided out among all the people. The inheritance has been evenly divided out.

divide up 1 *vi* (*break up into portions*) The cake divides up nicely. 2 *vt sep* (*apportion piece by piece*) They divided up the land among themselves.

do away with *vt fus* (a) (*abolish, get rid of*) They have done away with those old laws, you know. I want them to do away with this barbarous custom. (b) (*Fam: murder*) They say he did away with her by poisoning her food.

do by *vt fus* (*treat*) I hope you will do well by him. He maintains that he is very hard done by. *Idiom:* to do as you would be done by = to treat others as you would like them to treat you.

do down *vt sep* (*Fam: humiliate*) They will do you down if they can.

do for *vt fus* (a) (*Fam: clean a place for*) She does for the people in that flat. (b) (*Fam: kill, assault violently*) I'll do for him one of these days!

do in *vt sep* (*Fam: kill*) They did (*Dial* done) him in.

do out *vt sep* (a) (*clean*) She did the rooms out completely. *n* **a doing-out** = a thorough clean. (b) (*Fig: deprive*) He thinks that they did him out of that job.

do over *vt sep* (a) (*clean, decorate*) He has done the walls over in pale blue. (b) (*Sl: beat up*) The gang did him over.

do up 1 *vi* (*fasten by design*) This dress does up at the back. 2 *vt sep* (a) (*fasten*) She did up the dress. Do up your shoes!

She forgot to do up the zip. (*b*) (*parcel together*) The books have been done up in brown paper. (*c*) (*renovate, improve appearance*) She decided to do up the house. She did herself up for the occasion. (*d*) (*Fam, usu pass: exhausted*) I feel really done up after that walk.

do with   *vt fus*   (*a*) (*with 'can', 'could'=want, need*) Oh, I could do with a cup of tea. He said he could do with a wash. This silver could do with a polish. (*b*) (*in Neg, with 'can', 'could'=tolerate*) I just can't do with whining children. (*c*) (*with 'have' =be acquainted with, work with*) You shouldn't have anything to do with those people. He has to do with electronics. *Idioms:* (*i*) What has that got to do with the problem?=How is that connected with the problem? (*ii*) That has got nothing to do with the matter!=That has no connection with the matter. (*iii*) This has nothing to do with you=This is not your concern. (*d*) (*make do, be content with*) You will just have to do with what you've got.

do without   *vt fus*   (*manage without*) I can do without your advice, thank you. We could well have done without that happening. If you don't like it, you'll just have to do without. Do without then!

dock off   *vt   sep*   (*Fam: deduct*) The management keeps docking things off from our wages. Something seems to get docked off your pay packet every week. The government docks off a lot in taxes.

*dodge + particle   *vt sep*   (*dodge, change position, with direction*) The men dodged about in the bushes, trying to hide. A fast car was dodging in and out of the traffic. He stepped out, then dodged back again before he was seen.

dole out   *vt sep*   (*hand out as a dole or charity*) The food was doled out to the refugees. They dole out just enough for each family. The government doles out something to help the victims of emergencies. You can't expect us to dole out money like a public charity.

doll up   *vt sep*   (*Fam: dress up smartly*) She dolled herself up for the party. They are all dolled up and ready to go.

*double + particle   *vi*   (*move at double pace, with direction*) The soldiers doubled along, carrying all their equipment. He doubled over to where the victims lay.

double back   1 *vi*   (*a*) see ***double**. (*b*) (*return on exactly the same route*) The hunters doubled back the way they had come. 2 *vt sep* (*fold back*) She doubled back the bedclothes.

double up   1 *vi*   (*a*) see ***double**. (*b*) (*fold up violently at the waist*) He doubled up in agony. He doubled up when he was struck in the belly. (*c*) (*live two together in a room or flat*) They don't

mind doubling up. You two will have to double up tonight.
2 *vt sep* (a) (*fold*) She doubled the blanket up. (b) (*cause
to bend or fold violently at the waist*) The impact of the blow
doubled him up. The bullet doubled him up.

doze off *vi* (*fall asleep*) The old man dozed off by the fire. Oh,
I must have just dozed off for a minute or two.

draft out *vt sep* (*write out a preliminary version*) He drafted out
his letter of resignation. Can you draft out a plan for us?

*drag + particle *vt sep* (*pull, with direction*) He dragged the bags
along behind him. The children have dragged all their toys
out again. The cat has dragged something in. We dragged
them apart to stop the fight.

drag down *vt sep* (a) *see* ***drag**. (b) (*debilitate*) His illness is
dragging him down.

drag in *vt sep* (a) *see* ***drag**. (b) (*Fam: introduce with an effort*)
Why must you always drag this subject in when we are talking?

drag on 1 *vi* (*last an unpleasantly long time*) The meeting dragged
on. 2 *vt sep* *see* ***drag**.

drag up *vt sep* (a) *see* ***drag**. (b) (*introduce unpleasantly*) Must
you drag up all these old scandals? (c) (*Fam: raise badly*)
These children appear to have been dragged up rather than
brought up.

drain away 1 *vi* (*go away through some kind of drain or drainage
system*) (a) (*Lit*) The flood waters have drained away at last.
(b) (*Fig*) I feel as though all my strength has drained away.
2 *vt sep* (*release through some kind of drain or drainage system*)
(a) (*Lit*) They drained away the waters. (b) (*Fig*) This work
has drained my enthusiasm away.

drain off 1 *vi* (*run off through some kind of drain*) The liquid has
drained off into the ground. 2 *vt sep* (*remove through some kind
of drain*) They have drained off the liquid they want.

*draw + particle *vt sep* (*pull, with direction*) He drew the cloth
away. She drew the curtains back. He drew the blinds down.
The croupier drew the money in. The barman drew off a pint
of beer.

draw apart 1 *vi* (*separate*) Husband and wife have drawn apart
over the months. These wooden covers draw apart if you pull
them. 2 *vt sep* (a) (*pull apart*) You can draw the covers apart
if you wish. (b) (*take to one side*) He drew me apart to tell me
what he had heard.

draw aside=draw apart 2 (b).

draw away 1 *vi* (a) (*move off*) The car drew away as we approached. (b) (*move ahead*) The faster car drew away. The

best runner was beginning to draw away. *(c)* *(isolate oneself)*
She has drawn away lately and we can't find out why. 2 *vt sep*
see ***draw**.

draw back 1 *vi* *(a)* *(Lit: move backwards)* The cat drew back as
we approached. *(b)* *(Fig: withdraw, retire)* She has drawn back
from us all and we don't know why. 2 *vt sep* *(a)* *see* ***draw.**
(b) *Idiomatic:* n **a drawback**=a shortcoming, problem or
defect.

draw down *vt sep* *(a)* *see* ***draw**. *(b)* *(Fig: bring down)* She has
drawn down blame on her own head. They seek to draw
down ridicule on us.

draw in 1 *vi* *(a)* *(Aut: slow to a halt beside a kerb)* The car drew in.
(b) *(get shorter)* The autumn days are drawing in. 2 *vt sep*
(a) *see* ***draw**. *(b)* *(take in)* He drew in some air. The
ventilators draw in plenty of fresh air. *(c)* *(attract, bring in)*
This play is drawing in large crowds every night. *(d)* *(pull in)*
He drew in the horse's reins. *(e)* *Idioms:* *(i)* to draw in one's
horns=to be less aggressive and more careful. *(ii)* to draw in
one's claws=to stop attacking.

draw off 1 *vi* *(Mil: move to one side, withdraw)* The army drew off
to await fresh developments elsewhere. 2 *vt sep* *(a)* *see* ***draw**.
(b) *(distract)* They drew my attention off at the crucial moment.

draw on 1 *vi* *(come nearer)* Night was drawing on. The fateful
date drew on. 2 *vt sep* *(a)* *see* ***draw**. *(b)* *(encourage,
especially to say something)* She drew him on to tell her about
what had happened.

draw out 1 *vi* *(become longer: of days)* The spring days are drawing
out. 2 *vt sep* *(a)* *see* ***draw**. *(b)* *(obtain)* She drew some
money out (of the bank). They drew their savings out before
they went on holiday. *(c)* *(prolong)* This meeting has been
drawn out long enough. The singer draws her notes out too
much. *(d)* *(encourage or cause to speak)* She managed to draw
him out. He's shy and needs to be drawn out. *Idiom:* to
draw someone out of his shell=to coax and encourage someone
to be less shy. *(e)* *(discover)* They drew out the secret from her.
(f) *(formulate)* The general drew out his plan of action. *(g)*
(make thinner and longer) The little boy drew the elastic out as far
as it would stretch. *Idiom:* a long-drawn-out scream, sermon
etc=a scream, sermon etc that continues for some time.

draw up 1 *vi* *(stop a car)* The police drew up outside the house.
2 *vt sep* *(a)* *(formulate, set out)* The lawyer has drawn up the
agreement. We must draw up a contract. *(b)* *(set in line)*
The troops were drawn up, ready for inspection. *(c)* *(pull up
on to the shore)* The boat was drawn up. *(d)* *Idiom:* to draw
oneself up (to one's full height)=(i) to stand erect. *(ii)* to

indicate one's pride.

dream away 1 *vi* (*dream continuously*) She just sits by the window and dreams away. 2 *vt sep* (*spend in dreaming*) She dreams the time away.

dream up *vt sep* (*Fig Fam: think up, concoct*) He dreams up some very odd ideas. Where on earth did you dream that up?

dredge up *vt sep* (*bring to the surface by dredging or deep scooping*) (*a*) (*Lit*) The excavator has dredged up nothing but mud. (*b*) (*Fig*) He likes to dredge up unpleasant little facts about important people.

dress down *vt sep* (*a*) (*groom*) She dressed down the horse. (*b*) (*reprimand, scold*) He dressed us down in no uncertain terms. *Idiom:* to give someone a good dressing down=to reprimand someone severely.

dress up 1 *vi* (*a*) (*put on smart clothes*) They dressed up for the occasion. There's no need to dress up—it will all be very informal. *Idiom:* to be dressed up to the nines=to be dressed as smartly as possible. (*b*) (*put on fancy dress, for fun or a party*) The children love to dress up. He is going dressed up as a pirate. 2 *vt sep* (*a*) (*decorate*) You should dress yourself up a bit. (*b*) (*Fig: improve*) This scheme should be dressed up to look more attractive. (*c*) (*disguise*) He was dressed up as some kind of Indian prince.

***drift + particle** *vi* (*move aimlessly, with direction*) The rudderless boat was drifting along on the current. The wreckage slowly drifted away. Something was drifting up on the tide. (*Fig*) Those boys drift about doing nothing. He has drifted back and forth between Europe and Asia several times.

drill down *vi* (*dig or bore down with a drill*) The prospectors have been drilling down into the bedrock, hoping to strike oil.

drink away 1 *vi* (*drink continuously*) He has been drinking away for hours. 2 *vt sep* (*relieve by taking alcoholic drink*) He is trying to drink his trouble away. You can't drink your sorrows away. He tried to drink the memory away.

drink down *vt sep* (*drink in one gulp*) He drank the draught down. His mother got him to drink the medicine down. Come on, drink it down!

drink in *vt sep* (*a*) (*absorb readily*) These plants just drink the water in. The dry soil drinks the rain in. (*b*) (*Fig: absorb, receive with rapture*) The children just drink in his stories. She stood and drank in the panorama.

drink off *vt sep* (*quaff, drink in one long swallow*) He drank off the flagon of wine amid their cheers.

drink up 1 *vi* (*drink until finished*) She told the children to drink up. The barman asked the men to drink up. Drink up! 2 *vt sep* (*drink until all gone*) Children, drink up your milk.

*dribble + particle *vi* (*move in small quantities, with direction*) A few people dribbled along to see what was happening. The water has begun to dribble away. The saliva in his mouth was dribbling out. The boys dribbled back in ones and twos.

drip down *vi* (*fall in small drops*) The water dripped down from the trees.

drip off *vi* (*fall off in drips*) As the snow on the roofs melted, water started dripping off.

*drive + particle (*drive, with direction*) 1 *vi* The man got into his car and drove off. The car drove away. She drove out of the garage. I watched them drive in. 2 *vt sep* (a) He drove the beggars away from the gate. I watched them drive the cattle out. The men drove the sheep in. (b) He drove the car away. She drove everyone back after the party. He drove the car in (to the garage).

drive at *vt fus* (*Fig: intend, mean*) I don't know what you are driving at. What was he driving at? *cf* get at. (d)

drive back 1 *vi see* ***drive.** 2 *vt sep* (a) *see* ***drive.** (b) (*repel, repulse*) The soldiers drove back the enemy with heavy losses.

drive in 1 *vi see* ***drive.** *n cpd* **drive-in cinema, café**=a cinema or café where one remains in one's car. 2 *vt sep* (a) *see* ***drive.** (b) (*Tech: hammer in*) He drove the nails in. (c) (*Fig: introduce by force*) He drove the idea in somehow, and hoped that his pupils would retain it.

drive off 1 *vi* (a) *see* ***drive.** (b) (*Golf: hit the ball from the tee*) The first player drove off. 2 *vt sep* (a) *see* ***drive.** (b) (*Mil: repel, repulse*). The defenders drove the enemy off with heavy losses.

drive on 1 *vi* (a) *see* ***drive.** (b) (*continue to drive*) The man drove on through the night. 2 *vt sep* (a) *see* ***drive.** (b) (*incite, encourage*) She drove him on to commit murder.

drive out 1 *vi see* ***drive.** 2 *vt sep* (a) *see* ***drive.** (b) (*expel*) The soldiers drove out the defenders by repeated attacks. She tried to drive the evil thoughts out of her mind. He claims to be able to drive out demons.

drizzle down *vi* (*intensive of* **drizzle**) The rain has been drizzling down for hours.

drone away, drone on *vi* (*continue to drone or talk monotonously*) He can drone away for hours about his pet subjects.

droop down *vi* (*flag, hang down*) The flowers drooped down to the ground, because of the heat.

drop across *vi* (*Fam: come across to visit*) Drop across and have coffee sometime.

drop away *vi* (*a*) (*fall sheer*) The cliff drops away at that point. (*b*) (*become less*) The attendance has dropped away in recent months.

drop back 1 *vi* (*a*) (*fall back*) The hook which he had thrown did not catch on the rocks, and dropped back to the ground. (*b*) (*Fig: fall back in position*) He has dropped back to fifth in his class. (*c*) (*lessen*) Production has dropped back. The unemployment figures dropped back last month. 2 *vt sep* (*put back by dropping*) She dropped the letter back in the drawer.

drop behind *vi*=**drop back** (*b*).

drop down 1 *vi* (*come down suddenly*) The monkeys dropped down from the trees. The fruit has begun to drop down. After the crash, onlookers said that the plane had suddenly dropped down out of the sky. She dropped down into an armchair, exhausted. 2 *vt sep* (*release suddenly, intensive of* **drop**) She dropped the bag down and he caught it.

drop in 1 *vi* (*a*) (*fall in*) The roof dropped in on us. (*b*) (*Fam: visit casually*) They often drop in for coffee. He usually drops in at my place on his way home. 2 *vt sep* (*put in by dropping*) He stopped at the pillar-box and dropped the letter in. I'll drop the book in to you on my way home.

drop off 1 *vi* (*a*) (*fall off*) The handle of the door has dropped off. (*b*) (*Fam: fall asleep*) The old man has dropped off by the fire. (*c*) (*decline*) Interest in the book has dropped off. Sales have been dropping off badly. 2 *vt sep* (*a*) (*Fam: set down*) We can drop you off at your place on our way home. He said he would drop the parcel off at the post office.

drop out 1 *vi* (*a*) (*fall out*) The window was open, and the pot just dropped out. (*b*) (*Fig: cease participation*) He says he has dropped out, and won't attend college any more. They have dropped out of society. *n* **a drop-out**=a person who drops out. 2 *vt sep* (*release by dropping*) He opened the window and dropped the bag out.

drop out of *vt fus* (*withdraw from*) He has dropped out of the competition.

drop over= **drop across, drop in** 1 *vi* (*b*).

drown out *vt sep* (*make inaudible*) Her screams were drowned out by the noise of the storm. The amplified music drowned out everything else.

drum in *vt sep* (*a*) (*Fig: emphasize*) I would like to drum this one point in. I don't want to keep drumming it in, but it is very important. (*b*) (*force into someone's head or attention*) The teacher was determined to drum some elementary arithmetic in.

drum out *vt sep* (*usu Mil: expel*) He has been drummed out of the army. We drummed him out of the club. They have been drummed out of town.

drum up *vt sep* (*Fig orig Mil: summon*) They are trying to drum up public enthusiasm for the candidate. He can't drum up any support for his plans.

dry down *vt sep* (*dry completely*) He dried himself down after a shower.

dry off 1 *vi* (*become dry*) He has left the paint to dry off. Your clothes should have dried off by this time. 2 *vt sep* (*make dry*) She dried off the towel.

dry out 1 *vi* (*a*)=**dry off**. (*b*) (*Sl: of an alcoholic, become better*) He seems to have dried out. 2 *vt sep* (*a*)=**dry off**. (*b*) (*Sl: of an alcoholic, make better*) They appear to have dried him out.

dry up 1 *vi* (*a*) (*Lit: become completely dry*) The well has dried up. The little lake has dried up. The moisture has all dried up. The cow has dried up and no longer gives milk. (*b*) (*Fam: dry the dishes*) It's your turn to dry up. (*c*) (*Fam: lose inspiration, fail to produce words*) The speaker suddenly dried up in the middle of his speech. The actor dried up and looked blank. (*d*) (*Sl: be quiet*) I wish she would dry up. Oh, dry up! 2 *vt sep* (*make dry*) She dried up the mess on the floor. The sun has dried up all the puddles.

duck down *vi* (*intensive of* **duck**) The soldier ducked down behind a wall as bullets began to fly.

dust down *vt sep* (*a*) (*dust completely, clear completely of dust*) She dusted down the furniture. After his fall he rose and dusted himself down. (*b*) (*Fam: reprimand*) The colonel dusted his men down for inefficiency. *n a* **dusting-down**=a severe reprimand.

dust off *vt sep* (*clean off by dusting, sweep the dust from*) She dusted off the hat and put it on.

dust out *vt sep* (*clean out by dusting*) She dusted out the cupboards.

dust-up (*Idiomatic n*=*a quarrel.*) *Example:* There was a bit of a dust-up at the office, about who was to do what.

dwell (up)on *vt fus* (*Fig: spend time on, discuss too much*) I have no wish to dwell upon the unpleasant side of this business. He dwelt upon all the nasty aspects with considerable satisfaction.

dwindle away *vi* (*diminish, become smaller or fewer*) The money has just dwindled away to nothing. The numbers attending these meetings have dwindled away terribly.

dwindle down=dwindle away.

*ease + particle   *vt sep*   (*ease, move slowly and gently, with direction*)
He eased the screws out of the old wood with great care.   The
nurse eased away the bandage from the wound.

ease off   1 *vi*=**ease up.**   2 *vt sep*   (*remove slowly and gently*) The
nurse eased the bandage off.   He eased the stamp off carefully.

ease up   *vi*   (*a*)   (*slow down, decelerate*) Ease up, we're going too
fast!   (*b*)   (*become less tense*) I hope he will ease up now that he has
got promotion.   The situation should ease up now that the two
sides are prepared to talk.   The pain began to ease up after she
was given a sedative.

eat away   1 *vi*   (*eat steadily or continuously*)   They have been eating
away for more than an hour.   2 *vt sep*   (*destroy by, or as if by,
eating*) The acid has been eating away the sides of the container.
The sea water is eating away the base of the cliff.   The rats
have eaten the woodwork away.   This part has been eaten
away by insects.

eat in   *vi*   (*eat at home*) We aren't going out, we're eating in
tonight.   Most of the students eat in.

eat into   *vt fus*   (*destroy, through action of acids etc*) The substance has
begun eating into the woodwork.

eat out   *vi*   (*a*)   (*dine in a restaurant*) We need a baby-sitter tonight,
because we are eating out.   It's a long time since she last ate
out.   (*b*)   *Idiom:* to eat one's heart out (for someone, something)
=to long desperately (for someone, something).

eat up   (*eat until all finished*)   1 *vi*   Come on, children, eat up!
2 *vt*   (*a*) (*Lit*) Come on, children, eat up your food!   (*b*) (*Fig:
devour, consume*) This car just eats up the miles.   The central
heating eats up a lot of electricity.

ebb away   *vi*   (*flow away from a given position*)   (*a*) (*Lit*) The tide
ebbed away, leaving behind seaweed and debris.   (*b*) (*Fig*)
Her enthusiasm slowly ebbed away.   He felt his strength
ebbing away.

*echo + particle   *vi*   (*resound, with direction*) The shot echoed out.
Her shout echoed back from the mountain.

*edge + particle   *vi*   (*move hesitantly or in small stages, with direction*)
The cat edged along, its eyes fixed on the bird.   The suspicious-
looking fellow edged up to us, and asked us for money.   The
climbers edged slowly down from the summit of the mountain.

edge out   1 *vi*   *see* *edge.   2 *vt sep*   (*supplant*) They have been
trying to edge him out of his position of power for several years.
In the last election they succeeded in edging their opponents
out (of office) by a small margin.

edit out *vt sep* (*remove by editing*) He edited out the offensive paragraph.

egg on *vt sep* (*Fam: encourage*) They egged him on to fight those other boys. We don't want to do it, so stop egging us on.

eke out *vt sep* (*extend or maintain by care, rationing etc*) We must try to eke out our water supply until help comes. She ekes out a living somehow. Please try to eke the money out till the end of the month.

*elbow + particle *Idiom:* to elbow one's way=to push with the elbows in order to pass. The men elbowed their way back into the crowd. He elbowed his way over to where we stood.

empty out 1 *vi* (*empty completely*) The tank slowly emptied out. 2 *vt sep* He emptied out the tank. They emptied their pockets out, to show that they had no weapons.

end off *vt sep* (*finish*) We ended the work off with a flourish.

end up *vi* (*a*) (*Fam: come to an end, usu unsatisfactory*) If you drive your car like that, you'll end up in hospital. They ended up after five years with nothing to show for their effort. (*b*) (*finish by*) I ended up (by) telling him everything although I tried not to. Despite his strenuous efforts, he ended up unsuccessful after all.

enter in *vi* (*Old: intensive of* **enter**) The courtiers entered in at the palace gates.

enter into *vt fus* (*a*) (*begin, of correspondence, relations etc*) They entered into negotiations with their business rivals. She entered into a five-year contract. They hope that he will enter into an alliance in order to topple the opposition. (*b*) (*share; participate in*) I can never enter into his jokes. (*c*) (*figure in*) I'm afraid he does not enter into our plans. That possibility didn't enter into our calculations. The amount of money did not enter into their decision at all. What you think just doesn't enter into it! (*d*) *Idiom:* to enter into the spirit of something= to participate fully in something.

enter up *vt fus* (*state, list or write down, usu in a book kept for a special purpose*) Would you please enter up these names in the register? All this information is entered up in the appropriate places.

enter (up)on *vt fus* (*a*) (*begin*) The young man was just entering upon his career in teaching. The doctor is expected to enter upon his duties at the beginning of next month. (*b*) (*Old: take possession of*) She expects to enter upon her inheritance sometime next year.

*entice + particle *vt sep* (*lure, inveigle, with direction*) She enticed him along to the party. He hoped to entice the kitten down off the window ledge.

even out   1 *vi*   (*become level*) (*a*) (*Lit*) The ground should even out soon, and we can walk more easily.   (*b*) (*Fig*) He hopes that prices will even out next year.   2 *vt sep*   (*equalize, make equitable*) (*a*) (*Lit*) The road roller evens out the ground.   (*b*) (*Fig*) They expect to even out the tax burden among the people.

even up   *vt sep*   (*equalize*) If you give him an apple you must give his brother one to even things up.   He hopes to even up the score with his enemies soon.   This should even things up a bit.

explain away   *vt sep*   (*explain very plausibly, rationalize; attempt to satisfy with plausible explanations*) He is rather good at explaining away awkward situations.   It's no use trying to explain these things away.   He hoped to explain away the missing money, but was not particularly successful.

face about   *vi*   (*a*) ·(*usu Mil: turn completely round*) He told the men to face about.   Face about!   *Also imper:* About face!   (*b*) *Idiom:* He did an about-face=he reversed his opinion completely.

face out   *vt sep*   (*resist, oppose*) You should face out your problems. He's a bully, but you'd better face him out straight away.   He managed to face out their objections.

face up to   *vt fus*   (*Fam: confront, accept*) He faced up to the problem.   These are dangers which you must face up to.   She doesn't like facing up to things.   He won't face up to the fact that he is too old for the job.

fade away   *vi*   (*a*) (*Lit: fade steadily*) The colours faded away. The picture on the screen began to fade away.   The sounds faded away into nothing.   (*b*) (*Fig: become less substantial, thinner*) That old man is just fading away.   She faded away and died.   If you don't eat you'll start fading away!   (*c*) (*vanish quietly or discreetly*) He faded away quietly and we never saw him again.   He is an expert at fading away when he isn't needed. (*d*) (*vanish slowly, become defunct in stages*) These customs are fading away now.

fade in   (*Cine, TV*)   1 *vi*   (*come in slowly until clear*) The scene faded in.   Fade in to a scene in the office.   2 *vt sep*   (*bring in slowly until clear*) Fade the scene in now.   *n* **a fade-in**.

fade out   1 *vi*   (*fade completely, die out*) (*a*) The picture on the TV screen suddenly faded out.   The sounds faded out gradually. (*b*) (*Cine, TV*) Fade out to the next scene.   (*c*) (*Fig: vanish, become obsolete or defunct*) These practices have faded out.   2 *vt sep* (*Cine, TV*) Fade the scene out and then fade in to the street scene.   *n* **a fade-out**.

fag away   *vi*   (*Fam: work hard and continuously*) He fags away for a pittance.

fag out *vt sep* (*Fam: tire, exhaust completely*) This work will fag you out. Don't fag yourself out on their account. I'm really fagged out.

faint away *vi* (*faint completely*) When she saw him she fainted (clean) away.

fake up *vt sep* (*Fam:invent, fabricate*) He faked up the whole thing —none of it was true. The painting was beautifully faked up.

fall about *vi* (*Sl: laugh hysterically*) (*a*) They were falling about (laughing). (*b*) *Idiom:* to fall about in the aisles=to laugh uncontrollably.

fall away *vi* (*a*) (*fall out and down*) The stones have fallen away from the side of the house. (*b*) (*Geog: sink or go down*) The ground falls away steeply at this point. (*c*) (*dwindle, diminish*) The number of people coming to the club has fallen away a lot. Attendances are falling away steadily. The old customs have fallen away into disuse.

fall back *vi* (*a*) (*recoil*) He fell back in surprise. She fell back in dismay when she saw him. (*b*) (*Mil: retreat*) The army has begun falling back to prepared lines of defence.

fall back (up)on *vt fus* (*go back to for support, have as a reserve*) We have some money to fall back on. It's good to have a friend to fall back upon.

fall behind *vi* (*a*) (*Lit: fail to maintain one's position*) The racehorse fell behind. Several of the runners fell behind in the race. (*b*) (*Fig: fail to maintain a schedule*) She is falling behind with her payments for the cooker. They fell behind with the rent.

fall down *vi* (*a*) (*fall to the ground or downward, drop*) The injured horse fell down. He fell down dead. (*b*) (*be in a state of dereliction*) That building is falling down. The house is falling down from lack of attention. (*c*) (*Fam: fail, come to nothing*) His plans have fallen down. (*d*) *Idiom:* He has fallen down on the job=he has failed.

fall for *vt fus* (*a*) (*Fam: accept as true, be duped by*) Don't tell me you fell for that old trick! Everyone seems to fall for his charming manner. (*b*) (*Fam: become keen on*) She has fallen for him (in a big way). I have quite fallen for this year's purple colours.

fall in *vi* (*a*) (*fall into something*) The child was near the river and I was frightened he would fall in. Be careful you don't fall in. (*b*) (*collapse inwards*) The walls fell in. They are afraid that the whole building will fall in on them. *n* a **fall-in**. (*c*) (*Mil: make or join the ranks or a parade*) He ordered the men to fall in. Fall in! (*d*) (*expire*) The lease of the land has fallen in. His debts have fallen in.

fall in with   *vt fus   (accept, agree with, concur with)*   I have decided to fall in with your plan.   They have fallen in with the general policy.   *(b) (Fam: join, associate oneself with)*   He has fallen in with some strange people.

fall off   *vi   (a) (fall from a position)*   Hold tight to the handle bars and be careful you don't fall off.   He fell off.   *(b) (decline in numbers)*   Attendances have fallen off.   His support has greatly fallen off.   The numbers have fallen off badly.   Sales are falling off for no apparent reason.   *(c) (decrease)*   His zeal has fallen off considerably.   Their enthusiasm seems to be falling off a bit.

fall out   1 *vi   (a) (fall outwards and downwards)*   The window opened as he leaned on it, and he fell out.   When he picked up the box, some papers fell out.   *(b) (Fig: quarrel)*   I think they have fallen out again.   I don't want to fall out with you.   We're not going to fall out over this, are we?   *(c) (Mil: leave the ranks or a parade)*   He was told to fall out.   Company, fall out!   *(d) (Impers: come to pass, happen)*   It fell out that the men were not needed.   I don't know how it will all fall out.   It fell out as we expected.   *(e) (Atomic Physics: drop from the upper atmosphere on to the earth)*   Many people are afraid of what happens when radioactive particles fall out from nuclear explosions.   *n* **(atomic) fallout** = *(i)* the action of particles falling out.   *(ii)* the result of the action, a residue of radioactive matter in the air, sea or soil.   2 *vt sep   (Mil: dismiss from the ranks or a parade)*   Sergeant, fall the men out.   Fall out!

fall over   1 *vi   (topple to the ground)*   The tree fell over when its roots were exposed.   The soldier fell over dead.   2 *vt fus   (a) (trip over)*   He fell over a chair and hurt his leg.   That clumsy child is always falling over himself.   *(b) Idiom:*   He was falling over himself to be polite and helpful = he was making an immense effort to be polite.

fall through   *vi   (a) (drop through)*   The floor collapsed and they fell through.   *(b) (Fig Fam: fail to develop, abort)*   All their plans have fallen through.

fall to   1 *vi   (start eating)*   They fell to (with a will).   2 *vt fus   (a) (begin)*   I fell to thinking about old times together.   *(b) (Impers: be responsible for)*   It falls to you to do the work this week.   I'm afraid it falls to me to break the news.

fall under   *vt fus   (be classified under)*   Which category does this item fall under?   It falls under 'Miscellaneous' in the files.

fall (up)on   *vt fus   (attack)*   The robbers fell on the unsuspecting travellers.   They fell upon him and killed him.

falter out   *vt sep   (say or speak hesitantly)*   She faltered out her name.   He faltered out something about being lost.

fan out (*spread out like a fan*) 1 *vi* The searchers fanned out across the mountainside, to cover as much ground as possible. He ordered the men to fan out. Fan out! 2 *vt sep* The cards were fanned out face downward on the table. He fanned his search party out across the hills.

farm out *vt sep* (*a*) (*pass on responsibility*) She farmed the children out on her neighbours. (*b*) (*delegate, distribute*) The work has been farmed out to various people. We must stop them farming out the information to all the other agencies. (*c*) (*usu pass: exhausted for farming*) This land has been farmed out. The area was farmed out long ago.

fasten down *vt sep* (*fix down*) The windows have been fastened down. He fastened down the collar of his coat. They fastened the flaps down.

fasten on *vt sep* (*fix on*) She fastened the badge on. Fasten it on here, please. Is it firmly fastened on to the saddle?

fasten on to=**fasten (up)on.**

fasten up *vt sep* (*do up, fix into place by fastening*) She fastened the dress up. Fasten up the buttons, please. Can you fasten me up, please?

fasten (up)on *vt fus* (*Fig: latch on to, adopt quickly*) She fastened upon his suggestion as an excuse for her actions. Don't fasten upon his ideas so uncritically. She fastened upon the idea of going to London.

fathom out *vt sep* (*Fig Fam: understand, explain, comprehend*) I just can't fathom out his intentions. She couldn't fathom him out at all.

fatten up 1 *vi*=**fatten out** 1. 2 *vt sep* (*make fat, usu for sale*) They are fattening the sheep up. These animals need fattening up.

fatten out 1 *vi* (*become fat*) He has fattened out a lot. Those sheep have fattened out since I last saw them. 2 *vt sep* (*increase in quantity, lengthen*) It isn't a large piece of work, and needs fattening out.

fawn (up)on *vt fus* (*flatter slavishly, ingratiate oneself with*) They like to fawn upon great writers. She fawns upon anyone with influence.

feast away 1 *vi* (*feast continuously*) They were feasting away in the great hall. 2 *vt sep* (*spend in feasting*) They intended to feast the night away.

fed up *Idiomatic adj* (*a*) (*Fam: tired, bored, depressed*) I'm fed up (with) waiting for him. They are really fed up with the whole thing. (*b*) *Idiom:* to be fed up to the back teeth=to be completely frustrated.

feed back *vt sep* *(return in stages)* He fed the information back to us. The machine feeds back everything you need to know. *n* **feedback**=(*i*) the return of specific information. (*ii*) the information obtained from operating anything, used to improve, correct or control further operations.

feed in *vt sep* *(introduce steadily)* He fed the tape in (to the machine). Feed the wire in here. If you feed the data in, you get the analysis a few minutes later.

feed up *vt sep* *(feed as fully as possible)* She fed him up on the best food she could get. We'll have to feed you up after your illness. *Idiomatic adj* **fed up** (see above).

feel about/around *vi* *(search about by touching)* He felt about in the dark for the door handle. She felt about for the light switch.

feel for *vt fus* *(sympathize with)* I really feel for him in all these troubles. He felt for her in her sorrow.

feel up to *vt fus* *(usu with neg or conditional: feel capable of, feel equal to)* He doesn't feel up to the job. I don't feel up to things today. We could go on now if you feel up to it.

fence in *vt sep* *(enclose with a fence)* (*a*) (*Lit*) He fenced in his land. The area has been fenced in. (*b*) (*Fig*) I feel fenced in by all these restrictions. Don't fence me in.

fence off *vt sep* (*a*) *(separate with a fence)* He fenced off the whole plot of land. The area has been fenced off. (*b*) *(parry or resist)* (*Lit*) He fenced off their attack/the blow. The speaker neatly fenced off the question.

fend off *vt sep* *(parry, resist, deflect)* (*a*) (*Lit*) He was able to fend off the blow with his arm. Nothing could fend off that attack. (*b*) (*Fig*) The speaker fended off the questions.

ferret about/around *vi* *(search about)* The police ferreted about for clues. He has been ferreting about, trying to get some information.

ferret out *vt sep* *(elicit, bring out like a ferret)* He managed to ferret out quite a lot of information. She'll ferret it out for us if it's humanly possible.

*ferry + particle *(move on a ferry, with direction)* 1 *vi* They ferried across to the other side. They ferried back and forth. 2 *vt sep* (*a*) (*Lit*) He ferried them across to the other side. They were willing to ferry me over. Can you ferry them up to the landing-stage? They ferried dozens of men in from the wreck. (*b*) (*Fig*) He ferried people back and forth in his car all day.

*fetch + particle *vt sep* *(fetch, with direction)* He fetched the box in. They fetched their friends over to meet us. Can you fetch it out and show me it? Fetch him up to have a chat.

fetch up 1 *vi* (*Fam: end up*) They fetched up in Singapore eventually. 2 *vt sep see* *fetch.

fiddle about/around *vi* (*Fig Fam: play about, toy*) He was fiddling about with the car engine. Stop fiddling about with that radio set and listen to me!

fiddle away 1 *vi* (*play a fiddle continuously*) An old man was fiddling away at the street corner. 2 *vt sep* (*Fig: waste*) He's been fiddling his time away in London when we needed him here. She has fiddled away a fortune in the last few months.

fidget about/around *vi* (*move about restlessly, uneasily*) Stop fidgeting about! That child fidgets about all the time.

fight back (*resist*) 1 *vi* The enemy fought back ferociously. They will fight back, they won't surrender. 2 *vt sep* (*a*) (*Lit*) We shall fight them back if they attack. (*b*) (*repress*) She fought back her tears.

fight down *vt sep* (*Fam: suppress, restrain*) He fought down his anxiety. She tried to fight down her rising terror.

fight on *vi* (*continue fighting*) The battalion fought on stubbornly, although surrounded and outnumbered. We shall fight on until death.

fight out *vt sep* (*usually with 'it': fight to the end*) (*a*) (*Lit*) They fought it out with knives. (*b*) (*Fig*) We had better fight this thing out.

fight together *vi* (*a*) (*fight as comrades*) We fought together against many enemies. (*b*) (*fight as enemies*) They were fighting together in the public bar.

figure on *vt fus* (*Fam: count on*) I figure on him helping us.

figure out *vt sep* (*a*) (*work out, estimate*) I can't figure out how much money I owe them. (*b*) (*work out, understand*) She figured out how he had arranged the matter. I wish I could figure out how their minds work. She couldn't figure him out at all.

*file + particle *vi* (*walk in line, with direction*) The men filed away silently. I watched the soldiers file out. Silent mourners filed past, paying their last respects.

file away 1 *vi* (*a*) (*scrape continuously with a file or abrasive tool*) He filed away at the metal bar. (*b*) *see* *file. 2 *vt sep* (*a*) (*put away in a file or filing system*) The secretary filed the letter away. (*b*) *Idiom:* to file something away in one's memory.

file down 1 *vi* *see* *file. 2 *vt sep* (*reduce by filing, or by means of a file*) He filed the surface down. The end of the bar had been filed down to a point.

fill in 1 *vi* (*stand or serve as a substitute*) We'll find someone to fill in for you. I'll fill in if absolutely necessary. 2 *vt sep* (*a*) (*fill until level or full*) The workmen filled the hole in. (*b*) (*complete*) Fill in these forms, please. She filled the form in. (*c*) (*provide, in full*) Can you fill in the details for us? Fill in your name and address here. (*d*) (*inform in full*) Would someone please fill me in on this point?

fill out 1 *vi* (*a*) (*fill with wind etc*) The sails filled out as the breeze caught them. (*b*) (*get fatter*) He has filled out a lot since I last saw him. Her cheeks have filled out. 2 *vt sep* = **fill in** 2 (*b*).

fill up 1 *vi* (*Aut: fill with petrol*) He filled up at the next petrol station. 2 *vt sep* (*a*) (*fill to the full*) She filled his glass up a second time. (*b*) (*Aut Fam: fill the tank with petrol*) Fill her up! *n* a **fill-up.** (*c*) = **fill in** 2 (*b*).

film over *vi* (*become covered with a thin layer*) The windscreen has filmed over with some kind of oil.

***filter + particle** (*pass through a filter or in small quantities, with direction*) 1 *vi* (*a*) (*Lit*) Water has begun filtering through into the bottle. The liquid filters out into this receptacle. (*b*) (*Fig*) The soldiers filtered up one by one into the enemy position on the hill. News has filtered down to us that there is trouble among the directors. 2 *vt sep* We think the stuff can be filtered off without difficulty. The impurities have been filtered out.

find out 1 *vi* (*discover the truth*) She is afraid he will find out. I hope she doesn't find out. 2 *vt sep* (*a*) (*discover*) They have found out the truth. If you do try to see her, be careful you're not found out. She will find out all his secrets. I finally found out what he was really like. (*b*) (*make enquiries about*) Will you try to find out when the trains leave? Find out his address, please.

fine down *vt sep* (*smooth or file down until very fine*) The craftsman fined the wood down very gently.

finish off 1 *vi* (*terminate something*) Let's finish off now; it's time to go home. Well, we can finish off with a glass of brandy. The meeting finished off with a prayer. 2 *vt sep* (*a*) (*end, conclude*) He finished the work off yesterday. I'll be glad to finish this off. Finish off the letter and I'll post it. Finish off your food! (*b*) (*kill*) They finished off the wounded animal. The soldiers finished the enemy off. Her illness last year nearly finished her off.

finish up 1 *vi* (*a*) = **finish off** 1. (*b*) = **end up** (*a*) and (*b*). 2 *vt sep* (*finish completely*) Oh, finish it up now! I wish he would finish the whole thing up and forget about it.

***fire + particle** 1 *vi* (*shoot with direction*) The soldiers fired down on the men below. They fired up at the windows

He ran to the window and fired in. Someone was firing out from the clump of trees. 2 *vt sep* (*project by firing, with direction*) They fired a flare up into the night sky. They are firing shells out and down into the valley. The guard fired off several rounds of ammunition.

fire away 1 *vi* (*a*) see *****fire. (*b*) (*fire or shoot continuously*) The troops were firing away at the advancing enemy. (*c*) (*Fig Fam: begin, usu telling a story*) We're ready to listen, so fire away! 2 *vt sep* see *****fire.

fire ahead=**fire away** 1 (*c*).

firm up 1 *vi* (*become solid*) The ground has firmed up a lot since it was properly drained. 2 *vt sep* (*make secure*) We should try to firm this arrangement up a bit before putting money into the scheme.

fish for *vt fus* (*Fam: seek*) She is always fishing for compliments. There's no good fishing for information, I can't tell you anything.

fish out *vt sep* (*a*) (*Fig Fam: bring out like a fish*) He fell into the river and we had to fish him out. They fished a lot of rubbish out (of that pool). (*b*) (*Fig Fam: bring out*) He fished out a piece of string from his pocket. (*c*) (*usu pass: be exhausted of fish*) The lake was fished out long ago. This river is in danger of being fished out.

fish up *vt sep* (*bring up like a fish*) The men have fished up something very peculiar in their nets. She put her hand into her bag and fished up several books.

fit in 1 *vi* (*a*) (*go properly into position*) I've filled the box, and all the books fit in nicely. (*b*) (*accord, harmonize*) This information does not fit in with what I was told yesterday. It all fits in now! (*c*) (*blend, harmonize*) The house fits in beautifully with its surroundings. I hope this picture will fit in with your general décor. (*d*) (*take a proper place, co-operate*) He tried to fit in with the others, but it was difficult. She doesn't fit in here, I'm afraid. 2 *vt sep* (*a*) (*fix in*) The cupboards have now been fitted in. I fitted the panels in myself. (*b*) (*get in*) Somehow she managed to fit everything in the suitcase. (*c*) (*include*) She has succeeded in fitting everything in her busy schedule. (*d*) (*harmonize*) We must fit our plans in with yours. (*e*) (*provide a place for*) I'm sure you can fit me in somewhere. Isn't there enough space to fit the children in?

fit on 1 *vi* (*adhere, go into position*) This bottle top won't fit on. The catch of the door doesn't fit on any more. 2 *vt sep* (*put or fix on*) The dressmaker fitted the dress on and made some minor adjustments. The carpenter fitted some extra hooks on.

fit out *vt sep* (*equip*) The ship has been fitted out with a new engine.　The warship was fitted out with bigger guns.　We must fit the expedition out with the best equipment.

fit up　*vt sep*　(*a*) (*fix or put up*) The carpenter fitted up the wall cupboards.　(*b*) (*fit, fix completely*) The place has been fitted up with all modern conveniences (all mod cons).　It's well fitted up.

fix on　1 *vt fus*　(*Fig Fam: choose, select*) They finally fixed on 2 p.m. as the best time.　Well, we'd better fix on a date for the meeting. 2 *vt sep*　(*fit or put on*) Can you fix this lid on, it keeps coming off. Fix the top on firmly.　He fixed the badge on at the correct angle.

fix up　1 *vi*　(*arrange*) We've fixed up to go out tonight.　They have fixed up to visit us next month.　I fixed up to go abroad for a holiday.　I have fixed up for a plumber to come to-morrow.　2 *vt sep*　(*a*) (*fit or put up*) The carpenter fixed up the wall cupboards.　(*b*) (*arrange*) I'll try to fix something up that suits everyone.　Let's fix it all up now.　(*c*) (*provide an opportunity or work for*) Can you fix him up?　They fixed me up with this job.　(*d*) (*accommodate*) They fixed him up in a small hotel. Can you fix her up for the night?

fizz up　*vi*　(*rise while fizzing or effervescing*) The lemonade fizzed up

fizzle out　*vi*　(*come to nothing, usu abjectly*) (*a*) (*Lit*) The firework didn't work properly, but just fizzled out.　(*b*) (*Fig*) His schemes seem to have fizzled out.　I hope the whole project doesn't just fizzle out. All his enthusiasm soon fizzled out.

flag down　*vt sep*　(*stop, by using a flag, or making a flagging action*) The guards flagged the car down.　He flagged the taxi down.

flake off　*vi*　(*come off in flakes*) The paint has begun to flake off. The surface is flaking off.

flake out　*vi*　(*Fam*)　(*a*) (*faint*) She flaked out when she heard the news.　(*b*) (*fall instantly asleep through exhaustion*) They just flaked out when they got back.

flame out　*vi*　(*burst out in flames, flare out*) A beacon flamed out against the night sky.

flame up　*vt sep*　(*burst out in flames, flare up*) (*a*) (*Lit*) The fire flamed up instantly.　(*b*) (*Fig*) His anger flamed up again.

***flap + particle**　*vi*　(*fly with flapping wings, with direction*) The big bird slowly flapped away.　Birds were flapping about everywhere.　The vulture flapped off.

flare up　*vi*　(*burst into fire, come up in a sudden glow*) (*a*) (*Lit*) Lights flared up in the darkness.　The bonfire flared up as I poured petrol on to it.　(*b*) (*Fig*) His temper flared up when he heard how much money had been spent.　Trouble may flare up at any time in the city. *n* a **flare-up**=a burst of fire/ anger/trouble.

*flash + particle *vi* (*Fam: move very fast, or with a flash, with direction*) The car flashed past. He flashed in to tell us what happened, then flashed out again. They flashed off somewhere in their new car.

flash about/around 1 *vi see* ***flash** (2) *vt sep* (*Sl: exhibit, display*) They are always flashing their money about. I wish she wouldn't flash her diamonds about so much.

flash back *vi* (a) *see* ***flash** (b) (*Cine, TV, Writing: return or revert briefly to an earlier point in the story*) The film suddenly flashed back to the hero's youth. *n* a **flashback**=a device for taking a story back in time. *Example:* There was a flashback to his youth.

flash forward *vi* (a) *see* ***flash** (b) (*Cine, TV, Writing: move briefly to a later point in a story*) The film flashed forward to show the deaths of the soldiers. *n* a **flash-forward**=a device for taking a story on in time. *Example:* The author likes an occasional flash-forward to show the results of a character's decisions.

flatten out 1 *vi* (*become flat or flatter*) The countryside flattens out beyond that ridge. 2 *vt sep* (*make flat or flatter*) She flattened out the dough with a rolling pin. The roadroller flattened out the bumps in the road.

flesh out *vt sep* (*Fig Fam: to fill or fatten*) This story isn't detailed enough, it needs to be fleshed out.

flick off *vt sep* (*knock off lightly*) She flicked the dust off with a cloth. He flicked off the cigarette ash.

flick out 1 *vi* (*come out quickly and/or briefly*) The snake's tongue flicked out. 2 *vt sep* (*throw out lightly or casually*) He flicked the cigarette butt out (of the window).

flick over *vt sep* (*turn rapidly*) She flicked over the pages of the book.

*fling + particle *vt sep* (*throw with an effort, with direction*) He flung the book away in disgust. These old clothes should be flung out. He opened the window and flung his sweater in. He flung off his jacket as he came in.

fling away *vt sep* (a) *see* ***fling**. (b) (*Fig Fam: waste*) She just flings her money away. She told her daughter not to fling herself away on that dull job.

fling off 1 *vi* (*leave abruptly*) She flung off in a fury. 2 *vt sep* (a) *see* ***fling**. (b) (*Fam: produce casually*) He just flung off a remark about getting a new job. (c) (*discard, rid oneself of*) She has decided to fling off all restraints. I wish I could fling off all these petty considerations.

fling out   1 *vi* = **fling off**.   2 *vt sep*   (*a*) *see* ***fling**.   (*b*) (*discard, dispose of*) He flung out everything he didn't need.

fling up   *vt sep*   (*a*) *see* ***fling**.   (*b*) *Fig Fam: give up, resign from*) He says he'll fling up the whole thing if they don't give him more money.   I feel like flinging it all up.   (*c*) *Idiom:* to fling up ones' hands in horror = to be horrified, to express horror freely.   She flung up her hands with horror on hearing about the murder.

*flip + particle   *vt sep*   (*toss, jerk, with direction*) He flipped the cigarette across to me.   She flipped the cigarette ash off onto the floor.   He flipped the stone over with his foot.

flip through   *vt fus*   (*examine rapidly*) She flipped through the book. He flipped through the papers but could not find what he was looking for.

*flit + particle   *vi*   (*move lightly, with direction*) Butterflies were flitting in and out among the bushes.   I watched a brilliant little bird flit past.   The little girl was flitting about in the garden, picking flowers.   The figure flitted off into the darkness

*float + particle   (*move on, or as on, a liquid, with direction*)   1 *vi*   The raft floated away.   Something was floating in on the tide.   I watched the rudderless dinghy float past.   2 *vt sep*   They floated the boat off when the tide came in.   We managed to float the barrels out to the ship.

*flock + particle   *vi*   (*move in a crowd*) People were flocking in from the surrounding countryside.   We all flocked out to watch the display.   Crowds were flocking past.   Pilgrims flocked up towards the hilltop shrine.   The children flocked round to listen.   The sheep flocked together for warmth.

*flood + particle   *vi*   (*move like a flood, with direction*)   (*a*) (*Lit*) The water flooded back.   The waves came flooding in.   (*b*) (*Fig*) The sunlight flooded in when she opened the curtains. People were flooding in from the surrounding countryside. Men and women flooded out into the streets.

flood out   1 *vi   see* ***flood**.   2 *vt sep*   (*a*) (*inundate*) The rains may flood the place out.   The villages were flooded out. (*b*) (*force to leave a place through flooding*) We were flooded out (of the house).

*flop + particle   *vi*   (*move with clumsy actions, with direction*) The dying fish flopped about on the riverbank.   The tired girl flopped down in a comfortable chair.   The head of the doll flopped back and forth grotesquely.

*flow + particle   *vi*   (*flow, with direction*)   (*a*) (*Lit*) The water flowed past.   The tide flowed in rapidly.   He watched the liquid flow out. (*b*) (*Fig*) Resources are flowing out too fast. Profits began to flow in later the same year. *n* **overflow, inflow, outflow.**

***flounce + particle** *vi* (*flounce, move in a jerky, sweeping manner, with direction*) She flounced out in a huff. The girls flounced in to show their new dresses.

***flounder + particle** *vi* (*flounder, move sluggishly, ineffectually, with direction*) (*a*) (*Lit*) Stop floundering about and think of something to do! We floundered along in the mud. (*b*) (*Fig*) He floundered on in his bad French. I suppose she'll flounder out of her problems somehow.

flush away *vt sep* (*dispose by means of a rush of water*) He flushed the waste materials away.

flush out *vt sep* (*a*) (*clear or clean out by flushing*) She flushed the sink out with warm water. Flush the bottle out (thoroughly) before re-using. (*b*) (*remove or expel by flushing*) He flushed the dirt and stones out with a hosepipe. All the rubbish has been flushed out. (*c*) (*Fig: expose, bring out of concealment*) The police intend to flush the bandits out. The security forces say they will flush out all the troublemakers.

***flutter + particle** *vi* (*fly, or move with small flapping movements, with direction*) (*a*) (*Lit*) The bird fluttered about, trying to get out of the room. A seagull fluttered down with an injured wing. A sparrow fluttered in, looking for food. (*b*) (*Fig*) Stop fluttering about getting in everyone's way! She flutters back and forward like an excited hen. The old lady fluttered in nervously.

***fly + particle** (*fly, with direction*) 1 *vi* The bird flew down from the branch. The sparrows flew away when the cat appeared. When the door was opened, something flew out. The aeroplanes flew over in formation. Fighter-bombers flew in low over the city. 2 *vt sep* He flew the aeroplane over to France. Can you fly us up to Alaska? The airline will fly you out on time.

fly apart *vi* (*come apart violently, disintegrate under pressure*) The machine shook so much that I thought it would fly apart. The engine flew apart while they were testing it.

fly into *vt fus* (*Fig Fam: suddenly develop or exhibit*) He flew into a rage. Now, don't fly into a temper with me!

fly off 1 *vi* (*a*) *see* ***fly.** (*b*) (*come off suddenly and/or violently*) The wheel flew off and narrowly missed me. I'm afraid in case bits start flying off when the engine starts! 2 *vt sep* *see* ***fly.** 3 *Idiom:* to fly off the handle= to lose one's temper.

fly past *vi* (*a*) *see* ***fly.** (*b*) (*specifically Air Force: fly past in*

formation) The aeroplanes flew past.   *n* a **fly-past**=a ceremonial
flight, usu part of a military display or parade.

foam up   *vi*   (*come or pour up foaming*) The froth and bubbles
foamed up.   When he poured the warm beer, it foamed up
(out of the glass).

fob off   *vt sep*   (*a*)   (*cheat, placate temporarily*) He intends to fob us
off again.   Stop fobbing everyone off with false promises.
(*b*)   (*palm off, pass with deliberate deception*) Are you trying to fob
this rubbish off on us?   You aren't fobbing inferior goods off
here!

foist off=**fob off** (*b*).

fold away   1 *vi*   (*fold to one side or for easy storage*) The bed folds
away.   This kind of table folds away easily.   2 *vt sep*   (*put
away folded*) She folded the clothes away.   Can you fold the
bed away?   *n cpd* a **foldaway table/chair**=a table/chair that
can be folded away.

fold back   1 *vi*   (*fold to one side or out of the way*) The bed folds back.
2 *vt sep*   (*put back by folding*) She folded back the bedclothes.
Fold back the shutters, please.

fold down   1 *vi*   (*go flat by folding*) The flap folds down.   2 *vt sep*
(*put down by folding*) Fold the flap down.   He folded down the
corner of the page.

fold up   1 *vi*   (*a*)   (*Fig Fam: end in failure*) The business folded up.
The play folded up.   Most of his ambitious schemes fold up on
him.   (*b*)   (*double up*) He folded up with laughter.   2 *vt sep*
(*make smaller by folding*) She folded up the papers.   Fold up
your clothes tidily please.

*follow + particle   *vt sep*   (*follow, with direction*) Can you follow
them in?   He followed the others out.   They went to the
second floor flat, and he followed them up.

follow on   1 *vi*   (*continue to follow*) He followed on despite every
difficulty.   (*b*)   (*continue*) The story follows on from the death of
the heroine.   The later books follow on from the earlier ones.
We shall follow on from where he left off.   2 *vt sep*   (*a*)   *see*
*follow.   (*b*)   (*specifically Theatre: come on after*) He goes on
(to the stage) first, and then you follow him on.

follow out   *vt sep*   (*a*)   *see* ***follow**.   (*b*)=**follow through**.   2 *vt sep*

follow through   1 *vi*   (*continue, maintain the offensive*)   (*a*)   (*Lit*)
The boxer followed through with a left to the chin.   The
soldiers followed through with an infantry assault.   (*b*)   (*Fig*)
The manager followed through with a special bonus scheme.
The politician followed through with an attack on his opponent.
2 *vt sep*   (*pursue, develop*) He followed the plan through to the
end.   If you follow the policy through to its logical conclusion

you will find that it will succeed.

follow up 1 *vi* (*a*) (*pursue an advantage*) She followed up with a suggestion that he take her out to dinner. They followed up with a request for money. 2 *vt sep* (*a*) (*get benefit from, pursue*) We should follow up his suggestion about getting money from the government. The general followed up the success by attacking the enemy on all fronts. (*b*) (*not lose track of, keep a check on*) We must follow up this business contact. They followed the matter up until they got results. (*c*) (*reinforce*) They followed up the programme with another just as good. *n* **follow-up** =reinforcement, development and consolidation. *n* **a follow-up**=an instance of such reinforcement etc.

fool about/around *vi* (*a*) (*waste time*) Stop fooling about and do something useful! (*b*) (*play the fool*) They love fooling around. He's always fooling about. (*c*) (*behave stupidly*) I don't like the way you fool about with that gun. Stop fooling about with my equipment!

***force + particle** *vt sep* (*force, compel, with direction*) The guards forced him along at gunpoint. The police forced him out into the yard. This door has been forced in. We were forced back by the flames.

forge ahead *vi* (*make good progress*) (*a*) (*Lit*) The ship forged ahead under a favourable wind. (*b*) (*Fig*) The students have forged ahead with their work. She seems to be forging ahead in her new job.

fork out 1 *vi* (*Fam: pay, usu unwillingly*) I had to fork out again, to get her what she wanted. He doesn't like forking out. 2 *vt sep* (*a*) (*remove or expel with a fork*) He forked the weeds out. (*b*) (*Fig Fam: pay, provide, usu unwillingly*) I don't like forking out any more money than absolutely necessary. He won't fork out a penny more.

fork up 1 *vi* (*Fig Fam: pay up, usu unwillingly*) Come on, fork up! 2 *vt sep* (*a*) (*dig up and loosen with a fork*) He forked up the soil. (*b*)=**fork out** 2 (*b*)

foul up *vt sep* (*a*) (*Lit: make dirty*) The whole river has been fouled up with oil. This place has been really fouled up. Trust that dog to foul the place up! (*b*) (*Fig: spoil*) They have really fouled up their chances of success. The whole business has been fouled up by his stupidity. Trust him to foul things up!

frame up *vt sep* (*a*) (*put in a frame*) We must frame up that picture (*b*) *Sl n* **a frame-up**=a faked impression that someone has committed a crime, whereas in fact he has not. *Example:* I didn't do it, it's a frame-up!

fray away *vt sep* (*fray slowly*) The rope has been frayed away and could snap if pulled suddenly.

freak out · *vi* (*Sl: have a drug trip, have hallucinations*) He freaked out for several hours. *n* **a freakout**=a state of drug-induced hallucination.

freeze in *vt sep* (*usu pass: restrict to a place through freezing weather conditions*) The whole village was frozen in for a week. The ship was frozen in as the ice thickened.

freeze off *vt sep* (*Fig: show no enthusiasm for*) He offered his help, but they froze him off. They froze off his offers of help.

freeze on to *vt fus* (*Sl: attach oneself to*) He froze on to them and wouldn't go away.

freeze out *vt sep* (*a*) (*Lit: drive out from cold*) They left their cottage, frozen out by the hard winter. It's so cold in this room we're nearly frozen out. (*b*) (*Fam: boycott, blackball, ignore*) They froze him out (of everything they did). I don't know why they freeze him out.

freeze over *vi* (*become covered with ice*) The lake froze over Even the river froze over that winter.

freeze up 1 *vi* (*freeze completely*) The whole village froze up. The waterpipes froze up. 2 *vt sep* (*usu pass: freeze completely*) We were frozen up last year and had burst waterpipes afterwards. *n* **a freeze-up.**

freshen up 1 *vi* (*become fresh or fresher*) The weather has freshened up after the rain. She went up to the bathroom to freshen up. 2 *vt sep* (*make fresh or fresher*) The shower freshened me up. I feel freshened up after that little sleep. Go and freshen yourself up before the guests arrive.

fret away *vt sep* (*worry continuously*) She frets away all the time when he isn't at home. Stop fretting away and expecting the worst!

*frighten + particle *vt sep* (*frighten, make afraid, with direction*) The noise frightened the children away. His shotgun frightened off the birds. The gathering darkness frightened them in. Something frightened them out (of that house).

*frisk + particle *vi* (*move lightly and happily, with direction*) The young animals were frisking about. The children frisked in, yelling and singing.

fritter away *vt sep* (*waste, spend in a stupid way*) She frittered away all her money. He has frittered away every chance he ever got.

frizzle up 1 *vi* (*grow dry from heat*) The sandwiches are frizzling up in the sun. I forgot about the oven and the roast has frizzled up. 2 *vt sep* (*grill, dry or burn completely*) The heat of the sun frizzled everything up. The steak got all frizzled up.

*frolic + particle= ***frisk.**

frown (up)on *vt fus* (*disapprove of, condemn*) He frowns upon things like that.   Doesn't she frown upon that kind of behaviour? This is the kind of thing they frown on here.

fry up *vt sep* (*a*) (*fry completely, until destroyed*) The sun seems to have fried everything up.   (*b*) (*fry quickly*) She said she could fry something up for them to eat.   *n* **a fry-up** = (*i*) a quick meal of fried food.   (*ii*) the preparation of such a meal.

fumble about/around *vi* (*search about clumsily*) He fumbled about in his pocket for his keys.   Stop fumbling around!   What are you fumbling about for?

fuse together 1 *vi* (*stick together, coalesce*) The metals fused together. 2 *vt sep* (*stick together, coalesce*) Can you fuse the two materials together?   The metals had been fused together by the great heat.

fuss about/around *vi* · (*fuss generally, vaguely*) She fussed around all the time.   Oh, stop fussing about and sit down!

gabble away *vi* (*a*) (*Lit: jabber, chatter inarticulately and continuously*) The geese were gabbling away furiously.   (*b*) (*Fig: talk away in a rowdy and rather incoherent manner*) The guests at the cocktail party were gabbling away.

gabble on *vi* (*Fig: continue to gabble, like geese*) They gabbled on about their holiday plans till I could have screamed.

gad about/around *vi* (*go about in a gay, light-hearted way*) He gads about without a care in the world.   They gad about a lot, going to expensive restaurants and shows.   *n* **a gadabout** = a person who gads about.

gain over *vt sep* (*win over, convert*) They have gained him over. They expect to gain over a lot of converts.

gain (up)on *vt fus* (*catch up with, come closer to*) (*a*) (*Lit*) The horsemen were rapidly gaining on their enemy.   Hurry up, they are gaining on us!   (*b*) (*Fig*) The company is gaining upon its rivals in volume of sales.

gallivant about/around *vi* (*go about in a frivolous pleasure-seeking manner*) He gallivants about as if he had all the time and money in the world.   Oh, stop all this gallivanting about, and settle down to something!

gallivant off *vi* (*go off in a rather frivolous way*) She has gallivanted off somewhere with her friends.

*gallop + particle (*move at the fastest pace of a horse, or very rapidly, with direction*) 1 *vi* (*a*) (*Lit*) The horses galloped away.   The riders galloped up to the inn.   The gates of the fort opened and the messenger galloped in.   (*b*) (*Fam*) Do stop galloping about so much, and sit still for a little while. 2 *vt sep* The cavalrymen galloped their horses across. You can test this animal by galloping him down to the river and back.

gamble away 1 *vi* (*gamble continuously*) They have been gambling away for days, almost forgetting to eat. 2 *vt sep* (*lose by gambling, forfeit*) He has gambled his whole fortune away. She has gambled away our chances of success.

*gambol + particle *vi* (*cavort and play, with direction*) The lambs were gambolling about in the fields. The children like to gambol around in the garden. The foal gambolled up and took the sugar from my hand.

gang up *vi* (*form a gang*) The boys seem to have ganged up. He says they are all ganging up against us. I hope they won't all gang up on her and make her life miserable. He has ganged up with some very disreputable types.

gasp away 1 *vi* (*gasp, take short breaths continuously*) He was gasping away, finding it very hard to breathe properly. She gasps away till she can get a cigarette. 2 *vt sep* (*lose while gasping*) The fish lay on the river bank, gasping its life away. The dying man gasped his last minutes away.

gasp out 1 *vi* (*intensive of* **gasp**) When he saw the photograph he gasped out in disbelief. 2 *vt sep* (*emit with gasps*) He gasped out the news before losing consciousness. She gasped out something about nearly drowning.

gather in *vt sep* (*collect as fully and closely as possible*) The shepherd gathered in his sheep. The seamstress gathered in the cloth.

gather round *vi* (*come together in a crowd*) Gather round, friends, and hear the news! The people gathered round, curious to know what was happening.

gather together 1 *vi*=**gather round.** 2 *vt sep* (*bring together in a group*) He gathered the animals together. They gathered their belongings together, and set off. She gathered some friends together.

gather up *vt sep* (*pick up into one bundle, collect*) She gathered up the children's toys. He gathered the books up and put them away.

gaze about/around *vi* (*look about*) She gazed about at the strange landscape. He gazed about, trying to decide where the danger lay.

gaze away *vi* (*a*) (*look continuously*) I love this painting, and could gaze away at it for hours. (*b*) (*gaze into the far distance*) She stands on the cliff and gazes away out to sea.

gaze out *vi* (*look out*) The men were gazing out to sea. She stood at the window, gazing out.

gear up *vt sep* (a) (*Lit: fit with gears*) The machine is now geared up and ready for use. (b) (*Fig: make ready*) The team is geared up, fit for anything. I hope you are all geared up for the new sales campaign. He geared himself up for the interview.

gen up (*Mil Sl*) 1 *vi* (*provide oneself with fullest possible information*) He genned up on all the problems. 2 *vt sep* (*provide with fullest possible information*) The air force commander genned his men up for the mission. He's all genned up about what to do and when to do it. He's really genned up on this kind of machine.

*gesture + particle *vt sep* (*invite or order by means of gestures, with direction*) She gestured him over. He gestured them up to where he was standing. They were gestured back, so that they wouldn't be seen.

get about/around *vi* (a) (*move or go about*) He gets about quite well, despite his rheumatism. She is getting about again after her illness. She really does get about! (b) (*Fam: spread*) The news got about that he was leaving. Bad news certainly gets about. The report has got about that you won't help us. It must not get about that he is ill.

get above *vt fus* Idiom: **to get above oneself**=pretend to a superior social position. *Examples:* Oh, she really is getting above herself! He does get above himself sometimes.

get across 1 *vi* (a) (*cross, traverse*) When the traffic lessened, they managed to get across. The mountaineers have finally managed to get across to the other side. (b) (*Fam: manage to communicate one's ideas*) He gets across well, doesn't he? The meaning of the play certainly gets across. The message got across all right. 2 *vt sep* (a) (*transport or carry across*) They got the load across without difficulty. We got her across all right. (b) (*Fam: communicate successfully*) They got the message across, didn't they? She managed to get the feeling across that she wasn't happy. He got his meaning across. 3 *vt fus* (*annoy*) They really get across me! She got across the headmaster, who made life very difficult for her.

get ahead *vi* (a) (*Lit: go well in advance*) That ship has got ahead of the others. (b) (*Fig: progress well*) He's certainly getting ahead in his profession. We are getting ahead well with the project.

get along 1 *vi* (a) (*Fam: go*) Well, I must be getting along now. I'd better be getting along, or my husband will be wondering what's happened to me. (b) (*Fam: manage*) Oh, they're getting along very well. The firm is getting along all right. Don't worry, I'll get along without you. He manages to get along without much money. (c) (*Fam: progress*) They are getting along well with the programme. I'm getting along

nicely, thank you.   His broken arm is getting along quite well.
(d) (*be on good terms*) These two boys just don't get along at all.
We get along with them very well.   They get along very nicely
(with each other).   (e) *Idiom, imper:* get along with you!=oh,
stop teasing!   2 *vt sep*   (*move or convey along*) I'll get the books
along to you as soon as I can.

get around to=**get round to.**

get at   *vt fus*   (a) (*reach*) This village is pretty difficult to get at.
I can't get at him on the telephone.   If I get at you, I'll wring
your neck!   (b) (*gain access to*) They are having trouble getting
at the information.   The files are difficult to get at.   He is a
hard man to get at.   *Idiomatic adjs (Fam); **getatable, ungetat-
able.**   (c) (*obtain, ascertain*) The truth is difficult to get at.   We
have finally managed to get at the facts (of the matter).   (d)
(*suggest, hint, imply*) Just what are you getting at?   I am not
sure what she was getting at.   (e) (*Fam: criticize adversely*) She
is always getting at him.   Who are you getting at now?   I'm
getting at you!   (f) (*bribe, usu pass*) The officials appear to have
been got at.

get away   1 *vi*   (a) (*leave*) I really must get away from this place
for a few days.   The girls get away from work at five p.m.
She didn't get away until nine last night.   (b) (*escape*) The
convict got away from his guards.   The thief got away with a
lot of money.   *n* **a getaway**=an escape.   *n cpd* **a getaway
car**=a car used in a getaway.   *n phr* **a clean getaway**=a
getaway achieved smoothly and successfully.   *Idioms:* (i)
There's no getting away from it=it cannot be denied or dismissed
easily.   (ii) You can't get away from it=you can't dodge or
deny the matter.   2 *vt sep*   (a) (*convey away*) We managed to
get him away before anyone came.   They got the boxes away.
(b) (*snatch away*) I got the book away from him.   (c) (*post*) I
must get this letter away tonight.

get away with   *vt fus*   (a) (*abscond with, decamp with*) The cashier
has got away with the takings.   He has got away with a huge
sum in diamonds.   (b) (*escape just punishment while doing*) He has
got away with it after all.   That man could get away with
murder.   You aren't going to let them get away with it, are
you?   He mustn't get away with this!   It was a pretty rotten
thing to do, but he got away with an apology and no other
punishment.

get back   1 *vi*   (a) (*return*) When do they get back?   I expect them
to get back about eight tonight.   He got back home dead tired.
She got back to bed after making a drink.   (b) (*keep back*) The
soldiers told the people to get back.   Get back!   2 *vt sep*   (a)
(*recover, regain*) He has got back the land his family lost.   He got
the book back.   You can't get back your youth once it's gone.

She has got her strength back after her illness. They got the money back. I don't think she'll get him back now that he's found someone more compatible. (b) (*replace, return*) I got the book back before he noticed it was missing. They got him back home before his wife realized he was drunk.

get back at *vt fus* (*gain revenge on*) I'll get back at them somehow for this! He got back at her for spoiling his evening. She got back at him by showing me the letter.

get by *vi* (a) (*pass*) Let me get by, please. Can I get by? (b) (*Fam: be tolerable, be passable*) This work will get by, but that's all. It may just get by. (c) (*manage*) She gets by on a remarkably small income. We get by somehow, but it's not easy.

get down 1 *vi* (a) (*descend*) The old lady got down from the bus. We get down at the next station. (b) (*kneel*) It would be better if you got down and begged for mercy. Get down (on your knees)! He got down and began to pray. 2 *vt sep* (a) (*bring down*) She got the book down (from the shelf). They got the pictures down. (b) (*swallow, usu unwillingly*) The child got the medicine down. I got the food down somehow. (c) (*make a note of*) I hope you managed to get it all down. His secretary got it down. (d) (*succeed in shooting down*) The hunters got down a number of birds. They got down two enemy aircraft. (e) (*Fam: depress*) The news certainly got her down. All these phrasal verbs get me down! You mustn't let it get you down.

get down to *vt fus* (*start to work seriously on*) I really must get down to some study. She decided to get down to her French. When you get down to it, it isn't so difficult.

get forward 1 *vi* (*move forward*) They got forward to the front line without any enemy response. 2 *vt sep* (*convey forward*) We got it forward on time.

get in 1 *vi* (*come in, enter*) He got in before the rain started. The sun gets in through these windows. Water gets in through this crack in the wall. (b) (*interpose oneself*) He got in between the other two people. (c) (*be admitted*) The child got in (to the school) after a special test. I think he will get in without too much trouble. (d) (*Fam: get home*) She said she would get in late tonight. What time does he get in? (e) (*Pol: be elected*) Their candidate got in all right. The party expects to get in at the next election. 2 *vt sep* (a) (*bring in*) He got the chairs in from the garden before the rain started. The farmers have begun getting in the harvest. She went out to get the washing in. The company is trying to get in all its outstanding debts. The government gets the taxes in quite efficiently. (b) (*push or screw in*) I can't get this nail in. Can you get this rod in without tools? (c) (*Gardening: put in the ground*) It's time to get the bulbs in. He has got his seeds in already. (d) (*bring in as a* *supply*) She has got the groceries in for the whole week. He has gone out to get the coal in. (*e*) (*summon in*) They have got the doctor in to look at the child. She got the electrician in to check the wiring. We must get a joiner in to fix this cupboard.

get into   *vt fus*   (*a*) (*Fam: be affected by, or involved in*) He gets into a terrible rage if you just mention politics. Don't get into such a panic! These books have got into an awful mess. The children are always getting into trouble/mischief. (*b*) *Idiom:* to get into the habit of = to become used to doing.

get in with   *vt fus*   (*get into the good graces of, propitiate*) He is trying hard to get in with those people, because he thinks they can help him.

get off   1 *vi*   (*a*) (*dismount*) They stopped the bus and got off. She got off at the next stop. Please tell me where to get off. *Idiom* (*Fam*): I told him where to get off = I told him what I thought of him and it was not very complimentary. (*b*) (*depart*) The plane got off on time. We must get off before it gets dark. (*c*) (*Fam: escape punishment*) He got off with a warning. They got off lightly. The petty thief got off with a fine. You won't get off so easily next time. (*d*) *Idiom:* to get off to sleep = to fall asleep. *Example:* It sometimes takes me ages to get off to sleep. 2 *vt fus* (*a*) (*dismount from*) She got off the bus. The dog got off the couch. (*b*) (*leave*) Let's get off this topic of conversation. Can we get off this subject now? (*c*) (*escape from*) She managed to get off washing the dishes. He gets off doing the dirty work. 3 *vt sep* (*a*) (*remove, take off*) She got her hat and coat off. They managed to get the stains off. He got the cover off without too much trouble. (*b*) (*Fam: despatch, send off*) She got the children off to school. They got the mail off without too much delay. She got the orders off promptly. (*c*) (*Fam: save from punishment*) The barrister got his client off. They managed to get him off with only a fine and a warning. You won't get him off so easily next time. (*d*) (*learn by heart, memorise*) He got off several of Shakespeare's sonnets. (*e*) (*Naut: refloat*) The boat had run aground, but they managed to get her off again. (*f*) (*Naut: rescue*) The crew of the stranded yacht were in danger but we got them off.

get off with   *vt fus*   (*a*) = **get away with.** (*b*) (*Fam: start having an affair with*) He got off with that blonde. She got off with a millionaire.

get on   1 *vi*   (*a*) (*climb or step on*) The bus stopped and we got on. You can get on when the doors open. (*b*) (*Fam: advance, make progress*) How are you getting on now? The work is getting on splendidly. I am afraid she isn't getting on very well at school. (*c*) (*succeed*) He has certainly got on in the world. Some people get on, and others don't. (*d*) (*Fam: agree, concur, work or live* *together in harmony*) They get on very well. I was surprised at how well you all get on. Some people get on, and others don't. We get on with them very well. *Idiom:* They get on like a house on fire=they like each other very much. (*e*) (*Fam: proceed, go on one's way*) Well, we must be getting on now. Better get on while there is still light. (*f*) (*Fam: grow old*) Well, he's getting on now, and isn't as agile as he was. She is getting on in years. They are all getting on, but won't admit it. (*g*) (*pass*) Well, time's getting on, and we haven't done all the work yet. (*h*) *Idiom imper:* Get on with you!=stop teasing! 2 *vt fus* (*a*) (*mount, climb on*) He got on the horse. She got on her bicycle and cycled off. They got on a bus/train. (*b*) *Idiom:* to get on one's feet again=(*i*) to recover after an illness. (*ii*) to recover after a setback in business or in one's career. 3 *vt sep* (*put on*) She got her hat and coat on. They've got their coats on and are all ready to go. She's got the kettle on for a cup of tea. He's got the coffee on.

get on for *vt fus* (*Fam: come close to, draw near to*) He must be getting on for forty now. She's getting on for 35 if she's a day! That old fellow is getting on for 100. It's getting on for midnight, and we really ought to be going home.

get on to *vt fus* (*a*) (*Fam: recognize, trace, find*) The police will get on to him very soon. (*b*) (*Fam: nag*) She's always getting on to me about something. (*c*) (*Fam: contact, get in touch with*) I'll get on to them straight away and find out what is happening. He'll get on to us if anything goes wrong. Get on to your consul and ask his advice.

get on with *vt fus* (*continue, proceed with*) I expect you all to get on with your work while I'm away. Get on with it! This is quite enough work to be getting on with.

get out 1 *vi* (*a*) (*leave*) They decided to get out while there was still time. I'd better get out before I'm thrown out. Get out! (*b*) (*escape*) The prisoners got out through that window. The cat has got out again. (*c*) (*Fig: leak out, become known*) The news has got out that you are leaving. Don't let it get out that he is coming. 2 *vt sep* (*a*) (*remove, usu with an effort*) He got the cork out by pulling hard. The dentist managed to get the tooth out. She couldn't get the stain out. (*b*) (*Fam: bring out, make ready*) I'll get the car out and we can be off. They got the horses out. She got a bed out for her unexpected guest. (*c*) (*manage to produce*) He was very embarrassed, but somehow he got the apology out. She sometimes finds it difficult to get her words out. (*d*) (*Fam: publish*) We expect to get the next edition out on time. They got the book out quickly. (*e*) (*Fam: borrow from a library etc*) She got the book out for a fortnight. (*f*) (*Fam: prepare and present*) They managed to get the plans out on time. He has got out a very interesting scheme. The accountant got the

balance sheets out. When will you get the accounts out?
(g) (*Fam: solve, calculate successfully*) He managed to get that
puzzle out. I can't get this sum out.

get out of   *vt fus*   (a) (*leave*) He got out of the car. She got out of
bed.   (b) *Idiom:* to get out of the way=to move to one side, to
stop interfering or obstructing.   (c) *Idiom:* to get out of one's
depth=to become involved in something beyond one's ability
to handle it.   *Example:* He got out of his depth in that financial
argument, because the other fellow knew the facts.   (d) (*Fam:
avoid*) I can't get out of going to see them. I wish I could get
out of it. He hoped to get out of doing the work.

get over   1 *vi*   (a) (*cross*) He got over while the traffic was stopped.
They came to a river and wondered how to get over.   (b)
(*communicate something*) He gets over well when he wants to.
The play really gets over (to you), doesn't it? That actor gets
over beautifully.   2 *vt fus*   (a) (*Lit: cross*) They got over the
river. He got over the obstacles.   (b) (*Fig: overcome*) He got over
his difficulties. She seems to have got over her problems. They
don't appear to have got over their disappointment.   (c) (*Fam:
manage to suppress one's surprise etc*) I just can't get over it! He
couldn't get over her doing something like that.   (d) (*cover a
distance of*) They only managed to get over ten kilometres.
3 *vt sep*   (a) (*help to cross*) They got him over somehow. We
had to get the animals over first.   (b) (*swallow*) He got the
medicine over   (c) (*finish, have done with*) Well, let's get it over
(with). They got the work over as quickly as possible.   (d)
(*manage to communicate*) They got the play over all right. She
gets her songs over. They can't get their message over. I
couldn't get it over to him that I meant to come.

get round   1 *vi*   (a)=**get about/around**   (b) (*by-pass an obstacle*)
The damaged trucks were in the way, but our driver got round
somehow. It may take time, but we'll get round.   2 *vt sep*
(a) (*Fam: revive, restore to consciousness*) The doctor got the man
round quite quickly after the accident.   (b) (*convert, persuade*)
We should have very little difficulty getting him round to our
way of thinking. They'll get her round, don't worry.   *cf*
bring round 2.   3 *vt fus*   (a) (*evade, circumvent*) He is trying to
get round paying his taxes. You just can't get round the
regulations in this way. There is no getting round the need for
money.   (b) (*Fam: coax, persuade usu to help*) She is so good at
getting round him that she'll get the money all right. That
child can always get round you and get what it wants.

get round to   *vt fus*   (*find time to do*) He says he'll get round to it
next week. I just can't get round to it. I always wanted to
write, but have never got round to it. Perhaps we'll get round
to doing it some day.

get through 1 *vi* (*a*) (*pass through*) He got through into the flooded mineshaft, and rescued the men. The water gets through every time it rains. (*b*) (*arrive successfully*) The column of soldiers got through and relieved the besieged garrison. The news finally got through to us. (*c*) (*Fam: be accepted, succeed in passing an examination*) The candidates didn't all get through. The bill has got through and will soon be an Act of Parliament. (*d*) (*Tel: make contact with someone*) I managed to get through all right. She couldn't get through (on that line). 2 *vt fus* (*a*) (*Fam: finish, complete*) We got through the work all right. He got through the book in one evening. (*b*) (*Fam: exhaust, use up completely*) She has got through all the money her father left her. We got through the coal too quickly. 3 *vt sep* (*a*) (*help to pass through*) Don't worry, we'll get you through when the ropes come. She got the thread through by gentle coaxing. (*b*) (*Fam: help to pass an examination or vote*) I'll get you all through. Their teacher got them through without any failures. The members of parliament united to get the bill through. (*c*) (*Tel: help to contact someone*) The operator finally got me through.

get through with *vt fus* (*Fam: finish completely, usu with a feeling of relief*) He finally got through with the subject. I'll be glad to get through with this whole project.

get together 1 *vi* (*Fam: meet, usu informally*) The family is getting together for the anniversary. Some of the lads get together at the pub once a week. We must get together and discuss this. *n* a **get-together**=an informal meeting or gathering. 2 *vt sep* (*bring together, assemble*) He got them together to talk matters over. It is difficult to get them all together under one roof. He tried to get all his thoughts together.

get up 1 *vi* (*a*) (*rise*) The men got up and began working again. She gets up at six a.m. every morning. Please don't get up, I can find my own way out. There is a strong wind getting up. A heavy swell is getting up just beyond the bay. (*b*) (*mount, climb*) He got up on the horse. How do you get up on to an elephant? 2 *vt fus* (*climb*) He got up the tree without difficulty. The old man got up the stairs slowly. 3 *vt sep* (*a*) (*make rise*) She got him up at six a.m. They got the soldiers up well before dawn. (*b*) (*bring or move up*) The workmen got the tools up from below. (*c*) (*bring or move nearer*) The soldiers have got their equipment up to the front line. (*d*) (*accumulate, gather*) The engine has got up steam. The cars got up speed on the straight. (*e*) *Idiom:* to get someone's back up=to irritate or anger someone very much. (*f*) (*Fam: organize*) They got up a play to amuse the children. He is good at getting things up for parties. Some authors can get up plots easier than others. (*g*) (*Fam: prepare, arrange*) She got up the dress for sale. The book has been got up very nicely by the designers and printers.

She got herself up very attractively. (*h*) (*dress*) They got themselves up as pirates for the fancy dress ball. *n* (*Fam*) **a get-up**=clothes (usually odd or eccentric) (*i*) (*Fam: study*) He is getting up his maths for the exam. I must start getting up my lecture notes.

get up to *vt fus* (*a*) (*catch up with, come level with*) I had just got up to their boat when a strong wind hit us. (*b*) (*Fam: reach*) I've got up to page 110 in the book. (*c*) (*involve oneself in*) He has got up to some new mischief. I wonder what she'll get up to next?

gibber away *vi* (*a*) (*Lit: jabber continuously*) The chimpanzees were gibbering away to each other. (*b*) (*Fig: chatter away like an ape*) He gibbered away about his crazy ideas.

giggle away *vi* (*laugh stupidly and continuously*) The girls were giggling away together. I don't know what they were giggling away about.

ginger up *vt sep* (*a*) (*Lit: spice*) The food was rather insipid, and needed gingering up. (*b*) (*Fig Fam: instil with life or enthusiasm*) He said he would ginger the boys up a bit. They are rather lazy, and need gingering up.

gird on *vt sep* (*Old: put on with a belt, belt on*) He girded on his father's sword.

gird up *vt sep* (*a*) (*Old: fix up with a belt*) He girded up his tunic. (*b*) (*Old Fig: prepare for action*) He girded himself up. *Biblical Idiom:* to gird up the loins of your endeavour=to get ready, to prepare for effort.

give away *vt sep* (*a*) (*bestow*) He gave the money away. I have given the book away. (*b*) (*distribute*) She gave the money away to the poor. The guest gave away the prizes. (*c*) (*betray*) The soldier gave away the secrets when the enemy tortured him. She's not giving away anything he told her. *n* (*Fam*) **a give-away**=something which gives away a secret. *Example:* Her guilty expression was a real give-away. *Idiom:* to give the game/show away=to reveal or betray a secret or a confidence. (*d*) *Idiom:* to give away the bride=to serve as father or guardian at a wedding, leading the bride to her intended husband.

give back *vt sep* (*a*) (*restore*) He gave back everything he had taken. Give the book back to your brother! They gave the people back their freedom. Living here has given me back my health. (*b*) (*return, reflect*) This chamber gives back a marvellous echo. The mirrors gave back hundreds of parallel images.

give forth *vt sep* (*Old, Formal*)=**give out.** 2 *vt sep*

give in 1 *vi* (*Fam: yield, surrender*) I give in. If we can't continue with the struggle, we may as well give in now. 2 *vt sep* (*hand,* *put or bring in*) They gave in the documents as requested. **Where** do we give in our names?

give off *vt fus* (*emit, serve as the source of*) The steel plates were giving off a great deal of heat. This rotting vegetation gives off a terrible smell.

give on to *vt fus* (*lead on to, provide access to*) This door gives on to the courtyard.

give out 1 *vi* (*a*) (*Fam: come to an end*) The supplies are beginning to give out. Her patience gave out long ago. Has the money given out at last? (*b*) (*stop functioning*) The engine gave out. (*c*) (*announce*) He gave out that they weren't coming. 2 *vt sep* (*a*) (*distribute*) The teacher gave out the books. He will give out the money soon. (*b*) (*announce*) He gave the news out in a grave voice. 3 *vt fus* = **give off.**

give over 1 *vi* (*Sl: stop doing something*) I wish she would give over for a bit. Do give over! 2 *vt sep* (*transfer, hand over*) They gave the building over for use as an office. It's been given over to a charity. *Idiom:* to give oneself over to drink/drugs/ pleasure etc = to devote all one's time to these things, to become addicted to them.

give up 1 *vi* (*Fam: wish to stop, lose interest*) Don't give up just because it's difficult. Oh, I give up! 2 *vt sep* (*a*) (*hand or pass up*) He gave the books up to her. (*b*) (*surrender, part with*) She doesn't want to give the job up. Why should we give up all our old friends? He gave up his seat on the bus to an old lady. They gave up their tickets as they left the train. He gave himself up to the police. *Idiom:* to give up the ghost = to die. (*c*) (*devote*) She has given up her life to nursing the sick. They have given themselves up to this task. (*d*) (*renounce; stop*) She has given the idea up. He gave up his title to the estate. I want to give the job up. She is trying to give up smoking. They gave up their subscriptions to the club. He gave up trying to help. I shall give up offering to go. (*e*) (*deliver up, hand over*) He gave up authority last month. They gave up the keys to the city. (*f*) (*with persons and things = abandon*) We gave them up as dead. He was given up as dead. They had given you up for lost.

*glance+particle *vi* (*look quickly, with direction*) He glanced back to see if they were following. She glanced up from her work to see who had come in. He glanced in as he passed.

glance off *vi* (*a*) *see* ***glance.** (*b*) (*strike lightly or in passing; strike and ricochet*) The bullets struck the steel armour and glanced off. The spear harmlessly glanced off.

glass in *vt sep* (*cover in with glass*) The area has been completely glassed in. I like the glassed-in effect.

glass over   *vi*   (*cover over with glass*) The space has been glassed over.

gleam out   *vi*   (*shine suddenly and brightly*) A light gleamed out in the darkness. His torch gleamed out.

*glide + particle   *vi*   (*glide, move smoothly and swiftly, with direction*) The ship glided along swiftly. The snake glided away into the undergrowth. She glided up to me and offered me a drink.

glimmer out   *vi*   (*shine or gleam out weakly*) A light glimmered out, hardly affecting the darkness.

gloom about/around   *vi*   (*go about dejectedly*) They have been glooming about for days, since they were told they couldn't go.

gloss over   *vt sep*   (*a*) (*Lit: cover over with a shiny layer*) The surface has been beautifully glossed over.   (*b*) (*Fig: hide or obscure with plausible arguments; seek to conceal by passing on to another subject*) He glossed over the various points raised by his critics. You can't just gloss it over like that! He always glosses these things over.

glow away   *vi*   (*shine continuously*) The light glowed away in the darkness, reassuring everyone.

glow on   *vi*   (*continue to glow*) The fire glowed on for several hours after it had lost its heat.

glow out   *vi*   (*glow suddenly and brightly*) An intense light glowed out from the window of the house.

glue down   *vt sep*   (*stick down with glue*) They glued the wood down.

glue on   *vt sep*   (*stick on with glue*) He glued the paper on.

glue together   *vt sep*   (*stick together with glue*) She glued the papers together. The materials are all glued together.

gnaw away   1 *vi*   (*gnaw, chew continuously*) The dog gnawed away on the bone. 2 *vt sep*   (*remove or deface by gnawing*) The rats have gnawed the boards away. Something has gnawed the surface away.

*go + particle   *vi*   (*go, with direction*) He went away. She went in. They went out. I shall go back.

go about/around   1 *vi*   (*a*) (*move about, circulate*) They go about together. They go about in gangs.   (*b*) (*move about as usual*) He went about for ages without knowing it had happened. She's going about again after her illness.   (*c*) (*travel, circulate*) The rumours are going about again.   (*d*) (*Naut, with about: change direction*) The ship went about. The captain ordered them to go about. 2 *vt fus*   (*a*) (*approach, undertake*) He knows how to go about these things. She goes about it very efficiently. How shall we go about it? We must go about it very carefully.

They go about their duties quietly. (*b*) (*Fam: be occupied with*) The people were going about their everyday affairs. Just go about your work as if nothing had happened.

go about/around with *vt fus* (*keep company with*) (*a*) (*for friendship*) He goes about with a nice group of boys. (*b*) (*for courting*) She goes about with that boy. He's going about with a very pretty girl.

go across *vi* (*a*) *see* **go.* (*b*) (*specifically, cross, traverse*) They went across to the other side.

go after *vt fus* (*try to win*) He is going after the championship. Why don't you go after her? They both went after the same job/girl/prize.

go against *vt fus* (*a*) (*prove hostile to*) Luck has gone against us. Events went against them. (*b*) (*be contrary to*) This action goes against my conscience. Your conclusions go against all established opinions. (*c*) (*oppose*) Do not go against your father's wishes. (*d*) (*have an adverse affect on*) This misbehaviour will certainly go against his chances of promotion.

go ahead *vi* (*a*) *see* **go.* (*b*) (*specifically, move steadily forward*) The ship went ahead against the enemy bombardment. *Naut Idiom=* to go full steam ahead=to go forward at the greatest possible speed. (*c*) (*Fam: continue, proceed*) They went ahead and told us what had happened. Go ahead, tell me. (*d*) (*carry on, proceed*) She just went ahead and did it. Please don't go ahead with it till you've seen me again.

go along *vi* (*a*) *see* **go.* (*b*) (*work through something*) I check the spelling as I go along.

go along with *vt fus* (*Fig: concur, agree with*) I can't go along with you in this matter. He could go along with it most of the way, but not entirely. I go along with you all the way.

go at *vt fus* (*a*) (*attack*) He went at him with an axe. (*b*) (*undertake vigorously*) You should see her go at the job. He went at it with a will.

go away *vi* (*a*) *see* **go.* (*b*) (*specifically, depart*) They went away and did not return. (*c*) (*Fam: elope*) He went away with his friend's wife. They went away together.

go back *vi* (*a*) *see* **go.* (*b*) (*specifically, return*) He went back for his hat. They went back to the scenes of their childhood. (*c*) (*revert*) Let us go back to the subject we were discussing. She has gone back to her old habits. (*d*) (*retreat*) The soldiers went back under heavy artillery fire. (*e*) (*take the mind back in time*) He went back to his childhood. Let me go back to a date in 1953. My memory doesn't go back that far. (*f*) (*date back*) Our family goes back to the Norman Conquest.

This festival goes back to Roman times. (g) (Biol etc: revert) Species do not usually go back to earlier forms. He seems to have gone back to the actions of his infancy. (h) (extend back in space) The garden goes (right) back to that wall. Our land goes all the way back to the field over there.

go back on vt fus (a) (rescind, retract) He never goes back on his promises. I won't go back on my word. (b) (betray) They have sometimes gone back on their friends. You can't go back on me now!

go below vi (Naut: go below decks) The captain went below.

go (on) before vi (Old Euph: die) We must remember those who have gone on before.

go beyond 1 vi (a) see *go. (b) (Old Euph: die) He has gone beyond. 2 Idiom: to go beyond a joke = to cease to be funny and become a serious matter.

go by 1 vi (a) see *go. (b) (specifically, pass by) They went by without stopping. 2 vt fus (base a judgement on) There is very little to go by. We can't go by looks alone. Don't go by what I say. To go by appearances, I would say all is not well. If we go by instructions, then we must leave now. You can never go by what he says.

go down vi (a) see *go. (b) (specifically, descend) They opened the cellar door and went down. Go down and see who is at the door, please. (c) (Naut: sink) The ship went down with all hands. The boat went down without a trace. (d) (recede) The flood waters have gone down. (e) (fall, collapse) The wall went down with a crash. He went down on his knees and begged for mercy. Prices on the stock exchange have begun to go down. (f) (fall on a scale) The pressure has gone down. Her temperature has gone down. (g) (diminish, lose value or tone) This neighbourhood has gone down a lot. The pictures have gone down in value considerably. (h) (set) The sun/moon has gone down. (i) (become deflated) The tyre/balloon has gone down. (Med) The swelling has gone down a lot. (j) (University: break up at end of term) The students have all gone down (for the summer etc). (k) (Fam: be swallowed) The food has gone down. A mouthful went down the wrong way and made him choke. (l) (Fam: be accepted, approved) The idea went down well/ badly (with them). That sort of behaviour won't go down at all well with your neighbours. (m) (Music: fall to a lower pitch) He went down an octave. (n) (go as far as) This history book goes down to the French Revolution. Go down to the bottom of the page and then stop. (o) (fail in an exam) I'm afraid he has gone down again. (p) (Bridge: fail to make contract) She went down and lost the rubber. (q) (be noted, remembered) That remark will go down in history. This tradition should go down unchanged to posterity. (r) *Theatre Idiom:* The curtain went down on something=something came to an end.

go down with *vt fus* (*Med: contract or become ill with*) He has gone down with 'flu. The children have gone down with measles.

go for *vt fus* (a) (*attack*) She went for him with a hatchet. Be careful or the dog will go for you. (b) (*attack, criticize severely*) The newspapers have certainly gone for him. (c) (*admire*) I don't much go for blondes. She doesn't go for beards. He really goes for miniskirts. The newspapers have certainly gone for him (in a big way). (d) (*strive for*) She really went for that prize.

go forth *vi* (*Old*) (a) *see* *go. (b) (*specifically: march or journey out*) The army went forth amid great cheering and applause. He went forth upon a journey to a far land. (c) (*be sent out*) The command went forth that all men of a certain age should be killed.

go forward *vi* (a) *see* *go. (b) (*specifically, Mil: advance*) The soldiers went forward at dawn. (c) (*be put forward*) The suggestion went forward to the committee.

go in *vi* (a) *see* *go. (b) (*specifically: begin, begin work*) What time does the school/theatre go in? (c) (*specifically Mil: attack a special place*) The infantry went in. The bombers will go in soon. (d) (*Met: go behind clouds*) The sun has gone in.

go in for *vt fus* (a) (*enter for, be a candidate for*) He has gone in for the civil service exams. She has gone in for the beauty competition. Are you going in for the three-legged race? (b) (*Fam: enjoy, have as a hobby*) She goes in for badminton and tennis. He goes in for athletics. I go in for stamp collecting and judo. She doesn't go in for walking much. (c) (*become occupied or concerned with*) One day he may go in for politics. He goes in for biology. (d) (*like, enjoy*) We don't go in for that sort of thing here. Some people go in for football in a big way.

go into *vt fus* (a) (*Fig: investigate, take up*) The police intend to go into the matter very carefully. Our Member of Parliament says he will go into it for us. (b) (*examine or state in detail*) He was willing to go into the history of the city for us. She went into a full explanation of the purpose of the machines. (c) (*Fam: dispute the details and merits of*) Don't let's go into it here, please! They went into it for several hours, without much satisfaction on either side. (d) (*begin to wear, put on*) She went into mourning on the death of her father. (e) (*Fam: start upon, become subject to*) He went into fits of laughter. She went into hysterics. He went into a fit of depression after the news. She went into a decline and nothing the doctor could do would help.

go off 1 *vi* (a) *see* *go. (b) (*specifically: depart*) They went off

without telling me (where they were going). (c) (*elope*) She
went off with the gardener's son. (d) (*decamp, abscond*) The
accountant went off with all the money. (e) (*ignite, explode*) The
bomb went off, killing three people. The fireworks went off in
a cascade of colour. The guns went off. (f) (*go bad, become
rancid etc*) The meat has gone off. The milk has gone off
because of the heat. (g) (*Fig: lose one's skill*) The football team
seemed to go off. The lecturer used to do well, but he seems to
have gone off. (h) (*wear off, disappear*) The effects of the sedative
have gone off now. (i) (*fall asleep*) The old man has gone off
by the fire. She went off all right after a hot drink. (j) (*take
place*) The events went off well/all right/badly. The party went
off as planned. 2 *vt fus* (*lose one's liking for*) I'm afraid I've
gone off Chinese food. He has gone off her, and doesn't want
to see her again. I've gone off Dickens and the other Victorian
novelists.

go on 1 *vi* (a) *see* ***go.** (b) (*continue going*) The travellers went on
through the night. They went on to the next town. (c) (*Lit
and Fig: proceed*) They went on to the next town. They went
on to the next item on the agenda. (d) (*continue talking*) She
went on about her illness (until I was tired listening). Some
people just go on and on (and on). He went on to say that we
were welcome any time we cared to come. (e) (*continue*) The
war went on till 1918. This work is quite enough to be going
on with. (f) (*happen*) Just what's going on here? They told
me what had been going on. (g) (*pass*) Time goes on. (h)
(*Pej Fam: behave*) What a silly way to go on! If you go on like
that, you must expect trouble. *n* (*Fam*) **goings-on** (*pl*) =
shocking behaviour. (i) (*Fam:stop teasing*) Oh, go on (with
you)! (j) (*Theatre: perform on stage*) She went on as a witch in
'Macbeth'. (k) (*Sport: take one's turn*) You go on next. It's
your turn to go on. 2 *vt fus* (a) (*accept, be guided by*) The police
have very little to go on in this case. We can't go on evidence
like that. Give us something to go on. (b) (*US Fam: like*)
I don't go on that at all.

go on for *vt fus* (*Fam: approach*) He must be going on for forty!
It's going on for midnight.

go out *vi* (a) *see* ***go.** (b) (*specifically, leave*) She went out. They
didn't tell me they were going out. (c) (*be extinguished*) The
lights have gone out. The fire went out. (d) (*Fig: fade and die,
cease*) The light has gone out of her life. Her love has slowly
gone out. (e) *Idiom:* to go out like a light = to fall quickly and
deeply asleep. (f) (*cease to be important or fashionable*) Short skirts
have gone out. (g) *Idiom:* to go out of print = to be unavailable
in print (of books). (h) (*leave home for occupational reasons*) She
goes out as a cleaner. She goes out to work now. (i) (*Fam:
emigrate*) The whole family have gone out to Canada. (j) (*flow*

back or away) The tide has gone out.   (*k*) (*Sport: cease to function, usu in a competition*) That team went out in the third round. (*l*) (*be circulated*) Forms have gone out to all our sub-offices. Voting papers went out to everyone in the society. (*m*) (*end*) The year has gone out.   April went out like a lion.   (*n*) *Idiom:* my heart went out to her = I sympathized with her very much.

go over   1 *vi*   (*a*) *see* ***go.**   (*b*) (*specifically, cross*) He went over to the other side of the street.   They have gone over to France. (*c*) (*Fig: change one's allegiance*) They have gone over to the enemy.   He went over to the liberals.   (*d*) (*be overturned*) The car went over into a ditch.   (*e*) (*be received*) The news went over without much comment.   His speech went over well/all right/ badly.   2 *vt fus*   (*a*) (*examine, study*) The auditors went over the accounts with care.   The police went over his story.   (*b*) (*search*) The police went over her room.   (*c*) (*repeat*) I asked her to go over her lines again.   The teacher went over the lesson for revision purposes.   (*d*) (*review, consider*) Let us go over the facts as we know them.   She likes going over her friend's faults. I wish you would stop going over my mistakes.   (*e*) (*touch up, improve*) He went over the painting, giving it the finishing touches.   Someone has gone over this photograph.

go through   1 *vi*   (*a*) *see* ***go.**   (*b*) (*be satisfactorily concluded, succeed*) The bill has gone through and become an Act of Parliament. The law has now gone through.   The deal went through all right.   2 *vt fus*   (*a*) (*suffer, endure*) She has gone through a lot since her husband was killed.   No one knows what I've had to go through.   (*b*) (*examine*) The auditors went through the accounts.   The lawyers went through the evidence.   He has gone through his mail.   (*c*) (*search*) The police went through the suspect's clothes.   He went through my pockets.   The Customs men went through our suitcases.   (*d*) (*use up, consume*) He has managed to go through a lot of money in a week.   They have gone through two pairs of shoes since then.   The boy has gone through the seat of his trousers.   The machine goes through a lot of wood pulp.   The book has gone through several editions in one year.   (*e*) (*perform successfully*) He went through his lessons.   We have all gone through the required formalities.   They went through the appropriate marriage procedure.   (*f*) *Idiom:* to go through the motions of doing something = to give the appearance of doing something (without really doing it).

go through with   *vt fus*   (*complete*) She says that she can't go through with the examination.   He couldn't go through with the deal.   I can go through with it if you can.

go together   *vi*   (*a*) *see* ***go.**   (*b*) (*Fam: court, keep company*) That fellow and that girl go together.   (*c*) (*harmonize*) The colours go together (very well). These people go together all right. (d) (*entail each other*) These events go together. Such conditions always seem to go together. Medical symptoms of this kind often go together.

go towards *vt fus* (*Fig: serve as a contribution for*) This money will go towards the rehabilitation of the refugees.

go under *vi* (a) *see* ***go.** (b) (*specifically Naut: sink*) The ship slowly went under. (c) (*Fig: sink*) The sun slowly went under. (d) (*Fig: fail*) His business has gone under. He has completely gone under.

go up *vi* (a) *see* ***go.** (b) (*specifically, rise*) The smoke went up. (c) (*specifically, climb*) The men went up towards the peak. The aeroplane went up. (d) *Theatre Idioms:* (i) The curtain went up=the play or performance began. (ii) The curtain went up on something.=something began. (e) (*Fig: rise, increase, improve*) He has gone up in my estimation since he did that. The goods have gone up in quality. The goods have gone up in price. (f) (*explode*) The bomb went up, killing three people. The whole building went up when the bomb exploded. The house went up in flames. (g) (*University: enter*) He went up (to Oxford/Cambridge) in 1971. (h) (*go forward as a candidate*) She has gone up for the exam.

go with *vt fus* (a) (*Fig: accompany, occur with*) Poverty goes with laziness. The goodwill goes with the business. The house goes with the job. (b) *Idioms:* (i) to go with the times=to stay in fashion. (ii) to go with the crowd=to think and behave as the majority does. (c) (*harmonize with*) The colours go with each other. Her new hat doesn't go with her dress. His voice doesn't quite go with his appearance. (d) (*Fam: keep company with*) He goes with her. She is the girl I go with.

go without *vt fus* (*manage without*) If you can't save the money, then you'll just have to go without a new coat. That old man often goes without food for days.

goad on *vt sep* (*force on with a goad, incite*) (a) (*Lit*) The driver goaded the oxen on. (b) (*Fig*) He goaded his opponents on to attack him. Stop goading them on.

gobble away *vi* (a) (*gobble, eat quickly in large pieces, continuously*) The men gobbled away until all the food was gone. (b) (*make a gobbling noise continuously*) The turkeys were gobbling away.

gobble down *vt sep* (*gobble or cram down, swallow quickly in large quantities*) He just gobbles his food down. The animal gobbled down everything it was given.

gobble up *vt sep* (*gobble till all gone: eat up greedily*) (a) (*Lit*) He gobbled up the food as though he had been starving for a month. (*b*) (*Fig*) This project just gobbles up money.

goof off *vi* (*US Sl: shirk responsibility*) If you ask him to do anything, he will just goof off.

goof up *vt sep* (*US Sl: spoil*) I'm afraid I've goofed it up. He always goofs things up.

grab away 1 *vi* (*make continuous grabbing movements*) The monkey kept grabbing away at the food. 2 *vt sep* (*snatch away violently*) He grabbed the toy away from his companion.

grade down *vt sep* (*put in a lower grade or position*) (*a*) They have been graded down because of their physical condition. (*b*) **downgrade.**

grade up *vt sep* (*put in a higher grade or position*) (*a*) They have been graded up because of their special abilities. (*b*) **upgrade.**

grate up *vt sep* (*intensive of* **grate**, *shred*) She grated up the cheese. Would you grate these vegetables up?

grind down *vt sep* (*a*) (*Lit*) (*reduce, usu to a powder, by grinding*) The stones have been slowly ground down. Rock that has been ground down by the elements becomes soil. She ground the nutmeg down into powder. (*b*) (*Fig: oppress, weaken*) The dictator ground the people down. Some people say that capitalists like to grind down the poor.

grind out *vt sep* (*a*) (*produce through a grinding process*) The powder is ground out through this machinery and into these containers. (*b*) (*Music: produce mechanically*) The tunes are ground out by this old barrel organ. (*c*) (*Music: keep on playing, usu badly*) The musicians ground out their favourite melodies until we were tired of them. (*d*) (*Fig: produce, churn out*) The public relations people keep grinding out more information about how wonderful their companies are. I wish they would stop grinding out the same old propaganda.

grind up *vt sep* (*grind thoroughly*) The materials have been ground up into a fine powder. This machine grinds all the refuse up.

groan out 1 *vi* (*emit a groan*) She groaned out in her sleep. The sick man groaned out in pain. 2 *vt sep* (*emit as a groan*) The exhausted man groaned out his complaints. They heard him groan out something about an enemy attack. She groaned out that she never had any luck.

*grope + particle *vi* (*search, feel blindly with direction*) She groped about in the dark for the matches. He groped up from the cellar to the top of the stairs. They groped along until they came to a door.

group together 1 *vi* (*come together in a group*) The people grouped together to await events. It's natural for people to group together for comfort and reassurance. 2 *vt sep* (*bring together as a group*) He grouped the guests together according to their special interests. I don't know what method was used to group them together. The objects were grouped together according to colour and shape.

grow away *vi* (*a*) (*Lit: grow outwards*) The plant has begun to grow away from the wall. (*b*) (*Fig: detach oneself: develop a separate life*) He has been growing away from these habits. She has slowly grown away from us, and we don't know why.

grow in *vi* (*a*) (*grow inward*) The creeper is growing in towards the gutters, and should be cleared away. The doctor said that the toe-nail was growing in (to the flesh). *n phr* **an in-grown** or **in-growing toe-nail.** (*b*) (*grow back into place*) The plants are growing in again, despite the drought. Her hair is growing in again after the accident.

grow out *vi* (*grow in an outward direction*) The plants are beginning to grow out towards the sun.

grow out of *vt fus* 1 (*become too big for*) (*a*) (*Lit*) He has grown out of all his clothes. (*b*) (*Fig*) I have grown out of these childish habits. 2 **to outgrow** = (*i*) to grow quicker than (someone or something else). (*ii*) grow out of.

grow together *vi* (*a*) (*come together while growing*) These bushes and creepers have slowly grown together. (*b*) (*Fig: come closer together as time passed*) The two of them have grown together over the years. We were not always such close friends, but have grown together during these difficult times.

grow up *vi* (*a*) (*grow in an upward direction*) Plants grow up towards the sunlight. This bush has grown up a lot in the last few months. (*b*) (*mature*) Your children seem to have grown up quickly. She's very grown up now. He tries to act grown up but doesn't always manage. *n* **a grown-up** = an adult *pl* **grown-ups.** *n cpd* **grown-up attitudes** = attitudes typical of adults or mature people. (*c*) (*Fam: behave in a grown-up manner*) I sometimes wish he would grow up. Oh, grow up (for heaven's sake)!

grub about/around *vi* (*Fig Fam: search diligently about like a bird looking for grubs*) She was grubbing about for something in her handbag. Stop grubbing about there and tell me what you're looking for. He's been grubbing about for a job, without success.

grub up *vt sep* (*dig up*) (*a*) (*Lit*) The animal was grubbing up insects and other tasty titbits. (*b*) (*Fig Fam*) Where did you grub these people up? It's something he grubbed up somewhere.

*guide + **particle** *vt sep* (*guide or conduct, with direction*) The usher guided us in. We were guided out without difficulty. A man on the far side of the river guided them over.

gulp back *vt sep* (*restrain with an effort*) She gulped back her tears. He gulped back the furious reply he wanted to make.

gulp down *vt sep* (*swallow greedily*) They gulped the water down. He gulped down his beer.

gum on *vt sep* (*fix or put on with gum or glue*) He gummed on the stamp. She gummed the label (back) on after it came off.

gum up *vt sep* (a) (*Lit: cover with gum or glue*) The works of the machine were gummed up with some kind of thick viscous material. (b) (*Fig: cause to stop, bring to a halt as if with gum or glue*) This has really gummed things up. All our plans are gummed up for want of capital.

gun down *vt sep* (*shoot down with a gun*) The bandit gunned the guards down. I saw them gun down innocent women and children.

*gurgle + particle *vi* (*make a gurgling sound, with direction*) The little stream gurgled along through the woods. Water was gurgling back up the waste-pipe. The liquid gurgled away.

*gush + particle *vi* (*gush, pour, with direction*) The water gushed away through the huge hole. Oil was gushing up out of the ground. Blood gushed out (of the wound).

guzzle away *vi* (*eat or drink greedily, continuously*) They guzzle away like pigs whenever they get the chance.

hack down *vt sep* (*cut down or fell, violently or unevenly*) He hacked down the undergrowth to clear a path. They hacked down several bushes out of sheer vandalism.

hack out *vt sep* (*cut violently or unevenly*) The settlers hacked out a clearing in the wilderness where they would eventually build their homes.

hack up *vt sep* (*cut up violently or unevenly*) The rioters hacked up the furniture in the embassy and smashed the windows.

hail down 1 *vi* (*pour down fiercely*) Stones hailed down on them. 2 *vt sep* (*Old: call down or summon*) The prophet hailed down curses on the heads of the men who would not heed him.

hammer away *vi* (a) (*Lit: hammer continuously*) He has been hammering away in the shed for hours. (b) (*Fig: work hard*) They have been hammering away at the prime minister for weeks, trying to change his mind. We shall hammer away at this problem till we get a solution.

hammer down *vt sep* (a) (*fix down with nails, by hammering*) He hammered the planks down. (b) (*shape by continuous hammering*)

He hammered down the metal till it was the shape he wanted.

hammer in *vt sep* (a) (*fix in, by hammering*) He hammered in the nail. (b) (*Lit: knock in by heavy blows*) They hammered in the door and then charged into the room. (c) (*Fig: inculcate or emphasize by continuous hard effort*) I'll hammer some information in whether that child likes it or not. He intends to hammer in the point that his men will not accept the offer.

hammer out *vt sep* 1 (*Lit*) (a) (*shape by hammering*) He hammered out the metal bar. (b) (*remove by hammering*) They hammered out the dents in the metal sheet. 2 (*Fig: achieve by strong continuous discussion and bargaining*) They hammered out a new policy which would satisfy both sides in the quarrel. I expect to hammer out some kind of solution, given time.

hand back *vt sep* (*restore, return*) They intend to hand back the money. The pupils handed back the books at the end of the lesson. I expect them to hand back the land they seized during the war.

hand down *vt sep* (a) (*Lit: given down by hand*) He handed (me) down the book from the shelf. (b) (*Fig: pass on, as a tradition*) The story was handed down from father to son. They expect to hand these traditions down almost unchanged from generation to generation. (c) *Idiomatic n:* **a hand-me-down**=a garment passed on by someone who can no longer wear it.

hand in *vt sep* (*give in by hand*) Please hand this message in at the office as you go past. Someone handed in some money he had found in the street.

hand on=**hand down** *vt sep* (b).

hand out *vt sep* (a) (*Lit: give out by hand*) They were standing in the street, handing out leaflets to passers-by. The teacher handed out the books at the beginning of the lesson. (b) (*Fig Fam: offer, dispense*) He likes handing out advice to everyone. The government doesn't want to look as though it is handing out charity.

hand over *vt sep* (*pass over by hand, give, surrender*) He handed over the book when I asked for it. The police handed over the man to the prison authorities. They expect to hand over power at the end of the month. He doesn't want to hand over the property to anyone. *n* **a hand-over**=act or moment of exchange.

hand round *vt sep* (*distribute among a gathering*) She handed round the coffee and cakes. He handed round the various papers which they would need.

hand up *vt sep* (*Old: help up by hand*) He handed her up into the carriage. *n* **a hand-up**. *Example:* If you give me a hand-up

I can get over the wall all right.

hang about/around *vi* (*Fam: remain idling in a place*) Those young fellows have been hanging about for hours. I wish he would stop hanging about and do something useful. You shouldn't keep these people hanging about waiting for you. He hung about, hoping to see someone he knew.

hang back 1 *vi* (*hesitate*) She hung back from asking the questions. I don't know why he always hangs back when he gets the chance to do something. 2 *vt sep* (*restore to a hanging position*) They didn't need the clothes, so they hung them back in the wardrobe.

hang behind *vi* (*Fam: lag behind, linger behind*) That child hangs behind everywhere we go. She was hanging behind, too shy to speak.

hang down *vi* (*dangle down*) The rope hung down from the ceiling.

hang on 1 *vi* (*a*) (*Lit: hold on, sometimes precariously*) The climber on the ledge hung on precariously, waiting for help. (*b*) (*Fig Fam: wait*) Hang on till I get help. Hang on and I'll come with you. 2 *vt fus* (*a*) (*Fig: wait (up)on, depend (up)on*) Everything hangs on his decision. It all hangs on whether he is willing to help us. (*b*) (*Fig: listen with fascination*) The girl hung on his every word.

hang on to *vt fus* (*a*) (*hold on to*) She hung on to his arm. (*b*) (*Fam: retain, often with determination*) You should hang on to that painting, because it may be worth a lot of money.

hang out *vi* (*a*) (*Lit*) The dog's tongue was hanging out. His shirt tail was hanging out. (*b*) (*Fig*) His tongue was hanging out for the chance to go to Paris＝he really wanted to go to Paris. (*c*) (*Fig Sl: live*) Where does she hang out? (*d*) (*Fig: hold on*) The striking workers hung out for more money before resuming work. I expect him to hang out until he gets what he wants.

hang over *vt fus* (*a*) (*Fam: continue*) I expect this situation to hang over till Monday. (*b*) *Idiomatic n* a **hangover**＝the after-effects of too much alcohol.

hang together *vi* (*a*) (*Lit*) All the shirts hang together in the same wardrobe. (*b*) (*Fig: keep the same company, stay united*) They all hang together in that village. I hope we shall all hang together in this emergency. (*c*) (*Fig: present an appearance of truth or consistency*) His story hangs together well, I must say. The argument was a good one and hung together.

hang up 1 *vi* (*a*) (*US Sl: have a psychological problem*) He's hung up on drugs. She's hung up on the way her parents never showed any love for her as a child. *n* a **hang-up**=a psychological problem. (*b*) (*Fam: close a telephone conversation abruptly*) I was telling her all about it and then she just hung up (on me). 2 *vt sep* They hung the pictures up on the walls. You can hang up your coat on that hook.

hang (up)on=hang on 2. *vt fus*

hanker after/for *vt fus* (*long for, desire*) He hankers after the old days. Sometimes I really hanker after home cooking.

happen (up)on *vt fus* (*come upon by chance*) I happened upon that old picture yesterday, you know, the one we were talking about.

harden up 1 *vi* (*become hard*) The ground has hardened up. 2 *vt sep* (*make hard*) Potted plants should be hardened up before planting out.

*****hare + particle** *vi* (*move quickly, like a hare*) The animals were haring along. The boys hared out to see the new arrivals.

hark back *vi* (*refer back*) He harked back to his youth. They are always harking back to their days in the army.

harp on *vi* (*talk continually, moan*) He harps on about how he has been cheated. I wish you wouldn't harp on about it all the time.

hash over *vt sep* (*Fam: discuss*) They hashed over all their old problems.

hash up *vt sep* (*Fam: spoil*) He's hashed up our plans again.

*****hasten + particle** *vi* (*Literary: hurry, with direction*) They hastened away. She hastened back to meet us.

hatch out 1 *vi* (*emerge from an egg*) The chicks have hatched out. 2 *vt sep* (*Fig: form, develop*) He has hatched out a new plan.

haul down *vt sep* (*pull down violently or with some effort*) They hauled the material down from the shelf. (*Sailing*) The sailors hauled down the flag/sails.

haul up *vt sep* (*a*) (*pull up violently or with some effort*) They hauled the materials up from the cellar. (*Naut*) The sailors hauled up the flag/sails. The sailors hauled up the small boat on to the deck of the ship. The boat was hauled up on to the beach. (*b*) (*Sl: summon*) He has been hauled up before the magistrate on a charge of assault.

have at *vt fus* (*Old: attack*) Have at them! (*Fencing*) Have at you!

have down *vt sep* (*entertain by invitation, often in the country*) We are having the Smiths down for a few days.

have in *vt sep* (*a*) (*entertain in the home by invitation*) We are having the Smiths in for dinner tonight. *(b)* *(send for, summon)* I think we had better have the doctor in.

have on *vt sep* *(a)* *(wear)* She had nothing on. He had on a raincoat and boots. *(b)* *(be engaged in doing)* He has a lot on at the moment, but should be free next week. I have nothing on (for) this evening. *(c)* *(Fam: deceive, tease, mislead)* I'm afraid he must have been having you on. Stop having us on, please!

have out *vt sep* *(a)* *(have removed or extracted)* He had a tooth out yesterday. *(b)* *(discuss or argue towards a conclusion)* They had it all out last night and cleared the air a little. I must have the whole matter out with them next time I see them. *(c)* *(continue till complete)* She should be left to have her sleep out.

have up *vt sep* *(a)* *(bring, order or invite up from a lower place)* We had them up for coffee last night. I had him up to see me, to explain what he was doing. *(b)* *(Fam Law, usu pass: summons)* He was had up (by the police) for dangerous driving.

head back *vi* *(go back, return)* We changed our minds and headed back to London.

head for *vt fus* *(have as a destination)* *(a)* *(Lit)* The ship was heading for Southampton. The car was heading for Glasgow. The police expected the criminals to head for the coast. *(b)* *(Fig)* You're heading for trouble if you go on behaving like that.

head off *vt sep* *(divert from an intended direction)* *(a)* *(Lit)* The hunters decided to head the animals off. We tried to head the men off, and get to the treasure first. *(b)* *(Fig)* The speaker seemed intent on heading off awkward questions.

heap up *vt sep* *(form into a pile)* *(a)* *(Lit)* The gardener began to heap up the fallen leaves. *(b)* *(Fig)* If you neglect these things, you will just heap up problems for yourself later on.

hear of *vt fus* *(listen to, countenance)* Mother just won't hear of such an idea. I will not hear of you making a trip to that place.

hear out *vt sep* *(hear to the end, to a conclusion)* We decided to hear him out before making any judgements on what he had done. They heard the story out in silence.

heat up 1 *vi* *(become hot)* The room was cold when we arrived, but soon began to heat up. 2 *vt sep* *(make hot)* She decided to heat up some soup.

*heave + particle *vt sep* *(push or move violently or with some effort, with direction)* They heaved the sacks out of the shed. I asked them to stop heaving those heavy bags around.

heave to *(Naut)* 1 *vi* *(come to anchor)* The ship hove to. 2 *vt sep* *(bring to anchor)* They hove the boat to.

heave up 1 *vi* *(a)* *(rise in sudden or large quantities)* The waters were heaving up in great swells. (b) (*Sl: be sick, vomit*) After drinking too much, he went to the lavatory and heaved up. 2 *vt sep* (*rise or lift with some effort*) A large creature heaved itself up out of the mud. They heaved him up on to the wall.

hedge about/around *vt sep* (*surround, as with a hedge*) The king hedged himself about with guards. They hedged the place about with all sorts of petty restrictions.

hedge in *vt sep* (a) (*Lit: enclose with a hedge*) The field was completely hedged in. (b) (*Fig: enclose or surround, as with a hedge*) The whole matter is hedged in with difficulties.

hedge off *vt sep* (*mark off or delineate with a hedge*) They decided to hedge the area off from the rest of the estate.

hedge round *vt sep*=**hedge in.**

heel over *vi* (*lean over*) The ship heeled over at a dangerous angle under the force of the wind.

*help + particle *vt sep* (*assist, with direction*) They helped the old lady out of the car. She helped the children up on to the seesaw.

help out 1 *vi* (*assist as much as possible*) We asked them if they would help out at the meeting. 2 *vt sep* (a) see ***help.** (b) (*assist in a useful way*) They helped us out a lot during those difficult months. Would £5 help you out?

hem in *vt sep* (*Fig: enclose, as with a hem*) The soldiers hemmed the enemy in and invited them to surrender. I feel hemmed in by these thick walls.

*herd + particle *vt sep* (*gather and move in a herd or flock, with direction*) The men herded the animals up and moved them into a corral. We were herded in like sheep. They herded everyone together for their general protection.

hew down *vt sep* (*cut down forcefully*) They hewed the trees down. He hewed his opponent down with one stroke of his sword.

hew off *vt sep* (*cut off forcefully*) He hewed off the larger branches of the tree with an axe.

hew out *vt sep* (a) (*Lit: cut out forcefully*) They hewed out the stones for the cathedral from nearby quarries. (b) (*Fig: develop in a forceful way*) They sat down and hewed out a new sales policy.

hew up *vt sep* (*cut up forcefully*) They hewed up plenty of wood for their winter supply.

hide away 1 *vi* (*conceal oneself*) The little girl hid away in the cellar. 2 *vt sep* (*conceal*) We hid the toys away in the attic, where the children would not find them. The villagers hid the smuggler away until the revenue men had gone.

hide out *vi* (*conceal oneself for a period of time*) The outlaw hid out in the hills for months. The police knew that the wanted men were hiding out somewhere in the town. *n* **a hideout**=a place to hide.

hide up *vi* (*US*)=**hide out.**

hire out *vt sep* (*give out on hire, lend for payment*) The company hires out cars. They hire out machinery for this kind of work.

hit back 1 *vi* (*Fig: resist actively*) We must hit back against this tyranny. He hit back at his opponents in the debate. 2 *vt sep* (*strike in return*) The little boy hit the big boy back.

hit off *vt sep* (*a*) (*Fig: achieve, mainly in imitation*) He hit off a perfect likeness when he drew his friend's face. He imitates voices, and can hit off some famous people beautifully. (*b*) (*Fig Fam usu with 'it' or 'things': be friendly*) He hit it off with them from the start. *Idioms:* (*i*) to hit it off well (with someone)= to become friendly. (*ii*) Not to hit things off very well=not to become very friendly.

hit out *vi* (*attack violently, and often without skill*) (*a*) (*Lit*) He began to hit out despairingly at his attackers. (*b*) (*Fig*) The men are angry and ready to hit out in almost any direction. The MP hit out at Government policy on unemployment.

hit up (*Fam*) *Idiom:* to hit it up=to celebrate, have a good time.

hit (up)on *vt fus* (*Fig: find, discover*) He hit upon the solution to the problem almost by accident. I hope someone hits on a way out of this difficulty soon.

hitch up *vt sep* (*a*) (*harness*) The farmer hitched up the horses to the cart. The men hitched the oxen up and started the long, slow journey in the wagons. (*b*) (*lift into proper position*) He hitched up his trousers, which were rather loose.

hive off 1 *vi* (*Fam: go off suddenly*) (*a*) (*Lit*) He hived off into the garden and we have hardly seen him all day. (*b*) (*Fig*) Since his electronics business was so successful he has hived off into lecturing and other work. 2 *vt sep* (*Fig Comm: separate, as if bees in a new hive*) The government has decided to hive off some parts of the nationalized industries to private enterprise.

hoard up *vt sep* (*gather in a hoard, preserve for the future*) The old man must have hoarded up a lot of money over the years. They don't spend much, so I suppose they just hoard it all up.

*hobble + particle *vi* (*walk or move with short difficult steps, with direction*) The old man hobbled along, leaning on his stick. The injured men hobbled over to the emergency centre. The lame horse hobbled up.

*hoist + particle   *vt*   (*lift, by some contrivance, with direction*) They tried to hoist the huge stones up with a rope, but failed.   The dockside cranes soon hoisted the cargo off.

hold back 1 *vi*   (*restrain oneself*) (*a*) (*Lit*) The shy little girl held back from meeting us.   (*b*) (*Fig*) I held back as long as I could from telling him what I thought of him.   2 *vt sep*   (*a*) (*Lit: restrain*) The policemen held back the crowds, who were pressing forward to see the visitors.   She was very upset, but held back her tears for as long as she could.   They are accustomed to holding back their emotions.   (*b*) (*Fig: keep a secret*) We were sure he was holding something back from us.   Don't hold anything back, you must tell me everything.

hold by *vt fus*   (*adhere to; accept*) I don't hold by such foolish ideas.

hold down *vt sep*   (*a*) (*keep on the ground or in place*) They held the man down, to prevent him escaping.   It was necessary to hold the tents down because of the strong wind.   (*b*) (*Fam: have*) He holds down quite a good job in the city.

hold forth 1 *vi*   (*perorate, make a speech*) The chairman held forth for several minutes on the dangers of indecision.   2 *vt fus* (*Formal: offer*) The management holds forth the prospect of rapid promotion to young men with enthusiasm and initiative.

hold in *vt sep*   (*a*) (*Lit: restrain*) The rider held in his horse, although it clearly wanted to gallop.   (*b*) (*Fig: restrain, suppress*) She is very good at holding in her emotions.

hold off 1 *vi*   (*a*) (*Lit, Naut: keep at a suitable distance*) The ship held off from the shore because of dangerous crosswinds.   (*b*) (*Weather: fail to appear*) The rain held off for the whole morning, although we had all expected a storm.   (*c*) (*restrain oneself*) She holds off from close friendships.   2 *vt sep*   (*Fig: resist successfully*) The regiment held off superior enemy attacks for three days.

hold on 1 *vi*   (*a*) (*Lit: maintain a grip or footing*) They hoped the climber would be able to hold on until rescuers reached him.   (*b*) (*Fig Fam: endure*) The soldiers held on in that isolated position until reinforcements arrived.   (*c*) (*Fam: wait*) Hold on a minute till I put my coat on.   The telephone operator asked the caller to hold on until a connection was made.   2 *vt sep* (*secure*) This screw holds the lid of the box on.   The child's hat was held on by an elastic strap.

hold out 1 *vi*   (*a*) (*Fig: continue, last*) How long will our food supply hold out?   (*b*) (*continue to resist*) The battalion held out for a week in the face of heavy enemy assaults.   (*c*) (*maintain a negotiating position*) The trade union intends to hold out for better pay and conditions.   2 *vt sep*   (*a*) (*Lit: extend*) She held out her arms to embrace the little girl.   (*b*) (*Fig: offer*) I'm afraid that his case holds out very little hope.

hold out on *vt fus* (*Fam: keep something secret from*) He must know more than he will admit—I think he's holding out on us.

hold over *vt sep* (*Fig: postpone, delay*) The meeting was held over until Friday.

hold to *vt fus* (*adhere*) I hold to everything I said at the meeting. He has always held to his religious beliefs very firmly.

hold together 1 *vi* (*remain in one piece, remain united*) This old coat hardly holds together any more. I expect the family to hold together in an emergency like this. 2 *vt sep* (*a*) (*Lit: keep together usu with the hands*) He held the wires together while his companion fitted them into place. (*b*) (*Fig: keep united*) He hopes to hold the family together through this difficult period.

hold up 1 *vi* (*stay erect*) This building holds up well despite its age. 2 *vt sep* (*a*) (*raise*) The pupil held up his hand to ask the teacher a question. (*b*) (*support*) The pillar holds up the roof. (*c*) (*stop; delay*) The traffic was held up by an accident. *n a* **hold-up**. (*d*) (*confront, in order to rob*) The thieves held up a van carrying a factory payroll, and escaped with the money. *n a* **hold-up**. (*e*) (*exhibit, expose*) He was quite willing to hold anyone up to ridicule, even his friends.

hold with *vt fus* (*Fam: approve of, condone*) I do not hold with heavy drinking and wild parties.

hole out *vi* (*Golf: to hit the ball into a hole*) He holed out in four, one under par.

hole up *vi* (*Sl: hide, conceal oneself*) The thieves holed up in a mountain hut after their escape from the police.

hollow out *vt sep* (*make a hollow or cavity*) The animal hollowed out a place for itself and lay down. The men hollowed out a tree-trunk in order to make a canoe.

home in *vi* (*Tech: come in towards 'home' or base*) The pilot homed in by means of radar, despite the poor visibility.

home in on *vt fus* (*Tech: move towards with the accuracy of a homing pigeon*) The missile is built so as to home in on the hot exhaust of jet planes, and destroy them.

home on to=home in on.

hook on 1 *vi* (*attach itself by means of a hook*) The top cover hooks on to the material underneath. 2 *vt sep* (*attach with a hook*) You can hook the cover on to the material underneath.

hook up 1 *vi* (*fix itself in position with hooks*) The back of the dress hooks up. 2 *vt sep* (*a*) (*fix in position with hooks*) You can hook up the dress at the back. (*b*) (*Tel: make a link*) The engineers plan to hook up the whole area soon. *n* a **hook-up.**

*hop + particle *vi* (*move in small, quick jumps, with direction*) The small boy hopped over into the garden. The bird hopped up on to the windowsill, looking for crumbs. The children were hopping along in the street.

hop off *vi* (*a*) *see* ***hop.** (*b*) (*Sl: go away hurriedly*) He just hopped off without telling us he was going.

horn in *vi* (*Sl: join in, without invitation, like an animal using its horns*) Those gangsters just horned in on legitimate business in the state, and started running things.

horse about/around *vi* (*Sl: behave in an aimless, rather rough way, usu said of young people*) The boys were horsing about in the back garden, making a lot of noise and getting dirty.

hose down *vt⸱sep* (*clean down with water from a hose*) They hosed down the cars and then polished them.

hose out *vt sep* (*clean out with water from a hose*) He hosed out the stable.

hot up (*cf* **heat up**) 1 *vi* (*a*) (*Lit: become hot*) The soup soon began hotting up. (*b*) (*Fig: become dangerous*) Things are beginning to hot up in the Middle East again. (*c*) (*Fig: become fast or more exciting*) The music began to hot up. The pace of the investigation began to hot up, as the police closed in on the criminals. 2 *vt sep* (*Lit Fam: make hot*) She said she would hot up some soup.

hound down *vt sep* (*Fig: hunt down, as with dogs*) The police intend to hound down all dangerous criminals. He insisted that his political opponents were trying to hound him down and make him look responsible for the crisis.

hound out *vt sep* (*Fig: hunt out, as with dogs*) They are determined to hound out law-breakers.

hover about/around *vi* (*a*) (*Lit: hover in the area*) Many little birds were hovering about. (*b*) (*Fig: wait around in an apparently aimless way*) That fellow has been hovering about here for several days, and I would like to know what he wants.

howl away *vi* (*howl continuously*) The wolves have been howling away on the edge of the forest for hours.

howl down *vt sep* (*Fig: drown out with loud shouts of disapproval*) The students howled down the speaker, because they did not like his opinions.

howl out (*cry in a sudden and loud manner*) 1 *vi* The man howled out in pain. 2 *vt sep* They howled out their hatred.

hunch up *vt sep* (*form into a hunch or hump*) He hunched up his shoulders against the cold, driving rain. The figure was hunched up in a corner of the room.

hunt after/for *vt fus* (*seek, look for*) The men had been hunting after that animal for weeks, without success. She was hunting after a particular kind of coat and finally found it.

hunt down *vt sep* (*hunt with determination*) The men hunted down the mad dog until they cornered and shot it. The police were intent upon hunting down the escaped convict.

hunt out *vt sep* (*seeking with determination*) She has been hunting out all the old family photographs. They go into town at this time every year and hunt out bargains in the shops.

hunt up *vt sep* (*Fam: seek by some kind of research or investigation*) Where did you hunt up all this information? They have been trying to hunt him up for some time. She has been busy hunting up the origins of her family.

huddle away *vi* (*crowd together out of sight*) The children huddled away in a corner.

huddle down *vi* (*intensive of* **huddle**) The child huddled down in the bed, listening to the sound of the storm.

huddle together *vi* The animals huddled together for warmth.

huddle up *vi* (*gather in a tight group*) The refugees huddled up in one part of the house, frightened and uncertain.

*hurl + particle *vt sep* (*throw violently or with great effort, with direction*) The men hurled the rocks down on their attackers. He picked up a stone and hurled it out of the window.

*hurry + particle (*move quickly, with direction*) 1 *vi* The people hurried along. They hurried in. Please hurry up! 2 *vt sep* The guards hurried the prisoners up. The escort hurried the men out.

*hurtle + particle *vi* (*move at very great speed, with direction*) The train hurtled along at 120 mph. The rocket hurtled upwards towards the moon. The meteorite hurtled downwards and struck the earth.

hush up 1 *vi* (*Fam: be quiet*) Oh, do hush up! 2 *vt sep* (*suppress*) They tried to hush up the scandal, but news soon leaked out. The politicians hushed the whole affair up.

*hustle + particle *vt sep* (*move in a quick, busy fashion*) The men were hustled along by their guide. An eager official hustled us out after our meeting with the famous man.

ice in *vt sep* (*enclose or surround with ice*) We can't move the machinery, because it is iced in.

ice over *vi* (*become covered with ice*) The weather has turned very cold and the lake has iced over. The windows of the car are icing over.

ice up 1 *vi* (*become completely covered with or full of ice*) The wings of the aircraft have iced up. The car windscreen is beginning to ice up. 2 *vt sep* The water pipes are all iced up.

idle about/around *vi* (*move about in an lazy way*) I asked him to stop idling about and do something useful.

idle away 1 *vi* (*operate continuously, while disengaged*) The car engine has been idling away for several minutes, to get it warm. 2 *vt sep* (*waste*) He has been idling his time away on the beach, lying around and doing nothing.

***inch + particle** (*move slowly, by inches, with direction*) 1 *vi* The car inched along through the dense fog. The cat inched forward, its eyes fixed on the bird. 2 *vt sep* He inched the car along through the dense fog. They inched the pipe up into position, and then connected it to the main pipe.

ink in *vt sep* (*fill in, using ink*) She inked in the outlines on the paper. He did the outline work and then she inked the rest of the drawing in.

ink out *vt sep* (*delete, using ink*) He inked out the mistakes in the typescript.

ink over *vt sep* (*go over with a pen*) You must ink over your signature, pencil writing is not allowed.

inquire after *vt fus* (*ask for information about*) They have been inquiring after houses in this neighbourhood. He inquired after your health. They were inquiring after a Mr. Smith but I knew nothing about him.

inquire into *vt fus* (*investigate*) The police decided to inquire into the events leading up to the accident. I expect that you will want to inquire into the reasons for this decision.

invalid out *vt sep* (*permit or require demobilization or resignation, because of status as an invalid*) He has been invalided out of the Army. Because of his illness, he expects to be invalided out (of the service) at the end of the year.

***invite + particle** *vt sep* (*offer hospitality, with direction*) We invited them up to have coffee with us. They invited us out to dinner. She hopes to invite all her friends along to a reunion party.

iron out *vt sep* (a) (*Lit: smooth, using a hot iron*) She ironed out all the creases in the shirt. (b) (*Fig: smooth, as if using a hot iron; resolve*) He expects to iron out these difficulties at a special conference next week. They are experts at ironing out the problems that arise at international gatherings.

issue forth *vi* *(Old: emerge, pour forth or out)* The soldiers issued forth from a side gate in the wall, and attacked their besiegers. A stream of foul language issued forth from her lips.

*jab + particle 1 *vi* *(stick or poke, with direction)* The boy jabbed the stick in. 2 *vt* *(move by means of jabbing or poking, with direction)* He jabbed the beetle out with a stick.

jabber away *vi* *(talk repetitious nonsense)* The monkey jabbered away in a corner. I'm tired of these politicians jabbering away about matters of which they have no knowledge.

jabber out *vt sep* *(jabber aloud; say so rapidly as to reduce to nonsense)* She jabbered out her prayers, to finish them as quickly as possible.

jack in *vt sep* *(Sl: conclude, stop, usu with a suggestion of irritation or frustration)* It's time we jacked this work in. I've had enough —I'm going to jack it in now.

jack up *vt sep* *(a)* *(Lit Tech: raise by means of a jack)* He jacked up the wheel of the car, in order to repair the puncture. *(b)* *(Fig: raise, increase)* Prices have been jacked up a lot this year.

*jam + particle *vt sep* *(push hard, with direction)* He jammed the stick through until it appeared on the other side of the wall. He jammed his hat on and went out. He jammed the material in until the cavity was full.

jam in *vt sep* *(a)* see ***jam**. *(b)* *(usu pass: be caught in a jam, be unable to move in any direction)* My car has been jammed in by several lorries, and I can't get it out.

jam on *vt sep* *(a)* see ***jam**. *(b)* *(apply firmly)* The driver jammed on his brakes, to prevent an accident.

jar (up)on *vt fus* *(have a harsh impact on)* This noise jars on my ears. Her constant complaining jars upon my nerves.

jaunt about/around *vi* *(Fam: move around nonchalantly, casually)* They jaunt about quite a lot, especially during the summer. He spends a lot of time jaunting about on the continent.

jaw away *vi* *(Fam: talk continuously, as if using the jaw too much)* I got tired of him jawing away all the time.

jazz up *vt sep* *(Sl)* *(a)* *(express as a form of jazz music)* They have begun jazzing up the Classics now. I wish they wouldn't jazz up all the old traditional tunes. *(b)* *(make more exciting, revitalize)* The boys want to jazz up the house, change the décor, have brighter colours. *(c)* *(improve, give an appearance of improvement)* I've tried to jazz up the old car with a spot of paint and some accessories.

jib at *vt fus* *(refuse to accept, reject)* The horse jibbed at that high fence. I jib at providing all this information in order to prove that I'm creditworthy.

*jig + particle *vi* (*move as though doing a lively dance, with direction*)
The girls were jigging about in the living-room, all very excited.
The little boy ran along, jigging in and out through the crowd.

jockey about/around *vi* (*move in order to achieve a desired position*)
(*a*) (*Lit*) The men on the horses were jockeying about to get into
a proper line. (*b*) (*Fig*) The politicians jockeyed about in order
to establish relative power within the party.

*jog + particle *vi* (*move at a slow steady run, with direction*) The
athletes were jogging along. To get fit, he jogs up and down in
the park almost every evening.

join in 1 *vi* (*Fam: take part, participate*) You will be expected to
join in at club parties. 2 *vt fus* He joined in the children's
game. I invited her to join in the conversation. They joined
in the general protest.

join on 1 *vi* (*attach oneself to*) The people were hurrying to see the
parade, and we joined on at the rear. 2 *vt sep* (*attach*) They
joined the wires on and made the necessary new connection.

join up 1 *vi* (*Mil: offer oneself as a recruit, cf* **sign on**) He has
joined up in the Parachute Regiment. 2 *vt sep* (*connect, link
together*) The electrician joined the wires up.

jolly along *vt sep* (*Sl: encourage to move more quickly*) Would you
jolly those people along a bit, please?

jolly up *vt sep* (*Sl: encourage or cause to be more active*) It's time we
jollied those people up and got the work done.

*jostle + particle *vi* (*move within a crowd, with direction*) They
jostled through to the exit. The people were jostling along
towards the city square.

jot down *vt sep* (*write down in a short quick note*) He jotted down
our telephone number.

*journey + particle *vi* (*travel, with direction*) They journeyed
along through the wine country. We journeyed up from the
coast at a leisurely pace.

juggle around/about *vt sep* (*move or switch suddenly from one
position to another*) (*a*) (*Lit*) He juggled the objects around so
quickly that I could not see what was happening. (*b*) (*Fig*)
I wish they would stop juggling the bus-times around and settle
on a fixed timetable.

jumble together *vt sep* (*mix together, compound*) He jumbled all
the names together in a hat and asked her to draw one out.

jumble up *vt sep* (*mix completely, said of solid objects, not liquids*)
(*a*) (*Lit*) I'm afraid I have jumbled these pieces of paper up.

These numbers are not in sequence, they're all jumbled up. (b) (Fig) The whole thing is jumbled up in my memory and I can't give you exact details of it. His thoughts seem to be jumbled up.

*jump + particle vi (jump, with direction) The little boy was jumping up and down. The bus stopped and he jumped off. The train stopped and I jumped on.

jump at vt fus (accept with enthusiasm) He said he would jump at the chance of going abroad. She jumped at the offer of a job.

jump on vt fus (criticize sharply or suddenly) I told her what I had thought of doing, and she just jumped on me and said it was ridiculous.

jut out vi (protrude, stick out) The stones jut out from the side of the building. His teeth tend to jut out a little.

keel over vi (capsize, begin to capsize) The boat keeled over.

*keep + particle 1 vi (remain, with direction) The police warned the people to keep away. We were asked to keep back from the entrance to the house. Keep down or the bullets will hit you! Danger, keep off! 2 vt sep (keep, with direction) They kept us out. She kept the boy in. Would you keep that dog away, please?

keep at vt fus (a) (Fam: persist with) He kept at the job till finished. Keep at it! (b) (maintain pressure on) Keep at him till he pays you.

keep away 1 vi (a) see *keep. (b) (abstain) He keeps away from liquor and tobacco. 2 vt sep see *keep.

keep back 1 vi see *keep. 2 vt sep (a) see *keep. (b) (withhold) National Insurance keeps back 5% of my wages. They are keeping back the names of the victims. (c) (have as a secret, conceal) You are keeping something back from us. (d) (hinder) I don't want to keep you back (from your work).

keep down 1 vi see *keep. 2 vt sep (a) see *keep. (b) (control) The government intends to keep down the revolutionaries. You can't keep down a whole population if they don't want to be kept down. You should try to keep down your anger. (c) (limit) She is managing to keep down her spending. The government wants to keep prices down. (d) (retain in the stomach) The sick man can't keep anything down. (e) Idiom: You can't keep a good man down=a capable person will succeed whatever you do to stop him.

keep from vt fus (refrain, abstain from) He keeps from alcohol. I hope you will keep from doing anything rash.

keep in 1 vi (a) see *keep. (b) (Sl: stay friendly, try to stay in *favour*) I'm trying to keep in with them. You should keep in with him as he is very influential. 2 *vt sep* (*a*) *see* ***keep.** (*b*) (*restrain*) He tries to keep his emotions in. (*c*) (*restrict to a place*) The teacher has decided to keep them in all afternoon, as a punishment for bad behaviour. (*d*) (*hold or pull in*) Keep your stomach in!

keep off 1 *vi* (*stay away*) I hope the rain keeps off. Keep off! 2 *vt sep* (*a*) *see* ***keep.** (*b*) *Idiom:* To keep one's hands off = to leave something alone, not to interfere.

keep on 1 *vi* (*a*) (*continue*) He kept on till the work was finished. (*b*) (*continue to move*) The soldiers kept on towards their objective. 2 *vt sep* (*a*) *see* ***keep.** *Idiom* (*Sl*): Keep your hair on! = don't get upset or excited. (*b*) (*continue to employ*) I intend to keep these men on at the factory. (*c*) (*continue to use or possess*) We are keeping on the house in France.

keep on about *vt fus* (*keep talking irritatingly about*) She always keeps on about the cost of living.

keep on at *vt fus* (*nag*) I wish you wouldn't keep on at me the whole time.

keep out 1 *vi see* ***keep.** 2 *vt sep* (*a*) *see* ***keep.** (*b*) (*maintain or have outside*) They keep the dog out most of the time. (*c*) (*provide insulation against*) That coat should keep out the cold.

keep out of *vt fus* (*not become involved in*) You should keep out of these things. Keep out of what doesn't concern you.

keep to *vt fus* (*a*) (*adhere to*) He always keeps to his promises. (*b*) (*stay in*) He has decided to keep to his bed.

keep together 1 *vi see* ***keep.** 2 *vt sep* (*maintain unity as a group*) He hopes to keep the family together.

keep under *vt sep* (*a*) (*suppress*) He has kept his feelings under for too long. (*b*) (*repress, hold back*) You won't keep her under for much longer.

keep up 1 *vi* (*a*) (*remain, stay in position*) The younger boys were not able to keep up in the race. The old yacht couldn't keep up with the others. (*b*) (*Fig Fam: stay buoyant, bright*) Her spirits have kept up very well, despite all her bad luck. I hope the weather will keep up. (*c*) (*maintain a friendship or correspondence*) I'm afraid we haven't kept up at all since she went abroad. (*d*) *Idiom:* (*i*) To keep up with the Joneses = to maintain or advance one's social position with an effort. (*ii*) To keep up with the times = to stay in fashion, to be progressive. 2 *vt sep* (*a*) (*maintain, continue*) You should try to keep up these old traditions. They keep up a steady correspondence. I want to keep up my subscription to that magazine. She wishes she had kept up her Latin. Keep it up! (*b*) (*maintain in good repair*) They have succeeded in keeping the house up. The local authorities have kept the roads up well. *n* **upkeep**=maintenance.

key up *vt sep* (*Fig, usu pass: excited or worked up*) She's all keyed up because of the latest bulletin. They are keyed up to a high pitch of expectancy.

*kick + particle *vt sep* (*propel with the foot, with direction*) The boys were kicking an old ball about. I asked for the ball and he kicked it over. The little boy was kicking a tin can along.

kick about/around 1 *vi* (*Sl: lie or remain about, without importance*) That old book has been kicking about for weeks, gathering dust. Some lads were kicking around, not doing anything much. 2 *vt sep* (a) *see* ***kick**. (b) (*Sl: bully, abuse*) He had better stop trying to kick us around.

kick against *vt fus* (*resist*) He has been kicking against this transfer for weeks. *Idiom:* To kick against the pricks=to resist a goad or any pressure.

kick away 1 *vi* (*kick continuously*) The little boy was kicking away at the woodwork. 2 *vt sep* (a) *see* ***kick**. (b) (*remove as a support, by kicking*) They kicked away the wooden posts and brought the whole thing down.

kick back 1 *vi* (*recoil*) The engine kicked back. 2 *vt sep* (a) *see* ***kick**. (b) *Idiomatic:* *n* **a kickback**=a cut or share in some deal, usu illegal.

kick in *vt sep* (a) *see* ***kick**. (b) (*knock or break in by kicking*) The attackers kicked the door in. The thugs kicked his teeth in.

kick off 1 *vi* (*Football: begin the game by kicking the ball*) (a) (*Lit Fam*) They kicked off bang on time. *n* **the kick-off**=the start of a game. (b) (*Fig Fam: begin, start*) When should we kick off? The party kicked off in great style. 2 *vt sep* *see* ***kick**.

kick out 1 *vi* (*strike out with the foot or with hoofs*) The horse kicked out at them. 2 *vt sep* (a) *see* ***kick**. (b) (*Sl: expel*) If I were you, I would kick those people out (of the house).

kick up *vt sep* (a) *see* ***kick**. (b) (*Fig Fam: cause*) The boys were kicking up a terrific row. She kicked up a fuss because we didn't go.

kid on *vt sep* (*Sl: tease*) Stop kidding us all on.

kill off *vt sep* (*reduce steadily in numbers by killing*) The hunters killed off most of the animals in that area. That species has been almost completely killed off.

kip down *vi* (*Sl: settle to sleep*) I think I'll kip down here for the night.

kiss away *vt sep* (*remove by kissing*) He tried to kiss away her tears. He promised to kiss away her worries.

kiss back *vt sep* (*kiss in return*) He kissed her and she kissed him back.

kit out *vt sep* (a) (*Mil: provide with kit*) The new intake of soldiers has just been kitted out. (b) (*Fam: dress*) He was kitted out in new clothes from head to foot.

kit up *vt sep* (*Mil: dress or load in full kit*) The soldiers are kitted up and ready to go.

kneel down *vi* (*go down on one's knee or knees*) They kneeled (knelt) down to pray. He kneeled (knelt) down to pick up the letter.

knit up 1 *vi* (*be knitted*) This nylon doesn't knit up as well as pure wool. 2 *vt sep* (*knit entirely*) She had knitted up the front before she ran out of wool.

*knock + particle *vt sep* (*knock or strike, with direction*) He knocked her hand aside. They knocked the poles down. She knocked the vase off by accident. He knocked his assailant over. They weren't playing tennis—just knocking the ball about.

knock about/around 1 *vi* (*Fam: wander, usu as a vagabond, or with no fixed aim*) He has knocked about quite a bit. 2 *vt fus* (*travel, usu with no fixed aim*) He has knocked about the world for many years. 3 *vt sep* (a) *see* ***knock.** (b) (*Fam: ill-treat*) He knocks his wife about a bit. I wish they'd stop knocking their children about. (c) (*damage*) The harvest was badly knocked about by that freak storm.

knock back 1 *vi* (*knock in return*) He knocked on the wall, and she knocked back. 2 *vt sep* (a) *see* ***knock.** (b) (*Sl: consume quickly*) He knocked back two double whiskies. (c) (*Sl: cost*) That new watch must have knocked her back a few quid. (d) (*Fam: shock, stun*) This kind of news knocks you back a bit, doesn't it?

knock down *vt sep* (a) *see* ***knock.** (b) (*demolish*) They are going to knock down those old buildings soon. (c) (*strike and cause to fall, used of traffic*) A bus knocked her down. He was knocked down by a taxi. (d) (*assign for sale, at an auction*) The auctioneer knocked the lot down to him.

knock in *vt sep* (a) *see* ***knock.** (b) (*hammer in*) He knocked the nail in.

knock off 1 *vi* (*Sl: stop work*) The men knock off at six. Let's knock off now. 2 *vt sep* (a) *see* ***knock.** (b) *Idiom:* To knock someone's block off=to assault someone savagely. (c) (*reduce the price by*) I'll knock off £10 just for you. (d) (*Fam: do quickly*) He just knocks these things off in his spare time. She knocked that article off in no time at all. (e) (Sl, usu imper: stop) Knock it off! (f) (Sl: steal) He knocked off that gold watch when the shop assistant wasn't looking.

knock out vt sep (a) see *knock. (b) (displace by hammering) He knocked the screw out. (c) (empty by knocking) He knocked his pipe out on the edge of the ash-tray. (d) (stun, render unconscious) The boxer knocked his opponent out. n a **knockout.** n cpd a **knockout blow.** (e) (Fam: eliminate from a competition) He has now knocked out most of the other competitors. n cpd a **knockout competition**=a competition where the competitors are successively eliminated until only the finalists remain.

knock together 1 vi (a) (strike together) The two pieces of wood knocked together. (b) Idiom: His knees were knocking together =he was very frightened 2 vt sep (a) see *knock. (b) Idiom: You should knock their silly heads together=try to make them see sense.

knock up 1 vi (Sport: prepare casually for a game) They knocked up together for a few minutes. Idiom: to have a **knock-up.** 2 vt sep (a) see *knock. (b) (waken by knocking) They knocked us up at six a.m. (c) (Fam: prepare hurriedly) She knocked up a snack for all of us. They knocked that building up pretty quickly. (d) (Fam, usu pass: be exhausted, ill) She looks quite knocked up. Take care not to knock yourself up. (e) (Cricket: score) The batsman knocked up over a hundred runs.

knock up against vt fus (a) (strike by chance) She knocked up against the table. (b) (Fig: meet by chance) We knocked up against him last week, in town.

knot together vt sep (tie together with a knot or knots) He knotted together the ends of the ropes.

knuckle down vi (Fam: submit, discipline oneself) You'll just have to knuckle down and get the work done as required. You really must knuckle down to it.

knuckle under vi (Fam: submit abjectly) They expect me to knuckle under and do just what I'm told.

labour along vi (move along laboriously, with effort) The man laboured along, groaning in pain. The damaged car was labouring along.

labour on vi (a) (continue to labour or work) The men laboured on into the night. (b) (move on laboriously, with effort) The refugees laboured on towards safety.

labour under vt fus (suffer from) I think you must be labouring under a misapprehension. He is labouring under the illusion that we can help him.

lace up vt sep (do up with laces) He laced up his boots.

laden down=**loaded down**   (*see* **load down**).

ladle out   *vt sep*   (*serve with a large spoon*) (*a*) (*Lit*) She ladled out the soup.   (*b*) (*Fig*) He likes to ladle out advice.

lag behind   *vi*   (*dawdle or linger behind*) The girls lagged behind, picking flowers.   Some members of the convoy were beginning to lag behind.

lam into   *vt fus*   (*Sl: attack*) (*a*) (*Lit*) The boxer lammed into his opponent.   (*b*) (*Fig*) She lammed into me about the mistake I had made.

¹and up   *vi*   (*end up, finish*) He landed up in New York.   Be careful or you'll land up in jail.   He landed up sacked from the job after all.

lap over   *vi*   (*overlap, sit one partly on another*) The tiles lap over.

lap up   *vt sep*   (*a*) (*scoop up with the tongue*) The cat lapped up the milk.   (*b*) (*Fig Fam: enjoy, accept happily*) He just laps up flattery. They lapped up the special treatment given them.

lark about/around   *vi*   (*Fam: play or romp about, usu in a rather noisy manner*) The boys were larking about on the street corner.

lash about/around   *vi*   (*move or thrash about violently*) The animal lashed about in pain.   The prisoner lashed about, but could not break his bonds.

lash down   1 *vi*   (*fall violently*) The rain was lashing down.   2 *vt sep*   (*tie down tightly with ropes*) The cargo was lashed down on the deck of the ship.

lash out   *vi*   (*attack*) (*a*) (*Lit*) He lashed out at the burglar with a stick.   (*b*) (*Fig*) The politicians lashed out at the opposition policy.   (*c*) (*Fam: spend lavishly*) Her father has really lashed out on her education.

lash up   *vt sep*   (*tie up tightly with ropes*) The equipment is lashed up and ready to go.

last out   1 *vi*   (*endure, survive*) I think they will last out till they are rescued.   2 *vt sep*   (*survive*) I don't think the old man will last out the winter.

latch on   *vi*   (*a*) (*seize hold*) The dog latched on and wouldn't let go.   (*b*) (*Fig Fam: understand*) I don't think he has latched on to what we are doing.   She just hasn't latched on.

latch on to   *vt fus*   (*Fam: acquire*) He has latched on to some very valuable pieces of property.

laugh at   *vt fus*   (*a*) (*get amused about*) What are you laughing at? That is nothing to laugh at.   (*b*) (*mock*) She was laughing at us all the time.   (*c*) (*Fam: dismiss as unimportant*) They laughed at the idea.

laugh away 1 *vi* (*laugh continuously*) He was laughing away to himself all the time. 2 *vt sep* (*dismiss with laughter, scorn*) He laughed away the dangers.

laugh down *vt sep* (*defeat, dismiss or silence by laughing*) The audience laughed the speaker down.

laugh off=**laugh away** 2 *vt sep.*

launch forth 1 *vi* (*begin with vigour or drama*) He launched forth into a colourful description of his journey. 2 *vt sep* (*Fig: send out with great vigour or display*) This party should launch them forth into society.

launch out *vi* (*a*)=**launch forth**. (*b*) (*start vigorously*) He has launched out into a new line of business.

*lay + particle *vt sep* (*put or place, with direction*) He laid the box down. She laid the book aside for a moment. They laid the materials back in the cupboard.

lay about 1 *vi* (*a*) (*strike violently*) He laid about with a stick. (*b*) (*Dial*)=**lie about**. *Idiomatic n* **a layabout**=an idle person. 2 *vt fus* (*attack violently*) He laid about them with a stick.

lay alongside *vt sep* (*Sailing: place beside*) They brought the ship up to the others and laid her alongside.

lay aside *vt sep* (*a*) *see* ***lay**. (*b*) (*abandon*) I want you to lay aside these useless prejudices. He laid aside his scruples and joined the gang.

lay by *vt fus* (*a*)=**lay aside**. (*b*) (*save*) The old woman had laid by a little money. (*c*) *Idiomatic n* **a layby**=a parking place at the side of a main road.

lay down *vt sep* (*a*) *see* ***lay**. (*b*) *Idiom:* Lay down one's arms= surrender. (*c*) *Idiom:* Lay down one's life=sacrifice one's life. (*d*) (*resign, give up*) The old man has laid down his office, to make way for a younger man. (*e*) (*impose, institute*) He has laid down certain conditions which you must follow. It is laid down that no changes can be made after a committee decision. *Idiom:* To lay down the law=to state the law firmly, to impose one's will. (*f*) (*store in a cellar, of wine*) He has laid down some excellent vintages.

lay in *vt sep* (*a*) *see* ***lay**. (*b*) (*make a store of*) He has laid in plenty of water and food. She has laid in provisions against a shortage.

lay into *vt fus* (*Fam*) (*a*) (*attack*) He laid into the defenders and scored a goal. (*b*) (*criticize*) At the committee meeting the experts laid into each other fiercely.

lay off 1 *vi* (*Sl: stop doing something unpleasant*) I wish you would lay off! 2 *vt sep* (*Industry: dispense with*) The factory has laid

off workers because of the drop in sales. The work force has
been laid off. 3 *vt fus* (*a*) (*Sl: stop*) Would you lay off that!
Lay off it! (*b*) (*Sl: stop annoying*) Lay off that girl! Just lay off
me will you!

lay on 1 *vi* (*Old: begin an attack*) The soldiers laid on with a will.
2 *vt sep* (*a*) *see* ***lay.** (*b*) (*impose*) The government has laid
on a new tax. The firm is laying on higher prices. (*c*) (*provide*)
Gas and electricity are now being laid on. They lay on all
essential services. The entertainment has been laid on by our
hosts. (*d*) (*apply*) He laid on the varnish. She laid the paint on
thickly. *Idiom:* To lay something on thick=to exaggerate or
overemphasize something.

lay out *vt sep* (*a*) *see* ***lay.** (*b*) (*prepare*) The servants laid out his
meals carefully. Her clothes were laid out for her. The
undertaker laid out the corpse prior to burial. (*c*) (*organize*)
He has laid out the garden quite nicely. (*d*) (*disburse*) She laid
out a lot of money on this house. *n* **outlay**=disbursement,
expenditure. (*e*) (*plan, design*) The gardens are beautifully
laid out. *n* **layout**=plan (of a house, town etc).

lay to (*Naut:*) 1 *vi* (*come to anchor*) The ship lay to off the coast.
2 *vt sep* (*bring to anchor*) He laid the ship to, off the coast.

lay up 1 *vi* (*Dial*)=**lie up.** 2 *vt sep* (*a*) (*store as fully as possible*)
They have laid up large supplies of food. (*b*) (*Fig: accumulate*)
He is just laying up a lot of trouble for himself. (*c*) (*put into
storage*) He has laid up his car for a few weeks. The ships have
been laid up. (*d*) (*Fam: confine or be confined to bed*) He has been
laid up with the 'flu. You'll lay yourself up if you go on like
this.

laze about/around *vi* (*move or lie about lazily*) That boy has been
lazing about too much lately. Stop lazing about and do
something!

laze away 1 *vi* (*laze, be lazy or idle, continuously*) It's lovely just to
laze away in the sun. 2 *vt sep* (*pass lazily*) They lazed away
the whole afternoon. I'd like to laze the summer away.

***lead + particle** *vt sep* (*take or conduct, with direction*) She led
them in. He led them out. We were led aside and told the
bad news. The guards led the prisoners away. The men led
the animals back to their stalls.

lead in 1 *vi* (*Elec: come in, enter*) The wires lead in through this
hole. 2 *vt sep* (*a*) *see* ***lead.** (*b*) (*Elec: bring in*) They intend
to lead the wires in through this hole. This wire leads the
current in.

lead into *vt fus* (*a*) (*enter*) This road leads into the main road two
miles further on. (*b*) (*Fig*) A policy of this type could lead into

serious complications.

lead off 1 *vi* (*start*) He led off by kicking the ball to his partner. The singer led off with a popular ballad. 2 *vt sep see* ***lead.**

lead on 1 *vi* (*usu imper: lead forward, with vigour*) Lead on! 2 *vt sep* (*a*) *see* ***lead.** (*b*) (*Fam: tease*) Stop leading us on and tell us what you are going to do. (*c*) (*raise the hopes of*) He has been leading those people on for some weeks now.

lead out 1 *vi* (*go out first*) The men on the left will lead out. 2 *vt sep see* ***lead.**

lead to = lead into

lead up 1 *vi* (*go up*) This staircase leads up to the roof. 2 *vt sep see* ***lead.**

lead up to *vt fus* (*a*) (*Fam: introduce, serve to introduce*) His speech was clearly leading up to a major announcement of policy. (*b*) (*Fam: prepare to say*) What are you leading up to?

leaf through *vt fus* (*look through by turning the leaves or pages*) He casually leafed through the book.

leak out 1 *vi* (*a*) (*Lit: escape by leaking*) The oil has leaked out into the surrounding soil. (*b*) (*Fig: become known, probably by some unofficial means*) The news has leaked out. 2 *vt sep* (*Fig: make known, probably by some unofficial means*) They have leaked the information out to the press.

lean back 1 *vi* (*bend gently backward*) The trees leaned back under a stiff breeze. He leaned back against the wall. 2 *vt sep* (*cause to bend or lie back*) We leaned the poles back against the wall.

lean forward 1 *vi* (*bend gently forward*) He leaned forward and looked into the hole. She leaned forward and whispered the news. 2 *vt sep* (*cause to bend or lie forward*) He leaned his head forward.

lean out *vi* (*bend out, put one's head out*) Please don't lean out (of the window).

lean over *vi* (*bend over gently*) He went to the parapet and leaned over. *Idiom:* To lean over backwards = to make every possible effort (to do something).

*leap + particle *vi* (*leap or jump, with direction*) The boys leapt in and out of the broken window. The monkey was leaping up and down. When the bus slowed down the men leapt off.

learn off *vt sep* (*learn by heart, by rote*) She has learned the poem off. The actor has learned off his lines.

learn up *vt sep* (*learn as thoroughly as possible*) She has learned up as much French as she could for the trip. They have learned up all they can about the subject.

lease out vt sep (give out on a contract) They have leased the premises out to an oil company.

*leave + particle vt sep (leave, with direction) He left the car behind. Let us leave that matter aside for a moment. The others went in and left him out in the garden. They have left a lot of litter about.

leave behind vt sep (a) see ***leave**. (b) (outstrip) The best runner was rapidly leaving the others behind. In this subject, he leaves everyone else way behind. (c) (forget to take) He left behind a pair of glasses and some books.

leave in vt sep (a) see ***leave**. (b) (permit to stay) They have left those words in after all.

leave off 1 vi (stop, usu by interrupting) I think we should leave off now and have some coffee. Oh, leave off, will you. 2 vt sep (a) (refrain from putting on) She left her coat off when she went out. (b) (avoid doing) I'm afraid he has left it off again.

leave on vt sep (a) (allow to stay in place or position) He left the button on. She left her hat on. (b) (not switch off) Don't leave the light on when you go out.

leave out vt sep (a) see ***leave**. (b) (omit) I hope you won't leave this excellent material out. He left that part of the speech out. (c) (exclude) We ought to leave these people out from the invitations. I suppose this decision leaves me out? (d) (leave available) If you aren't home when I go to bed, I'll leave some food out for you.

leave over vt sep (a) (postpone) Let's leave the meeting over till next month. (b) (usu pass, remain) No food has been left over after the meal. There aren't any bits of cloth left over. n pl **leftovers**=remnants (usu of food).

lend out vt sep (give out temporarily) They have lent out the car to some friends.

lengthen out 1 vi (become steadily longer) The winter days are beginning to lengthen out. 2 vt sep (make longer) They have lengthened his speech out considerably.

*let + particle vt sep (permit, with direction) The doctor is letting her up out of bed for a few hours. He let the cat in, and later let it out again. The guard let us over to speak to one of the prisoners.

let down vt sep (a) see ***let**. (b) (release, open downwards) He let the window down. (c) (flatten by removing air, deflate) He let the tyre down. (d) (loosen and let fall) She let her hair down. Idiom: To let one's hair down=to become completely uninhibited. (e) (lengthen) She let the dress down several centimetres. (f) (help down) They let him down on a rope. He let himself down slowly by means of a rope. (g) (*disappoint*) I hope you won't let us down over this party. Don't let me down. We are counting on you not to let us down. *n* **a letdown**=a disappointment.

let in 1 *vi* (*admit water*) These shoes are letting in badly. The tent is letting in. 2 *vt sep* (a) *see* ***let.** (b) *Idiom:* To let someone in for something=to cause something (usually unpleasant) to happen to someone. *Examples:* If I'd known what you were letting me in for I should never have come. He's letting himself in for a lot of trouble. (c) *Idiom:* To let someone in on something=to allow someone to know about something. *Examples:* Do let me in on your secret! We mustn't let him in on our plans.

let off *vt sep* (a) *see* ***let.** (b) (*release*) The engine let off steam in sudden, blasts. *Idiom:* To let off steam=to release surplus power, energy or tension. (c) (*forgive, release*) The headmaster let the boy off with a warning. I'll let you off this time. The offender was let off with a small fine. The Customs officials let us off lightly. (d) (*explode*) They are letting off fireworks in the park tonight. The terrorists let off a bomb near the building.

let on 1 *vi* (*Fam: tell, admit*) Don't let on about what they did. She never let on that she had met him. 2 *vt* *see* ***let.**

let out 1 *vi* (*strike out*) He let out wildly at the thief. 2 *vt sep* (a) *see* ***let.** (b) (*release*) They have let the prisoner out a year early for good conduct. Someone has let the news out. *Idiom:* To let the cat out of the bag=to reveal a secret. (c) (*widen*) She let the dress out several centimetres. (d) (*emit, give out*) He let out a loud groan.

let up 1 *vi* (*diminish, slacken off*) The rain began to let up. His team worked on without letting up. He never lets up for a moment. *n phr* **no let-up**=no respite or relaxation. 2 *vt sep* *see* ***let.**

level down *vt sep* (*make level by lowering the height of*) (a) (*Lit*) The men have levelled the soil down and made the whole area flat. (b) (*Fig*) I hope we shall not design an educational system for levelling everyone down.

level off 1 *vi* (*become level*) (a) (*Lit*) The ground levels off beyond those trees. (b) (*Fig*) Production has levelled off now and we don't expect to increase it. 2 *vt sep* (*make level*) The gardener has levelled the ground off.

level out 1 *vi* (a)=**level off.** (b) (*flatten out, of a moving object*) The aeroplanes levelled out over their targets and began to drop bombs. 2 *vt sep* (*Fig: neutralize*) Some people hope to level out the differences between the rich and the poor.

level up *vt sep* (*make level by raising the height of* (a) (*Lit*) (The men have levelled the soil up and made the whole area flat. (*b*) (*Fig*: This educational system is intended to level people up to higher standards of attainment.

lever out *vt sep* (*remove by means of a lever*) (*a*) (*Lit*) He levered the stone out. (*b*) (*Fig*) They have tried to lever him out of his powerful position. (*c*) (*lift out*) He levered himself out of the chair.

lever up *vt sep* (*raise by means of a lever*) They managed to lever up the stone slab and look underneath.

lick off *vt sep* (*remove by licking with the tongue*) She licked the cream off.

lick up *vt sep* (*lift by licking*) The dog licked up the gravy.

lie about/around *vi* (*a*) (*be strewn about*) The objects were lying about on the grass. (*b*) (*be lying unused or unwanted*) That old book was lying about for weeks before I finally threw it away. (*c*) (*lie idly doing nothing*) I wish you wouldn't just lie about all day.

lie back *vi* (*recline*) (*a*) (*Lit*) He lay back in the comfortable chair. She lay back in bed. (*b*) (*Fig*) Just lie back and enjoy yourself here.

lie down *vi* (*a*) (*settle, to rest, sleep or wait*) She lay down for half an hour. The dog lay down. (*b*) (*Fig: accept, submit*) I hope you don't expect me just to lie down and take his insults. *Idiom:* (*i*) To take something lying down=to accept something meekly. (*ii*) He won't take that lying down=he won't submit to that. (*iii*) To lie down under an insult=to submit to an insult.

lie in *vi* (*a*) (*stay in bed*) He is lying in this morning. *n* (*Fam*) **a lie-in.** (*b*) (*be confined for childbirth*) She is lying in. *n cpd* **a lying-in hospital**=a maternity hospital.

lie off *vi* (*Naut: rest nearby*) The ship is now lying off, ready to load up.

lie over *vi* (*be postponed, be adjourned*) The decision must lie over until the next executive meeting.

lie to *vi* (*Naut*) (*a*) (*be moored, anchored*) The ship was lying to outside the harbour. (*b*) (*come into position for anchoring*) The ship lay to.

lie up *vi* (*a*)=**lie in** (*a*). (*b*) (*rest*) He intends to lie up for a time. (*c*) (*remain in hiding*) The criminals are lying up somewhere in those hills. (*d*) (*be out of use*) My car has been lying up all winter.

lift down *vt sep* (*lift and then bring down*) He lifted the books down from the top shelf.

lift off 1 *vi* (*leave the ground*) The heavy bombers slowly lifted off.

The rocket lifted off from its launching pad. 2 *vt sep* (*raise and remove*) He lifted off the lid of the pot.

lift up *vt sep* (*raise, pick up*) He lifted the suitcases up. Don't shuffle, lift up your feet.

light up 1 *vi* (a) (*Lit: fill with light*) The room suddenly lit up. The neon signs lit up. (b) (*glow*) Her face lit up when she heard the news. (c) (*Fam: start smoking*) The men settled down in their chairs and lit up. 2 *vt sep* (a) (*Lit: fill with light*) The lamp lit up the room. The searchlight lit up the whole area. (b) (*Fig: brighten*) A smile lit up her face. (c) *Sl Idiom:* To get lit up=to get happily drunk.

limber up *vi* (*Sport: take exercise to loosen up*) The athletes were limbering up before the competition.

***limp + particle** *vi* (*limp, walk with difficulty, with direction*) The injured man limped along slowly. The beggar limped up and asked for money. He can almost walk again, and limps about with the help of a stick.

line up 1 *vi* (a) (*Lit: stand or queue in a line*) The people lined up at the ticket office. *n* a **line-up**. (b) (*Fig: take up a position, for elections etc*) The political parties have lined up behind their candidates. 2 *vt sep* (a) (*Lit: to arrange in a line*) She lined the boxes up. (b) (*Fig: obtain, contrive*) They have lined up a lot of support for their candidate. (c) (*Sport*) *n* a **line-up**=(i) a list of players in a game. (ii) the players themselves.

linger about/around *vi* (*wait about, usu reluctant to leave*) The people lingered about near the theatre, hoping to get a glimpse of their favourite actors.

linger on *vi* (a) (*wait on and on*) Some of the guests lingered on until well after two a.m. (b) (*continue to live painfully*) Although we had expected him to die months ago, he has lingered on (in pain).

link up 1 *vi* (*join together*) The two parties linked up and went on together. 2 *vt sep* (*Radio, TV, Tel: bring together*) He linked up the two areas by telephone. *n* a **link-up**. *n cpd* a **telephone/ radio link-up**.

lisp out *vt sep* (*speak out with a lisp or speech defect*) The child lisped out his name.

listen in *vi* (*listen on a radio receiver or telephone*) We listened in to some very interesting programmes last night. Someone has been listening in to our telephone conversation. *n* a **listener-in**.

litter up *vt sep* (*fill, clog up or cover with litter or rubbish*) The whole picnic area is littered up. Please don't litter the place up.

live down *vt sep* (*Fig Fam: survive, manage to forget*) It will be difficult to live down this humiliation. You'll never live it down!

live in *vi* (*live in a place, as an employee or member of an institution*) The servants live in. Students of this college are expected to live in.

live off *vt fus* (*a*) (*survive on*) He lives off fruit and nuts. (*b*) (*find food in*) The army is expected to live off the land. (*c*) (*depend on for sustenance and shelter*) She still lives off her parents.

live on *vi* (*survive, continue*) He has lived on into an age which he does not understand. These traditions will live on for centuries.

live out 1 *vi* (*live outside a place of work or institution*) The servants live out. Students can live out (of college) if they wish. 2 *vt sep* (*survive*) I doubt if she'll live out the winter.

live through *vt fus* (*survive*) I don't think he'll manage to live through another bad winter. She has lived through two world wars. I couldn't live through another day like that.

live up *vt sep* (*Sl*) *Idiom:* To live it up = to have a wonderful time.

live up to *vt fus* (*a*) (*maintain*) You should try to live up to your father's principles. They hope he will live up to their expectations. (*b*) (*emulate*) I doubt if he can live up to his brother.

liven up 1 *vi* (*become lively*) He livened up when the dancing girls appeared. The party livened up after the pop group started to play. 2 *vt sep* (*make lively*) The pop group livened the party up.

load up 1 *vi* (*become or get something loaded*) The lorry driver loaded up at the depot. 2 *vt sep* (*load completely, fill*) They loaded up the lorry. The vehicles were loaded up.

load down *vt sep* (*load heavily*) They loaded us down with gifts. The ship was loaded (or laden) down with extra cargo.

loaf about/around *vi* (*Fam idle around*) The boys were loafing around, doing nothing in particular. Stop loafing about!

lock away *vt sep* (*secure by locking*) He has locked away the jewels in the safe. The prisoner is securely locked away.

lock in *vt sep* (*restrict to a place by locking*) The guard locked the prisoners in for the night. I locked him in by mistake.

lock on *vi* (*join by locking*) The two space vehicles locked on (to each other).

lock out *vt sep* (*a*) (*exclude from a place by locking*) They have deliberately locked us out. I locked myself out by mistake. (*b*) (*Industry: prevent from starting work, by locking out*) The management has locked the men out. *n* **a lockout**.

lock up *vt sep* (a) (*lock securely*) He locked up the box. *n* **a
lock-up**=a shop or a garage with no living quarters attached.
n cpd **a lock-up shop, a lock-up garage.** (b) (*protect by
locking securely*) He locked up the jewels in a box.   They have
locked the prisoners up in their cells.   *n* **a lock-up**=a prison.
(c) (*Fin: invest, perhaps unwisely*) They have locked up all their
capital in that enterprise.

log off *vi* (*Computer: end work*) We logged off at nine p.m.

log on *vi* (*Computer: begin work*) We logged on at six p.m.

log out *vi* (*register departure in a log-book*) The men logged out two
hours ago.

log up *vt sep* (a) (*Naut: mark up in a log-book*) They have logged
up the ship's position regularly.   (b) (*Fig: achieve*) We have
logged up a remarkable series of gains.

loiter about/around *vi* (*walk about idly*) Some suspicious-looking
men were loitering about near the house.

loll about/around *vi* (*lie about, in a lazy and slovenly manner*) The
boy was lolling about on the couch, eating sweets.

loll back *vi* (*lie back, in a lazy and slovenly manner*) The men lolled
back in their armchairs, drinking beer.

long for/after *vt fus* (*yearn for*) He has been longing for her ever
since she left.   I long for the time when I don't have to work as
hard as this.

*look + particle *vi* (*look, with direction*) He looked up and saw
her.   She looked away quickly.   He opened the window and
looked out.

look after *vt fus* (a) (*take care of*) I hope you will look after these
animals properly.   She has looked after her elderly parents for
many years.   They don't look after themselves very well.
Look after yourself!   (b) (*be temporarily responsible for*) I am
looking after her children this morning.   They look after the
shop when he goes away.

look at *vt fus* (a) (*inspect, study, examine*) Would you look at this
paper, please?   Just look at this!   *Idiom:* This house isn't much
to look at=it is not a very attractive-looking house.   (b) (*Fig:
view*) He looks at life differently from you and me.   Her way of
looking at things is not yours.   (c) (*usu neg: consider, accept*) I'm
afraid I just wouldn't look at an offer from those people.   The
landlady won't look at foreigners.   I wouldn't look at a job
like that.

look back *vi* (a) *see* ***look.** (b) (*reminisce*) They like to look back
on old times.   Never look back.

look down on *vt fus* (*Fig: hold in contempt, disdain*) She looks down on people like that. I wish you wouldn't look down on this kind of work.

look for *vt fus* *(seek)* We are looking for an ambitious young assistant. Don't look for any help from him.

look forward to *vt fus* *(anticipate eagerly)* We are looking forward to seeing you again. I am looking forward to the party.

look in *vi* *(a) see* *look. *(b) (call, visit)* The doctor looked in for a few minutes just to see if everything was all right. Look in again soon! I'll look in at the shop on my way home. *(c) Idiom:* He hasn't got a look-in=he hasn't got a chance (of doing or gaining something).

look into *vt fus* *(investigate)* The police are looking into the matter. I shall look into your complaints.

look on 1 *vi* *(watch, usu idly)* They stood looking on while the man was robbed. *n* **an on-looker** 2 *vt fus*=**look (up)on.**

look on to *vt fus* *(face)* This building looks on to the public square.

look out 1 *vi* *(a) see* *look. *(b) (usu imper: take care, be careful)* Look out! *(c) (keep watch) see* **look out for** *(b).* *n* *(Mil etc)* **a look-out**=soldier, person, on watch. *n cpds* **a look-out post/station/tower.** 2 *vt sep* *(search for)* I'll look out the photographs you want to see. 3 *Idiomatic warning:* It's your lookout=It will be your problem. 4 *n* **outlook**=future state of the weather/one's career etc. *Example;* I'm afraid the outlook for tomorrow is rather grim.

look out for *vt fus* *(a) (seek)* I'm looking out for a new house. *(b) (keep a watch for)* I want you to look out for them at the meeting. *Idiom:* keep a sharp look out=*(i)* observe everything carefully. *(ii)* watch carefully what you are doing.

look out on to=**look on to.**

look over 1 *vi* *see* *look. 2 *vt sep* *(a) (examine carefully or fully)* He has looked over your work and has some comments to make. I would like you to look over these documents. Would you look the applicants over and tell me what you think of them. *(b) (revise)* She is looking over her notes before the exam. *Note* The verb **overlook** has the opposite meaning: *ignore, choose not to notice. Example:* We decided to overlook his mistake.

look round 1 *vi* *see* *look. 2 *vt fus* *(visit, inspect, tour)* The party was looking round the factory. We want to look round the town.

look through *vt fus*=**look over** *vt sep.*

look to *vt fus* *(a) (take care of)* Would you look to the children, please. *(b) (rely on)* I look to my parents when I need help.

(c) *Idiom:* Look to it that it doesn't happen again=Make sure that it doesn't happen again.

look up 1 *vi see* ***look**. (b) (*improve*) The weather is looking up. His prospects in life seem to be looking up. Business is looking up. Things are looking up now. 2 *vt sep* (a) (*go to visit*) I want to look them up sometime. (b) (*seek, search for, look for*) I shall look up their number in the telephone directory. He looked the word up in the dictionary.

look (up)on *vt fus* (*regard, view, consider*) We look upon these people as our most dangerous rivals. I shall look upon your son favourably when he comes.

look up to *vt fus* (*admire, respect*) I really look up to him.

loom up *vi* (*appear ominously*) The ship loomed up out of the fog.

loop back 1 *vi* (*return in a loop or circle*) The wires loop back at this point. 2 *vt sep* (*take back in a loop*) He looped the wires back.

loosen up 1 *vi* (*become loose, relax*) (a) (*Lit*) This rope has loosened up. My muscles have begun to loosen up again. (b) (*Fig*) The government has considerably loosened up on taxation. 2 *vt sep* (*loosen as muchas possible*) He has loosened the soil up with a fork.

lop off *vt sep* (*cut off quickly*) They lopped a lot of old branches off. The soldiers lopped off their prisoners' heads.

lose out *vi* (*Fam: lose badly*) I think we have lost out. We certainly lost out on that deal.

***lounge + particle** *vi* (*Fam: move lazily, with direction*) The big fellow was lounging around on the couch. One of the young men lounged up and started to ask personal questions.

louse up *vt sep* (*Sl: spoil*) I'm afraid he's loused the whole thing up. Trust you to louse things up.

***lug + particle** *vt sep* (*pull with some effort, with direction*) He lugged the box over to us. Can you lug that thing in here?

***lumber + particle** *vi* (*move steadily and heavily, with direction*) The elephants lumbered along. One of the big creatures lumbered up in a threatening way. We watched the tanks lumbering out.

lump together *vt sep* (*take together as a lump*) He has lumped everyone together. We don't want to be lumped together in one group.

lunch in *vi* (*have lunch at home, in an office, place of work etc*) We are lunching in today.

lunch out *vi* (*have lunch in a restaurant*) I don't often lunch out.

***lurch + particle** *vi* (*move in a sudden, unpredictable fashion, with* *direction*) The drunk man was lurching along. He lurched up to us and began singing. The ship lurched about in the storm.

*lure + particle *vt sep* (*trick or entice, with direction*) The animals were lured in with a special bait. The police lured the bandits out and shot them. We hope to lure the wolf away from this place.

lure on *vt sep* (*a*) *see* ***lure.** (*b*) (*lure or entice continuously*) She will lure that poor fellow on until he does just what she wants.

lurk about/around *vi* (*linger or loiter about secretively*) Some men were lurking about in the bushes, so we called the police.

lust for/after *vt fus* (*desire fiercely*) Some men lust for women, and others lust for gold.

make after *vt fus* (*Old: pursue*) They made after him on horse-back.

make at *vt fus* (*Old: attack*) He made at her with a knife.

make away *vi* = **make off.**

make away with *vt fus* (*murder secretly*) They made away with their opponents.

make for *vt fus* (*a*) (*go towards, as a destination*) The party was making for London. The ship made for Southampton. (*b*) (*have as a result, provide basis for*) This kind of thing makes for good human relations.

make off *vi* (*escape*) When the police arrived, the thieves made off.

make off with *vt fus* (*steal, decamp with*) The manager has made off with the company profits.

make out 1 *vi* (*Fam: get on, do*) How are you making out these days? 2 *vt sep* (*a*) (*write, fill out*) He made out a cheque for the required amount of money. We shall make out the bill immediately. The necessary documents will be made out in good time. (*b*) (*distinguish*) We couldn't make the people out in that poor light. I could just make out where the road was in the fog. (*c*) (*decipher*) It was difficult to make out his hand-writing. (*d*) (*disentangle, understand*) It isn't easy to make out his ideas. I can't make out what he wants. (*e*) (*claim, assert*) They make out that we knew what was happening. (*f*) (*establish, demonstrate*) How do you make that out? (*g*) *Idioms:* (*i*) They make him out to be a fool = They would like you to believe that he is a fool. (*ii*) He makes himself out to be a doctor = He is claiming to be a doctor. (*iii*) The play makes her out to be naive = In the play she is meant to appear naive.

make over *vt sep* (*a*) (*assign*) He has made the estate over to his eldest son. He has made the money over to charity. (*b*) (*remake*) She has made the coat over and it looks quite fashionable now.

make up 1 *vi* (*a*) (*re-establish good relations*) They have made up. Let's kiss and make up. (*b*) (*apply cosmetics*) The actors were making up when we arrived. *n* **make-up**=cosmetics. (*c*) (*Sport: gain*) He managed to make up on the other runners in the race. 2 *vt sep* (*a*) (*counterbalance, adjust*) The government says it will make up your loss in profits this year. He gave us £10 to make up the deficit. (*b*) (*invent, fabricate*) He made the story up. *Adj* It's a **made-up** story from beginning to end. (*c*) (*put together*) The pharmacist made up the prescription. The shop assistant made up the parcel expertly. (*d*) (*sew, tailor*) They make up clothes as well as sell material. 'Customers' own material made up here'. (*e*) (*arrange, form*) She made up the beds. The various parts make up a coherent whole. The book will be made up by expert printers. (*f*) (*compile*) The lists have now been made up. Customers' accounts are made up once a month. (*g*) (*compensate for*) We hope to make up lost time quickly after the strike. (*h*) (*with 'it': recompense*) I'll make it up to you (for all you have suffered). (*i*) (*re-establish good relations; settle*) Let's make it up. They have made up their quarrel at last. (*j*) (*apply cosmetics to*) She made her face up. They were making up the actors' faces before the play. (*k*) *Idiom:* to make up one's mind=to come to a decision.

make up for *vt fus* (*compensate for*) He tried to make up for all the trouble/worry he had caused.

make up to *vt fus* (*Fam: flatter*) She makes up to her boss all the time.

mangle up *vt sep* (*crush thoroughly*) The bodies of the accident victims were all mangled up.

*****manipulate + particle** *vt sep* (*arrange at will, with direction*) They manipulated the parts up into place. We may manage to manipulate the pieces out. I don't like people who try to manipulate you about to suit themselves.

*****manoeuvre + particle** (*US maneuver*) (*move deliberately, usu Mil, with direction*) 1 *vi* The tanks were manoeuvring about on the plain. The patrol manoeuvred up to within a few yards of the enemy position. 2 *vt sep* He manoeuvred the tanks around. The general manoeuvred the enemy away from the city.

map out *vt sep* (*a*) (*Lit: mark out on a map*) The scouts mapped the area out thoroughly. (*b*) (*Fig: plan*) We have mapped out a plan of campaign. He has mapped out what he will do.

*march + particle *(march, with direction)* 1 *vi* The men marched along. Several soldiers marched up. They marched away. 2 *vt sep* The sergeant marched the men in. He marched the prisoner out. The captain marched his company forward.

march past *vi* (*a*) *see* ***march.** (*b*) *(go past in ceremonial formation)* The contingents of the army, navy and air force marched past. *n* **a marchpast.**

mark down *vt sep* (*a*) *(note down with a mark)* Would you mark these points down? (*b*) *(reduce in price)* All these items have been marked down. (*c*) *(single out)* He has been marked down for assassination. They marked him down for promotion.

mark on *vt sep* *(put on with a mark)* They have marked the prices on.

mark off *vt sep* *(delimit, indicate the boundaries by marking)* This area has been marked off for athletic practice.

mark out *vt sep* (*a*) *(Lit: delineate)* The tennis court has been freshly marked out. (*b*) *(Fig: indicate)* They have marked out exactly what they intend to do. (*c*) *(note)* He has been marked out for early promotion.

mark up *vt sep* (*a*) *(put up with a mark)* They marked up the score on the scoreboard. (*b*) *(put a price on)* They have marked up all these items. (*c*) *(raise in price)* These items have now been marked up.

marry off *vt sep* *(arrange the marriage of)* He has married off his daughter to a rich young lawyer. They couldn't marry her off.

mash up *vt sep* *(mash thoroughly, reduce to a pulp)* (*a*) *(Lit)* The potatoes have been mashed up. (*b*) *(Fig)* His face was mashed up in the accident.

match up 1 *vi* (*a*) *(correspond)* These colours match up nicely. (*b*) *(be equal)* He matched up to the situation. 2 *vt sep* *(bring into correspondence or harmony)* She has matched the patterns up very well.

*meander + particle *vi* *(move slowly and erratically, with direction)* The river meandered along. The party of pilgrims meandered back and forward in the temple grounds.

measure off *vt sep* *(delimit or mark off by measuring)* They measured off the area in which they would work.

measure up 1 *vi* (*a*) *(be good enough)* It's a tough assignment, and I hope he'll measure up (to it). She'll measure up, don't worry. (*b*) *(take measurement)* Will you measure up or shall I? 2 *vt sep* (*a*) *(measure fully)* He measured up the wood before he started. (*b*) *(Tailoring: measure for a suit etc)* I'll just measure you up, sir, if I may? (c) (*Fig: assess*) We've been trying to measure up his chances.

meet up *vi* (*intensive of* **meet**) They met up again in Rome. He met up with some old friends.

meet with *vt fus* (*encounter*) He has met with some unexpected difficulties. They met with violent deaths. She met with a curt refusal. He met with a warm reception. The ship met with a gale.

melt away *vi* (a) (*Lit: thaw*) The ice melted away. (b) (*Fig: vanish*) His money has just melted away. The crowd quickly melted away when police asked for the names of witnesses. The fog melted away.

melt down *vt sep* (*reduce by melting*) They melted down the gold ingots. A lot of this scrap metal can be melted down and used again.

merge together 1 *vi* (*blend together*) The shadows slowly merged together. 2 *vt sep* (*bring into a blend*) They merged the colours together.

mess about/around 1 *vi* (a) (*Fam: behave in an irritating way*) The children were messing about in my room. Stop messing about! (b) (*work or play in a messy situation*) I love messing about in boats. 2 *vt sep* (*Fam: upset, disturb*) They have messed me about a lot lately. His plants have been messed about a bit by the wind. Stop messing me about!

mess up *vt sep* (a) (*Lit Fam: spoil, make a mess of*) She warned him not to mess up her hair. The kids have messed the garden up. (b) (*Fig Fam: spoil*) His plans have been messed up. This strike will mess his business up.

mete out *vt sep* (*apportion, dispense*) The judge meted out punishment impartially. It is not my intention to mete out praise or blame.

mill about/around *vi* (*crowd about in confusion*) The frightened animals were milling about in their pens. The people in the streets milled about.

***mince + particle** *vi* (*walk or move in an affected or effeminate way, with direction*) The dandies minced along in their most colourful clothes. A young fop minced up and introduced himself.

mince up 1 *vi* *see* ***mince.** 2 *vt sep* (*reduce to mince*) The butcher minced the meat up.

mind out *vi* (*Fam, usu imper: take care*) Mind out or you'll get hurt!

miss out 1 *vi* (*Fam: miss completely, lose*) I'm afraid I missed out on that deal. 2 *vt sep* (*omit*) We missed your name out by mistake.   They decided to miss out the last part of the play.

mist over   *vi*   (*become misty*) The windscreen of the car misted over.

mist up   1 *vi*=**mist over.**   2 *vt sep*   (*make misty*) The condensation has begun to mist up the windows.

mix in   1 *vi*   (*take part in things*) She doesn't mix in very well. 2 *vt sep*   (*add by mixing*) She mixed in the eggs.   He carefully mixed the powder in.

mix round   *vt sep*   (*stir and mix*) He mixed round the contents of the pot.

mix together   1 *vi*   (*mingle*) The people mixed together amicably. 2 *vt sep*   (*put together by mixing*) You should mix the ingredients together.

mix up   *vt sep*   (a) (*prepare by mixing thoroughly*) She mixed their medicine up in a glass.   (b) (*muddle, confuse*) I'm afraid I have mixed your names up.   She had mixed him up with someone else.   *n* **a mix-up**=a muddle.   (c) (*Fam: involve*) Don't mix me up in your affairs.   We are sorry we got mixed up in that business.   He got mixed up in politics.   They were mixed up with a lot of criminals.   (d) (*usu pass: be confused*) I'm really mixed up.   The facts are all mixed up.   He's a silly mixed-up sort of fellow.

mock-up   *n* (*Mil: a scale model*) They made a mock-up of the campaign.   The architect showed a mock-up of his plans.

monkey about/around   *vi*   (*act like a monkey or foolishly*) Those boys have been monkeying about with my tools again.   Stop monkeying about!

*mooch + particle   *vi*   (*Fam: move in an aimless, sullen, slovenly manner, with direction*) The disgruntled boys mooched off.   He mooched along with his hands in his pockets.   Those fellows have been mooching around here too much.

moon about/around   *vi*   (*go about in a listless manner*) She has been mooning about all day, thinking about her boy-friend.

mop down   *vt sep*   (*clean down with a mop*) She mopped the walls down.

mop over   *vt sep*   (*clean over with a mop*) She mopped over the floors

mop up   1 *vi*   (*clean up with a mop*) Don't worry about the mess; I'll mop it up.   2 *vt sep*   (a) (*Lit: clean up with a mop*) He mopped up the water.   (b) (*Fig Fam: eliminate*) The army has now mopped up the enemy.   *n cpd Mil* **mopping-up operations** =operations for ending enemy resistance.

mosey along/on   *vi*   (*US Fam: go informally along*) I guess I'd better mosey along out of here.

***motor** + **particle** *vi* (*travel by car, with direction*) He is motoring down to the coast.   They intend to motor up to London.   Oh, he motored off somewhere for the weekend.

mount up *vi* (*increase*) His debts are beginning to mount up.

***move** + **particle** (*move, with direction*) 1 *vi* They bought a new house and moved in immediately.   Our neighbours have begun to move out.   The people moved aside to allow the procession past.   The car slowly moved away. 2 *vt sep* The men moved the rock aside.   We decided to move the luggage in while there was time.   He moved the furniture up in pieces and assembled it afterwards.

move about/around 1 *vi* (*a*) *see* ***move**. (*b*) (*travel about*) They moved about a lot. (*c*) (*fidget*) The children kept moving about. 2 *vt sep* *see* ***move**.

move along 1 *vi* (*a*) *see* ***move**. (*b*) (*policeman's order*) Move along now!   Move along there, please! 2 *vt sep* *see* ***move**.

move away 1 *vi* (*a*) *see* ***move**. (*b*) (*leave an area or a house*) They moved away a year ago. 2 *vt sep* *see* ***move**.

move back 1 *vi* (*a*) *see* ***move**. (*b*) (*return to a place*) They have moved back to London. 2 *vt sep* (*a*) *see* ***move**. (*b*) (*restore or return to an original position*)) They moved the furniture back. The general moved his men back.

move forward 1 *vi* (*a*) *see* ***move**. (*b*) (*Mil: advance*) The troops moved forward at dawn. 2 *vt sep* (*a*) *see* ***move**. (*b*) (*Mil: advance*) The general moved his troops forward.

move in 1 *vi* (*a*) *see* ***move**. (*b*) (*take possession of a place*) The enemy moved in last night. 2 *vt sep* *see* ***move**.

move in on *vt fus* (*a*) (*Mil: surround and squeeze*) The army has begun to move in on the defenders. (*b*) (*Sl: take control of*) The gang has decided to move in on the slot machine business.

move off 1 *vi* (*a*) *see* ***move**. (*b*) (*begin to depart*) The train moved off.   The troops have started moving off. 2 *vt sep* *see* ***move**.

move on 1 *vi* *see* ***move**. 2 *vt sep* (*a*) *see* ***move**. (*b*) (*advance*) He moved on the hands of the clock.

move out 1 *vi* (*a*) *see* ***move**. (*b*) (*quit, leave*) The company has moved out.   Our neighbours are moving out. 2 *vt sep* *see* ***move**.

move up 1 *vi* (*a*) *see* ***move**. (*b*) (*rise in rank*) He is moving up. 2 *vt sep* (*a*) *see* ***move**. (*b*) (*promote*) They are moving him up.

mow down *vt sep* (*Fig Mil: kill quickly in large numbers*) The machine-guns mowed down the advancing lines of infantrymen.

muck about/around *vi* (a) (*Fam: do aimless things*) The boys were mucking about in their room. Stop mucking about! (b) (*meddle*) He keeps mucking about with things he doesn't understand. (c) (*tinker for amusement*) I'm just mucking about with this old watch. 2 *vt sep* (*Sl: irritate*) He seems to enjoy mucking me about. Stop mucking us about!

muck in *vi* (*Fam: take part*) Come on, muck in! Everyone mucks in here.

muck out *vt sep* (*clean thoroughly*) They mucked out the stables.

muck up *vt sep* (a) (*Lit: make dirty*) The children have mucked the whole place up. (b) (*Fig Fam: spoil*) They have mucked my plans up completely.

muddle along *vi* (*Fam: manage somehow*) Oh, we muddle along, you know, though we're not rich.

muddle on *vi* (*continue to muddle, manage*) They muddle on in their own way.

muddle through *vi* (a)=**muddle along**. (b) (*survive or win somehow*) We'll muddle through, don't worry.

muddle up *vt sep* (*mix up, confuse*) Their names have been muddled up. I'm feeling rather muddled up. Don't muddle me up.

muffle up 1 *vi* (*cover up fully*) Make sure you muffle up properly, because it's pretty cold outside. 2 *vt sep* (*muffle up completely; silence or reduce by muffling*) They muffled up the noise with blankets. His voice sounded muffled up.

mug up *vt sep* (*Fam: learn thoroughly, usu for an exam*) He has been mugging up his Latin.

mull over *vt sep* (*think over, consider carefully*) He mulled the idea over in his mind.

mumble away *vi* (*speak indistinctly and continuously*) The old man mumbled away to himself. She was mumbling away about her problems.

munch up *vt sep* (*chew up vigorously*) He munched up the celery.

muscle in *vi* (*Sl: force one's way in*) They muscled in on the meeting. The gang has muscled in on their rivals' territory. He intends to muscle in (on their business).

muster up *vt sep* (a) (*Old: recruit*) They mustered up as many men as possible. (b) (*Fig: gather, summon*) He mustered up all his courage for the ordeal.

nag away/on *vi* (*nag continuously*) She has been nagging away at him for years.

nail down *vt sep* (a) (*Lit: fix down with nails*) He nailed the lid down. (b) (*Fig: make agree*) I nailed him down to coming at six. (c) (*force to take a firm position*) We will eventually nail you down on this point.

nail up *vt sep* (a) (*fix up with nails*) He nailed the picture up (on the wall). (b) (*seal with nails*) He nailed the door up. He nailed the goods up in a crate.

narrow down 1 *vi* (a) (*Lit: become narrow*) The path has narrowed down a lot since I was last here. (b) (*Fig: become restricted*) The field of inquiry has narrowed down to five people. The choice has narrowed down to three. 2 *vt sep* (*make narrow*) They have narrowed the search down to this area of the town.

natter away *vi* (*Sl: talk or chatter away amiably*) The two of them often natter away for hours.

*navigate + particle (*steer, guide, with direction*) 1 *vi* He navigated out of the channel. They navigated through successfully. 2 *vt sep* He navigated the ship out of the channel. They navigated the boat through successfully.

*need + particle *vt sep* (*need, with direction*) I need her over to help me with the children. I need this tooth out. Do you need the book back tomorrow?

nestle down *vi* (*snuggle down comfortably*) The children nestled down in their beds.

nestle in *vi* (*snuggle in comfortably*) The animals nestled in against their mother.

nestle up *vi* (*snuggle affectionately close*) She nestled up to him. He nestled up as close as he could get.

nibble away 1 *vi* (*nibble by eating in small pieces continuously*) That child is always nibbling away at something. 2 *vt sep* (*remove by nibbling*) (a) (*Lit*) The mice have nibbled away the edges of these papers. (b) (*Fig*) Neighbouring countries have been nibbling territory away for years.

nibble off *vt sep* (*cut off or separate by nibbling*) The rats have nibbled the tops off and left the rest.

nick in *vi* (*Fam: slip suddenly in front of*) The car nicked in ahead of the lorry and almost caused an accident.

*nip + particle *vi* (*Sl: move very quickly, with direction*) They nipped off without telling us where they were going. Nip up and tell him to come down for his breakfast. They are constantly nipping in and out of each other's houses.

nip away 1 *vi* *see* ***nip**. 2 *vt sep* (*remove by nipping or pinching*) He nipped away the ends with a pair of pliers.

nip in 1 *vi* *see* ***nip**. 2 *vt sep* (*take in or make narrow by a nipping or pinching action*) She nipped the waist of the dress in.

nip off 1 *vi* *see* *****nip.** 2 *vt sep* (*cut off with a nipping action*) You should nip off the flowers so that the rest of the plant can grow more vigorously.

nip out 1 *vi* *see* *****nip.** 2 *vt sep* (*take out or remove fully by a nipping action*) You should nip these weeds out before they become a real nuisance.

nod off *vi* (*Fam: begin to fall asleep*) The old man was nodding off by the fire.

noise about/around/abroad *vt sep* (*spread around as news*) They have noised the agreement about already, without waiting for permission.

*****nose + particle** 1 *vi* (*Fam: investigate, as if with the nose, with direction*) They have been nosing about here again. I don't like those men nosing in and out all day, asking questions. 2 *vt sep* (*bring or drive nose first, with direction*) He nosed the car out into the road. She carefully nosed the vacuum cleaner into all the corners.

nosh up *vi* (*Sl: eat greedily*) They've been noshing up again. *n* **a nosh-up**=a feast.

notch up *vt sep* (*mark up in notches or cuts*) (*a*) (*Lit*) The gunman notched up five victims on the handle of his gun. (*b*) (*Fig: achieve, gain*) He has notched up quite a few triumphs lately.

note down *vt sep* (*take down in note form*) The students noted down everything he said. His secretary noted down the details of the plan. I expect you've noted down the main points.

*****nudge + particle** *vt sep* (*move by nudges or small pushes, with direction*) The men nudged us along. The bigger boy nudged him aside and went in first. He nudged me out.

number off (*mark off by numbers or in sequence*) 1 *vi* The soldiers numbered off from the right. 2 *vt sep* The sergeant numbered his men off from the right.

nurse through *vt sep* (*assist to survive or to get better by nursing*) (*a*) (*Lit*) She nursed him through. (*b*) (*Fig*) I hope you will help to nurse this project through.

nuzzle in *vi* (*become comfortable by small wriggling actions*) The children nuzzled in under the blankets.

nuzzle up *vi* (*become close and comfortable by small wriggling actions*) The children nuzzled up against their sleeping mother.

offer up *vt sep* (*offer to a superior person or power*) They offered up sacrifices once a year to the gods. The priest offered up prayers of thanksgiving to God. I suppose he expects us to offer up praise and adoration to him because he's our boss.

oil over *vt sep* *(cover completely with oil)* He oiled the tools over and put them away in the shed. The athlete oiled himself over.

*ooze + particle *vi* *(move out slowly, said of liquids, with direction)* The oil began to ooze out through the tiny hole. I imagine the flood waters will ooze away over the next few days. *(Fig)* His enthusiasm slowly began to ooze away in the face of their hostility.

open on to *vt fus* *(open outward, towards)* The french windows open on to a beautiful old lawn.

open out 1 *vi* *(a)* *(open wide)* The flower opened out when the sun came out. *(b)* *(become less shy)* The young girl began to open out once we had got to know her better. *(c)* *(spread as a panorama)* The countryside opens out beyond those trees, and you can see for miles. 2 *vt sep* *(unfold)* He opened out the map and studied our position.

open up 1 *vi* *(a)* *(open completely)* The flowers slowly opened up in the warmth of the sun. *(b)* *(speak frankly)* The girl decided to open up and tell us everything. *(c)* *(emerge, develop)* New prospects have opened up for us this year. 2 *vt sep* *(a)* *(open completely)* He opened up the packing-cases and found that they were full of valuable old books. *(b)* *(make accessible, develop)* The pioneers opened up this land over a hundred years ago. The company has decided to open up this area for housing. *(c)* *(start)* They decided to open up a business in the town.

opt in *vi* *(choose to be included)* He had known about the scheme for some time, but only opted in at the last minute.

opt out *vi* *(choose to be excluded)* He doesn't like the scheme and has decided to opt out.

*order + particle *vt sep* *(order, with direction)* The general ordered up more men as reinforcements. They wanted us to go and so they ordered us out immediately. She ordered the little boy down from the high ladder. He doesn't like being ordered about by anyone.

own up *vi* *(confess, admit, own)* He owned up to the crime. They hoped he would own up to having told the lie. Come on, own up!

*pace + particle *vi* *(walk with measured steps, with direction)* The worried man paced up and down.

pace out 1 *vi* *see* ***pace.** 2 *vt sep* *(measure by paces or strides)* They paced out the distance between the houses.

pack away *vt sep* *(a)* *(Lit: store away)* She packed away the clothes until they would be needed again. *(b)* *(Fig: eat)* He can pack away more food than anyone else I know.

pack in 1 *vi* (*a*) (*crowd in*) The people packed in as tightly as they could. (*b*) (*Sl: stop working, resign*) I'm sorry to say he has packed in. (*c*) (*Sl: stop functioning*) The car engine packed in at the top of the big hill. 2 *vt sep* (*a*) (*push in*) She packed all the clothes in after much trouble. They packed the people in as tightly as they could. (*b*) (*Sl: stop, give up*) After a couple of weeks he packed the job in. Pack it in, for heaven's sake! (*c*) (*Sl: give up, lose interest in*) I believe he's packed his studies in.

pack off *vt sep* (*a*) (*send as a package or in a package*) He has packed the books off to his friend. (*b*) (*Fam: dismiss, send*) She always packs the children off to bed about seven.

pack up 1 *vi* (*a*) (*do one's luggage*) I've been packing up, ready to go. (*b*) (*Sl: stop*) The men have packed up and gone home. (*c*) (*Sl: stop functioning*)=**pack in** (*c*). (*d*) (*become transportable*) My books pack up easily.

*pad + particle *vi* (*move softly on pads or as if on pads, with direction*) The cat padded along. A lion was padding up and down inside the cage. He pads round in carpet slippers all day.

pad out 1 *vi* *see* ***pad.** 2 *vt sep* (*fill out with extra material*) (*a*) (*Lit*) The tailor padded out the shoulders of the coat. (*b*) (*Fig*) The editor asked him to stop padding out his articles.

*paddle + particle 1 *vi* (*a*) (*move while wading in shallow water, with direction*) The little boys paddled along through the stream. She paddled in gingerly, hoping the water was warm. (*b*) (*move by means of a paddle or paddling actions, with direction*) They paddled in towards the shore. The boat paddled along through the muddy waters. 2 *vt sep* (*cause to move, using a paddle*) They paddled the canoe in towards the shore. They paddled the boat away.

paint in *vt sep* (*include or add by painting*) They painted in the sections which had been left empty.

paint on 1 *vi* (*continue to paint*) He painted on through the night. 2 *vt sep* (*add on by painting*) They painted on the name of the ship.

paint out *vt sep* (*remove or delete by using paint*) They painted out the names on the shop front.

paint up *vt sep* (*improve by using paint*) They have painted the place up since I was last here.

pair off 1 *vi* (*separate into pairs*) The young people soon paired off. 2 *vt sep* (*a*) (*divide or separate into pairs*) The students have been paired off. He has been paired off with me. They paired us off for the purpose of the exercise. (*b*) (*couple for reproductive purposes*) They paired the animals off.

pal up *vi* (*Fam: become friendly*) They have palled up again after the quarrel. I hope the two boys will pal up. He has palled up with some rather disreputable types.

palm off *vt sep* (*pass by trickery*) He has palmed these shoddy goods off on to us. There should be a law against people palming off rubbish like this.

*pan + particle (*TV, Cine: move to present a panorama*) 1 *vi* The camera panned out over the crowd. The TV cameraman panned up to bring in the aeroplanes. 2 *vt sep* Pan the camera over to include those people. Can you pan it down(wards) and then over to the left.

pan out *vi* (a) (*Fam: turn out, develop*) Things didn't pan out well for them. Events may pan out better than expected. (b) *see* ***pan.**

paper over *vt sep* (a) (*Lit: cover with paper*) They papered over the cracks in the wall. (b) (*Fig: attempt to conceal*) I think we must try to paper over this disagreement.

parcel out *vt sep* (*share out in portions*) (a) (*Lit*) They parcelled out the food for the refugees. (b) (*Fig*) The inheritance has not been kept together, but has been parcelled out among the family.

parcel up *vt sep* (*wrap up in or as a parcel*) They parcelled up the books and posted them.

pare down *vt sep* (a) (*Lit: trim down by paring, probably with a knife*) They pared down the sticks. She pared her nails down. (b) (*Fig: reduce*) It will be necessary to pare this budget down considerably. She has had to pare down her living expenses.

partition off *vt sep* (*close off or separate with a partition*) They partitioned off a little room for him to use as an office. The room was partitioned off into several cubicles.

*pass + particle 1 *vi* (*move past, with direction*) The people were passing in and out of the main door. They opened the gate and the procession passed through. 2 *vt sep* (*send, push or direct past, with direction*) He passed the wine along to the people lower down the table. She passed the papers back to them. He passed the leaflets out.

pass away *vi* (a) *see* ***pass.** (b) (*Fig Euph: die*) He passed away at midnight last night. (c) (*vanish, disappear*) The old cultural values have passed away.

pass by 1 *vi* (*pass to one side*) I saw him passing by. *n* **a passer-by** *pl* **passers-by.** The road passes by on that side of the village. *n* **a by-pass**=a road for traffic to avoid a town. 2 *vt sep* (*ignore, overlook*) I'm afraid they have passed him by for promotion. Life has passed me by.

pass down 1 *vi* *see* ***pass.** 2 *vt sep* (a) *see* ***pass.** (b) (*Fig: hand down, transmit*) The tradition has been passed down from father to son. (*c*) (*send down through a hierarchy or organization*) The story has been passed down that he bungled the negotiations.

pass for   *vt fus*   (*be taken for, be recognized as*) She would pass for an American very easily.   You surely don't think I could pass for him, do you?   She's 40, but I think she could pass for 25 without much trouble.

pass off   1 *vi*   (*go away*) I was feeling sick, but the feeling has passed off.   2 *vt sep*   (*succeed in presenting*) She passed herself off as an American.   They passed him off as a much younger man.

pass on   1 *vi*   (*a*) *see* *****pass**.   (*b*) (*Fig Euph: die*) He passed on in his sleep.   (*c*) (*Fig: move on*) Let us pass on to a new subject.   2 *vt sep*   (*a*) *see* *****pass**.   (*b*) (*Fig: tell someone else*) Pass the news on that he is coming tomorrow.

pass out   1 *vi*   (*a*) *see* *****pass**.   (*b*) (*faint*) She passed out when she heard the bad news.   He passed out from too much drinking.   (*c*) (*graduate*) He has passed out with honours.   *n cpd* (*Mil*) **a passing-out parade.**   (*d*) (*Fig: go on and away, move from*) He has passed out of our lives completely.   2 *vt sep*   *see* *****pass**.

pass over   1 *vi*   (*Fig Euph: die*) He passed over in his sleep.   2 *vt sep*=**pass by** 2 *vt sep*.

pass up   *vt sep*   (*a*) *see* *****pass**.   (*b*) (*Fam: forgo, waive*) He passed up the chance to go to France this summer.   You should never pass up opportunities like these.

paste in   *vt sep*   (*put in, insert or include by using paste*) He pasted the pictures in.

paste on   *vt sep*   (*put on, by using paste*) He pasted the stickers on.

paste up   *vt sep*   (*put up, by using paste*) He pasted the notice up.

patch up   *vt sep*   (*mend with patches*) (*a*) (*Lit*) He has succeeded in patching up the old car.   She patched up the dress.   (*b*) (*Fig*) They have tried to patch up their differences.   It would be better to stop patching the situation up every few months and make radical changes.

*****patter** + **particle**   *vi*   (*move or occur with light quick sounds, with direction*) The children pattered about happily.   The rain pattered down on the tin roof.   He heard the sounds of feet pattering away into the distance.

pay back   *vt sep*   (*a*) (*return, as payment of a debt*) He paid the money back promptly.   I wish he would pay me back the money.   (*b*) (*Fig: be avenged on*) I'll pay them back for this treatment.

pay down   *vt sep*   (*a*) (*pay on the spot, immediately*) He paid the money down and took the goods.   (*b*) (*pay as a deposit*) He paid £10 down and agreed to pay the rest in monthly instalments.

pay in   *vt sep*   (*give in, put in*) He has paid the money in and we are happy about it. She paid the cash in to her bank account. He went to the bank and paid the cheque in.

pay off 1 *vi* (*prove profitable*) The gamble has paid off. His scheme has paid off handsomely. The trick has more than paid off. 2 *vt sep* (*a*) (*settle*) He paid off his debts quickly. (*b*) (*give money to, as settlement of a debt*) He has paid off his creditors. (*c*) (*discharge with a payment*) He paid his servants off. The manager personally paid off the redundant employees. The ship's crew were paid off at the end of the voyage. (*d*) (*Naut: release steadily*) They paid the ship off from the jetty. (*e*) (*avenge, settle*) He has managed to pay off old scores. *n* **the pay-off**=time for revenge, time for settling things.

pay out *vt sep* (*a*) (*release steadily or in stages*) They paid out the rope. (*b*) (*give out, usu as pay or in payment of bills*) They have paid out a lot on repairing that house. The cashier paid the money out efficiently.

pay up 1 *vi* (*pay promptly*) I asked him to pay up. Pay up! 2 *vt sep* (*a*) (*settle promptly or fully*) Please pay up all you owe. *Adj* He is a fully **paid-up** member of this club. (*b*) (*Stock Exchange: free*) The shares have been paid up.

peak off *vi* (*Stat: reach a maximum and fall off*) The numbers have begun to peak off. The sales peak off at this point.

peal out *vi* (*ring out in peals, resound*) The bells pealed out.

peck out *vt sep* (*remove or destroy by pecking*) The crows pecked out the eyes of the dead sheep.

*pedal + particle *vi* (*move by pedalling or using pedals, with direction*) The boy got on his bicycle and pedalled away. The girl was pedalling up and down in the street.

peel away 1 *vi* (*a*) (*Lit: separate as a surface layer*) The skin was beginning to peel away. The covering was old and had peeled away. (*b*) (*Fig: separate from a mass*) The fighter planes, flying in formation, one by one peeled away to left and right. 2 *vt sep* (*remove by stripping off*) He peeled away the wrapper.

peel back *vt sep* (*remove by stripping to one side*) He peeled back the plastic film.

peel off 1 *vi* (*a*)=**peel away** 2 (*b*) (*Sl: undress*) She peeled off and went to bed. 2 *vt sep* (*a*)=**peel away.** (*b*) (*Sl: remove*) She peeled off her clothes and went to bed.

*peep + particle *vi* (*look quickly and often furtively, with direction*) He raised the edge of the curtain and we peeped through. He could see the children peeping in through the window.

*peer + particle *vi* (*look intently, with direction*) He was peering about in the dark, looking for something. The children peered out through the windows.

peg away   *vi*   (*Sl: continue working*) He has been pegging away at that material for months.

peg down   *vt sep*   (*hold or fix down with pegs*) They pegged the tent down securely.

peg out   1 *vi*   (*Sl: die, stop functioning*) The old man pegged out. This engine is going to peg out soon, if you don't do something. 2 *vt sep*   (*mark out with pegs*) They pegged the area out.

*pelt + particle   *vi*   (*Fam: move very rapidly, with direction*) The car pelted along.   I opened the door and the little boys pelted out.

pelt down   *vi*   (a) see ***pelt**.   (b) (*Lit: pour down violently*) The rain was pelting down (for all it was worth).

pension off   *vt sep*   (*superannuate; dismiss from service with a pension*) Has he been pensioned off yet?   I think they will pension him off soon.   We do not want to be pensioned off and forgotten.

pent-up   *pp no regular verb form*   (*suppressed, repressed*) He is full of pent-up resentments.   They give you an impression of pent-up power.

pep up   1 *vi*   (*Fam: become cheerful*) She pepped up considerably when she heard the news.   2 *vt sep*   (*Fam: make more cheerful, improve, fill with pep and energy*) He pepped me up a lot with his comments.   He pepped the party up with his jokes.   She asked him to pep her drink up with something stronger.

perk up   1 *vi*   (a) (*Fam: cheer up, become cheerful*) She perked up considerably when she heard the news.   (b) (*show interest*) He perked up at the news and began to ask questions.   2 *vt sep* (a) (*raise sharply*) The dog perked its ears up, and stood listening. (b) (*make smarter in appearance*) He perked himself up before going out.

*permit + particle   *vt sep*   (*allow, with direction*) The doctor permits her up now for several hours a day, because of her steady improvement.   Would you permit them in for a few minutes, to talk to you?   The escort stood back from the door and permitted them through.

permit of   *vt fus*   (*allow, intensive of* **permit**) This situation does not permit of an easy solution.

*persuade + particle   *vt sep*   (*move by persuading, with direction*) Do you think you could persuade them over to see me?   She persuaded him up for a cup of coffee.   They persuaded me in to shelter from the rain.

peter out   *vi*   (*become exhausted, empty*) (a) (*Lit*) The supply of coal has just petered out.   The goldmine petered out years ago.

(b) (*Fig*) His ambitions slowly petered out in the face of opposition. Her enthusiasm for the project has completely petered out.

phase in   *vt sep*   (*introduce in phases or stages*) They have decided to phase the new techniques in immediately. It will take years to phase in all these developments.

phase out   *vt sep*   (*remove by phases or stages*) We really ought to phase these less successful products out. It will take a long time to phase out the obsolete laws.

phone in/off=**telephone in/off**

pick at   *vt fus*   (a) (*eat in tiny portions*) The birds picked at the bread crumbs.   (b) (*eat listlessly*) He has just been picking at his food lately.   (c) (*keep touching and scratching*) Stop picking at that scab. She picks at her face all the time.   (d) (*adversely criticize in small ways*) He has been picking at your work for some time now.

pick away   *vt*   (*remove or alter by small stages*) Some animal has picked away the side of the fence. If you pick away the covering, you can see the inscriptions underneath.

pick away at   *vt fus*   *intensive of* **pick at**.

pick off   *vt sep*   (a) (*Lit: collect or remove by picking*) They have picked off all the apples.   (b) (*Fig Mil: shoot individually*) The sniper picked off two of our sentries this morning. The marksman picked the enemy off one by one.

pick on   *vt fus*   (a) (*single out, select*) They picked on him for the work.   (b) (*single out or isolate for criticism*) Why do they keep picking on us? She picks on him all the time. Pick on someone your own size! Stop picking on her!

pick out   *vt sep*   (a) (*remove or select by picking*) He picked out the small stones.   (b) (*choose*) They have picked out the best items on the menu. Would you pick out the one you want?   (c) (*distinguish*) He was not able to pick out the figures clearly.   (d) (*Music: attempt to play, probably in an amateurish way*) She picked out the tune on the piano.   (e) (*Art, often pass: highlight*) The design was picked out in bright blue.

pick over   *vt sep*   (*inspect, usu by lifting and feeling with the fingers*) She picked over the fruit. Customers were picking over the remnants left after the sale.

pick through   *vt fus*=**pick over** *vt sep*.

pick up   1 *vi*   (*Fam*) (a) (*recover, after an illness*) He is picking up again, I'm glad to say.   (b) (*fall into company*) He has picked up with a bad bunch of people.   (c) (*continue*) After the interruption, we picked up where we had left off.   2 *vt sep*   (a) (*lift*)

He picked the box up. She picked herself up after the fall. It's the sort of book you can pick up and enjoy any time. (b) (*Fam: get, acquire*) He picked up some bargains at that sale. Where did you pick up that lovely old vase? He has picked up some bad habits at that club. The car picked up speed quickly. (c) (*learn or acquire without difficulty*) He has picked up elementary French in three months. While living there, she picked up the local accent. They have picked up a lot of information about this area. (d) (*make casual acquaintance of*) He just picked her up at a dance. n **a pick-up**=a casually acquired girl-friend. (e) (*correct, reprimand*) The teacher picked him up for grammatical mistakes. (f) (*Radio: receive*) We can pick up many foreign stations on this set. The operator picked up distress signals from a damaged ship. (g) (*spotlight, focus on*) The car headlights picked up a rabbit. (h) (*Aut: give lift to*) The driver stopped to pick up a hitch-hiker. (i) (*Fam: catch*) The police picked up the man they wanted just outside London. (j) (*collect*) I'll pick up an evening newspaper on the way home. Could you pick up some bottled beer at the pub as you go past? (k) (*regain*) He has picked up his strength again after his illness. (l) (*make better, more cheerful*) Have some whisky—it will pick you up again. *Idiomatic n* **a pick-me-up**=a tonic.

piece together *vt sep* (*put together piece by piece*) (a) (*Lit*) They pieced together the broken vase. The pottery dug up at that archaeological site needs to be carefully pieced together. (b) (*Fig*) The detectives have slowly pieced together the whole astonishing story. I managed to piece together what had happened from what he told me.

pierce through *vt sep* (*pierce, penetrate completely*) The arrow pierced him through.

pile off *vi* (*Fam: jump off in a crowd*) The lorries stopped and the men piled off.

pile on 1 *vi* (*Fam: jump on in a crowd*) The lorries drew up and the waiting soldiers piled on. 2 *vt sep* (a) (*put on in a heap*) He piled the stones on. (b) (*Fig: intensify*) They seem to enjoy piling on the bad news. *Idiom:* To pile on the agony=to try to make bad things worse. (c) (*Fam, with 'it': exaggerate*) Stop piling it on. She certainly piles it on.

pile up 1 *vi* (*accumulate*) (a) (*Lit*) The debris has piled up against that wall. (b) (*Fig*) His debts have been piling up for quite some time. His work has piled up while he's been away. 2 *vt sep* (*accumulate*) (a) (*Lit*) They had piled up a lot of earth in one corner of the garden. She piled up plenty of tinned food in case of an emergency. (b) (*Fig*) He has piled up a lot of troubles for himself.

*pilot + particle *vt sep* (*guide, with direction*) The man piloted the ship in. Can you find someone to pilot us out of here?

pin down *vt sep* (a) (*secure with a pin*) She pinned the paper down, to prevent it blowing away. (b) (*trap in position*) The huge tree had fallen and pinned him down. He had been pinned down by fallen rafters. (c) (*Fig: limit, restrict, confine*) They managed to pin him down to a particular time and place. I can't pin him down to a promise like that. (d) (*Fig Fam: locate*) We haven't been able to pin them down anywhere.

pin on *vt sep* (*secure to something with a pin*) She pinned the brooch on (to her lapel).

pin up *vt sep* (*fix up with a pin*) She pinned the photo up (on the wall). She pinned up her hair. She pinned up the hem of the dress. He likes pinning up pictures of beautiful girls. *n cpd* **a pin-up (girl)**=a girl whose photographs are pinned up, a beauty.

pinch back *vt sep* (*Gardening: cut off by a pinching action*) He decided to pinch back the buds on the plant.

pinch off *vt sep*=**pinch back** *vt sep*.

pine away *vi* (*pine continuously*) She has been pining away since you left. That dog is pining away for its master.

*****pipe + particle** *vt sep* (*move by means of a pipe, with direction*) They piped the water away. The water was piped up from the valley. They decided to pipe the supply in from the next valley. The oil is piped out from this point.

pipe away 1 *vi* (*play a woodwind instrument continuously*) He has been piping away for the last two hours. 2 *vt sep* *see* ***pipe.**

pipe down 1 *vi* (*Sl: be quiet*) I wish he would pipe down. Pipe down! 2 *vt sep* *see* ***pipe.**

pipe in *vt sep* (a) *see* ***pipe.** (b) (*Scot: bring in, accompanied by bagpipe music*) The haggis was piped in. The regimental band triumphantly piped the soldiers in.

pipe up 1 *vi* (a) (*Fam: speak up in a piping voice*) The child suddenly piped up that he wanted to go home. (b) (*Fam: speak up*) He piped up near the end of the meeting. 2 *vt sep* *see* ***pipe.**

*****pitch + particle** *vt sep* (a) (*throw or compel, with direction*) He pitched the ball out (of the court). They pitched the materials in. (b) (*Fam:*) He was pitched out of that club. Pitch the paper over to me, please.

pitch in 1 *vi* (*Fam: participate*) I like the way he always pitches in and helps. Right, folks, pitch in! 2 *vt sep* *see* ***pitch.**

pitch into *vt fus* (*Sl: attack*) (a) (*Lit*) The gang pitched into him and left him badly injured. (b) (*Fig*) The opposition politicians pitched into his speech, criticizing it point by point.

pitch out *vt sep* (*a*) *see* ***pitch.** (*b*) (*Fam: eject*) The car overturned and the driver was pitched out. (*c*) (*Fam: get rid of*)
It's time you pitched those books out.

plan out *vt sep* (*plan as fully as possible*) They planned out the trip
(with care).

plane down 1 *vi* (*Aviat: descend in or like an aeroplane*) The glider
planed down towards the meadow. 2 *vt sep* (*smooth down with
a plane*) The carpenter planed the wood down.

plank down *vt sep* (*Fam: put down, deposit briskly*) He planked the
money down on the counter and asked for more beer.

plant out *vt sep* (*Gardening: lift and re-plant in the open*) These bulbs
should now be planted out. When will you plant the flowers
out in beds?

plaster down *vt sep* (*stick, smooth down with plaster*) (*a*) (*Lit*) He
plastered the material down. (*b*) (*Fig*) He plastered his hair
down (with a new hair oil).

plaster on *vt sep* (*put on thickly like plaster*) He plastered the
butter on. He plastered on the hair oil.

plaster over, plaster up *vt sep* (*cover with plaster*) (*a*) (*Lit*) They
have managed to plaster over all those large cracks in the wall.
(*b*) (*Fig*) I hope he doesn't expect us to plaster over the cracks
in his policy.

play about/around *vi* (*a*) (*play in an area*) The children are
playing around in the garden. (*b*) (*Fam: toy, divert oneself*) I
wish you wouldn't play about with his affections. Stop playing
about with that plate.

play along 1 *vi* (*Fam: co-operate*) I'll play along with them and
see what they want. I'm glad you've decided to play along.
2 *vt sep* (*Fam: keep waiting in suspense*) They have played him
along for some time now, without telling him what they really
want.

play back *vt sep* (*re-play*) When we've finished the recording
we'll play it back to you. *n* **play-back**=action of playing
back.

play down *vt sep* (*Fam: depreciate, reduce in force or value*) They
have consistently tried to play down his part in the scheme.
In a crisis it is best to play down the emotional issues.

play in *vt sep* (*a*) (*Sport: prepare for playing*) The team took a
few minutes to play itself in. (*b*) (*Music: introduce or lead in by
playing music*) The band played the guests in.

play off *vt sep* (a) (*Sport: succeed in playing*) They have now played off all the important games in the league fixtures. (b) (*Fig: oppose, set*) He likes to play one person off against another. He has played his enemies off against each other.

play out *vt sep* (a) (*Theatre, Music: play to the end*) They played the whole thing out. (b) (*accompany while going out*) The organ played the people out. (c) (*Sl usu pass: be exhausted, be finished*) The argument is completely played out. I feel really played out after that game.

play over/through *vt sep* (*play fully or in entirety*) They played over the whole symphony.

play up 1 *vi* (a) (*Sport Fam: play well*) I expect them to play up this afternoon. Come on, chaps, play up! (b) (*Sl: cause trouble*) The old wound has been playing up again lately. The engine began playing up. *cf* **act up**. 2 *vt sep* (*Sl: cause trouble or inconvenience for*) The child is always playing his father up.

play (up)on *vt fus* (*influence, manipulate*) He loves playing upon people's emotions. *Idiom:* To play on words=to make puns, witty jokes.

play up to *vt fus* (*flatter, ingratiate oneself with*) She is always playing up to people who may be able to help her.

*plod + particle *vi* (*walk slowly and heavily, with direction*) The oxen plodded on. The horse plodded back and forth.

plonk down 1 *vi* (*Fam: fall suddenly*) The apple plonked down on her lap. 2 *vt sep*=**plank down.**

plot out *vt sep* (a) (*design fully or clearly*) They plotted out a plan of action. (b) (*Naut: mark out*) He plotted out the course which the ship should follow.

*plough + particle *vi* (*move as if ploughing, with direction*) The ship ploughed along through the heavy seas. The bulldozer was ploughing up and down.

plough back *vt sep* (a) (*Lit: return to the soil by ploughing*) The remains of the crop should be ploughed back to increase the fertility of the soil. (b) (*Fig: re-invest*) Some of the profits should be ploughed back to help develop the company. They ploughed back a lot of their surplus.

plough in *vt sep* (*mix in by ploughing*) They decided to plough the sand in. The builders ploughed in a lot of young trees when clearing this area for development.

plough under *vt sep*=**plough in.**

plough up *vt sep* (a) (*plough thoroughly*) This land should be ploughed up. The farmer ploughed up the whole area. (b) (*churn up*) The tanks have ploughed up a lot of mud.

*pluck + particle *vt sep* *(pull, gently or with small hand movements, with direction)* They plucked me aside from the others. She plucked the hairs out. They plucked the surplus wool off. The gardener plucked all the weeds up.

pluck up *vt sep* *(a) see* ***pluck.** *(b) (Fam: find, develop)* The boy tried to pluck up enough courage to face the bully. I wish I could pluck up enough energy to do this work.

plug away *vi* *(Sl: continue working)* He has been plugging away at that job for hours.

plug in 1 *vi* *(attach with an electric plug)* Have you plugged in yet? 2 *vt sep* *(fix in with a plug)* Would you plug the light in? She wants to plug the radio in.

plug up *vt sep* *(close or seal by means of plugs)* They have plugged up those holes under the wall.

plump for *vt fus* *(Fam: choose)* I'll plump for bacon and eggs rather than breakfast cereal. He always plumps for the best that's going.

plump up *vt sep* *(a) (fatten)* We have really plumped up these chickens. *(b) (fluff out, make appear fat)* She took the cushions and plumped them up a bit.

*plunge + particle *vi* *(plunge, rush, with direction)* The boys ran to the edge of the swimming pool and plunged in. The frightened horse plunged aside. Dolphins were plunging about in the bay.

plunge in 1 *vi* *(a) see* ***plunge.** *(b) (Fig: take part eagerly)* They asked me to help, so I just plunged in. 2 *vt sep* *(thrust in violently or with some effort)* He plunged the dagger in to the hilt.

plunk down=plank down.

*point + particle *vi* *(indicate, usu with a finger, with direction)* They pointed up to where the man was climbing. She pointed back to where the others were following. He pointed forward.

point out 1 *vi* *see* ***point.** 2 *vt sep* *(a) (show)* Can you point him out to me, please? *(b) (mention)* I pointed out the difficulties. He pointed out that the work was nearly complete.

point up 1 *vi* *see* ***point.** 2 *vt sep* *(emphasize)* His rudeness just points up her good manners.

*poke + particle *(push or prod, usu with a pointed instrument, with direction)* 1 *vi* He poked about for some time with a stick, but found nothing. The ends of the poles were poking through. 2 *vt sep* He poked the ants out with his finger. They poked the bamboos up into the thatched roofs.

poke about/around *vi* *(a) see* ***poke.** *(b) (Fig: make unwanted inquiries)* Those detectives have been poking about here again.

poke in 1 *vi* (*a*) *see* *poke. (*b*) (*Fig: introduce, usu without welcome*) He has been poking in again, trying to find things out. 2 *vt sep* (*a*) *see* *poke. (*b*) *Idiom:* To poke one's nose in (where it isn't wanted)=to interfere.

poke up 1 *vi* *see* *poke. 2 *vt sep* (*a*) *see* *poke. (*b*) (*stir with a poker*) Can you poke up the fire?

polish off *vt sep* (*Sl: finish completely*) He polished off the food.

polish up *vt sep* (*a*) (*Lit: polish thoroughly*) They polished up the silverware till it shone. (*b*) (*Fig: improve*) I'll have to polish up my French before the holidays.

*pop + particle 1 *vi* (*Fam: go quickly, with direction*) I'll just pop along to the shop for some bread. He popped in for a coffee. I'll pop out and get a newspaper. Would you please pop across and get that book? I'll pop back and tell you the results. 2 *vt sep* (*Fam: put quickly, with direction*) He popped the cap back on the bottle. She opened the oven and popped the cake in.

pop off 1 *vi* *see* *pop. 2 *vt sep* (*a*) *see* *pop. (*b*) (*Sl: die*) The old man will soon pop off.

pop out 1 *vi* *see* *pop. 2 *vt sep* (*a*) (*bulge, project*) His eyes were popping out with horror. (*b*) *see* *pop.

pop up 1 *vi* (*a*) *see* *pop. (*b*) (*emerge*) The head of the dolphin popped up quite near the boat. 2 *vt sep* *see* *pop.

pore over *vt fus* (*study carefully*) He sat poring over the documents.

posh up *vt sep* (*Sl: dress or decorate with great show*) She has really poshed herself up, hasn't she? They're all poshed up today.

post up *vt sep* (*put up for display*) He posted up the new regulations.

potter about/around *vi* (*go about doing small jobs*) He is pottering about in the garden.

pounce out *vi* (*leap out*) The cat pounced out on the bird.

*pound + particle *vi* (*move along quickly but heavily, with direction*) The herd of buffaloes pounded along. A horseman came pounding up with the news. The cavalry pounded down on the enemy.

pound down 1 *vi* *see* *pound. 2 *vt sep* (*pulverize, reduce by pounding*) They pounded down the stones to a fine powder.

pound up 1 *vi* *see* *pound. 2 *vt sep* (*reduce completely by pounding, pulverize thoroughly*) She pounded up the ingredients.

*pour + particle (*pour, with direction*) 1 *vi* The water poured out. The rain poured down. The troops poured past. Men and machines poured along the main highways. They opened the gates and supplies began to pour through. 2 *vt sep* She poured the water out. She poured the remains away. The general poured men in to replace the slaughtered battalions.

pour out 1 *vi* *see* *pour. 2 *vt sep* (*a*) *see* *pour. (*b*) (*Fig*) She poured out her troubles. He poured his heart out to us. She just poured out her feelings.

praise up *vt sep* (*praise fully*) They have been praising you up to everyone they meet.

*prance + particle *vi* (*leap and dance stiffly, with direction*) The little boys pranced about, pretending to be Red Indians. The witch-doctor was prancing up and down. She pranced in happily to tell us.

prattle away *vi* (*talk casually and continuously*) She was prattling away about how clever they had been. The child prattles away to herself.

*press + particle 1 *vi* (*move or push forcefully, with direction*) We pressed on towards the town. The people lower down pressed up towards us. The crowd pressed in through the cordon of guards. 2 *vt sep* (*a*) (*push, with direction*) She pressed down the lid. He pressed in the knob. (*b*) (*iron, with direction*) She pressed the collar back. She pressed the pleats down.

press down 1 *vi* (*a*) *see* *press. (*b*) (*Fig: demand action*) His creditors have been pressing down heavily on him. 2 *vt sep* *see* *press.

press for *vt fus* (*demand, insist upon*) They are pressing for reforms.

press on *vi* (*a*) *see* *press. (*b*) (*Fig Fam: continue energetically*) Let's press on with the work. She pressed on, regardless of opposition.

press out 1 *vi* *see* *press. 2 *vt sep* (*a*) *see* *press. (*b*) (*squeeze out*) The juice of the grapes is pressed out.

press up *vi* (*a*) *see* *press. (*b*) (*Sport: lie face down on floor and push upwards with hands, but more usually in form 'do press-ups'*) He was busy doing his press-ups.

pretty up *vt sep* (*Fam: make pretty*) She prettied herself up for the party. It would be nice if we could pretty the place up a bit.

prick out *vt sep* (*a*) (*Gardening: remove, pick*) He pricked out every second plant at the third leaf. (*b*) (*outline with pricks*) She pricked out the design from the pattern.

prick up *vt sep* (*Lit: raise sharply*) The dog pricked up its ears, and listened intently. *Idiom:* To prick up one's ears = to listen with sudden interest.

print in *vt sep* (*put in, in print*) They want to print in some extra information.

print out *vt sep* (*a*) (*print and distribute*) They intend to print out thousands of these leaflets. (*b*) (*Computer: produce*) The computer has printed out the results you want. *n cpd* **a computer printout.**

prise out *vt sep* (*extract by levering*) (*a*) (*Lit*) He prised the nail out (of the door). (*b*) (*Fig*) They intend to prise the information out of him somehow.

prise up *vt sep* (*lift up by levering*) They want to prise up the flagstones and see what is underneath. He prised up the floorboards.

*prod + particle *vt sep* (*encourage to move by prodding or poking, with direction*) The oxen were prodded along. The sergeant prodded the men out of their beds. They opened the door and prodded the prisoner through.

promise away *vt sep* (*give away by promising*) He has promised most of the money away to various people.

prop up *vt sep* (*a*) (*Lit: support by means of props*) The men propped the old tunnel up with new timbers. (*b*) (*serve as a prop for*) The new timbers prop up the old mine tunnel. (*c*) (*Fig: support, maintain*) The régime has been propped up by several rich families.

*propel + particle *vt sep* (*direct, convey, with direction*) They propelled the men away. He propelled the car out.

prune away *vt sep* (*cut away systematically*) (*a*) (*Lit*) The gardener pruned away the ragged edges of the bush. (*b*) (*Fig*) We must prune away some of our surplus staff.

prune down *vt sep* (*cut down or reduce systematically*) (*a*) (*Lit*) The gardener pruned the bushes down in order to encourage better growth. (*b*) (*Fig*) He decided to prune down the budget for the coming year. We shall have to prune down our expenditure a bit.

pucker up *vi* (*intensive of* **pucker**) The child's face puckered up and she began to cry.

*puff + particle *vt sep* (*move by means of light gusts of wind, with direction*) The breeze puffed the boats across from one side of the pond to the other. The wind puffed the scraps of paper in and out among the trees.

puff away 1 *vi* (*a*) (*Fam: smoke continuously*) The old man puffed away at his pipe. He was puffing away on a big cigar. (*b*) (*move away with puffs of smoke*) The train puffed away. 2 *vt sep* see ***puff.**

puff out   *vt sep*   (*a*) *see* ***puff.**   (*b*) (*expand*) He puffed out his chest and told us about his victory.   She puffed out the story quite a lot.

puff up   *vi*   (*a*) *see* ***puff.**   (*b*) (*swell*) Her face has puffed up after being stung by a bee.   His eye looks very puffed up.

*pull + particle   1 *vi*   (*move under power, with direction*) The train pulled along steadily.   2 *vt sep*   (*impel by force, with direction*) He pulled the cork out of the bottle.   She pulled the box up to where she wanted it.   He pulled the materials over to his side of the table.

pull about   1 *vi*   *see* ***pull.**   2 *vt sep*   (*a*) *see* ***pull.**   (*b*) (*tug and shove*) They pulled him about rather violently.

pull away   1 *vi*   (*a*) **see *pull.**   (*b*) (*Fig: accelerate*) The car pulled away from the other vehicles.   (*c*) (*Naut: pull steadily*) The sailors pulled away on the oars.   2 *vt sep*   *see* ***pull.**

pull back   1 *vi*   (*a*) *see* ***pull.**   (*b*) (*Fig: hesitate, withdraw*) He pulled back from signing the document.   2 *vt sep*   (*a*) *see* ***pull.**   (*b*) (*Mil: withdraw*) The general decided to pull his men back.

pull down   2 *vt sep*   (*a*) *see* ***pull.**   (*b*) (*demolish*) They pulled the old building down.   (*c*) (*weaken*) This illness has pulled him down.   (*d*) (*Fig: humiliate, criticize*) They intend to pull him down a peg or two.

pull in   1 *vi*   (*a*) *see* ***pull.**   (*b*) (*arrive, of a vehicle*) The train pulled in.   (*c*) (*stop, of a vehicle*) The car pulled in at the garage.   2 *vt sep*   (*a*) *see* ***pull.**   (*b*) (*attract*) The play has pulled in large audiences.   (*c*) (*Fam: take into custody, capture*) The police pulled him in last night.   (*d*) (*Sport: restrain*) He pulled in the horse at the last minute.   (*e*) (*tighten*) He pulled in his stomach.   *Idioms:* (*i*) To pull in one's horns=to be more cautious.   (*ii*) To pull in one's belt=to economize.

pull off   *vt sep*   (*a*) *see* ***pull.**   (*b*) (*complete successfully*) He pulled that deal off beautifully.   They didn't manage to pull it off.

pull out   1 *vi*   (*a*) *see* ***pull.**   (*b*) (*depart*) The train pulled out.   (*c*) (*Fig: withdraw*) They have pulled out of/from the agreement. I'm going to pull out while there is still time.   (*d*) (*move out, usu to overtake*) The car pulled out from behind the bus.   The car pulled out in front of me before I knew what was happening.   2 *vt sep*   (*a*) *see* ***pull.**   (*b*) (*produce*) He pulled out a ten pound note.   He pulled out his fountain pen.   (*c*) (*release*) You had better pull out all the stops and really work.   *Sl Idiom:* To pull your finger out= to start working hard.

pull over   1 *vi*   (*a*) *see* ***pull.**   (*b*) (*move aside*) The car pulled over

to let the others past. 2 *vt sep see* ***pull.** 3 *n* **a pullover**=
a garment which is put on by pulling it over the head.

pull round 1 *vi* (*a*) *see* ***pull.** (*b*) (*get better after an illness or
indisposition*) I expect he'll pull round. 2 *vt sep* (*a*) *see* ***pull.**
(*b*) (*make better, after an illness or indisposition*) This brandy will
help pull you round.

pull through 1 *vi* (*a*) *see* ***pull.** (*b*) (*recover, from illness or
trouble*) Oh, don't worry, you'll pull through. He was badly
injured, but he'll pull through. 2 *vt sep* (*a*) *see* ***pull.** (*b*)
(*help recover*) Somehow or other we'll pull him through, despite
the injuries.

pull together 1 *vi* (*a*) *see* ***pull.** (*b*) (*Fig: co-operate*) I hope all
the members of staff will pull together. 2 *vt sep* (*a*) *see* ***pull.**
(*b*) (*Idiomatic reflexive*=*compose oneself*) I asked him to pull himself
together. After breaking down and weeping, she tried hard to
pull herself together. Pull yourself together!

pull up 1 *vi* (*a*) *see* ***pull.** (*b*) (*come to a halt, of a vehicle*) The car
pulled up.
2 *vt sep* (*a*) *see* ***pull.** (*b*) (*stop*) He pulled the horses up.
(*c*) (*check, reprimand*) The police pulled him up for speeding.
The soldier was pulled up for having an untidy uniform.

***pump + particle** *vt sep* (*transfer under pressure, with direction*) To
get the oil to the tank on the roof they had to pump it up. The
machine has been pumping away the water. The men tried to
pump the liquid out. The firemen began pumping water in.

pump up *vt sep* (*a*) *see* ***pump.** (*b*) (*inflate*) He pumped up the
bicycle tyre.

***punch + particle** *vt sep* (*punch, with direction*) He punched the
window in with his fist. They punched out little holes along
the edge of the paper. The goalkeeper punched the ball aside.
n **a punch-up** (*Sl: a fight with the fists*) They had a punch-up
over those girls. Don't start a punch-up here.

purse up *vt sep* (*tighten, like the top of a purse*) She pursed up her
lips.

***push + particle** 1 *vi* (*move forcefully, with direction*) He pushed
in through the crowd. They pushed on until darkness fell.
They pushed upwards until they reached the top. 2 *vt sep*
(*push, impel, with direction*) He pushed the barrow along. We
tried to push the lid down, but couldn't. He pushed the hatch
up. He opened the window and pushed himself out on to the
ledge. She was in a hurry and pushed the others aside. He
pushed the plate away.

push around/about *vt sep* (*a*) *see* ***push.** (*b*) (*Sl: bully*) Stop
pushing everybody about!

push for　*vt fus*　(*demand*) The men are pushing for higher wages.

push off　1 *vi*　(*a*) (*Naut: leave in a boat*) They pushed off from shore an hour ago.　(*b*) (*Sl: go away*) Well, I'll push off now. Oh, push off!　2 *vt sep*　*see* ***push.***

push on　1 *vi*　(*Fam: continue going*) Well, we'd better push on. The travellers pushed on without halting.　2 *vt sep*　(*a*) *see* ***push.***　(*b*) (*Fig: exhort, egg on*) They are pushing him on to take the exam.

push out　*vt sep*　(*a*) *see* ***push.***　(*b*) (*sprout*) The plant is pushing out shoots.

push over　*vt sep*　(*a*) *see* ***push.***　(*b*) *Idiomatic n phr* It's a **push-over**=it's very easy.

put + particle　*vt sep*　(*put, with direction*) She put the box in. He put the cat out.　I asked her to put her books away.　He put the books aside and listened to me.　She put the cutlery back where she had got it.

put about　1 *vi*　(*Naut: turn*) The ship put about and headed for safety.　2 *vt sep*　(*a*) (*circulate*) Someone has been putting rumours about that we are leaving.　(*b*) (*inconvenience*) Please don't put yourself about because of me.　(*c*) (*Naut: turn*) The captain put the ship about and headed for safety.

put across　*vt sep*　(*a*) *see* ***put.***　(*b*) (*Sl: make a success of*) He managed to put the deal across okay.　(*c*) (*communicate success-fully*) She puts her ideas across well.　He was having difficulty putting his case across.

put aside　*vt sep*　(*a*) *see* ***put.***　(*b*) (*Fig: abandon*) He put aside his anger.　She put aside her grief and went to work.　(*c*) (*save*) She has managed to put aside a little money.

put away　*vt sep*　(*a*) *see* ***put.***　(*b*) (*store, tidy*) She put her clothes away.　(*c*) (*garage*) I'll just put the car away.　(*d*) (*save*=**put aside**) They have put away some money in the bank.　(*e*) (*Fam: confine, in a mental home, or prison*) He has been put away.　They put her away.　(*f*) (*Fam: eat or drink copiously*) He really puts it away! They put away a lot.　(*g*) (*put to death, usu of animals*) He put away the old dog.　(*h*) (*renounce, give up*) I asked him to put away such foolish ideas.

put back　1 *vi*　(*Naut: return to port*) The ship put back.　They will put back when they get news of the hurricane.　2 *vt sep*　(*a*) *see* ***put.***　(*b*) (*specifically replace*) She put the book back.　(*c*) (*move backwards*) He put the clock back an hour.　(*d*) (*impede, delay*) The strike has put back production considerably.

put by　*vt sep*=**put aside** (*c*), **put away** (*d*).

put down　*vt sep*　(*a*) *see* ***put.***　(*b*) (*Fig: suppress, quell*) The largene swore that he would soon put down the rebellion. (c) (*note down*) He put down everything in writing. (d) (*assign*) I would put his bad manners down to tiredness. (e) *Idiom:* He put his foot down=he took up a strong position, made an ultimatum. (f)=**put away** (f)

put down for *vt fus* (*request, in writing*) We have put down for a better council house.

put forward *vt sep* (a) *see* *put. (b) (*advance, offer*) He put forward several interesting ideas.

put in *vt sep* (a) *see* *put. (b) (*insert, add*) He put in several more paragraphs. He put in some remarks about politics. (c) (*enrol*) They have put him in for that exam.

put in for *vt fus* (*request*) They have put in for a change of doctor.

put off *vt sep* (a) *see* *put. (b) (*postpone*) They have put off the meeting because of the weather. (c) (*dismay, discourage*) Don't let his rough manner put you off. She has been put off by his offensive remarks.

put on *vt sep* (a) *see* *put. (b) (*don*) He put on his hat. (c) (*pretend*) You are just putting it on, aren't you? Stop putting it on! *n* a **put-on**=a pretence.

put out 1 *vi* (*Naut: leave harbour or the shore*) The ship put out to sea. 2 *vt sep* (a) *see* *put. (b) (*extinguish*) They put out the flames. (c) (*disturb, upset*) Don't put yourself out for me, please. She feels rather put out about the whole affair. (d) (*publish, issue*) The government is putting out a lot of new propaganda. Those documents have been put out by the authorities.

put over *vt sep* (a) *see* *put. (b)=**put across** (c). (c) *Sl Idiom:* put one over on someone=cheat him/her.

put through *vt sep* (a) *see* *put. (b) (*Tel: connect*) The operator will put you through now. Would you put me through to him now? (c) (*succeed in accomplishing*) They have put through some clever business deals in their time.

put up 1 *vi* (*stay, live*) He puts up at a little hotel in the old part of the town. 2 *vt sep* (a) *see* *put. (b) (*erect*) The workmen put the hut up quickly. (c) (*raise*) The boy put his hand up to ask a question. (d) (*accommodate*) Would you put them up here for the night? *Idiomatic n* a **put-you-up**=a camp bed, or a couch which may be used as a bed. (e) (*Fam: offer as a contribution*) The millionaire put up several thousand dollars for this project. He put up a new proposal. (f) (*encourage, egg on*) They have put him up to doing it. He has been put up to this. (g) *Idiomatic n cpd* a **put-up job**=a contrived situation or action.

put up with *vt fus* (*tolerate*) She puts up with a lot of insolence from those people. I wouldn't put up with his nonsense if I were you.

put upon *vt fus* (*be coerced, forced, usu pass*) I will not be put upon!

puzzle out *vt sep* (*puzzle or work out, to a solution*) They could not puzzle out his intentions.   I wish I could puzzle out why he did it.

queue up *vi* (*form a queue*) The people began to queue up.   We have been queuing up here for hours.

quicken up 1 *vi* (*accelerate, increase*) The man's pace quickened up.   2 *vt sep* (*speed up, accelerate*) He quickened up his pace. The tempo of production has quickened up factory output.

quieten down 1 *vi* (*become quiet, calm*) The noise of the wind has quietened down.   He was very angry, but he has quietened down now.   2 *vt sep* (*make quiet*) I want you to quieten those children down.

*race + particle 1 *vi* (*race, with direction*) He raced up.   She raced away.   They raced in with the news.   2 *vt sep* (a) (*cause to move fast, with direction*) He raced the men over to where they were needed.   They raced the supplies across.   She raced the horse along.   (b) (*compete in racing, with direction*) I'll race you back.   They raced me across.   We raced each other down to the shop.

rack up *vt sep* (*Fam: score or log up*) He racked up a large number of points.

rail in *vt sep* (*enclose with rails or a railing*) They railed the area in.

rail off *vt sep* (*mark off or separate with rails or a railing*) They have railed off the enclosure.

raise up *vt sep* (*Old, intensive of* **raise**) He has raised up a family of champions.   He claimed he could raise up devils.

*rake + particle *vt sep* (*furrow or move with a rake, with direction*) The gardener raked the stones aside.   The ground has been thoroughly raked over.   They have raked the leaves out.

rake in *vt sep* (a) *see* ***rake.** (b) (*Fig Fam: bring in in quantities*) That gambling casino just rakes money in.   He rakes in a lot of cash.

rake off *vt sep* (a) *see* ***rake.** (b) (*Fig Fam: remove as a special profit or fee*) They rake off 10% for themselves.   *n* **a rake-off**= a special profit.

rake over *vt sep* (a) *see* ***rake.** (b) (*Fig Fam: discuss, gossip about*) They like raking over old scandals.

rake up *vt sep* (a) *see* ***rake.** (b) (*Fig Fam: unearth, discover*) They enjoy raking up new scandals.   Where did you rake that story up?

rally round 1 *vi* (*come together to give help*) I expect the family to rally round in an emergency like this.   Oh, everyone will rally round and help.   2 *vt sep*   (*bring together to be of practical use*) He will rally all of them round.   It is essential to rally the people round.

*ram + particle   *vt sep*   (*push forcefully, with direction*) He rammed the bolt in.   They rammed the logs through.   He was rammed back against the wall by the rush of water.   (*Fig*) The government intends to ram this new legislation through.

*ramble + particle   *vi*   (*walk for enjoyment in the countryside, with direction*) They just rambled along.   A group of people rambled up.   They rambled on through the woods.

ramble on   *vi*   (*a*) *see* ***ramble.**   (*b*) (*Fig Fam: talk on without stopping, in a rather aimless way*) He rambled on about his unfulfilled ambitions.   I wish she wouldn't ramble on and on about her children.

rampage about/around   *vi*   (*go about in a dangerous, uncontrolled manner*) Gangs of teenagers were rampaging about, breaking things.   Looting soldiers rampaged about in the town centre.

rap out   *vt sep*   (*a*) (*signal by rapping or knocking*) He rapped out a morse message.   Something was rapping out sounds on the table.   (*b*) (*state clearly and briskly*) He rapped out a command.

rasp out   *vt sep*   (*say in a rasping, or harsh, voice*) The old man rasped out a warning.

ration out   *vt sep*   (*allocate as rations*) The food is being rationed out now.   They have been rationing out cloth.

*rattle + particle   *vi*   (*Fam: move quickly with a rattling noise, with direction*) The old car rattled along at 60 km/h.   The train rattled past, shaking everything.

rattle off   1 *vi*   *see* ***rattle.**   2 *vt sep* (*Fig Fam: reel off or state accurately at length*) He rattled off the names of several dozen important people in the business.   She can rattle off all the major dates of the French Revolution.

rattle on   1 *vi*   (*a*) *see* ***rattle.**   (*b*) (*Fig Fam: talk continuously*) He rattles on very fluently about electronics.

rattle through   1 *vi*   (*a*) *see* ***rattle.**   2 *vt fus*   (*Fig Fam: say or do rather quickly*) She rattled through her prayers.   He rattles through his work.

*reach + particle   *vi*   (*reach, with direction*) He reached up.   She reached down.   They reached in for the honey.   He reached over for his pipe.

reach back   *vi*   (*a*) *see* ***reach.**   (*b*) (*go back in the mind*) I asked him to reach back and try to re-capture the atmosphere of the place in his boyhood.

reach out   *vi*   (*a*) *see* ***reach.**   (*b*) (*Fig: extend an offer of help*) We have tried to reach out to these unfortunate people.

read back   *vt sep*   (*repeat a reading of; read in return*) He read back the list of names to me, and I checked them off one by one. Please read it back to me.

read in   *vt sep*   (*Fig: add in by inference*) You shouldn't try to read in (to this matter) things which aren't there.   Don't read things in to what I say.

read on   *vi*   (*a*) (*continue to read*) He read on through the afternoon. (*b*) (*read further*) When you have done the exercise, read on to page 45.   Now read on.

read out   *vt sep*   (*read aloud*) He read the proclamation out.   The pupils took turns in reading out their work.

read over   *vt sep*   (*read fully*) The editor read over the manuscript· I'd like you to read this over for me.

read through   *vt sep* = **read over.**

read up   *vt sep*   (*learn up by reading, study*) He has been reading the subject up.   I believe he has started reading up anthropology.

read up on   *vt fus* = **read up.**

rear up   1 *vi*   (*rise violently up*) (*a*) (*Lit*) The frightened horse reared up.   A huge creature reared up out of the marsh. (*b*) (*Fig*) Some serious problems have reared up since we last met. 2 *vt sep*   (*reflexive: rise up suddenly*) The creature reared itself up on to its hind legs.

reason out   *vt sep*   (*reason to the end, think out fully*) I intend to reason this matter out if it is humanly possible.   He isn't good at reasoning out even simple problems.

reckon in   *vt sep*   (*include*) Even if we reckon in profits from the new factory, we shan't be able to make an overall profit this year.

reckon on   *vt fus*   (*base one's assumptions on*) You should reckon on having to deal with more than one problem.   Does he seriously reckon on winning?   She didn't reckon on six extra dinner guests.

reckon up   *vt sep*   (*assess, count up*) He has begun reckoning up the odds against success.   Have you reckoned up the casualties of this attack?

reckon with   *vt fus*   (*expect to encounter*) I didn't reckon with this kind of opposition.   You shall have to reckon with her obstinacy.

reckon without   *vt fus*   (*expect not to have*) You must reckon without our help in this matter.   He reckoned without their interference.

***reel + particle**   *vi*   (*reel or move very unsteadily, with direction*) The drunk man reeled about in the street. I was dizzy after the accident, and everything was reeling back and forward. He reeled away in a dazed condition. Several drunk men reeled in. The enemy regiments reeled back in confusion.

reel in 1 *vi* (*a*) *see* *reel. (*b*) (*draw in a fishing line on its reel*) The man reeled in and went home without catching anything. 2 *vt sep* (*draw in on a fishing line with its reel*) He reeled in a beautiful trout.

reel off 1 *vi see* *reel. 2 *vt sep* (*Fig Fam: state quickly, accurately and at length*) He reeled off the names of all the people concerned in the affair. She can reel off great chunks of Shakespeare.

reel out 1 *vi see* *reel. 2 *vt sep* (*release or unwind on a reel*) The angler reeled out his fishing line. I reeled out more thread.

reel up 1 *vi see* *reel. 2 *vt sep* (*draw in on a reel*) They reeled up the line and stored it away.

refer back 1 *vi* (*a*) (*mention again*) I would like to refer back to the first of my three points. (*b*) (*check back through files*) We must refer back to the first letters which we received from him. 2 *vt sep* (*return*) You should refer this matter back to head office for a decision. This has been referred back to us again.

rein back 1 *vi* (*restrain a horse or harnessed animal*) The rider reined back. 2 *vt sep* (*a*) (*Lit: restrain by pulling on reins*) The rider reined his horse back. (*b*) (*Fig: restrain*) You should rein back your passions.

rein in = rein back.

rein up 1 *vi* (*stop a horse or harnessed animal*) The rider reined up. 2 *vt sep* (*stop by pulling on reins*) He reined up his horse.

remain in *vi* (*stay indoors*) We remained in because of the heavy rain.

remain out *vi* (*stay outside*) The children remained out because of the good weather.

remain up *vi* (*stay up after bedtime*) The children remained up because their uncle had come to see them.

render down *vt sep* (*reduce to an oil*) The fatty substances have been rendered down.

render up *vt sep* (*Old: surrender, give up*) The captain has rendered up his castle to the enemy.

rent out *vt sep* (*give out on receipt of rent*) I have rented the house out to a very nice family. He rents out villas in Italy.

report back 1 *vi* (*bring back a report*) Our correspondent has just reported back from the front line. I expect them to report back here as soon as they arrive. 2 *vt sep* (*send back in report* *form*) She reported the story back as soon as she could.

rest up *vi* (*have a complete rest*) She is resting up for a few weeks.

rev up *vt sep* (*increase the revs or revolutions in*) The mechanic revved up the engine. He loves revving that sports car up.

*ride + particle (*ride, with direction*) 1 *vi* They rode along. The horsemen rode up to the gate. She rode away. 2 *vt sep* He rode the horse back to the stable. They rode the animals away. She rode her cycle back to town.

ride down 1 *vi see* ***ride.** 2 *vt sep* (*a*) *see* ***ride.** (*b*) (*attack and knock down while riding*) The enemy cavalry rode our men down.

ride out 1 *vi* *see* ***ride.** 2 *vt sep* (*a*) *see* ***ride.** (*b*) (*Lit, Naut: survive by riding at anchor*) The ship rode out the storm. We can ride out the hurricane by staying here. (*c*) (*Fig: survive through patience or endurance*) She can ride this business out. The company has managed to ride out this trade depression.

ride up 1 *vi* (*a*) *see* ***ride.** (*b*) (*rise steadily up*) I don't like this skirt because it keeps riding up. 2 *vt sep* *see* ***ride.**

rig out *vt sep* (*Fam: clothe*) She rigged the children out in new dresses. He has been rigged out in a new uniform. *n* **a rig-out** = a set of clothes, a uniform.

rig up *vt sep* (*a*) (*Naut: fit up the rigging or ropework of*) They rigged the ship up efficiently. (*b*) (*fit up*) He can rig up all sorts of useful gadgets if you ask him. The terrorists rigged up a booby-trap for the security forces. (*c*) (*Fig: contrive*) Is this one of the schemes you like rigging up? I'm sure he has rigged something up for us.

ring back 1 *vi* (*Fam: call back on the telephone*) I'll ring back in ten minutes. 2 *vt sep* (*a*) (*Fam: re-contact by telephone*) I'll ring you back in ten minutes. (*b*) (*Theatre: open with a flourish*) They have rung back the curtains on a new show.

ring down *vt sep* *Theatre Idiom:* To ring down the curtain(s) = (*Lit*) to bring the curtains down and so finish a play for the evening. (*Fig*) (*i*) to bring a play to an end and not perform it again. (*Fig*) (*ii*) to bring anything to an end. *Example:* This event rang down the curtain on that astonishing epoch.

ring in 1 *vi* (*a*) = **telephone in.** (*b*) (*US Fam*) = **clock in.** 2 *vt sep* (*introduce by ringing bells*) The Scots like to ring in the New Year.

ring off *vi* (*close a telephone conversation*) I'd better ring off now.

ring out 1 *vi* (*a*) (*resound*) The bells rang out. (*b*) (*sound out loud and clear*) A shot rang out. His voice rings out across the whole school. 2 *vt sep* (*usher out by ringing bells*) The Scots like to ring the Old Year out and the New Year in. Ring out the old, ring in the new!

ring up 1 *vi* (*call on the telephone*) She rang up about an hour ago.
2 *vt sep* (*a*) (*contact on the telephone*) She rang you up about an
hour ago. (*b*) (*Theatre: raise*) We rang up the curtain on a new
show. *Idiom:* To ring up the curtain on something=to start
something completely new. (*c*) (*register on shop till*) The cashier
rang up 20p for the butter.

rinse out 1 *vi* (*come out through rinsing with water*) These colours
won't rinse out. 2 *vt sep* (*clean out by rinsing*) She rinsed out
the cups. He rinsed out his mouth. You must rinse the
shampoo out of your hair.

*rip + particle *vi* (*Sl: move quickly, with direction*) The motorbikes ripped along. He likes ripping up and down on his bicycle.
The sports car ripped away in a trail of exhaust.

rip off 1 *vi* (*a*) see ***rip.** (*b*) (*US Sl: steal*) He likes ripping off
when he can. *n* **a rip-off**=a theft. 2 *vt sep* (*a*) (*tear off with an
effort*) He ripped the paper off. (*b*) (*Old Fam: utter*) He ripped
off an oath.

rip out 1 *vi* see ***rip.** 2 *vt sep* (*tear out with an effort*) She ripped
out the pockets of the coat.

rip up 1 *vi* see ***rip.** 2 *vt sep* (*tear up with an effort*) He ripped up
the documents. They ripped up the floorboards.

rise up *vi* (*intensive of* rise) The hills rise up to six thousand feet.
A strange creature rose up out of the mud. Smoke rose up
from the crater of the volcano. The people may rise up and
destroy the tyrant.

*roam + particle *vi* (*wander, with direction*) The herds of buffalo
roam about freely. The tribes roamed up from the plains
to the mountains. I would love to roam away into those wonderful forests.

*roar + particle *vi* (*move with a roaring noise, with direction*) The
huge machines roared off. Cars were roaring away from the
starting-point. A jet plane roared in.

roar out 1 *vi* (*a*) see ***roar.** (*b*) (*give out a roar*) The lion roared
out. 2 *vt sep* (*give out with a roar, or in a roaring voice*) The lion
roared out its frustration. The champion roared out a challenge.

rock about/around 1 *vi* (*a*) (*rock, shake continuously*) The train
rocked about on the rails. The ship was rocking about horribly
in the rough seas. (*b*) (*Sl: dance about in time to rock music*) The
teenagers were rocking about. 2 *vt sep* (*move about with a
rocking motion*) The waves were rocking the little boat about.

*rocket + particle *vi* (*move in or like a rocket, with direction*) The
projectile rocketed away. Men have rocketed off to the moon.

The car rocketed out of the garage. (*Fig Fam*) The little fellow rocketed off to tell his friends what had happened.

rocket off 1 *vi* *see* ***rocket**. 2 *vt sep* (*send off in a rocket or like a rocket*) The men have been rocketed off to the moon. The car rocketed them off faster than they expected.

***roll + particle** (*roll, with direction*) 1 *vi* The ball rolled along. The stone rolled away. The tanks rolled past. (*Fig Fam*) Some of our friends rolled in for coffee. He always rolls up about this time. He rolled up in his new car. 2 *vt sep* The insect rolled the dung along. He rolled the papers up. She rolled out the dough. They rolled the carpet back. He rolled the barrel in. They rolled the kegs out.

roll away 1 *vi* (*a*) *see* ***roll**. (*b*) (*vanish by rolling away*) The clouds have rolled away. 2 *vt sep* *see* ***roll**.

roll by *vi* (*a*) *see* ***roll**. (*b*) (*Fig: pass*) The years have rolled by. She sits and watches the world roll by.

roll in 1 *vi* (*a*) *see* ***roll**. (*b*) (*Fig: come in, in quantities*) Money was just rolling in. 2 *vt sep* *see* ***roll**.

roll on 1 *vi* (*a*) *see* ***roll**. (*b*) (*Fig Fam usu imper: come soon*) Roll on the holidays! 2 *vt sep* (*a*) *see* ***roll**. (*b*) (*put on by rolling*) She rolled on the emulsion paint. *n* **a roll-on**=a woman's elasticated suspender belt.

roll up 1 *vi* (*a*) *see* ***roll**. (*b*) (*Fig Fam usu imper: come up in large numbers*) Roll up and see the sights! Roll up, roll up! 2 *vt sep* (*a*) *see* ***roll**. (*b*) (*wrap up*) He rolled himself up in a blanket. (*c*) *Idiom:* To roll up one's sleeves=to get ready for hard work.

***romp + particle** *vi* (*jump playfully, with direction*) The children are always romping about. He romped up to us in great excitement. She romped off somewhere just five minutes ago. He romped in with the news.

roof in *vt sep* (*cover over with a roof*) The area has now been roofed in.

roof over=**roof in**.

root about/around *vi* (*search about*) He has been rooting about for his college tie. She rooted around among her souvenirs.

root for *vt fus* (*Fam: cheer*) I always root for my favourite team. I'll be rooting for you on the great day.

root out *vt sep* (*remove by the roots*) (*a*) (*Lit*) He rooted out the weeds. (*b*) (*Fig: extirpate*) We must root out this evil. It is necessary to root out corruption in government.

root up *vt sep* (*pull up by the roots*) Pigs love rooting things up with their noses.

rope in *vt sep* (*a*) (*Lit: surround or ensnare with ropes*) The cattle

have been roped in. (*b*) (*mark off or enclose with ropes*) The
visitors' area has been roped in. (*c*) (*Fig: pull in as if with ropes,
inveigle, persuade, bring*) We must rope him in to help us. She
got herself roped in to serve tea at the fête.

rope off *vt sep* (*mark off or separate with ropes*) This area has been
roped off for the judges to use.

rope together *vt sep* (*bring or tie together with ropes*) The animals
have been roped together.

rope up 1 *vi* (*put on ropes as a group*) The climbers roped up and
began the ascent of the cliff-face. 2 *vt sep* (*tie together with
ropes*) He roped up the mules and led them off.

rot away 1 *vi* (*rot, decay slowly and completely*) The dead body
was rotting away. The wood had rotted away. 2 *vt sep* (*cause
to rot completely*) The damp rots everything away eventually.

rot off *vi* (*come off through rotting, decay*) The surface has rotted off.

rough in *vt sep* (*Drawing: fill in roughly*) He roughed in the rest of
the sketch with a piece of charcoal.

rough out *vt sep* (*sketch out roughly*) He roughed out the design,
just to give us an idea of what he intended.

rough up *vt sep* (*make rough*) He roughed up her hair. (*b*) (*Sl:
assault, but not too violently*) The gang decided to rough him up,
as a warning to others. He has been roughed up a bit.

roughen up *vt sep* (*make rough, usu objects*) The surface has to be
roughened up before you put the tiles on.

round down *vt sep* (*Comm: bring down to the lower whole figure*)
The prices of the goods have all been rounded down.

round off *vt sep* (*finish off well*) The debate was rounded off by
the chairman. They have rounded off their work and will
write a detailed report.

round out *vt sep* (*finish very fully*) He intends to round out his
work before presenting his final analysis. This is good stuff,
but it needs to be rounded out.

round up *vt fus* (*a*) (*herd together, gather in*) The cowboys rounded
up the cattle. The security forces are rounding up suspects.
n **a round-up.** *n cpds* (*i*) **round-up time**=the time when
cattle etc must be rounded up. (*ii*) **a cattle round-up**=the
actual rounding up of cattle. *Idiom:* to have a round-up=to
bring everything together, make a good summary of something.
(*b*) (*Comm: bring up to the next higher whole figure*) The prices of the
goods have all been rounded up to the nearest penny.

round (up)on *vt fus* (*attack, turn violently on*) (*a*) (*Lit*) The desperate
animal rounded upon its attackers. (*b*) (*Fig*) He rounded upon

his tormentors with furious countercharges. She rounded on her critics.

rout out *vt sep* (*a*)=**root out**. (*b*) (*get out of bed*) They routed the poor fellow out at six a.m.

rout up=**rout out** (*b*).

*row + particle (*row, with direction*) 1 *vi* He rowed along steadily. The oarsmen rowed up to the jetty. I watched the fishermen row in. 2 *vt sep* He rowed the boat along steadily. The oarsmen rowed the boat up to the jetty. They rowed their boat in.

rub along 1 *vi* (*Fig Fam: get along all right, manage*) He says he'll rub along somehow. I rubbed along with my French on holiday last year. 2 *vt sep* (*push along repetitively*) They rubbed the cloth along, to clean the edges of the panels.

rub away 1 *vi* (*rub continuously*) He rubbed away for hours to clean that old brass plate. 2 *vt sep* (*erode by rubbing*) Countless washerwomen have rubbed the stones away. The name on the brass plate has been rubbed away.

rub down *vt sep* (*a*) (*clean or dry down by rubbing*) She rubbed the horse down. *n* **a rubdown**. (*b*) (*smooth down*) He rubbed the wood down with sandpaper.

rub in *vt sep* (*a*) (*introduce by rubbing*) She rubbed the oil in. You should rub this liniment in hard. (*b*) (*Fig Fam: make worse, emphasize*) He rubbed in his victory. Don't rub it in!

rub off 1 *vi* (*a*) (*go away or remove through rubbing*) These marks won't rub off. The teacher wrote beside the blackboard exercise 'Please don't rub off'. (*b*) (*come off through rubbing*) The colours rub off on your hands. The pencil marks have rubbed off. (*c*) (*Fig: pass as if by rubbing from one to another*) I hope his good manners will rub off on his friend. 2 *vt sep* (*remove by rubbing*) The teacher rubbed the exercises off. The writing on the board has been rubbed off. It is difficult to rub off this dirt.

rub on *vt sep* (*put on by rubbing*) She rubbed the ointment on.

rub out 1 *vi* (*go away completely through rubbing*) The ink won't rub out. The marks rubbed out easily. 2 *vt sep* (*a*) (*erase*) He rubbed out what he had written. (*b*) (*Sl: kill*) The gangsters rubbed out their rivals. He was rubbed out.

rub up *vt sep* (*a*) (*polish by rubbing*) He rubbed the vase up until it shone. *Idiom:* To rub someone up the right/wrong way=to influence or affect someone successfully/badly. (*b*) (*Old Fam: improve*) I'll have to rub up my French before I go to Paris.

rub up against *vt fus* (*Fig Fam: come in contact with*) She rubs up against all sorts of people in her profession. I hadn't expected to rub up against them again.

ruffle up *vt sep* (a) (*ruffle, disturb completely*) He ruffled up her hair. Her clothes were badly ruffled up. (b) (*Fig Fam usu pass: angry, upset*) He got all ruffled up about the money. Don't get ruffled up (about it).

rule off *vt sep* (a) (*mark off with a ruled line*) The pupil ruled off the last exercise and started a new one. (b) (*Comm: close, end*) The account has been ruled off. The column of figures was ruled off.

rule out *vt sep* (a) (*Old lit: delete by putting a ruled line through*) The names have been ruled out. (b) (*Fig: exclude*) I cannot rule out the possibility of trouble. Don't just rule out his suggestions. That date must be ruled out. The age limit rules him out as a candidate. Sabotage cannot be entirely ruled out.

*rumble + particle *vi* (*move with a rumbling noise, with direction*) Heavy vehicles rumbled along through the night. The tanks rumbled past. Armoured columns rumbled into the town.

rumble out 1 *vi* (a) *see* ***rumble.** (b) (*sound out with a rumbling noise*) The volcano rumbled out. 2 *vt sep* (*give out in a rumbling voice*) He rumbled out a warning.

rummage about/around *vi* (*search untidily about*) She rummaged about in the drawer for a pencil. I like rummaging around in old shops.

rummage out *vt sep* (*get out by rummaging*) They rummaged out some old clothes for the jumble sale.

*run + particle *vi* (*run, with direction*) The children were running about happily. He ran away in fear. She ran up and hugged me. The boys ran out to play.

run about/around 1 *vi* *see* ***run.** *n* a runabout=a small car. 2 *vt sep* (a) (*convey about, usu in a car*) I'll be glad to run you about while you're in town. (b) (*Sl*) *Idiom:* To give someone the runaround=to make someone follow you in frustrated hope (usu a boy after a girl). To waste someone's time.

run across 1 *vi* *see* ***run.** 2 *vt sep* (*convey across*) I'll run you across in the car. He ran us across to the other side of the bay in his private launch. 3 *vt fus* (*Fig: come across by chance*) I ran across an old school friend yesterday whom I hadn't seen for years. He ran across some useful quotations which you may like to know about.

run after *vt fus* (a) (*pursue*) They have been running after him all day. He has been running after her for months, but she isn't interested in him at all. She runs after everything in trousers. (b) (*Fig Fam: serve, care for usu in a servile way*) She runs after her children all the time. I'm not going to spend my life running after you!

run against=**run across** 3 *vt fus.*

run at *vt fus* (*Old: attack, throw oneself upon*) He ran at them, sword in hand.

run along 1 *vi* (*a*) *see* ***run.** (*b*) (*Fam, usu imper for children: go away*) Run along! Run along now, children! 2 *vt sep* (*convey along, usu in a car*) I'll run you along to the station in a few minutes.

run away *vi* (*a*) *see* ***run.** (*b*) (*flee*) The enemy broke, and men began to run away in all directions. (*c*) (*run, out of control*) The horse reared, and then ran away. *n cpd* **a runaway horse/train.** (*d*) (*elope*) The young couple decided to run away and get married. *n pl* **the runaways.** *n cpd* **the runaway couple.** (*e*) (*escape*) He decided to run away. He ran away to sea. He ran away from boarding school. She ran away from home. (*f*) (*Fig Fam: leave*) Don't run away, I want to ask your advice. (*g*) (*flow away*) The water runs away through this pipe. His supply of money seems just to have run away. 2 *vt sep* (*allow to flow away*) He ran the water away.

run away with *vt fus* (*a*) (*Fig Fam: use up, consume*) This work just runs away with funds. The project has been running away with scarce resources. (*b*) (*Fam: steal*) The manager ran away with the funds. Someone has run away with my wallet. (*c*) (*Sport: win easily*) She has run away with the race. He ran away with the prize. (*d*) (*Fam: begin to suppose or think*) He has run away with the idea that you like him. Don't run away with the impression that we need money. (*e*) (*take possession of*) His temper sometimes runs away with him. Oh your imagination is running away with you.

run back 1 *vi* (*a*) *see* ***run.** (*b*) (*flow back*) The water began to run back into the depression as fast as they pumped it out. 2 *vt sep* (*a*) (*take back, usu in a car*) I'll run you back home after the show. (*b*) (*re-wind*) She ran the tape back after hearing it. The projectionist runs the film back at the end of every performance.

run down 1 *vi* (*a*) *see* ***run.** (*b*) (*flow down*) The water ran down steadily. (*c*) (*unwind to a stop*) The clock has run down. (*d*) (*lose a store of energy*) The batteries have run down. 2 *vt sep* (*a*) (*convey down, usu in a car*) I'll run you down to the station in a few minutes. (*b*) (*knock down, usu of cars*) She was frightened in case she would run someone down while driving. He was run down by a bus. (*c*) (*Naut: strike*) We were run down by a big merchant ship, and our dinghy was smashed. (*d*) (*Med pass: ill, debilitated*) I'm feeling run down, doctor. She looks run down. (*e*) (*Fig Fam: disparage*) They love running people down, you know. She runs everyone down. (*f*) (*pursue and* *capture*) The police ran him down eventually. The hounds ran the stag down. (*g*) (*slowly bring to a halt*) The management are running this factory down. We have been forced to run production down. (*h*) *n* **a run-down**=a summary. *Example:* He gave me a run-down on what had been happening while I was away.

run in 1 *vi* (*a*) *see* ***run.** (*b*) (*flow in*) Rivulets of water were running in everywhere. 2 *vt sep* (*a*) (*convey in, usu a car*) I'll run you in to the station in a few minutes. (*b*) (*bring slowly into full use*) He is running in his new car. New cars sometimes have a notice on them 'Running in, please pass'. (*c*) (*Fam: arrest*) The police have run him in again. (*d*) (*introduce*) They ran the liquid in through a tube.

run into *vt fus* (*a*) (*meet by chance*) I ran into some old friends I hadn't seen for years. (*b*) (*collide with*) The car ran into a lamp standard. He ran into the back of a bus. (*c*) (*Fig Fam: encounter*) You may run into some difficulties in that country. He has run into trouble in his job. (*d*) (*Fam: accumulate*) He has run into debt. (*e*) (*add up to*) His total income runs into six figures. Her book has run into four editions already.

run off 1 *vi* (*a*) *see* ***run.** (*b*) (*flow off*) The water runs off without leaving a trace. (*c*) (*flee*) The thief ran off before we could stop him. (*d*) (*decamp, abscond*) The accountant ran off with most of the firm's liquid assets. He ran off with his best friend's girl. 2 *vt sep* (*a*) (*allow to flow away*) He ran the water off. They ran off the excess liquid. (*b*) (*produce quickly*) He runs off several articles each day. (*c*) (*print*) They ran off five thousand copies. (*d*) (*Sport: conduct and conclude*) They ran off the heats and selected their representatives for the big competition.

run off with=**run away with** (*b*) (*d*).

run out 1 *vi* (*a*) *see* ***run.** (*b*) (*flow out*) The water runs out through this channel. (*c*) (*release itself*) The rope ran out through a slot. The chains ran out through special holes. (*d*) (*expire, come to an end*) His contract runs out shortly. The lease for that property will soon run out. (*e*) (*come to an end, become exhausted*) Supplies are beginning to run out. Your time has run out. *Idiom:* (*i*) The sands have run out=there is no more time. (*ii*) Someone's patience runs out=someone's patience comes to an end. 2 *vt sep* (*a*) (*convey out, usu in a car*) I'll happily run you out to see them. (*b*) (*pay out*) They ran the rope out as far as it would go. (*c*) (*Cricket, usu pass: put out of the game while running between wickets*) The batsman was run out. (*d*) (*reflexive, run until breathless*) He ran himself out, and had to rest. (*e*) *US Idiom:* To run someone out of town=to force someone to leave suddenly.

run out of *vt fus* (*begin to lose, lose*) We are running out of water.

He ran out of hope long ago.   I have run out of money.   *Idiom:*
to run out of time=to have no time left.

run over   1 *vi*   (*a*) *see* ***run.**   (*b*) (*flow over*) The water rose rapidly
and began to run over.   The bath is running over!   (*c*) (*visit
briefly*) She ran over to her neighbour's to borrow some milk.
I'll run over and see him tomorrow.   2 *vt fus*   (*a*) (*recapitulate*)
Let's just run over the story again.   (*Theatre*) I'll run over your
part with you.   They ran over what happened to refresh their
memories.   (*b*) (*re-read*) She quickly ran over her notes.   3 *vt sep*
(*a*) (*knock down, usu with a car*) The bus ran him over.   He was
run over by a bus.   (*b*) (*play usu fully*) He ran the tape over and
listened carefully.   I'll run it over once again.

run through   1 *vi*   (*a*) *see* ***run.**   (*b*) (*flow through*) The water runs
through by means of this conduit.   2 *vt fus*   (*a*) (*use up, consume*)
He ran through the family fortune in a year.   (*b*) (*read briefly*)
He ran through the text a few minutes before he was due to
speak.   (*c*) (*rehearse*) Let's just run through the thing one more
time.   They ran through it again to get it right.   *n* **a run-
through**=a brief rehearsal.   (*d*) (*recapitulate*) I would like just
to run through the important points again, if I may.   3 *vt sep*
(*a*) (*Old: transfix violently*) He ran his opponent through with a
sword.   (*b*) **run over** 3 (*b*).

run to   *vt fus*   (*a*) (*amount to*) His fortune runs to several hundred
thousand pounds.   The poem runs to several thousand lines.
(*b*) (*tend to*) This author runs to sentiment in many of his novels.
The garden is running to seed and badly needs attention.   She
naturally runs to fat.   *Idiom:* Someone's talents etc running to
waste=someone's talents etc not being used.   (*c*) (*Fam: afford*)
I just can't run to a new coat for you every month!   I think
the club funds will run to a party at the end of term.

run up   1 *vi*   *see* ***run.**   2 *vt sep*   (*a*) (*raise to the top of a pole*)
They ran up their national flag.   (*b*) (*accumulate*) He has run up
some astonishing debts.   She runs up rather large bills.   (*c*)
(*sew quickly*) She is willing to run me up a new dress.   She ran
the dress up in no time at all.

run up against   *vt fus*   (*encounter*) He ran up against trouble in his
new job.   I ran up against some old acquaintances last week.

*rush + particle   (*rush, with direction*)   1 *vi*   The children rushed
in.   She rushed out to get help.   He has rushed off somewhere
on business.   2 *vt sep*   I rushed her off to hospital.   He rushed
us through before we could see anything.   They want to rush
you out almost before you can get in.

rush at   *vt fus*   (*a*) (*attack*) They rushed at the enemy.   (*b*) (*tackle
too quickly*) You shouldn't rush at the job.   He rushed at it with
frantic energy.

rush through *vt sep* (a) *(hurry through, hasten)* They rushed the news through. You must rush this despatch through to head-quarters. (b) *(transport as quickly as possible)* They are rushing men through to the danger zone as fast as they can get trucks. We will rush someone through immediately.

rush up 1 *vi see* *rush. 2 *vt sep* (a) *see* *rush. (b) *(raise too quickly)* The construction company just rushed its buildings up.

rust in *vi* *(become fixed in through rust)* There is a risk that these screws will rust in.

rust up 1 *vi* *(become rusty)* The car has rusted up badly. 2 *vt sep* *(make rusty)* This damp climate rusts cars up in no time at all. The equipment is all rusted up.

rustle up *vt sep* *(Fig Fam: provide, obtain, get hold of)* Can you rustle up some men to help us? She said she would rustle up some coffee.

saddle up 1 *vi* *(put a saddle on a horse, preparatory to riding)* The men saddled up. 2 *vt sep* *(put a saddle on)* They saddled up their horses.

sag down *vi* *(intensive of sag)* The canvas was sagging down under the weight of water.

*sail + particle *(sail, with direction)* 1 *vi* The ship sailed away. The men sailed away in their ship. He sailed off somewhere in his dinghy. The liner sailed out in the early afternoon. *(Fig Fam)* She sailed out in a huff. They sailed off somewhere without telling me. 2 *vt sep* They sailed the ship in as close as they could get. The admiral sailed the fleet through with flags flying.

sail through 1 *vi see* *sail. 2 *vt fus* *(Fig: succeed easily in passing)* She sailed through her exams. 3 *vt sep see* *sail.

sally forth *vi* *(Old: sally out, come out eagerly or vigorously)* The defenders sallied forth to meet the foe. I sallied forth one fine morning to seek adventure.

sally out *vi* *(come out in a rush, come out confidently)* The defenders sallied out to attack the enemy.

salt away *vt sep* (a) *(Lit: put away, preserved in salt)* He salted the meat away. (b) *(Fig: store away, save, hoard)* She has salted away her money somewhere. The tycoon has salted his profits away in Switzerland.

salt down *vt sep* *(preserve with salt)* He salted down the meat and stored it away.

sandpaper down *vt sep* *(rub down or smooth down with sandpaper)* The carpenter sandpapered down the surface.

sandwich in *vt sep* *(Fig: squeeze in, like the meat in a sandwich)* I

was sandwiched in between two fat men.   The car was sandwiched in between two trucks.

*saunter + particle   *vi*   (*walk casually, with direction*) He sauntered
along, hands in pockets.   They sauntered off somewhere.   He
saunters about, doing nothing in particular.

save up   (*save as fully or as much as possible, put aside money for a purpose*)
1 *vi* I am saving up to buy a car.   You should save up and
get a house.   2 *vt sep* You should save some money up,
instead of spending it all.

saw away   1 *vi*   (*saw continuously*) He sawed away till he got tired.
2 *vt sep* = **saw off**.

saw off   *vt sep*   (*remove by sawing*) He sawed the branch off.

saw up   *vt sep*,   (*saw as fully as possible*) He sawed up the wood.
Ask him to saw up some logs for the fire.

scale down   *vt sep*   (*reduce in scale or size*) The enemy have scaled
down their attacks.   I asked him to scale down his proposals
to a manageable size.

scale up   *vt sep*   (*increase in scale or size*) The enemy have scaled
up their attacks.   I asked him to scale his proposals up, because
a more ambitious project was possible.

*scamper + particle   *vi*   (*run quickly or lightly, with direction*) The
mice scampered away.   The children scampered along to the
playground.   He heard the sound of little feet scampering off.

scare away   *vt sep*   (*frighten away*) The farmer scared the crows
away by firing his shotgun.   The children were scared away by
the look on his face.

scare off = **scare away**.

scatter about/around   (*scatter or distribute in an area*)   1 *vi* The
frightened people scattered about in all directions.   2 *vt sep* (*a*)
(*Lit*) He scattered the seeds about in the hope that some
would grow.   (*b*) (*Fig*) They scattered their ideas about in
the hope that someone might be interested in them.

scoop out   *vt sep*   (*get out with a scoop or a scooping movement*) He
scooped the dirt out with his hand.   She scooped the raisins
out (of the tin).

scoop up   *vt sep*   (*pick up with a scoop or a scooping movement*) She
scooped the raisins up from the floor.   He scooped up his small
son and carried him away.   The machine scoops up the earth
and dumps it over there.

*scoot + particle   *vi*   (*Fam: move swiftly, with direction*) Just scoot
along and tell them I'm coming.   The fish were scooting in and
out of the weeds.   Several little boats were scooting past.

*scorch + particle vi (*Fam: move very rapidly as if scorching the road, with direction*) The car just scorched along. The racing cars scorched off from the starting line. He scorched away on his motorbike.

score off 1 vt sep (*delete by drawing a line*) He scored their names off and wrote in some others. 2 vt fus (*Fig Fam: gain a victory against*) She likes to score off people when she can.

score out vt sep (*delete completely, by drawing a line*) He scored out the names. She scored out her mistakes.

score up vt sep (*Sport: mark up as part of a score*) They have scored up quite a lot of runs. The games were scored up on the board.

scour about/around vi (*search diligently about*) She has been scouring about all over town for a certain kind of sausage.

scour out vt sep (*clean out by scouring*) (a) (*Lit*) She scoured out the pots. (b) (*Fig*) The general hopes to scour the enemy out.

scout about/around vi (*move about like a scout, or for purposes of scouting*) They scouted about for a good place to camp. Scout about for something you like, get it, and send the bill to me.

scout out vt sep (a) (*investigate fully*) They scouted out the terrain ahead of the army. (b) (*hunt out, find, discover*) He has scouted out some excellent wines. Trust you to scout out the best bargains.

scrabble about/around vi (*scratch frantically about*) The man scrabbled about for a foothold on the cliff, but couldn't find one. She scrabbled about on the desk for her pen.

*scramble + particle vi (*scramble, move quickly on hands and feet, with direction*) They scrambled down from the top of the cliff. He scrambled up to the ledge. I watched them scramble along to where the injured man was lying.

scramble up 1 vi *see* *scramble. 2 vt sep (*mix up completely*) The materials were all scrambled up. The letters of the alphabet were scrambled up as part of the game.

*scrape + particle vi (a) (*move with a scratching sound, scrape while moving, with direction*) He could hear something scraping along outside the window. (b) (*manage to pass, with difficulty, scraping or as though scraping against the sides*) The gates were very narrow and the car just scraped in. The door was so small that the piano just managed to scrape through. The fence was very low but the dog scraped under. (c) (*Fig: manage to pass, with difficulty*) When I arrived the hall was nearly full and I just scraped in. The exam was so difficult that he only scraped through.

scrape along vi (a) *see* *scrape. (b) (*Fig Fam: manage to live*)

We scrape along somehow, although we've hardly any money.

scrape away 1 *vi* (*scrape continuously*) She scraped away at the
skin until it was clean. Those branches scrape away at the
window whenever a wind rises. 2 *vt sep* (*remove a veneer or
surface by scraping*) He scraped the dirt away and found lettering
underneath.

scrape off 1 *vi* *see* *scrape. 2 *vt sep* (*remove by scraping*) He
scraped the paint off to reveal metal underneath. She scraped
the food off into the dust bin.

scrape out 1 *vi* *see* *scrape. 2 *vt sep* (*get out by scraping*) She
scraped out the centre of the water melon.

scrape up *vt sep* (*a*) (*Lit: lift up by scraping*) She scraped up the
squashed fruit from the floor. (*b*) (*Fig: invent from very meagre
resources*) She scraped up a story about visiting her aunt, but no
one believed it. (*c*) (*obtain with difficulty*) We may manage to
scrape some cash up somewhere.

scratch along *vi*=**scrape along** *vi* (*b*).

scratch away 1 *vi* (*a*) (*scratch continuously*) He scratched away at
his pimples all the time. The chickens were scratching away
at the bare earth. 2 *vt sep* (*remove by scratching*) He scratched
away the surface with a knife, and found gold underneath.

scratch out *vt sep* (*a*) (*get out by scratching*) The chickens manage
to scratch some food out of the bare earth. (*b*) (*Fig: get, make*)
He said he could just scratch a living out of the soil. (*c*)
(*violently tear out*) She swore she would scratch his eyes out if she
saw him again. (*d*) (*outline with scratches*) He scratched out his
name on the bark of the tree.

scratch up *vt sep* (*dig up by scratching*) (*a*) (*Lit*) The birds scratch
up some worms from time to time. (*b*) (*Fig Fam: find*) I'll
manage to scratch some money up somehow. He scratched up
a team from various sources.

***scream + particle** *vi* (*scream, move with a screaming noise, with
direction*) The police cars screamed along. A squad car
screamed past. The ambulances screamed in from the highway.
A line of fighter planes came screaming down.

scream out 1 *vi* (*a*) *see* *scream. (*b*) (*emit a scream, shriek*) She
screamed out in terror. 2 *vt sep* (*emit as a scream*) She screamed
out a warning.

screen off *vt sep* (*partition with a screen*) The working area is screened off completely. The patient in the corner bed was screened
off from the other patients (in the hospital ward).

screw down *vt sep* (*fix down with screws or by screwing*) They
screwed the planks down and covered them with asbestos.

screw on *vt sep* (*fix on with screws or by screwing*) They screwed the planks on firmly.

screw in *vt sep* (*fix in as a screw or by screwing*) The joiner screwed the nails in. They screwed the light brackets in.

screw off *vt sep* (*remove by taking out the screws or unscrewing*) The joiner screwed the lamp brackets off and took them away.

screw up *vt sep* (a) (*Lit: tighten with screws*) The joiner screwed up the whole framework till it was firmly in position. (b) (*fix up with screws or by screwing*) They screwed the brackets up over the fireplace. (c) (*Fig Sl: spoil*) I'm afraid they've screwed the whole thing up. Your plan would screw it all up properly. It's all screwed up. (d) *Idiom:* To screw up one's courage = to make or prepare to make a very brave effort.

scribble away 1 *vi* (a) (*scribble, make meaningless marks continuously*) The little girl loves scribbling away on pieces of paper. (b) (*Pej: write continuously but badly*) He scribbles away year in year out, but no one will publish his stuff. 2 *vt sep* (*Pej: spend in writing*) He scribbles his time away when he could be doing something useful.

scribble down *vt sep* (*write down in a scribble*) He scribbled down some names and telephone numbers.

scribble out *vt sep* (*write out in a scribble*) He scribbled out a note and left it on the table.

scrub away 1 *vi* (*scrub continuously*) She scrubbed away at the doorstep until it was spotless. 2 *vt sep* (*remove by scrubbing*) I tried to scrub the stains away.

scrub down *vt sep* (*clean down by scrubbing or rubbing hard*) They scrubbed the walls down. He scrubbed himself down.

scrub off *vt sep* (*clean off by scrubbing*) They scrubbed the dirty marks off. I'll have to scrub off all the muck.

scrub out *vt sep* (*remove or delete fully by scrubbing*) He scrubbed the marks out with a wet cloth and a brush.

scrub up *vi* (*Med Fam: wash thoroughly, before treating a patient or performing an operation*) While the surgeon was scrubbing up, the anaesthetist gave the patient an injection.

*scud + particle *vi* (*usu of ships or clouds: move swiftly, with direction*) The little ship scudded in from the open sea. Clouds were scudding along in great streamers. Small boats were scudding back and forward.

*scuffle + particle *vi* (*walk with a scuffling of the feet, with direction*) The old tramp scuffled along. He scuffled in wearing rope sandals. The men scuffled out in silence.

*scurry + particle vi (*move hastily or quickly, with direction*) The
small animals scurried along.   The little girl scurried up breathlessly.   The boy scurried away to find his friends.

*scuttle + particle vi (*run with quick steps, with direction*) The
crabs scuttled out of the rocks.   The cockroaches scuttled about.
An armoured car scuttled along.   Some men, tiny in the distance,
were scuttling around near the houses.

seal in vt sep (*enclose or close in by sealing*) Some prisoners were
deliberately sealed in and abandoned.   The remains of the king
were sealed in (to the tomb).

seal up vt sep (*close up fully, by sealing*) (a) (*Lit*) The doors were
officially sealed up.   The entrance to the tomb was sealed up.
(b) (*Fig*) The whole matter is now sealed up and finished.   He
hopes to seal things up soon.

search about/around vi (*look around, search in an area*) The men
were searching about for something in the bushes.   The police
have been searching around all day, stopping people and asking
questions.

search after/for vt fus (*seek*) He is searching after something
unattainable.   She is searching for the truth.

search out=seek out.

see about vt fus (a) (*attend to*) She said she would see about the
electricity tomorrow.   We'll see about it as soon as possible.
(b) (*Ironic: consider whether something is really possible*) Well, well,
we'll see about that!

see in 1 vi (*look inside*) If you pull the curtain back, people will
see in.   2 vt sep (a) (*conduct in*) I'll see you safely in.   (b)
(*mainly Scot: celebrate the arrival of*) Let's stay up and see the
New Year in.

see into vt fus (*inquire into, investigate*) The police are seeing into
the matter.   We shall have to see into this.

see off vt sep (*accompany to a place of departure*) We'll come and see
you off.   They saw her off at the airport.

see out 1 vi (*look outwards*) These windows are so dirty that I
can't see out.   2 vt sep (*conduct out*) I'll see them out.   She saw
us all out.   Please don't get up, I'll see myself out.   (b) (*last*)
This coat will have to see the winter out.   I doubt whether the
old man will see another year out.

see over vt fus (*inspect*) I'd like to see over the house.

see through 1 vt fus (a) (*Fig Fam: assess as false*) I can see through
his little scheme.   You can easily see through it.   (b) n cpd **a
see-through blouse**=a blouse which is transparent.   2 vt sep
(a) (*help through a difficult time*) I hope £10 will see you through.

Don't worry, I'll see you through. (*b*) (*bring to a conclusion*) He said he would see the project through.

see to *vt fus* (*a*) (*undertake, attend to*) He sees to the various needs of the community. I'll see to it that you are not inconvenienced. (Please) see to it (immediately). (*b*) (*mend, fix, repair*) These shoes need seeing to. Your cough ought to be seen to before it gets any worse.

see up 1 *vi* (*look upwards*) We could see up into the loft from the bottom of the stairs. 2 *vt sep* (*escort or conduct up*) He saw us up to the main office.

seek after *vt fus* (*Old: intensive of* **seek**) She is seeking after a better life.

seek out *vt sep* (*go to find, look hard for*) I sought him out in the older part of the town. He seeks out all the new arrivals at the hotel and offers his services as a guide.

seep away *vi* (*escape through seepage, drain slowly away*) The water took a week to seep away.

seep in *vi* (*get in through seepage; drain slowly in*) Water has begun to seep in through these boards.

seep out *vi* (*get out through seepage, drain slowly out*) The liquid is seeping out (of its container) into the ground.

seize up *vi* (*Tech: lock hard into position*) The engine has seized up. (*Fam*) His back seized up when he bent down.

seize (up)on *vt fus* (*Fig: grasp hold of; intensive of* **seize**) He seized upon my offer in desperation. They will seize upon any help they are given. He will seize upon any excuse not to go.

sell off *vt sep* (*Comm: liquidate*) He has sold off his business. Everything has been sold off to pay his debts.

sell out 1 *vi* (*a*) (*Comm: liquidate stock*) He has sold out and moved to another part of the country. Do you expect me to sell out just when things are beginning to go well? (*b*) (*Comm: have no further stocks*) We have sold out of cottonwool. *Variations:* (*i*) To be sold out of something=to have no further stocks of something. *Example:* We are sold out of cottonwool. (*ii*) To be sold out=to be no longer in supply. *Example:* This record is entirely sold out. (*c*) (*betray a cause, surrender*) They have sold out to the enemy. *n* a **sellout**=a betrayal. 2 *vt sep* (*a*) (*Fin Comm*) They have sold out their assets. (*b*) (*betray*) He has sold us out. We have been sold out to our worst enemies.

sell up 1 *vi* (*sell one's major assets*) They have sold up and gone. I'll just have to sell up now, to get some ready cash. 2 *vt sep* (*a*) (*force to sell*) His creditors have sold him up. (*b*) (*intensive of* **sell**) They sold up the property.

*send + particle   vt sep   (send, with direction) When he arrived I
   sent him in.   If you talk any more I shall have to send you out.
   He sent his sister up to see their mother who was in bed.   They
   sent the boy back with their reply.

send after   vt fus   (send someone to search for) I've sent after him and
   hope he'll get the message.

send along   vt sep   (Fam: intensive of send) Would you send them
   along to see me when they come.   Just send him along, please.

send away   vt sep   (a) see *send.   (b) (despatch) They sent the
   goods away immediately.   cf send off.   (c) (banish, send elsewhere) I sent him away because I was tired of his idle chatter.
   Idiom: to send someone away with flea in his ear=to send
   someone away after severely reprimanding him.   (d) Idiom:
   To send the children away to school=to put the children in
   a boarding school.

send away for   vt fus   (request by post) I've sent away for it.   He
   wants to send away for some books.

send back   vt sep   (a) see *send.   (b) (return) They sent the
   manuscript back without comment.

send back for   vt fus   (Mil: demand, as from forward to rear) The
   troops at the front sent back for reinforcements.

send down   vt sep   (a) see *send.   (b) (University: expel) He has
   been sent down for riotous behaviour.

send down for   vt fus   (request, as from above to below) He sent down
   for more paint.   The head office have sent down for stationery.

send for   vt fus   (summon, order) They sent for the doctor.   The
   boss has sent for me.   He sent for a pint of beer.

send forth   vt sep   (Old)=send out.

send in   vt sep   (a) see *send.   (b) (submit or despatch to an authority)
   He has sent in his report.   The correspondent sent in his
   despatches regularly.   He sent in his application immediately.

send in for   vt fus   (request, as from exterior to interior) The painters
   sent in for more paint.

send off   vt sep   (a) see *send.   (b)=send away 2 (b) and (c).
   (c) (see off, accompany or attend while departing) There was a large
   crowd to send him off.   n a send-off.   Example: The send-off
   was heart-warming.

send off for   vt fus=send away for.

send on   vt sep   (a) (post or despatch to a new address) I'll send on any
   letters that come for you.   She sent the parcel on in the hope
   that he would eventually get it.   (b) (cause to go on, usu Theatre
   Sport etc) They sent him on although he was ill.   You should

never have sent on so inexperienced a player. (c) (cause to move on) They sent the traveller on to the next village.

send out vt sep (a) see *send. (b) (despatch) They sent him out to get the newspaper. (c) (circulate) The company is sending out leaflets to all its contacts. (d) (emit, give out) This lamp sends out a powerful beam. This fire sends out a lot of heat. cf **send forth.** Some stars send out vast quantities of radiation. That radio transmitter sends signals out constantly.

send out for vt fus (request, as from interior to exterior) The workmen in the building sent out for some sandwiches.

send up vt sep (a) (cause to go up) They have sent up several space ships this year. The climbers sent two men up to investigate the rockfall. The distressed ship sent up a flare. (b) (Fig Fam: satirize) The students here love to send up the staff. n a **send-up**=a satire or mocking representation. (c) (blow up, explode) The terrorists sent the bridge up.

send up for vt fus (request, as from below to above) The men in the hole sent up for more equipment.

separate out vt sep (intensive of **separate**) They separated out the various elements in the problem.

serve out vt sep (a) (distribute while serving) The waiters served out the second course. She served out very ample helpings to her guests. (b) (serve to the end) The prisoners must serve out their time (in jail).

serve up vt sep (a) (Lit: serve or bring to the table) She served up the food piping hot. I don't like serving things up cold. Are you ready to serve up? (b) (Fig: provide, deliver) He serves up some powerful propaganda.

set about vt fus (a) (begin, start) He set about the work systematic-ally. She set about writing the essay. I don't know how to set about it. How do you set about a thing like that? (b) (attack) The gang set about him and injured him badly. They set about each other furiously.

set apart vt sep (a) (Lit: place separately) These objects should be set apart from the others. (b) (Fig Fam: differentiate) These qualities set him apart from the rest of the group.

set aside vt sep (a)=**set apart** (a). (b) (place to one side) She set the magazine aside for reading later. (c) (reject, dismiss as insignificant) He set our objections aside and continued un-affected. I am afraid we must set aside your request for more equipment. (d) (Law: annul, nullify) The supreme court has set aside the judgement of the lower court. The government has now set aside those decrees.

set back *vt sep* (a) (*hinder, delay*) This interference is going to set us back considerably. The accident has set them back several weeks. This trouble will set his recovery back if we are not careful. *n* **a setback**=a hindrance, a delay. (b) (*retard mechanically*) The clock has been set back. *Idiom:* To set the clock back 50 years=to lose 50 years of progress. (c) (*lay back*) The mule set back its ears and would not move. (d) (*position well back*) The house is set back from the road. The planners have set the estate (well) back from the railway and the main roads. (e) (*Fam: cost*) This new house will set him back quite a bit. That car must have set you back (a packet)!

set by *vt sep* (*Old*)=**set aside** (a) (b).

set down *vt sep* (a) (*put down*) The bus set him down outside the office. The passengers will be set down at platform three. (b) (*write, put down in writing*) He tried to set his ideas down. If I can set it all down on paper, I shall. (c) (*attribute*) We set it down to his laziness. He set her attitude down to shyness.

set forth 1 *vi*=**set off** 1. 2 *vt sep* (*lay out for inspection*) He set the plan forth in a report. She willingly set forth her opinions.

set in 1 *vi* (a) (*begin, start*) Winter has set in. The tide has set in. A strong wind has set in. Some kind of rot appears to have set in. *Idiom:* The rot has set in=things are no longer as good as they were. (b) (*specifically Med: begin*) An unexpected complication has set in. Gangrene has set in. 2 *vt sep* (a) (*fix in*) The workmen set the panels in very carefully. (b) (*Typography: move inward*) Would you set the type in from the edge of the page?

set off 1 *vi* (*depart on or begin a journey*) The men set off. I watched the expedition as it set off. He set off on a lonely journey. 2 *vt sep* (a) (*start*) He set the whole thing off. I don't want to be the one to set it off again. He set her off crying. (b) (*enhance*) This dress sets off her complexion very well. (c) (*oppose*) This situation sets one family off against the other. (d) (*ignite, explode*) They set off the bombs/fireworks.

set on *vt sep* (*Old: encourage to act or attack*) Stop setting him on! They will set the dogs on in a moment.

set out 1 *vi* (a)=**set off** 1. (b) (*intend, propose*) He set out to do a lot of things, but didn't succeed. 2 *vt sep* (*display*) The goods were set out on the table. He has set out his ideas very clearly. They set out all their reasons. He set out the chessmen on the board.

set to *vi* (a) (*start work*) He set to enthusiastically. She set to with a will and soon finished it. (b) (*quarrel, fight*) They set to in earnest. The two men set to furiously.

set up 1 *vi* (*establish oneself*) He set up as a doctor in a little seaside town. 2 *vt sep* (*a*) (*place in position*) The men set up their tents well before darkness fell. We shall set up camp here. He set up a little stall to sell hamburgers. They set up a First Aid Post on the beach. (*b*) (*start, establish*) He set up a school for poor children. The government has set up a number of new colleges. (*c*) (*institute*) The government has set up a tribunal to examine the problem. I think they should set up an enquiry. (*d*) (*propose, put forward*) He has set up a theory/model. (*e*) (*Sport: establish*) The athletes set up several new records. (*f*) *Idioms*: (*i*) To set up house=to establish one's own home. (*ii*) To set up shop=to start business (of any kind). *Example*: He set up shop as a solicitor/old clothes man/piano teacher. (*iii*) To set someone up=to enable someone to begin a career/to provide someone with excellent facilities. *Example*: His father set him up as a dentist when he left college. He set himself up as a dentist. (*iv*) He's all set up=he is in a very satisfactory position. (*v*) I've set it all up for you=I've prepared it all for you/I've made it easier for you. (*g*) (*reflexive: pose falsely*) He set himself up as a doctor. (*h*) (*cause*) This trouble has set up an irritation. Your behaviour will only set up a quarrel. (*i*) (*Typography: compose*) He has set the text up. (*j*) (*equip*) He has been set up with all he needs. (*k*) (*improve health of*) This tonic will set you up again. A holiday will set you up after your illness. (*l*) *n* **a set-up**=an organization, arrangement. *n phr* (*Fam*) **a funny set-up**=a strange arrangement.

set (up)on *vt fus* (*attack*) The thieves set upon him and beat him senseless.

settle down 1 *vi* (*a*) (*come to rest on the ground*) The dust slowly settled down. The airship settled down in a field. (*b*) (*get into a comfortable position*) She settled down to read her book. (*c*) (*apply oneself*) He has settled down to the job. It will be all right once you settle down and get to work. (*d*) (*establish a home*) They have settled down near London. It is time you settled down. (*e*) (*calm down, become reasonable*) The children have settled down now. The situation has settled down. When things have settled down, we can talk about it. Marriage has made him settle down.

settle in *vi* (*Fam: instal oneself*) The new family have settled in. I hope you are all settling in satisfactorily.

settle up 1 *vi* (*bring a matter to a conclusion*) It's time we settled up. I'll settle up with them soon. 2 *vt sep* (*intensive of* **settle**, *pay*) He settled up the outstanding bills. Let's settle the bill up together.

settle (up)on *vt fus* (*decide on*) They have settled upon a house near the river. I don't know what dress she finally settled **on**.

sew on *vt sep* (*sew into position*) She sewed the buttons **on**.

sew up *vt sep* (*sew as completely as possible, close by sewing*) (*a*) (*Lit*) She sewed the tear **up**. The seams have been sewn **up**. The surgeon sewed **up** the wound. The materials were sewn **up** in a sack. (*b*) (*Fig Fam: finalize satisfactorily, organize efficiently*) He has the whole matter sewn **up**. It's all sewn **up**.

shade in 1 *vi* (*a*) (*blend in or harmonize in easy stages*) The lights shade **in** beautifully. (*b*) (*Art: fill in with pencil, charcoal etc*) When he finished the outlines, he started shading **in**. 2 *vt sep* (*bring in by stages*) (*a*) (*Lit*) The technicians shaded the light **in**. (*b*) (*Fig*) I imagine you can shade your activities **in** gradually, without anyone noticing. (*c*) (*Art: fill in with pencil or charcoal etc*) When he finished the outlines, he started to shade **in** the rest.

shade off *vi* (*move by stages, in a continuum*) The reds slowly shade **off** into pink.

shake down 1 *vi* (*Sl: sleep*) Let's shake **down** here. 2 *vt sep* (*cause to fall by shaking*) He tried to shake the apples **down** from the tree.

shake off *vt sep* (*a*) (*remove by shaking*) The dog shook **off** the drops of water. He shook the dust **off**. (*b*) (*Fig Fam: get rid of*) I just can't shake **off** this cold. It's a pity you won't shake **off** these expensive habits. (*c*) (*get rid of, avoid, lose*) The horsemen shook **off** their pursuers. He thought he had shaken **off** the search party.

shake out *vt sep* (*a*) (*get out by shaking*) He shook the sweets **out** (of the bag). She shook the insects **out**. (*b*) (*loosen or straighten by shaking*) He shook **out** the empty sack. They shook **out** canvas. The sails were shaken **out**.

shake up *vt sep* (*a*) (*shake as fully as possible*) She shook **up** (the contents of) the bottle before pouring. She shook **up** the pillows. (*b*) (*disturb, agitate*) This news has shaken me **up** considerably. The death of her father shook her **up** more than she cares to admit. I feel rather shaken **up** after the accident. (*c*) (*revolutionize*) He thinks he will shake the place **up**. You complacent people need shaking **up**. *n phr* **a good shaking-up** =a desirable and rapid series of changes. (*d*) *n* **a shake-up**= a reorganization.

*shamble + particle *vi* (*shamble, walk heavily, slowly, with direction*) The great hairy creature shambled **along**. The tired prisoners shambled **in** to their cells. Tired and wounded soldiers were shambling **past** in the gathering darkness.

shape up 1 *vi* (*Fam: make progress*) These students are shaping **up**

well. He will shape up into an excellent footballer. *Idiom:* Things are shaping up well=things are progressing. 2 *vt sep* (*shape as well as possible, form*) (*a*) (*Lit*) The potter shaped up the vase. (*b*) (*Fig*) Try to shape up your work in the next few weeks.

share out *vt sep* (*share evenly, distribute, divide out*) They shared out the food carefully. The money has been shared out. *n* **a share-out.**

sharpen up 1 *vi* (*become sharp or sharper*) The wind is sharpening up. 2 *vt sep* (*make sharp or sharper*) (*a*) (*Lit*) The men sharpened up their knives. (*b*) (*Fig*) This tension certainly sharpens up one's senses. You need to sharpen up your wits!

shave off *vt sep* (*remove by shaving or planing*) He shaved off his beard. I think you should shave off your moustache. The carpenter shaved some wood off (with a plane).

shear off 1 *vi* (*come off completely, break off, become suddenly detached*) The wheel sheared off and fell to the ground. 2 *vt sep* (*a*) (*cut off with shears*) He sheared the wool off. (*b*) (*cut off, remove by cutting*) They sheared off the ragged edges.

sheer off *vi* (*a*) (*usu Naut: alter route to avoid collision or contact*) The ship sheered off at the last minute. (*b*) (*Fig: shy off, keep away*) He sheers off from hard work.

shell out (*Fig Fam: pay out too much, usu unwillingly*) 1 *vi* Do you expect me to shell out every time you want something? They must have shelled out to get that car. 2 *vt sep* He shelled out a lot to get that car.

*shepherd + particle *vt sep* (*guide like a shepherd, lead, usher, with direction*) He shepherded us in. She shepherded her guests out. The warden shepherded everyone over to the window.

*shift + particle 1 *vi* (*move house, with direction*) They have shifted away from this area. When the tenants left he shifted down to the flat below. 2 *vt sep* (*shift, transfer, with direction*) He shifted the luggage up to his flat. I think I'll shift this cupboard down to the living-room. He has shifted the rug away from the window.

shift away 1 *vi* (*a*) *see* ***shift.** (*b*) (*transfer one's attention or interest*) He has shifted away from this policy. 2 *vt sep* *see* ***shift.**

shin down *vi* (*climb down*) The boys shinned down from the roof.

shin up *vi* (*climb up*) He shinned up onto the roof.

shine away 1 *vi* (*shine continuously*) The lamp in the window shone away for hours. 2 *vt sep* (*shine to one side*) Please shine that light away (from my eyes).

shine down 1 *vi* (*shine from above*) The sun shone down. 2 *vt sep* (*cause to shine from above*) Shine the torch down here, please.

shine in 1 *vi* (*shine from outside*) The light shone in. 2 *vt sep* (*cause to shine from outside*) Shine the torch in, please.

shine on 1 *vi* (*a*) (*continue to shine*) The stars shone on into a pale morning. The sun shone on for hours in a cloudless sky. (*b*) (*shine on to a position*) The light shines on from over there and illuminates the stage. 2 *vt sep* (*cause to shine on to a position*) Shine the torch on so that we can read the labels.

shine out 1 *vi* (*a*) (*shine from inside*) The rays of a lamp shone out through the window. (*b*) (*shine suddenly*) A light shone out in the dark wall of the house. 2 *vt sep* (*cause to shine from inside*) Shine the torch out, please.

shine up 1 *vi* (*shine from below*) The light shone up. 2 *vt sep* (*a*) (*cause to shine from below*) Shine the torch up into the rafters, please. (*b*) (*shine or polish as much as possible*) He shone his shoes up till they gleamed. I think I'll go and shine up the car a bit.

ship off *vt sep* (*send off by ship*) The men were shipped off to the Far East. He shipped the goods off as soon as he could. We shall ship the consignments off to you immediately.

ship out *vt sep* (*send out by ship*) They are shipping soldiers out to the Middle East. We can ship as much out (to you) as you need.

*shoo + particle *vt sep* (*move by shouting or by signalling with the face, lips and hands, with direction*) She shooed the children out (of the kitchen). He shooed the birds away (from the grass seed). She shooed the kids in for their bath. Can't you shoo those wretched cats off?

*shoot + particle *vi* (*move very fast, like a shot, with direction*) The car shot along doing ninety. The sports car shot away from the starting line. The rocket shot up into the sky. (*Fam*) He shot over to speak to me as soon as I came in.

shoot away 1 *vi* (*a*) *see* ***shoot.** (*b*) (*shoot continuously*) The soldiers began shooting away at the enemy positions. 2 *vt sep* (*detach by shooting*) The artillery shot away the church spire and most of one wall.

shoot down 1 *vi* (*a*) *see* ***shoot.** (*b*) (*shoot from above*) The soldiers shot down into the ravine. 2 *vt sep* (*bring down by shooting*) The anti-aircraft guns shot down three enemy planes. The aeroplanes were shot down in flames. (*b*) (*Fig: criticize very severely*) Why did you shoot him down (in flames) like that?

shoot off 1 *vi* *see* ***shoot.** 2 *vt sep* (*a*)=**shoot away** 2. (*b*) *Idiom:* to shoot one's mouth off=to boast loudly and foolishly.

shoot out 1 *vi* (*a*) *see* *shoot. (*b*) (*grow out quickly*) The new growth is just shooting out. (*c*) (*shoot from inside*) The trapped men shot out through the windows at their attackers. 2 *vt sep* (*a*) (*get out by shooting*) We shot them out of their hiding places. (*b*) (*settle or bring to an end by shooting*) The two men decided to shoot it out. *n* **a shootout**=a final gun battle.

shoot up 1 *vi* (*a*) *see* *shoot. (*b*) (*fire upwards*) The soldiers shot up at the second storey windows. (*c*) (*grow rapidly*) The plants are just shooting up. That boy has shot up since we last saw him. 2 *vt sep* (*a*) (*send up rapidly*) They shot the projectile up into the sky. (*b*) (*Fam: attack and wreck by shooting*) Some gang came in and shot the place up. (*c*) *Idiomatic n* **upshot**=result *Example:* The upshot of the affair was rather sad.

shop around *vi* (*Fam: look around in shops, seeking the best bargain*) (*a*) (*Lit*) You should shop around a bit before making a decision. I shopped around till I got what I wanted at a price I could afford. (*b*) (*Fig*) He was shopping around to see what support he could get for his proposals.

shore up *vt sep* (*prop up or support*) (*a*) (*Lit*) The whole wall needs shoring up with timber. This canal bank has been shored up. (*b*) (*Fig*) This government may need shoring up before the end of the year. He expects us to shore up his inefficient firm.

shout down *vt sep* (*silence by shouting*) The angry audience shouted the speaker down. They like to shout down the opposition.

shout out 1 *vi* (*shout aloud*) He shouted out in delight/pain. 2 *vt sep* (*announce by shouting*) They shouted out the results of the game. He shouted the news out.

*shove + particle *vt sep* (*push, with direction*) The postman shoved the letters in. The boy shoved the toys out. She shoved the food away, untouched. They shoved the boxes along, one by one.

shove off 1 *vi* (*Fam: leave, usu casually*) Well, we'd better be shoving off. He shoved off about an hour ago. Oh, shove off! 2 *vt sep* *see* *shove.

shove over 1 *vi* (*Fam: move over, usu to make room*) Shove over, I want to sit down. 2 *vt sep* *see* *shove.

*shovel + particle *vt sep* (*move with a shovel or spade, with direction*) He shovelled the earth away. They shovelled more soil in till the hole was filled. The workmen shovelled the stuff out.

*show + particle *vt sep* (*show, conduct, with direction*) The usher showed us in to our seats. The guards showed the visitors out. We were shown up to the new office. They were taken to the house and shown over/round.

show off 1 *vi* (*Fam: boast, display oneself for approval*) She loves showing off. Oh, stop showing off! He shows off a lot. *n* **a show-off**=a person who engages in showing off. 2 *vt sep* (*a*) *see* *****show.** (*b*) (*Fam: display, exhibit, highlight*) This colour shows your complexion off to the best advantage. These lights show the place off very nicely.

show over *vt sep* *see* *****show.**

show round *vt sep* *see* *****show.**

show up 1 *vi* (*Fam: appear, turn up*) He showed up when we least expected him. She'll show up when it suits her. They showed up again in Brazil a year later. I didn't expect you to show up here. 2 *vt sep* (*a*) *see* *****show.** (*b*) (*Fam: humiliate, shame*) She likes to show people up in public. Don't show us up by wearing something absurd. He showed his parents up rather badly.

shrivel up *vi* (*curl and dry up, usu to die*) (*a*) (*Lit*) The leaves are shrivelling up because of the terrific heat. The plant just shrivelled up. It turned yellow and shrivelled up. (*b*) (*Fig*) I just shrivelled up when he looked at me. Do you expect me to shrivel up just because you criticize me?

shrug off *vt sep* (*reject or dismiss with a shrug*) He shrugged off their complaints. She just shrugged the whole matter off. Please don't just shrug this off!

*****shuffle + particle** *vi* (*shuffle, move without raising feet, with direction*) The old man shuffled in. The prisoners shuffled dejectedly past. Several miserable refugees shuffled over, looking for food.

shuffle off 1 *vi* *see* *****shuffle.** 2 *vt sep* (*Old: discard, get rid of*) (*a*) (*Lit*) The snake shuffles off its skin once a year. (*b*) (*Fig*) He shuffled off his old friends when he became famous.

*****shunt + particle** (*divert, with direction*) 1 *vi* A train shunted past. The engines shunted in and halted. 2 *vt sep* (*a*) (*Lit*) The men shunted the engines in. He shunted the train out from the sidings. (*b*) (*Fam*) Can you shunt those papers over, please? He shunted the stuff across to us for examination.

*****shuttle + particle** *vi* (*move to and fro, with direction*) The train shuttled back and forward. The goods wagons shuttled in and out. Papers keep shuttling around in this place.

shut away *vt sep* (*lock away, isolate*) The animals are shut away in that hut all day long. They feel very shut away in that remote little cottage. He is afraid that the doctor will shut him away in a mental hospital.

shut down (*close completely*) 1 *vi* The shop has shut down because of lack of trade. 2 *vt sep* (*a*) They have shut the shop down. The factory has been shut down (from lack of orders).

n a **shutdown**=a closure, a complete stoppage. (*b*) She shut the lid down.

shut in *vt sep* (*seal or lock in, enclose*) She feels rather shut in in this house. If you close that door you can shut the noise in.

shut off *vt sep* (*a*) (*stop, shut completely, prevent from functioning*) Would you shut the electricity off, please? The current has been shut off. They have shut off the water supply. (*b*) (*separate, isolate*) They feel shut off from all human contact on this island. We are really shut off here.

shut out *vt sep* (*exclude, lock out*) (*a*) (*Lit*) If you close that door, you can shut out the noise. Close the door and shut out that draught! They have been shut out from the house. He shut the cat out. (*b*) (*Fig*) She has tried to shut the memories out. I can't shut out the picture of the accident. You really can't shut him out of your life so easily. It's impossible to shut out all news from the outside world.

shut to *vt sep* (*Old: close firmly*) Shut the door to!

shut up 1 *vi* (*Sl: be quiet, stop talking*) I asked them to shut up and let us hear the radio. I wish she would shut up! Oh, (for goodness' sake) shut up! 2 *vt sep* (*close completely, but not necessarily forever*) They shut the house up and went abroad. The shop has been shut up (temporarily). It's time to shut up shop and go home. (*also used idiomatically:* Shut up shop= stop work or a service).

shy away *vi* (*a*) (*react against something through fear, aversion or shyness*) The horse shied away. Don't shy away, please. (*b*) (*Fam: avoid*) He shies away from problems.

****sidle** + **particle** *vi* (*move in a sideways fashion, with direction*) The beggar sidled up and asked for money. The thief sidled past and was gone before we knew what had happened. A strange-looking fellow sidled in.

sift out *vt sep* (*separate out by using a sieve; isolate by using a sieve*) (*a*) (*Lit*) The farmers sifted out the good seed. He sifted out the wheat from the chaff. (*b*) (*Fig*) The detectives tried to sift out the useful information from the irrelevant.

sign away *vt sep* (*lose by signing, usu without sufficient thought*) You have just signed away a fortune. He signed away all his rights to the invention.

sign in 1 *vi* (*indicate one's arrival by signing a register*) They signed in last night around eleven o'clock. 2 *vt sep* (*help gain admittance by signing*) He signed us in to his club. Can you find someone to sign me in?

sign on 1 *vi* (*a*) (*join by signing*) He signed on yesterday and will start work on Monday. (*b*) (*specifically, join the army by signing* *a document*) He signed on for nine years in the infantry. When did you sign on? (*c*) (*Radio: begin to broadcast, by using a particular call-sign*) It's time for you to sign on. This is your favourite disc jockey signing on. 2 *vt sep* (*engage as an employee*) They signed on a large number of casual labourers last week. I don't expect him to sign anyone on.

sign off 1 *vi* (*a*) (*Radio: end a broadcast by using a particular signal or other indicator*) This is your favourite announcer signing off for tonight. (*b*) (*Fam: end a letter by signing*) I've written far too much and had better sign off.

sign out 1 *vi* (*indicate one's departure by signing a register*) He signed out at ten this morning. 2 *vt sep* (*assist a departure by signing*) I'll sign them out and guarantee their good behaviour.

sign up 1 *vi*=**sign on** 1 (*a*). 2 *vt sep* (*a*)=**sign on** 2. (*b*) (*arrange a contract with*) He has signed up a new star for the series. They manage to sign up all the best performers.

silt up 1 *vi* (*become full of silt*) The harbour is slowly silting up. 2 *vt sep* (*cause to be full of silt*) The current is a major factor in silting up the harbour.

simmer away *vi* (*simmer continuously*) (*a*) (*Lit*) The milk in the pot has been simmering away for some time. (*b*) (*Fig*) She's simmering away with rage.

simmer down *vi* (*become slowly cooler after boiling*) (*a*) (*Lit*) The water has simmered down a bit, and you can use it. (*b*) (*Fig*) His temper has simmered down and you may be able to reason with him. Come on, simmer down!

sing away 1 *vi* (*sing continuously*) She sings away for hours. The birds were singing away in the trees. 2 *vt sep* (*remove or dismiss by singing*) Sing all your troubles away.

sing on *vi* (*continue to sing*) They sang on for hours after the main party broke up.

sing out 1 *vi* (*sing loudly*) (*a*) (*Lit*) The choirmaster urged them to sing out (for all they were worth). (*b*) (*Fam: shout out, perhaps melodiously*) She sang out when she heard the good news. 2 *vt sep* (*a*) (*Lit*) The choir sang the words out with great vigour. (*b*) (*Fig*) He sang out something about getting promotion.

sing up *vi* (*sing more loudly*) Sing up, sopranos, I can't hear you!

single out *vt sep* (*distinguish or pick out for special treatment*) We singled him out as one of the most talented students. You have been singled out from all the others for this job. I don't know why they keep singling me out for abuse. He seems to have been singled out for all the nasty jobs.

sink down *vi* (*a*) (*intensive of* **sink**) The sun slowly sank down in the west. She sank down on her knees. (b) (*go down as fully as possible*) He sank down out of sight when the enemy patrol came past.

sink in 1 vi (a) (*sink into something*) The mud was soft and our feet sank in. It's a dangerous bog and you could easily sink in over your head. (b) (*Fam: become understood*) Has your plight sunk in yet? I don't think the facts have really sunk in. My explanation took a long time to sink in. It hasn't sunk in. 2 vt sep (*cause to sink into something*) They sank the metal rods in before the concrete set.

sip up vt sep (*sip as fully as possible or until all gone*) The little girl sipped up the lemonade.

siphon off vt sep (*remove or transfer by means of a siphon*) (a) (*Lit*) Someone has siphoned off my petrol! (b) (*Fig*) The department is good at siphoning off funds from one area to another. They have siphoned the money off for their own use.

sit about/around vi (*sit doing nothing in particular*) He just sits about all day. I wish I could just sit about and dream.

sit back vi (a) (*sit well back, lean back while sitting*) He sat back in his chair and looked at me. Sit back and listen to this. (b) (*Fig Fam: keep out of the way, become a spectator*) Do you expect me to sit back and do nothing? They won't sit back and let you do it.

sit down vi (*take a seat*) He sat down in the most comfortable chair. Ask them to sit down. *Idiom:* To sit down under an insult = to accept an insult meekly.

sit in vi (a) (*sit in a place, for a special purpose*) She sits in for me sometimes, when I go shopping. He sits in with the patients while the nurse has a rest. (b) (*replace*) I shall sit in for you while you go to the shops. He's sitting in for his friend today. (c) (*demonstrate by sitting in a place*) Some of the students are sitting in at the Faculty Office. n a **sit-in** = a passive seated demonstration.

sit in on vt fus (*Fam: attend, usu as a visitor*) I'd like you to sit in on this meeting. She sat in on the whole debate.

sit on 1 vi (*continue to sit*) The group of demonstrators sat on till morning. She sat on until someone agreed to help. 2 vt fus (a) (*Fig Fam: repress, suppress*) They are sitting on that particular idea. (b) (*Fig Fam: persecute, keep in one's place*) The committee sat on him. I don't like being sat on by the authorities. (c) (*Fig Fam: guard, protect*) I'll sit on the stuff for a few days.

sit out 1 vi (*sit outside in the open air*) They sat out until the sun went in. 2 vt sep (a) (*attend by sitting, until completely finished*) I somehow managed to sit the meeting out. They sat out the play. (*b*) (*Dancing: not take part in*) I'll sit this dance out. May I sit this one out?

sit up 1 *vi* (*a*) (*sit upright*) She sat up in bed, listening. He told the children to sit up and not slouch. Sit up! (*b*) (*stay out of bed*) He sat up till three a.m., reading. They sat up all night talking. I sat up with her, discussing her problems. (*c*) *Idiom:* To make someone sit up (and take notice)=to astonish or surprise someone (into taking notice of you). 2 *vt sep* (*cause to sit up*) The little girl sat all her dolls up. She sat the baby up and tried feeding him.

size up *vt sep* (*Fig Fam: judge, assess*) It isn't easy to size up the situation. She sized him up pretty quickly, and decided to keep away from him.

skate over/round *vt fus* (*Fig Fam: minimize, ignore, avoid*) He always tries to skate over difficulties. You won't be able to skate round this one.

sketch in *vt sep* (*Art: add in by sketching, or roughly*) (*a*) (*Lit*) He sketched in the details. She sketched in a face. (*b*) (*Fig*) Let me sketch in a little more of our plans.

sketch out *vt sep* (*a*) (*Art: draw roughly*) He sketched out the general picture first. (*b*) (*Fig: outline, state in general terms*) He sketched out his plans, so that we had some idea of what he would do.

*skim + particle *vi* (*skim or move lightly, usu over a surface, with direction*) The hydrofoil skimmed along. Little boats were skimming back and forward across the lake. The water birds skimmed across.

skim off 1 *vi* *see* ***skim.** 2 *vt sep* (*remove from the surface*) (*a*) (*Lit*) She skimmed the cream off the milk. (*b*) (*Fig*) He always skims off the best students for his classes.

skim through *vt fus* (*read quickly through, read superficially*) I don't have time to do more than skim through the book. He skimmed through the essay (quickly).

*skip + particle *vi* (*hop, with direction*) She skipped up and down. The others were skipping about excitedly. She skipped past on her way to school.

skip across *vi* (*a*) *see* ***skip.** (*b*) (*Fig Fam: visit quickly, and perhaps briefly*) He skipped across to Spain.

skip off *vi* (*a*) *see* ***skip.** (*b*) (*Fig Sl: decamp, abscond, make off*) The accountant skipped off with the money.

skip over 1 *vi*=**skip across.** 2 *vt fus* (*pass over, omit, ignore*) I'll skip over your rudeness. Let's skip over these points and come to the main argument.

skip through 1 *vi* *see* ***skip.** 2 *vt sep*=**skim through.**

skirt round *vt fus* (*try to avoid, circumvent*) (*a*) (*Lit*) They skirted round the town and made for the hills. (*b*) (*Fig*) They usually prefer to skirt round problems rather than face them squarely.

skive off *vi* (*Sl: go away, to avoid work*) He has skived off somewhere. Trust him to skive off when we need him.

***skulk + particle** *vi* (*walk in a stealthly way, with direction*) These men have been skulking about again. He skulked in, looking truculent. I watched them skulk off into the bushes.

slack off 1 *vi* (*a*) (*make a cable loose*) Slack off! (*b*) (*Fig Fam: tire, slowly stop working*) Don't slack off (now), just as we are getting to the end. 2 *vt sep* (*loosen*) Slack off those ropes. He slacked off the cable.

slack up *vi* (*Fam: stop working so hard*) It's time to slack up a bit.

slacken off 1 *vi* (*a*) (*diminish*) The pressure has slackened off. The wind has slackened off now. (*b*) (*stop working so hard*) Why don't you slacken off a bit. 2 *vt sep* (*a*)=**slack off** 2. (*b*) (*reduce*) He slackened off the pressure.

slacken up 1 *vi* (*relax*) It's nice to slacken up after such an effort. 2 *vt sep* (*loosen*) They slackened up the ropes.

slam down *vt sep* (*put down violently*) He slammed the book down. She slammed down the money and walked out.

slam to (*close violently*) 1 *vi* The door slammed to. 2 *vt sep* She slammed the door to.

slap down *vt sep* (*a*)=**slam down.** (*b*) (*Fig Fam: reduce in stature or humiliate, as if by slapping*) It's time someone slapped him down.

slap on *vt sep* (*put on or apply carelessly or in thick quantities*) He slapped on the paint. She just slaps her make-up on.

slap-up *adj*=(*Fig Fam: excellent*) *Examples:* It was a slap-up meal. They went to a slap-up hotel.

slash back 1 *vi* (*Fig: economize severely*) The government has slashed back on its spending. 2 *vt sep* (*a*) (*return a blow with equal violence, usu a sword or knife*) The bandit slashed back at his attacker. (*b*) (*cut back violently*) They slashed the vegetation back with their machetes. (*c*) (*Fig: cut back or reduce violently*) The government has slashed back its spending.

slash down 1 *vi* (*come down violently*) The sword slashed down on his neck. 2 *vt sep* (*cut down violently*) They slashed the plants down indiscriminately.

slash off *vt sep* (*cut off violently*) The boy slashed off the heads of the flowers with a stick.

sleep away 1 *vi* (*sleep continuously*) The baby is sleeping away quietly. 2 *vt sep* (*pass by sleeping*) She slept the morning away.

sleep in *vi* (*stay in bed deliberately or involuntarily*) He is sleeping in this morning. I'm sorry, I slept in (this morning).

sleep off *vt sep* (*Fam: recover from, by sleeping*) He slept the party off. You'll feel better when you've slept it off. It is usually possible to sleep these things off, and feel better afterwards.

sleep on 1 *vi* (*continue to sleep*) He was so tired that he slept on into the afternoon. Oh, let her sleep on. 2 *vt fus* (*Fig Fam: have a rest from a problem and return to it later*) Let's sleep on it and try again tomorrow.

sleep out *vi* (*a*) (*sleep in the open air*) It's so warm I feel I could sleep out. Some vagrants have to sleep out even in winter. (*b*) (*sleep in a tent*) They like sleeping out.

slew round *vi* (*swing round, veer*) The ship slewed round into the wind. The car violently slewed round and hit the wall.

slice off *vt sep* (*remove by slicing*) He sliced off several pieces of meat. The machine sliced the ham off evenly.

slice up *vt sep* (*cut up into slices*) She sliced the sausage up. First you should slice up the meat and the onions.

slick up *vt sep* (*a*) (*make slick or shiny*) He slicked up his hair. (*b*) (*Fam: improve*) The comedian was told to slick up his act. (*c*) (*Fam: smarten up*) This whole house needs slicking up. He slicked up his appearance.

*slide + particle (*slide, with direction*) 1 *vi* The snow slid down. The ship slid past. The plunger slides in and out easily. It slides up and down without trouble, if oiled properly. 2 *vt sep* He slid the money over to me. They slid the injured man down on a sledge. He slid the gun out (of its holster).

slide off 1 *vi* (*a*) *see* ***slide.** (*b*) (*Fam: leave*) I'd better slide off now. 2 *vt sep* *see* ***slide.**

slim down 1 *vi* (*become thinner*) She has slimmed down consider ably. 2 *vt sep* (*make slimmer, reduce*) (*a*) (*Lit*) This exercise will slim you down. (*b*) (*Fig*) The government has slimmed its budget down considerably.

*sling + particle *vt sep* (*Fam: throw violently or casually, with direction*) He slung the box out. I asked him to sling the hammer over. She slung it away in disgust. The equipment had been slung aside almost unused.

sling out *vt sep* (*a*) *see* ***sling.** (*b*) (*Fam: evict*) They have been slung out by their landlord. (*c*) (*Fam: sack*) His boss threatened to sling him out.

sling up   *vt sep*   (*a*) see ***sling.**   (*b*) (*hang up in or with a sling*) The equipment had been slung up on the wall.

*slink + particle   *vi*   (*a*) (*slink or move stealthily, with direction*) The cat slunk past.   A leopard slunk along through the undergrowth.   (*b*) (*move guiltily*) He had slunk in and sat in a corner. I watched them slink off unhappily.   Don't let him slink away.   *Idiom:* To slink off/out with your tail between your legs = to go away chastened or humbled, like a beaten dog.

*slip + particle   (*move gently, quickly and lightly, with direction*)   1 *vi* The boat slipped down into the water.   She slipped out to meet him.   He slipped in unobserved.   They slipped away together.   I'll slip back and get it.   2 *vt sep*   She slipped the ring off.   He slipped the message out through the window. He slipped the clutch in.   She slipped the dress on.

slip down   1 *vi*   (*a*) see ***slip.**   (*b*) (*slide down, usu accidentally*) He slipped down into the hole.   The paper slipped down between the seat and the back of the chair.   2 *vt sep*   see ***slip.**

slip up   1 *vi*   (*a*) see ***slip.**   (*b*) (*Fam: make a mistake or gaffe*) You slipped up over that problem.   He keeps slipping up on simple things.   Be careful you don't slip up through over-confidence. *n* **a slip-up** = a mistake.   2 *vt sep*   see ***slip.**

*slither+particle   *vi*   (*move in a sliding, slippery way, with direction*) The snake slithered along.   He slithered in like a snake.   The creature slowly slithered away.

slog away   *vi*   (*Fam: work away laboriously, slog continuously*) He has been slogging away for hours over his homework.   The athletes slogged away till exhausted.   She slogs away at her work.

slog on   *vi*   (*continue to slog or work laboriously*) He slogged on with his homework.   They slogged on until exhausted.

slop about   (*splash about*)   1 *vi*   The paint was slopping about in the bucket.   2 *vt sep*   Don't slop the milk about like that!

slop over   *vi*   (*splash or spill over*) The liquid slopped over on to the floor.

slope away   *vi*   (*continue in a slope*) The land slopes away towards the sea.

slope down   *vi*   (*go down in a steady slope or incline*) The land slopes down all the way to the river.

slope off   *vi*   (*Fig Fam: go away usu casually*) He sloped off somewhere with his friends.   Don't just slope off and leave us!

slosh about   1 *vi*   (*a*) = **slop about.**   1 (*b*) (*splash about*) He was sloshing about in the mud.   2 *vt sep* = **slop about** 2.

*slouch + particle *vi* (*move in a slouch, or slackly, with direction*) The boys slouched off sulkily. He slouched in, looking for trouble. Stop slouching about doing nothing!

slough off *vt sep* (*cast off, discard*) (*a*) (*Lit*) Snakes slough off their skins once a year. (*b*) (*Fig*) It's a habit he should slough off.

slow down 1 *vi* (*begin to slow, decelerate*) (*a*) (*Lit*) The car slowed down. The machine slowed down and stopped. (*b*) (*Fig*) You should slow down a bit and lead a less hectic life. (*c*) (*become slow, usually through age or illness*) He has slowed down a lot since his heart attack. 2 *vt sep* (*cause to slow or decelerate*) (*a*) (*Lit*) He slowed the car down as they approached the traffic lights. Can you slow this thing down? (*b*) (*Fig*) Their objections are slowing down the progress of the negotiations. This strike will slow down everything. *n* **a slowdown.**

slow up = slow down.

slug out *vt sep* (*Boxing: fight out steadily to the end*) The two men stood there and slugged it out. Go in and slug it out (with him)!

slump down *vi* (*collapse*) He slumped down dejectedly in a chair.

slump over *vi* (*collapse and fall*) When he touched the dead body, it slumped over on to the floor.

smarten up 1 *vi* (*become smart or smarter*) He has smartened up a lot in his general appearance. You have smartened up considerably. 2 *vt sep* (*make smart or smarter*) They have smartened the old house up a lot. I wish she would smarten herself up (and take a pride in her appearance).

smash in *vt sep* (*a*) (*break in violently*) The thieves had smashed the door in. (*b*) (*beat in violently*) The gang threatened to smash his face in.

smash up *vt sep* (*a*) (*break up violently, wreck*) The gang smashed the place up. The whole shop was smashed up. (*b*) (*crash and wreck*) He has smashed up his new car. *n* **a smash-up** = a collision, crash.

smell out *vt sep* (*find by the sense of smell*) (*a*) (*Lit*) The dogs smelled the fox out. The witch-doctor claimed to be able to smell out evil spirits. (*b*) (*Fig*) He says he can smell out trouble before it starts.

smoke out *vt sep* (*force out of a place by using smoke*) The soldiers smoked the enemy out of their hiding-places. The escaped convicts were smoked out of the house.

smooth away *vt sep* (*smooth until gone or alleviated*) She smoothed the wrinkles away. Her touch seemed to smooth away all his problems.

smooth back   *vt sep*   (*smooth and push back into position*) She smoothed back her hair from her forehead.

smooth down   *vt sep*   (*smooth or caress to lie flat*) (*a*) (*Lit*) He smoothed the fur down.   She smoothed her hair down.   (*b*) (*Fig*) I hope he can smooth the whole matter down.

smooth out   *vt sep*   (*smooth until flat*) (*a*) (*Lit*) She smoothed the creases out with an electric iron.   (*b*) (*Fig*) She is good at smoothing these little problems out.   I will try to smooth things out.

smooth over   *vt sep*   (*Fig Fam: make smooth, put right*) He was asked to smooth things over between them.   It will be difficult to smooth matters over now.

smuggle in   *vt sep*   (*bring in by smuggling, introduce illegally into a place*) The brandy was smuggled in.   They smuggled in some food for the prisoners.   A lot of opium is smuggled in every year.

smuggle out   *vt sep*   (*get out by smuggling, take out illegally*) The goods have been smuggled out by sea.   They smuggled him out before the police could stop them.

smuggle through   *vt sep*   (*get through by smuggling, or secretly and illegally*) The attempt to smuggle the diamonds through was a failure.   They hope to smuggle the guns through to their comrades.

snap at   *vt fus*   (*Fig: speak angrily to*) She snapped at him when he asked her what she was going to do.   Don't snap at me like that!

snap off   1 *vi*   (*break off sharply*) The branch snapped off.   2 *vt sep* (*a*) (*break off sharply*) He snapped the branch off.   (*b*) (*Mil: shoot, fire*) The sniper snapped off six rapid shots.   (*c*) (*Photo: take*) He snapped off several frames.

snap out   *vt sep*   (*say or speak sharply*) He snapped out an angry reply.

snap up   *vt sep*   (*Fig Fam: grab quickly*) He snapped up the offer. If there are any bargains going, she'll snap them up.

snarl up   *vt sep*   (*usu pass: mix or tangle up, confuse*) The wool is all snarled up.   The traffic gets snarled up very often at that roundabout.   *n* a **snarl-up.**

snatch up   *vt sep*   (*pick up quickly and/or roughly*) He snatched up some food and ran.   She snatched up the baby before she fled. The soldiers snatched up their rifles and prepared to fire.

*sneak + particle   (*sneak or move secretively, with direction*)   1 *vi* The thief sneaked quietly up.   Shadowy figures were sneaking along near the house.   I saw someone sneak away.   2 *vt sep* He

sneaked the girl away.   I expect she'll try to sneak some friends
in (to the party).   Don't sneak any liquor out!

sniff out   *vt sep* = **smell out.**

snip off   *vt sep*   (*cut off quickly and/or lightly*) She snipped some hair
off with a small pair of scissors.

snow in   *vt sep*   (*usu pass: surround with snow, and prevent from moving*)
The village has been snowed in for a week.   We were snowed
in for several days.

snow under   *vt sep*   (*Fig Fam usu pass: overload*) The firm is snowed
under with work.   We really are snowed under with new orders.

snow up   *vt sep*   (*usu pass: cover completely with snow*) The whole area
is snowed up.   The convoy was snowed up on the main road.
The mountain passes are snowed up.

snuff out   *vt sep*   (*extinguish completely*) (*a*) (*Lit*) They snuffed out
the candles.   Snuff out the lights.   (*b*) (*Fig Fam*) The men who
attacked that hill were snuffed out by machine-gun fire.

snuggle down   *vi*   (*sink and wriggle down comfortably*) Snuggle down
here beside me.   The children snuggled down in their beds.

snuggle in = **snuggle down.**

snuggle up   *vi*   (*come close for comfort*) She snuggled up to him.
Snuggle up and I'll tell you a story.

soak in   *vi*   (*permeate into every part*) The water has soaked in.   Put
some liquid on and let it soak in naturally.

soak up   *vt sep*   (*a*) (*Lit: draw up*) Sponges soak up water.   (*b*)
(*Fig Fam: learn quickly, absorb as much as possible*) She soaks up
everything you tell her.   The students soak it all up.   Don't
soak up everything uncritically.

soap down   *vt sep*   (*clean down with soap*) She soaped herself down
before getting into the bath.

soar away/off   *vi*   (*fly high into the distance*) The balloon soared
away on the wind.

soar up   *vi*   (*fly high, rise up with a rush*) The birds soared up into
the sky.   The balloon soared up on a gust of wind.

sob away   *vi*   (*sob continuously*) She has been sobbing away for
hours.

sob out   *vt sep*   (*say or tell while sobbing*) She sobbed out her account
of the accident.   *Idiom:* To sob one's heart out = to weep
bitterly.

sober up   1 *vi*   (*a*) (*become sober after being drunk*) He has sobered up.
She'll need time to sober up.   (*b*) (*become steady, serious or
reliable after a period of wildness*) That young fellow has begun to

sober up.   When on earth will you sober up?   2 *vt sep*   (*a*)
(*make sober after being drunk*) This shock will sober him up.
Drink this, it may sober you up enough to get home.   (*b*) (*make steady and reliable*) His father's death has sobered him up a lot.

soften up 1 *vi* (*become soft*) (*a*) (*Lit*) The material has begun to
soften up.   (*b*) (*Fig*) Her attitude has softened up a lot.   2
vt sep   (*make soft*) (*a*) (*Lit*) He softened up the plasticine with his
fingers.   (*b*) (*Fig*) If you talk to her nicely, you may manage to
soften her up.   Enemy resistance has been softened up by the
artillery bombardments.   Torture can soften a prisoner up and
make him co-operate.   *n cpd* **a softening-up process.**

soldier on *vi* (*Fam: carry on like a dutiful soldier, keep on working
steadily, persevere*) Well, it isn't easy, but we'll soldier on.   He'll
soldier on whatever happens.

sop up *vt sep* (*take up by soaking*) She sopped the gravy up with
bread.   They sopped up the water with cloths.

sort out *vt sep* (*a*) (*separate, arrange in classes*) He sorted out the
different kinds of flowers.   Can you sort these boxes out, please?
These things will take some sorting out!   (*b*) (*Sl: punish, be
avenged on*) Send the army in and sort the swine out.   This
should sort them out once and for all.   I'll sort you out (if you
aren't careful)!

sound off *vi* (*a*) (*sound a bugle*) The bugler sounded off.   Bugler,
sound off!   (*b*) (*Fam: boast*) He keeps sounding off about his
exploits in the Far East.

sound out *vt sep* (*test, check the opinions of*) Can you sound your
friends out and see whether they will help?   He will sound
them out for us.

soup up *vt sep* (*Sl: make more powerful*) He has souped the engine
up a lot.   He drives a souped-up version of this car.

space out *vt sep* (*arrange in regular spaces*) The foresters spaced the
seedlings out in rows.   Try to space the work out properly.

spark off *vt sep* (*Fig Fam: ignite, cause*) His speech seems to have
sparked off a real argument.   The management's attitude may
spark off a series of strikes.

speak for *vt fus* (*represent*) He says he will speak for us at the
committee meeting.   Have you got anyone to speak for you?

speak out 1 *vi* (*intensive of speak*) I expect you to speak out
against tyranny when the time comes.   He spoke out in favour
of reforms.   2 *vt sep* (*state, enunciate*) Speak it out clearly.   He
always speaks out his part in a ringing voice.

speak up *vi* (*speak louder*) The teacher asked the shy little girl to
speak up.   Would you please speak up, as we can't hear you?

Speak up!

*speed + particle (*speed with direction*) 1 *vi* The car sped along. The police cars came speeding past. The boys on their motorbikes were speeding up and down outside. 2 *vt sep* Would you speed the goods through to us immediately. I'll speed it over as soon as I get it. Speed the work along, please.

speed up 1 *vi* (*a*) *see* ***speed** (*with past participle* **sped**). (*b*) (*increase in speed, with past participle* **speeded**) The car speeded up to a hundred kilometres per hour. 2 *vt sep* (*increase in speed, with past participle* **speeded**) Can you speed things up at all? I asked them to speed the delivery up.

spell out *vt sep* (*a*) (*spell aloud*) He spelt out the names. (*b*) (*Fam: state clearly and fully*) The judges spelt out the consequences of a crime of this kind. Let me spell it out for you in words of one syllable. I wish someone would spell the proposals out for us.

spice up *vt sep* (*a*) (*add spices to*) She has spiced the soup up. I like spiced-up food. This dish has really been spiced up. (*b*) (*Fig Fam: brighten up, enliven*) Some music might spice the party up a bit. Let's spice things up!

spill out (*scatter out, pour out*) 1 *vi* The contents of the box spilled out on the floor. Careful the stuff doesn't spill out! 2 *vt sep* She spilled out the contents of the box onto the floor.

spill over *vi* (*overflow, pour over*) (*a*) (*Lit*) The milk in the pot boiled up and spilled over. (*b*) (*Fig*) The populations of many big cities have spilled over into the adjoining countryside. *n* **overspill**=excess population. *n cpd* **population overspill, overspill housing, overspill estate.**

*spin + particle 1 *vi* (*move while spinning, with direction*) The disc went spinning away into space. The wheel spun out of the door. 2 *vt sep* (*spin, with direction*) She spun the thread back. They spun the thread out. I want you to spin the fibres in (to the pattern). Spin the thread on at this end.

spin along *vi* (*a*) *see* ***spin** (*b*) (*Old Sl: go quickly along*) They were spinning along at fifty mph.

spin away 1 *vi* (*a*) *see* ***spin** (*b*) (*spin continuously*) She spins away for hours. (*c*) (*recoil or turn suddenly away*) The man spun away under the force of the blow. (*d*) (*move away, spinning*) The disc went spinning away into space. 2 *vt sep see* ***spin.**

spin off 1 *vi* (*a*) (*come off a reel*) The thread spun off at a terrific speed. (*b*) *see* ***spin** 2 *vt sep* (*a*) *see* ***spin.** (*b*) (*Fig: have as an addition*) When the work is finished, we should be able to spin off a few extras. *n* **a spin-off**=an unexpected bonus, an extra application.

spin out 1 *vi* (*come out on a reel*) The thread spun out quickly. 2 *vt sep* (*a*) *see* **spin.* (*b*) (*Fig Fam: extend, prolong*) He enjoys spinning a story out (for as long as possible). Don't spin it out any longer.

spiral down *vi* (*go down in a spiral*) (*a*) (*Lit*) The burning plane spiralled down into the sea. The stairs spiralled down into the depths of the building. (*b*) (*Fig*) Profits began to spiral down disastrously.

spiral up *vi* (*go up in a spiral*) (*a*) (*Lit*) The structure spiralled up towards the ceiling. (*b*) (*Fig*) Profits are spiralling up steadily.

spirit away *vt sep* (*remove by some mysterious means*) Someone seems to have spirited the documents away. Don't let anyone spirit you away until I get there.

spirit off=**spirit away.**

spit out *vt sep* (*a*) (*eject by spitting*) He spat the food out. It tasted bad, so she spat it out. (*b*) (*say or tell as if or while spitting*) She spat out her hatred. He spat the story out with bitter anger.

*splash + particle *vi* (*move with splashing as an accompaniment, with direction*) He splashed along through the puddles. The boy splashed back across the stream. They splashed away in the pouring rain. A big car splashed past, the spray soaking us.

splash down *vi* (*a*) *see* **splash.* (*b*) (*specifically, land in the sea*) The lunar capsule splashed down in the Pacific. The returning astronauts splashed down safely. *n* **a splashdown**=a landing in the sea (usu planned).

split on *vt fus* (*Sl: betray*) I'll never split on you! They split on us to the police.

split up 1 *vi* (*Fam: separate*) The team has split up. They split up some time ago, and are seeking a divorce. It's a pity when friends split up over trifles. *n* **a split-up**=a quarrel. 2 *vt sep* (*a*) (*divide*) They split up the work between them. We can split the food up. (*b*) (*separate*) I don't want to split a good team up. He split them up, and is being cited in the divorce proceedings. We must split up the twins to allow them to develop as individuals.

sponge down *vt sep* (*clean down with a sponge or by sponging with a cloth*) He sponged himself down rather than have a full bath. She sponged the sick child down and put her to bed.

sponge out *vt sep* (*clean out with a sponge*) She sponged the wound out gently.

sponge up *vt sep* (*clear up with a sponge*) He sponged up the mess on the floor.

sponge (up)on *vt fus* (*Sl: seek money from, live parasitically on*) She enjoys sponging upon them. Stop sponging upon us! He sponges shamelessly on his old parents.

spoon out *vt sep* (*ladle or serve out with or as though with a spoon*) (a) (*Lit*) She spooned out the syrup. (b) (*Fig*) (*Fam*) Stop spooning out second-rate propaganda.

spout out *vt sep* 1 *vi* (*come out in spouts or jets*) The water spouted out from the hole. 2 *vt sep* (*emit in spouts or jets*) (a) (*Lit*) The whale spouted out water. (b) (*Fig*) They spout out propaganda from that radio station.

spout up *vi* (*pour up in spouts or jets*) Lava spouted up from the erupting volcano.

spray on *vt sep* (*put on by spraying*) They sprayed the paint on. Spray on some weed-killer. You spray this hair lacquer on.

spray out 1 *vi* (*emerge in a spray or shower*) The water sprayed out of the nozzle of the hosepipe. 2 *vt sep* (*release in a spray or shower*) When he laughed he sprayed out the food in his mouth.

spread about, around 1 *vi* (*scatter, spread widely*) The papers were spread about on the desks and even on the floor. 2 *vt sep* (*disseminate, publicize*) Would you spread the news about that he is coming? They don't want the story spread around.

spread abroad *vt sep* (*Old: disseminate, publicize*) He has spread the news abroad that you are leaving. Spread it abroad!

spread out 1 *vi* (a) (*extend*) The wood spread out in all directions. (b) (*disperse, scatter*) The men spread out over a wide area. Spread out! (c) (*Comm: develop*) The business is spreading out in all directions. 2 *vt sep* (*stretch, extend*) He spread out his arms and legs. Spread the cloth out fully. They spread the payments out over three years. The resources are spread out too thin.

***spring + particle** *vi* (*leap lightly, with direction*) He sprang out at us. The animal sprang quickly away. She sprang back in alarm. The man sprang across to help me.

spring up *vi* (a) see ***spring**. (b) (*start to grow*) Weeds are springing up in the garden. New life was springing up everywhere. (c) (*begin*) Rumours have sprung up about us. Doubts sprang up in his mind. A friendship sprang up between them. A cool wind sprang up. Storms spring up easily in this region. (d) (*Fam: happen*) Something rather odd has sprung up. Well, these things spring up now and again.

sprinkle on *vt sep* (*put on lightly in droplets*) The priest sprinkled the holy water on. Sprinkle the liquid on carefully.

sprinkle out *vt sep* (*pour out lightly in droplets*) She sprinkled some water out. He sprinkled the liquid out carefully.

*sprint + particle *vi* (*run very fast, with direction*) The athletes sprinted past. He sprinted in, the winner. Several young men sprinted up to meet us.

sprout out *vi* (*burst out or grow*) Greenery has sprouted out in the derelict land behind the factory. Hairs sprouted out from his nostrils.

sprout up *vi* (*grow up quickly, rampantly*) Grass has sprouted up everywhere. Weeds are sprouting up.

spruce up 1 *vi* (*make oneself look better*) He has spruced up for the interview. 2 *vt sep* (*make look better*) He has spruced himself up for the interview. Let me spruce you up a bit.

spur on *vt sep* (*a*) (*Lit: goad with spurs*) He spurred the animal on to greater effort. The cavalry spurred their horses on. (*b*) (*Fig: encourage, exhort*) They spurred him on to greater effort. This success will only serve to spur her on.

spurt out *vi* (*come out in spurts or intermittent jets*) The water spurted out when he turned the tap. Blood was spurting out of the wound.

spurt up *vi* (*come up in spurts or intermittent jets*) Water spurted up out of the ground. The geysers spurted up at regular intervals.

sputter out *vi* (*go out in a series of flickers*) The fire sputtered out unattended. The candle sputtered out in the draught.

spy out *vt sep* (*study as a spy*) He was sent to spy out enemy positions. They spied out the exact location of the mortar. *Idiom:* To spy out the land = to study conditions.

squabble away *vi* (*quarrel continuously*) That couple squabble away all the time.

squander away *vt sep* (*waste completely, dissipate*) He has squandered away a fortune at cards. You seem to have squandered away every opportunity you ever got!

square up 1 *vi* (*a*) (*Boxing: stand face to face*) The fighters squared up and began to trade blows. (*b*) (*face*) The little boy bravely squared up to his tormentors. You'll have to square up to your problems. (*c*) (*clear one's debts*) Well, we've squared up (with him) at last. 2 *vt sep* (*a*) (*make square*) The outlines in the drawing had been squared up. The carpenter squared up the sides of the cupboards he was making. (*b*) (*settle*) I'll square the matter up for you. Who'll square up the damage he has done?

*squash + particle *vt sep* (*squash or squeeze strongly, with direction*) He squashed the earth down with his foot. The hat has been squashed in.

squat down   *vi*   *(settle down on one's heels)* The villagers squatted down to wait in the shade of a palm tree.   He squatted down and began to examine the soil.

*****squeeze + particle**   *(squeeze, with direction)*   1 *vi*   They squeezed along through the crowd.   Someone managed to squeeze past. He squeezed in before we could stop him.   2 *vt sep*   She squeezed the toothpaste out.   They managed to squeeze all the clothes in (to the suitcase).   They squeezed themselves through.

squeeze off   1 *vi*   *see* *****squeeze.**   2 *vt sep*   *(a) see* *****squeeze.**   *(b)* *(Mil: fire by squeezing the trigger)* The soldier squeezed off several rounds at the enemy patrol.

*****squelch + particle**   *vi*   *(move with a sucking sound of the feet, with direction)* The men squelched along through the mud.   He squelched in with his boots oozing dirty water.   They squelched away through the swamp.

*****squirm + particle**   *vi*   *(move with rapid wriggling actions, with direction)* The snake squirmed out of his hand.   The little boy squirmed about until he was released.   A man was squirming in through the window.

*****squirt + particle**   *vt*   *(squirt or send in thin jets, with direction)* He squirted the water in.   Squirt some water on here.   The elephant squirted the water up into the air.

stack up   *vt sep*   *(a)* *(pile up in stacks, heap up)* They stacked the blocks up against the wall.   Stack the materials up here.   *(b)* *(Fam: acquire, accumulate)* He has stacked up considerable profits in the last few months.

*****stagger + particle**   *vi*   *(move unsteadily, with direction)* The drunk man staggered along.   Several exhausted soldiers staggered in. He staggered off in a delirium.   He had enough strength to stagger out and collapse in the road.

stake out   *vt sep*   *(a)* *(mark out with stakes or wooden poles)* They staked out the area on which they intended to build.   The land has already been staked out.   *(b)* *(Fig: delineate, demarcate)* He has staked out his area of command.   The field of operations has been staked out.   *Idiom:* To stake out a claim (to . . .)=to assert one's entitlement (to . . .).

*****stalk + particle**   *vi*   *(walk stiffly, with direction)* He stalked past angrily, without looking at us.   She stalked off somewhere in a huff.   A superior-looking ostrich stalked along through the bush. A local official stalked up and demanded our passports.

stammer out   *vt sep*   *(say or tell while stammering)* She stammered out an excuse that no one could really believe.   He stammered out something about hoping he wasn't a nuisance.

*****stamp + particle**   *vi*   *(walk while stamping the feet, with direction)*

He stamped out in a rage. They stamped in, shouting and laughing. Armed men stamped past.

stamp on *vt sep* (*place on by means of a stamp*) The name of the company has been stamped on. Stamp the code numbers on.

stamp out 1 *vi* *see* ***stamp.** 2 *vt sep* (*a*) (*produce by a stamping process*) The machine stamps out various patterns on metal. (*b*) (*eradicate, destroy utterly*) We must stamp out this kind of crime. The defenders were stamped out in the last attack.

stand about/around *vi* (*stand idly in a particular area*) The unemployed men were just standing about with their hands in their pockets. Don't stand around doing nothing.

stand aside *vi* (*stand out of the way*) (*a*) (*Lit*) Stand aside and let us past! He just stood aside and allowed it to happen. (*b*) (*Fig*) I hope you don't expect me just to stand aside and allow this? He stood aside meekly when the new policy was proposed.

stand back *vi* (*stand to the rear, keep clear*) The policeman asked the spectators to stand (well) back. Stand back!

stand by *vi* (*a*) (*stand near but without involving oneself*) He stood by and watched. I hope you don't expect me to stand idly by while this happens? *Idiomatic n:* **a bystander**=person who watches but takes no part. (*b*) (*be prepared*) I told them to stand by for action. Stand by! *n* **a stand-by**=(*i*) a supporter. (*ii*) something which supports or helps; a remedy. (*iii*) a substitute. *n cpd* **stand-by passengers**=passengers waiting in the hope of obtaining cancelled places. *Idiom:* To keep something as a stand-by=to keep something in reserve.

stand down 1 *vi* (*a*) (*surrender one's place*) The second candidate has agreed to stand down. I am not going to stand down for him. (*b*) (*Mil: come off the alert*) The defenders stood down after the enemy disappeared. He ordered the men to stand down. The militia stood down. (*c*) (*Law: leave the witness box*) He asked the witness to stand down. 2 *vt sep* (*Mil: take off the alert, return to normal duties*) The militia was stood down. Stand those men down now, sergeant.

stand for *vt fus* (*a*) (*represent*) This symbol stands for strength and integrity. What on earth do these signs stand for? (*b*) (*tolerate, accept*) I won't stand for this nonsense (any longer) She stands for a lot of abuse from those children. (*c*) (*offer oneself as a candidate*) He is standing for parliament. They are standing for re-election. He is standing for chairman.

stand in *vi* (*replace, substitute oneself for, act as a substitute for*) She is standing in tonight. He said he would stand in for me any time. They are standing in while the others are unable to take part. *n* **a stand-in**=a person acting as a substitute.

stand in with   *vt fus*   (*Old: be in conspiracy with, be associated with*) He stands in with those people.

stand off   *vi*   (*Naut: keep or stay at a distance*) The ships stood off and waited for orders.   The two fleets were standing off from each other.   *Idiomatic adj* **stand-offish**=haughty, snobbish, distant.

stand out   *vi*   (*a*) (*step forward*) He ordered the soldier to stand out.   Stand out!   (*b*) (*project, protrude*) The stonework stands out from the rest of the wall.   (*c*) (*be conspicuous by contrast*) The primary colours stand out clearly from the others.   The bold print stands out very well.   Due to his height, he stands out in a crowd.   Her talents stand out in comparison with the others.   (*d*) (*hold out, continue resisting*) The garrison will stand out for some time.   He says he will stand out against this oppression. The workers are standing out for higher wages and better conditions.

stand over   1 *vi*   (*wait*) The project is to stand over till next year. 2 *vt fus*   (*supervise*) He works better when someone is standing over him.   I hate having someone standing over me all the time.

stand to   *vi*   (*prepare for action*) He told his men to stand to. Stand to!

stand up   1 *vi*   (*a*) (*stand erect, become erect*) He told the men to stand up straight.   She stood up when they came in.   (*b*) (*Law: resist attack*) This case will stand up (in court) all right. I'm afraid it won't stand up in court.   2 *vt sep*   (*a*) (*place in a standing position*) He stood the statue up in a corner.   Stand it up over here.   (*b*) (*Sl: fail to meet as agreed*) She often stands her boy-friends up.   Don't stand me up again!   (*c*) *Idiomatic n cpd* (*Lit* and *Fig*) **a stand-up fight**=a straight fight without subtlety.

stand up for   *vt fus*   (*defend, extol*) He stands up for women's rights.   Always stand up for your principles.   Will you stand up for me?

stand up to   *vt fus*   (*a*) (*resist, face*) The little boy stood up to the big bully.   Stand up to them!   (*b*) (*Fig: resist, survive*) Your report won't stand up to close scrutiny.   His position doesn't stand up to detailed examination.   Wool stands up to certain treatment better than other fibres.

stare out   1 *vi*   (*gaze outward*) She stared out over the sea.   They were staring out of the window.   2 *vt sep*   (*defeat by staring*) He stared the other fellow out.   Stop trying to stare me out. *cf* **outstare**.

staple together   *vt sep*   (*fix together by means of a staple or staples*) She stapled the pages together.

start back *vi* (*a*) (*start a return journey*) It's late, so we'd better start back now. They started back immediately when they got the news. (*b*) (*recoil, move back suddenly*) She started back in fear when she saw them. The noise made him start back.

start off 1 *vi* (*a*) (*begin a journey*) They started off at dawn next day. Don't start off without telling me. (*b*) (*begin*) I'll start off by using this piece of wood. The story-teller started off by describing a beautiful princess. (*c*) (*move quickly away*) A hare started off into the forest. 2 *vt sep* (*begin*) Let's start the party off with a song. He started the story off by describing a lovely princess.

start out *vi* = **start off** 1 (*a*).

start up 1 *vi* (*a*) (*jump or leap up suddenly*) A hare started up at his feet and raced off. He started up in alarm. (*b*) (*begin functioning*) The engine started up immediately. The machines all started up at the same time. 2 *vt sep* (*a*) (*cause to function*) He started up the engine. She started the car up. (*b*) (*begin, open, undertake*) He has started up a new business.

starve out *vt sep* (*a*) (*starve into leaving a place*) They decided to starve the enemy out. (*b*) (*reduce by hunger*) The refugees look starved out.

stash away *vt sep* (*Sl: hide away, conceal*) He is said to have stashed away a lot of money. Where did you stash the loot away?

stave in *vt sep* (*Old: break and/or push in*) The men staved in the door. The sides of the barrel have been staved in. (NOTE: *Preterit and Past Participle* **stove, staved**)

stave off *vt sep* (*resist, deflect, keep at bay*) This action may help to stave off later disasters of the same kind. It may be too late to stave off trouble.

stay away *vi* (*remain elsewhere*) She is deliberately staying away from the meetings. Why don't you stay away if you don't like us?

stay behind *vi* (*remain behind*) The pupil stayed behind to ask the teacher a question. He told them to stay behind for a few minutes.

stay down *vi* (*a*) *keep down*) The men in the trenches stayed down while the enemy shells were exploding. (*b*) (*specifically, remain below the surface of water*) The diver stayed down for some time. I didn't expect him to stay down so long (under water.) (*c*) (*Med: remain in stomach*) The food seems to have stayed down this time. He has stopped vomiting and his food should stay down now.

stay in   *vi*   (a) (*remain in position*) When the nails are screwed in, they will stay in.   I am not sure if these props will stay in long enough to do the work.   (b) (*remain at home*) She said she was staying in tonight to wash her hair.   He doesn't usually stay in on Friday evenings.

stay out   *vi*   (a) (*remain or keep out*) Please stay out till the work is finished.   I told him to stay out.   Stay out!   Get out and stay out!   (b) (*remain out of the home, office etc*) He usually stays out late on Friday nights.   It's unusual for them to stay out so long.

stay up   *vi*   (a) (*remain up in position*) Those rafters don't look strong enough to stay up.   The temporary roof won't stay up much longer.   (b) (*remain out of bed*) He stays up late most nights, reading business reports.   It's not like you to stay up after midnight.

*steam + particle   *vi*   (*move under steam power, with direction*) The ship steamed out of harbour.   I watched the liner steam past. The ferry steamed back and forward.   The larger ship steamed steadily ahead.

steam out   1 *vi   see* ***steam.**   2 *vt sep* (*remove by steaming*) The technique steams the dirt out (of clothes).

steam up   1 *vi*   (a) *see* ***steam.**   (b) (*become covered in condensation*) The windows have steamed up.   2 *vt sep*   (a) (*cover in condensation*) This humidity steams all the windows up.   (b) (*Fig Sl usu pass: be angry*) He's all steamed up about losing the contract. Don't get (so) steamed up about it.

*steer + particle   (*steer, navigate, guide, with direction*)   1 *vi*   Steer past on the inside.   The helmsman steered skilfully through. 2 *vt sep*   He steered the ship in to harbour.   The captain steered the ship out skilfully.   They relied on him to steer the boat away from the rocks.

*step + particle   *vi*   (*step, walk briskly, with direction*) The horses stepped past proudly.   Would you mind stepping in for a moment?   He just stepped out for a breath of fresh air.   Step aside and make room for us.   He stepped back to admire the painting.

step aside   *vi*   (a) *see* ***step.**   (b) (*Fig: move from a position of authority*) They expect him to step aside and make way for a younger man.   I'm not ready to step aside yet.

step back   *vi*   (a) *see* ***step.**   (b) (*Fig: move into an insignificant position*) He doesn't want to step back from the centre of things.

step down   *vi*   (a) *see* ***step.**   (b)=**step aside** (b).

step in   *vi*   (a) *see* ***step.**   (b) (*Fig: intervene*) The government may step in and try to settle the dispute.   The police are reluctant to step in.

step out 1 *vi* *see* ***step.** 2 *vt sep* *(with 'it': go very briskly)* Look at them stepping it out!

step up 1 *vi* *(a) see* ***step.** *(b) (Fig: be promoted)* He has stepped up into the management of the firm. 2 *vt sep* *(a) (increase, usu in steps or stages)* The factory has stepped up production. The tempo has been stepped up. *(b) (with 'it': increase in strength)* Step it up!

*stick + particle *vt sep* *(a) (stick or push, with direction)* The boy stuck the cane in (to the ground). He stuck his arm out (of the car window). They stuck the hooks up into the rafters of the room. *(b) (Fam: put, place, with direction)* She stuck the book away somewhere. Stick the papers in and close the drawer. Stick the stuff out in the garden for the moment. He stuck the letter back in its envelope. *(c) (cause to adhere, with direction)* Stick the stamps on and post the letter. Can you stick the label back where it was before? Stick the flap down with tape or glue or something.

stick around *vi* *(Sl: stay in the area, stay available till needed)* Why don't you stick around? Stick around, baby/honey.

stick at *vt fus* *(a) (keep at, keep working at)* He'll stick at it till he succeeds. Stick at it! *(b) (Neg: stop, hold back, have qualms of conscience about)* They won't stick at murder to get what they want. He'll stick at nothing to get complete power.

stick by *vt fus* *(stay loyal to)* I'll stick by him. She will stick by her friends whatever happens. They stuck by him to the end.

stick in 1 *vi* *(Fig Fam: persevere, work hard)* I told him to stick in and pass the exam. Stick in, you'll succeed! 2 *vt sep* *(a) see* ***stick** *(a) (b) (c).* *(b) (Sl: attack with, usu as means of assaulting)* Stick the boot in, pal!

stick on 1 *vt sep* *see* ***stick.** *(b) (c).* 2 *vt fus* *(hold back, have qualms about)* He may stick on the second clause in the contract. I hope you aren't going to stick on the question of money.

stick out 1 *vi* *(a) (project)* The woodwork sticks out from the main wall. An arm was sticking out from the hole. *(b) (Fam: hold out, remain obdurate for)* The men are sticking out for higher wages. 2 *vt sep* *(a) see* ***stick** *(a) (b).* *(b) (endure)* If you can stick it out a bit longer, everything will be all right. Stick it out! *(c) (protrude)* The doctor asked him to stick his tongue out. It's rude to stick your tongue out at people.

stick to *vt fus* *(adhere to, remain attached to)* He is sticking to his principles in this matter. I hope you will stick to the point in the debate. Oh, stick to the point. *(b) (stay with)* Stick to me closely or you might get lost. *(c) (remain loyal to)* She will stick to him whatever happens. He will stick to her through thick and thin.

stick up   1 *vi*   (*a*) (*protrude upwards*) The canes were sticking up from a box in the corner.   The lid was sticking up.   Her hair keeps sticking up no matter how often she combs it.   (*b*) (*Fam usu pass: trapped, located against one's will*) I hate being stuck up in a place like this.   She feels stuck up here, with nothing to do. 2 *vt sep*   (*a*) *see* *****stick** (*a*) (*b*) (*c*).   (*b*) (*specifically, Sl: hold up one's hand while being robbed*) Stick them up!   Stick 'em up! Stick up your hands!   *n* **a** **stick-up**=an armed robbery. (*c*) (*Fam: Idiomatic past participle*) **stuck-up**=snobbish, from 'having one's nose stuck up in the air'.   *Examples:* She really is stuck-up.   They are the stuck-up type.

stick up for   *vt fus*   (*Fam: defend*) He always sticks up for her. Can't you stick up for yourself sometimes?   Don't stick up for him!

stink out   *vt sep*   (*a*) (*stink completely, fill with a bad smell*) That animal stinks the place out!   (*b*) (*force out by causing a stink*) If you take the beast in there, it'll stink everybody out!

stink up   *vt sep*   (*fill with a stink or terrible smell*) Those rotten eggs have stunk the place up.

stir up   *vt sep*   (*a*) (*Lit: intensive of stir*) Would you stir up the paint a bit?   (*b*) (*Fig: agitate, disturb*) Stop stirring things up. She loves to stir people up.   (*c*) (*cause, provoke*) Someone is stirring up trouble in the old part of the city.   He hopes to stir up bloody revolution.

stitch on   *vt sep*   (*put or fix on by stitching*) She stitched the zip on (to the dress).

stitch up   *vt sep*   (*a*) (*stitch as fully as necessary*) She stitched the dress up.   She stitched up the tear in the dress.   (*b*) (*bind up or seal by stitching*) The surgeon stitched up the wound.   The packers stitched up the canvas bags and labelled them.

stock up   1 *vi*   (*make a stock, store*) We had better stock up with essential foodstuffs.   They stocked up for several months.   2 *vt sep*   (*provide with a stock or supply*) He has stocked the shop up very well.

stoke up   1 *vi*   (*Fam: provide oneself with nourishing food*) Let's stoke up while there's time.   Better stoke up against the cold.   2 *vt sep*   (*a*) (*Lit: stoke as fully as possible, stir into action*) The men stoked up the fires.   The furnaces have been stoked up.   (*b*) (*Fig: stir up, encourage*) He has been stoking up (the fires of) rebellion in the province.   Stop stoking things up!

*****stomp** + **particle**   *vi*   (*Fam: move heavily, with direction*) They stomped along in their big boots.   He stomped in for something to **eat.**   Somebody in the flat above keeps stomping up and down.

stoop down *vi* (*intensive of* **stoop**) The man stooped down and picked up the paper.

stop in *vi* (*remain or stay in*) I'll stop in and look after the kids. She usually stops in on Wednesday evenings. Don't stop in just for me.

stop out *vi* (*remain or stay out*) When she's angry with me, she stops out for hours. Don't stop out just because he's coming.

stop over *vi* (*stay, break a journey*) I expect he'll stop over with us for a day or two on his way to New York. She usually stops over with him in London. *n* a **stopover**=a break in a journey.

stop up 1 *vi* (*remain or stay out of bed*) She stops up till he gets home. Don't stop up for me, please. 2 *vt sep* (*a*) (*seal up*) The hole has been stopped up with putty. A cork should stop it up all right. She stopped up her ears to keep the noise out. (*b*) (*close completely*) My nose is stopped up with the cold. His ears were stopped up with wax.

store up *vt sep* (*keep in supply, store as fully as possible*) He has been storing up food for the winter. Squirrels store up nuts.

stow away 1 *vi* (*hide, to get a free passage*) He stowed away to Australia. People used to stow away on ships quite a lot. *n* a **stowaway**=a person hiding for a free passage. 2 *vt sep* (*put or store away*) She stowed the money away in a drawer. He keeps the cash stowed away in an old sock. Stow it away somewhere.

*straggle + particle *vi* (*walk slowly, some lagging behind others*) Refugees straggled in all day. Remnants of the army straggled back from the battle. Most of the athletes straggled along behind, taking it easy.

straighten out 1 *vi* (*become straight*) The road straightens out after this bend. 2 *vt sep* (*a*) (*Lit: make straight or straighter*) He tried to straighten out the bent wire. (*b*) (*Fig: put right*) Can you come and straighten things out between them? I'll try to straighten the matter out (once and for all). (*c*) (*Fig Fam: ensure a clear understanding of the facts*) He said we needed some straightening out on one or two points. I'll straighten them out on this matter.

straighten up 1 *vi* (*become erect or upright*) The man was bending over, but when we approached he straightened up. I told them to straighten up. Straighten up! 2 *vt sep* (*a*) (*make straight and upright*) He straightened himself up and looked them squarely in the eye. Straighten yourself up! (*b*) (*make square or recti-lineal, regularize*) He straightened up the papers. You had better straighten up those lines before you do any more work.

(*c*) (*Fig Fam: clarify, state clearly*) I'd like you to straighten a few things up for me.

strap down   *vt sep*   (*fix down with straps*) The patient was strapped down to the bed in case he injured himself by moving. Strap the lid down and then put the box in here.

strap in   *vt sep*   (*fix in with straps or a strap*) The driver was properly strapped in. Strap yourself in before starting the engine. I don't like being strapped in.

strap up   *vt sep*   (*a*) (*fix up with straps*) The equipment was strapped up on to the wall.   (*b*) (*restrict as fully as possible with straps*) The prisoner was safely strapped up.

*stream + particle   *vi*   (*move along in a stream or in large numbers, with direction*) Water was streaming in through a hole in the roof. The blood streamed down from the wound in his head. The people streamed past on their way to the square.

strengthen up   *vt sep*   (*make strong or stronger*) This food will strengthen you up after your illness.

stray away   *vi*   (*wander away and get lost*) (*a*) (*Lit*) Several sheep have strayed away.   (*b*) (*Fig*) The priest was afraid that some of his parishioners would stray away from the paths of virtue.

*streak + particle   *vi*   (*move like a streak or very fast, with direction*) The jets streaked over from the enemy positions. A dive-bomber streaked down towards our lines. The car streaked off in a cloud of dust. The cat streaked out when it saw the dog.

*stretch + particle   *vi*   (*stretch, with direction*) He stretched out and took an apple from the bowl. She stretched up and touched the picture. Not everyone can stretch down and touch their toes.

stretch out   1 *vi*   *see* ***stretch.**   2 *vt sep*   (*a*) (*extend*) She stretched her hand out and touched him. He stretched the elastic out as far as it would go.   (*b*) (*Fig: extend, prolong*) He stretched the story out. They don't want to stretch the meeting out.

strew about/around   *vt sep*   (*scatter about*) They strewed bread crumbs about for the birds. The papers were all strewn about. The burglar left their belongings strewn about everywhere.

*stride + particle   *vi*   (*walk with long, firm steps, with direction*) The giant strode along. He strode up and introduced himself. I watched the two men stride away down the hill.

*strike + particle   (*hit, with direction*)   1 *vi*   He struck out at his attacker. They struck down at his defenceless body. They struck back savagely when attacked.   2 *vt sep*   They struck him down and kicked him. He struck the window in with one blow. She struck his arm away angrily.

strike off *vt sep* (*a*) *see* ***strike**. (*b*) (*remove by cancelling or scoring off*) He struck their names off. (*c*) (*Med etc: remove from the professional register because of misconduct*) The doctor was struck off.

strike out 1 *vi* (*a*) *see* ***strike**. (*b*) (*set out*) The explorers struck out for the hills. (*c*) (*start swimming*) The swimmer struck out towards the shore. 2 *vt sep* (*a*) *see* ***strike**. (*b*) (*cancel out, score out*) Would you strike his remarks out, please? The names have been struck out at your request.

strike up 1 *vi* (*a*) *see* ***strike**. (*b*) (*Music: start playing*) The band struck up (with the national anthem). 2 *vt Idiom:* Strike up the band!=let the band start playing. 3 *vt fus* (*Fig Fam: make, form*) They struck up an acquaintance. I hope they will strike up a lasting friendship.

string along 1 *vi* (*Fam: follow*) I'll string along, if you don't object. Some ragged children strung along behind, hoping for money. 2 *vt sep* (*Fam: keep someone hoping for romance, sex, a reward etc*) She strings her boy-friends along. Stop stringing the poor girl along! They are stringing him along by offering him these occasional favours.

string out *vt sep* (*a*) (*Lit: put out on strings*) They strung the pieces of paper out to frighten birds away. (*b*) (*Fig usu pass: extend in lines or strings*) The refugees were strung out along the dusty roads for miles.

string up *vt sep* (*a*) (*put up in or with strings*) We strung the onions up. The nets were strung up under the rafters. (*b*) (*Fam: hang by the neck*) The mob strung up several of the men whom they suspected of murder. String them up!

strip down 1 *vi*=**strip off** 1. 2 *vt sep* (*a*) (*reflexive: take one's clothes off*) He stripped himself down. (*b*) (*Tech: dismantle as fully as possible*) The mechanic stripped the engine down· This motor needs to be stripped down.

strip off 1 *vi* (*take one's clothes off*) He stripped off and dived into the pool. 2 *vt sep* (*a*) (*remove in strips*) He stripped the tape off. They stripped the bandages off. (*b*) (*pull off quickly*) He stripped his shirt off.

*stroll + particle *vi* (*walk casually, with direction*) The people were strolling along, enjoying the evening air. He strolled around for an hour or so. They strolled off hand-in-hand. She strolled in an hour late.

struggle along *vi* (*manage along with a struggle, get along with difficulty*) (*a*) (*Lit*) The wounded man struggled along somehow. (*b*) (*Fig*) They struggled along for some years without much money.

struggle back *vi* (*return with difficulty* The soldiers struggled back to their lines despite heavy enemy attacks.

struggle on *vi* (*continue to struggle*) The partisans struggled on against the invaders even when there seemed little hope. We struggle on somehow, although there isn't much money.

*strut + **particle** *vi* (*walk with stiff pride, with direction*) The cockerel strutted along. A drill sergeant was strutting about on the parade ground.

stub out *vt sep* (*finish by crushing the stub or butt*) He stubbed out his cigarette (in the ash-tray).

stuff down *vt sep* (*push firmly down*) He stuffed the papers down into the box.

stuff in *vt sep* (*push firmly in*) He stuffed the papers in (to the drawer).

stuff up *vt sep* (a) (*push firmly up*) He stuffed the cloth up into the hole. (b) (*usu pass: fill completely*) The chimney seems to be stuffed up. My nose is stuffed up with the cold.

*stumble + **particle** *vi* (*walk as though about to fall, with direction*) The tired men stumbled along. People were stumbling about in the dark. He stumbled up to us, begging for help. I watched them stumble away over the rocks.

stumble across/(up)on *vt fus* (*come upon by chance, chance upon, find accidentally*) I stumbled across some information that may be useful to us. If you stumble upon the book, keep it for me.

stump up *vt* (*Sl: pay up, usu unwillingly*) I have to stump up £5 every year as a compulsory donation. They expect us to stump up whenever they need money.

*suck + **particle** *vt sep* (*pull by means of air suction, with direction*) The vacuum cleaner sucks the dirt up. The ventilators suck the fumes out. These windows seem to suck the dust in. He sucked up the lemonade (through a straw).

suck in 1 *vi* (*Sl: ingratiate oneself*) He is busy sucking in (with his new boss). Oh, stop sucking in! 2 *vt sep* *see* *suck.

suck up *vt sep* (a) *see* *suck. (b) (*Fig: absorb*) The plants suck up a lot of water. He sucks up all the information you give him.

suck up to *vt fus* (*Sl: ingratiate oneself with*) He shamelessly sucks up to important people.

sum up 1 *vi* (*come to a conclusion, summarize the main points*) Well, let's sum up. He summed up to everyone's satisfaction. 2 *vt sep* (a) (*bring to a conclusion*) He summed up the seminar with a few remarks of his own. (b) (*summarize*) He summed the matter up succinctly. Can you sum it all up for us? (c) (*Fam: assess, judge*) She is good at summing people up. I can't sum him up at all.

*summon + particle vt sep (*summon, with direction*) The captain summoned him in. The headmaster summoned them up. He summoned me over and demanded an explanation. They were summoned out to answer questions.

summon up vt sep (a) *see* ***summon.** (b) (*Fig: muster, gather, find*) She summoned up enough courage to tell them to leave her in peace. He couldn't summon up the strength to move. I can't summon up much enthusiasm for this book.

swab down vt sep (*clean down with a swab or mop*) The sailors swabbed the deck down.

swab out vt sep (*usu Med: clean out with a swab of absorbent material*) The nurse swabbed out the wound.

*swagger + particle vi (*walk with bravado, with direction*) The bully swaggered in. They swaggered out, victorious. I saw some soldiers swaggering along.

swallow down vt sep (*swallow, usu unwillingly*) He swallowed the medicine down.

swallow up vt sep (*swallow completely*) He is afraid that the ground will open and swallow him up.

swan off vi (*Sl: go off casually, wander off*) He has just swanned off somewhere.

*sway + particle vi (*move from side to side, usu gently, with direction*) The drunk man swayed about. The trees swayed back and forward in the breeze. The boxer swayed back to avoid the blow.

swear by vt fus (*think highly of, value*) He swears by that shop. I always swear by their products.

swear in vt sep (*Law: introduce by requiring to take or swear an oath*) He swore the witness in. The jury was sworn in.

swear off vt fus (*avoid*) He swore off doing it. I wish he would swear off alcohol.

sweat out vt sep (a) (*Lit: remove by sweating*) He wants to sweat the alcohol out of his system. (b) (*Fig usu with 'it': endure*) They'll just have to sweat it out (until help comes).

*sweep + particle (*sweep, with direction*) 1 vi The ship swept along proudly. She swept in like a queen. He swept out in a fury. The car swept past in a cloud of dust. 2 vt sep (a) (*Lit*) She swept up the mess. She swept the dirt out. Stop sweeping the rubbish in here! Sweep it away, please. (b) (*Fig*) The government has swept away much of the old system. They say they will sweep out the administration and introduce new methods.

sweeten up   *vt sep*   (*make sweet or sweeter*) (*a*) (*Lit*) He sweetened up the tea. (*b*) (*Fig*) Are you trying to sweeten me up with a bribe? She sweetened him up before asking for the money.

swell out   1 *vi* (*expand by swelling, become inflated*) (*Lit*) The sails swelled out in the strong wind. 2 *vt sep* (*Fig*) He swelled out his chest with pride.

swell up   *vi* (*become bloated*) The bodies of the dead have begun to swell up. The lump on his neck has swollen up considerably.

*swerve + particle   *vi* (*move in various curves, with direction*) The car was swerving about dangerously. He swerved in and out of the traffic. The fast boat swerved round towards the open sea.

swig away   *vi* (*Sl: take drinks continuously*) He keeps swigging away at that bottle of brandy.

swill down   *vt sep* (*a*) (*clean down with plenty of water*) They swilled the pigsty down. Swill it down with a hosepipe. (*b*) (*Sl: drink down, consume*) He has swilled down vast quantities of beer. He swilled the bread down with a mug of tea.

swill out   *vt sep* (*clean out with plenty of water*) This room is so filthy it needs swilling out. Swill the place out.

*swim + particle   *vi* (*swim, with direction*) The man swam up to the boat. They swam in for a rest, and then swam out again. I watched her swimming away. The children were swimming about in the pool.

*swing + particle   *vi* (*move with a swing, with direction*) The tall man swung along steadily. The monkey swung down from the tree. A jet plane swung round and began to dive over the town.

*swirl + particle   (*move in swirls or eddies, with direction*) 1 *vi* The water swirled past at great speed. Muddy water was swirling up from the great hole. Vapour was swirling out of the volcano. Great clouds came swirling in from the sea. 2 *vt sep* She swirled the cream round with a whisk. The typhoon swirled the sea up into a column of water.

*swish + particle   *vi* (*move with a swishing sound, with direction*) The bicycles swished along through the rain. The branches of the tree swished back and forward against the wall. The glider swished down gently towards the field.

switch back   1 *vi* (*a*) (*Lit: turn a switch back*) He switched the timings forward, and was told to switch back immediately. (*b*) (*Fig: revert, return*) I think we should switch back to the old system. We can't switch back now, it's too late. 2 *vt sep* (*restore to a previous position*) Would you switch the radio back to the other programme? Switch the machine back now. NOTE *n* a **switchback,** no connection with the phrasal verb. A switchback is a road whose surface or 'back' rises and falls.

switch off 1 *vi* (*disconnect by turning a switch off*) The programme on the radio was dull, so she switched off. We'd better switch off now. When the work was finished, they switched off. 2 *vt sep* (*a*) (*disconnect by turning a switch off*) He switched the radio off. Switch the machine off, please. (*b*) (*Sl: prevent or stop from talking*) Switch that fellow off!

switch on 1 *vi* (*connect by turning a switch on*) I want to switch on at nine, because there's a good programme. When I give the signal, switch on! 2 *vt sep* (*connect by turning a switch on*) Switch the radio on, please. He switched the machines on. The equipment is switched on automatically.

switch over 1 *vi* (*a*) (*convert by using switches*) You can switch over from one circuit to another without any difficulty. (*b*) (*Fig: convert to*) He switches over from French to Spanish without any hesitation. We are switching over to a new technique next year. Why don't you switch over to a more sensible method? *n* a **switch-over** (e.g. to decimal currency, metrication, driving on the right etc). 2 *vt sep* (*convert or transfer, usu by switching*) Can you switch the current over from one circuit to another? Why don't you switch your company over to making a different product?

*swoop + particle *vi* (*move suddenly with a swoop, with direction*) The hawk swooped down on its prey. His mother swooped in and caught him opening the cake tin. The enemy fighter plane came swooping out from a bank of clouds.

*swoosh + particle *vi* (*move with a swooshing noise, with direction*) The express train swooshed past. The rocket swooshed up and burst into a hundred coloured lights. The car swooshed along at 100 mph.

swot up 1 *vi* (*Fam: study very hard*) He is swotting up for his exams. I'll have to start swotting up soon. 2 *vt sep* (*learn up, study very seriously*) He is swotting the subject up for a professional exam. I must swot up my French.

*tack + particle *vi* (*Naut: change course across the wind, with direction*) The ship tacked along. It was necessary to tack back across the bay.

tack back 1 *vi see* ***tack.** 2 *vt sep* (*a*) (*fix back in position with tacks*) He tacked the carpet back. (*b*) (*fix to one side, by means of tacks*) He tacked the material back (out of the way).

tack down 1 *vi see* ***tack.** 2 *vt sep* (*a*) (*fix down with tacks*) She tacked the carpet down. (*b*) (*sew down with tacking stitches*) She tacked the pleats down.

tack on 1 *vi*   *see* ***tack***.   2 *vt sep*   (*fix on with a tack or tacks*) (*a*) (*Lit*) He tacked the sheets of paper on as carefully as possible. (*b*) (*Fig*) They tacked the information on at the end of the report.   (*c*) (*sew on with tacking stitches*) She tacked the pockets on.

tag along *vi*   (*Fam: come along as a follower*) Oh, I'll just tag along and watch you all playing.   She always tags along with them.

tag around with *vt fus*   (*Fam: accompany*) She tags around with him quite a lot.

tag on *vi*   (*Fam: follow*) He tagged on behind.   Stop tagging on to us all the time.

tag together *vt sep*   (*join together*) (*a*) (*Lit*) Tag these documents together, please.   (*b*) (*Fig*) I wouldn't tag those events together.

tail away *vi*   (*diminish*) The numbers in the procession began to tail away.   Attendances tailed away towards the end of the course.

tail off *vi*   (*diminish, lessen*) My enthusiasm has rather tailed off.

take + particle *vt sep*   (*take, with direction*) He took the children out.   She took the lost cat in.   The guards took the prisoners away.   The porter took us up to our room.   She took along all the documents she needed.   They took me aside and broke the news.

take aback *vt sep*   (*usu pass: surprised*) I was quite taken aback by his attitude.   Don't be taken aback by anything she says.

take after *vt fus*   (*Fam: resemble*) The baby really takes after his father.

take apart *vt sep*   (*a*) (*Old: separate from a main group*) He took his disciples apart and spoke with them.   (*b*) (*dismantle*) The mechanics took the engine apart.   (*c*) (*Sl: dismember, murder*) I'll take him apart if I lay my hands on him!

take away 1 *vi*   (*detract*) This kind of action takes away from his reputation.   2 *vt sep*   (*a*) (*Arith: subtract*) Take away 2 from 4 and you get 2.   (*b*) (*remove*) Take the knife away from that child before he cuts himself.   They took away his freedom. These books are not to be taken away.   The guards took the prisoner away to jail.

take back *vt sep*   (*a*) *see* ***take***.   (*b*) (*return*) He took the book back.   (*c*) (*retract*) He decided to take his threats back.   I shall take back my remarks if he will do the same.   (*d*) (*agree to receive back again*) She won't take her husband back now, even if he begs her.   The grocer took back the rancid butter.   (*e*) (*remind of earlier times*) These photographs really take me back (to my youth).

take down *vt sep*   (*a*) *see* ***take***.   (*b*) (*dismantle*) The workmen

are now taking down the scaffolding round the building. (*c*)
(*write down*) His secretary took down all the points he made.
(*d*) (*humble, humiliate*) They want to take him down a bit.
Idiom: To take someone down a peg or two=to humiliate
someone considerably.

take in *vt sep* (*a*) *see* ***take.** (*b*) (*receive in one's house*) They took
me in and fed me. He took the orphan in. (*c*) (*escort in to
dinner*) He took her in on his arm. (*d*) (*accept as business*) She
takes in washing. She sometimes takes in work to do at home.
(*e*) (*Sew: make narrower*) She decided to take the dress in. (*f*)
(*include, cover*) I think this list takes in everybody. These points
take in everything. The tour takes in all the larger towns.
(*g*) (*understand, grasp*) Things are happening so quickly, I can't
take it all in. Did you take in what he said? (*h*) (*see at a
glance*) He took in what was happening and decided to get away
quickly. (*i*) (*deceive, cheat*) The guide took the tourists in, and
managed to get extra money out of them. I wasn't taken in by
his stories. You can't take me in like that. (*j*) (*US Fam: see,
attend*) After eating lets take in a movie.

take off 1 *vi* (*a*) (*leave the ground*) The aeroplane took off smoothly.
(*b*) (*Fam: leave hurriedly*) They took off, abandoning all their
belongings. 2 *vt sep* (*a*) *see* ***take.** (*b*) (*remove*) She took off
her hat. (*c*) (*amputate*) The surgeon took off his arm. He had
a leg taken off. (*d*) (*remove from service or circulation*) Several
trains have been taken off this week. They have taken the
local bus off. (*e*) (*deduct*) As the cover of the book was torn,
the bookseller took 50p off. (*f*) (*lead away*) The guards took
him off to prison. I took myself off because they did not want
me there. (*g*) (*Fam: imitate*) He takes that comedian off
beautifully. He likes to take off politicians.

take on 1 *vi* (*a*) (*become popular, fashionable*) This song has really
taken on. (*b*) (*Fam: become upset*) Don't take on so! Oh, she
does take on. 2 *vt sep* (*a*) *see* ***take.** (*b*) (*accept*) He took on the
bet on. She has taken on too many responsibilities. (*c*)
(*Sport: accept as an opponent*) The boxer happily took the other
man on. (*d*) (*employ*) The factory is taking on more men.
(*e*) (*load*) The tanker took on water at that port. (*f*) (*absorb,
acquire*) The cloth took on blue from the overalls that were
washed in the same tub. His work has taken on a bizarre
quality lately.

take out *vt sep* (*a*) *see* ***take.** (*b*) (*escort away*) The policeman
took them out. (*c*) (*extract*) The dentist took out a tooth. The
surgeon took out my appendix. (*d*) (*remove, eliminate*) This
liquid is good for taking out stains. (*e*) (*acquire*) He has taken
out an insurance policy. Most people take out life insurance
nowadays. (*f*) (*Fam: vent, get rid of*) Don't take your bad
temper out on me. He took out his anger on the dog. (*g*)

(Fam) Idiom: This kind of thing takes it out of you=this kind of thing tires you. *(h) Idiom:* This should take you out of yourself =this should divert or entertain you for a while.

take over 1 *vi* *(accept duty)* I took over from him at six o'clock. The second shift has now taken over. 2 *vt sep* *(a) see* ***take.*** *(b) (Fin Comm absorb)* The bigger firm has taken over the smaller one. *n* **a takeover** *n cpd* **a takeover bid**=an attempt at a takeover. *(c) (assume responsibility for)* He took over the station last week. I'll take the children over now. He took the business over from his father. He has decided to take over her debts. The new doctor has taken over the duties of the old one.

take to *vt fus* *(a) (conceive a liking for, begin to like)* She has really taken to that child. *(b) (adopt as a hobby)* She has taken to painting in oils. He has taken to skiing. They have taken to drink (=alcohol). *Idiom:* To take to the road=to begin wandering, become a tramp. *(c) (have recourse to, usu for safety)* The people have taken to the hills. The men took to the boats. *Idiom:* To take to one's heels=to flee.

take up 1 *vi* *(improve)* The weather has taken up a bit. Business is taking up. 2 *vt sep* *(a) see* ***take.*** *(b) (lift, raise)* He has taken up the carpet. *(c) (shorten)* She has taken up that dress. *(d) (lift or displace for repairs)* The workmen have taken up that road. The pavement has been taken up again. *(e) (stop and accept, of vehicles)* The bus took us up at the corner. The cars took their passengers up outside the hotel. *(f) (occupy, fill)* That bed takes up a lot of room. This work will take up a lot of my time. It is taking up all his attention. She's very taken up these days with all her activities. *(g) (absorb)* Blotting paper takes up ink. *(h) (raise the question of)* I'll take that matter up with my member of parliament. *(i) (develop an interest in; adopt as a hobby)* My son has taken up stamp-collecting. She took up sculpture. He has taken up Spanish. They have taken up antiwar campaigning. *(j) (return to)* She took up the story from where she had left off. She took up her sewing after the visitor had gone. *(k) (Fin: buy, obtain)* He has taken up shares in that company. *(l) (exercise, accept)* They do not intend to take up their option on that site. He took up my offer of £3,000. *(m) (arrest)* The police took him up on a drugs charge. *(n) (interrupt, correct)* He took me up short on that point. I'd like to take you up on the point you just made. *(o) (understand)* Please don't take me up wrongly. *n* **uptake** *Idiom:* To be quick on the uptake=to understand pretty quickly. *(p) Idiom:* To take someone up on something=to accept someone's bet or challenge. *Example:* I'll take you up on that!

take up with *vt fus* *(a) (become friends with)* He has taken up with the older boys round the corner. I'm afraid she has taken up with bad company. (*b*) *Idiom:* To be (very) taken up with someone/something=to be (very) engrossed or interested in someone/something.

talk away 1 *vi* (*talk continuously*) She talks away for hours without stopping. 2 *vt sep* (*force to go away by talking*) I'm afraid you won't talk this problem away. He can't talk away his enormous debts.

talk back *vi* (*reply insolently*) Don't talk back like that! It is appalling the way that child talks back to his parents.

talk down *vt sep* (*a*) (*reduce to silence by talking*) He is an expert at talking the opposition down. (*b*) (*Aviat: bring safely down by continuous instructions*) They talked the pilot down to a perfect landing, despite the fog.

talk down to *vt fus* (*patronize*) She talks down to everyone, but particularly young people.

talk on=talk away 1 *vi.*

talk out *vt sep* (*a*) (*discuss fully*) We really ought to talk this matter out sometime soon. (*b*) (*Parl: prevent from becoming legislation by spending all the parliamentary time talking*) They have succeeded in talking out that piece of reform.

talk over *vt sep* (*a*) (*discuss in detail*) We must talk that matter over. It's best to talk these things over quietly. (*b*)=**talk round** 1 *vt sep.*

talk round 1 *vt sep* (*persuade, convince*) I may be able to talk him round, but I doubt it. They finally managed to talk her round. 2 *vt fus* (*discuss, without ever being specific*) They talked round the problem for hours. He is expert at talking round things without coming to any decision.

talk to *vt fus* (*reprimand*) He talked to them very sharply. She needs to be talked to. *Idiom:* A good talking-to=a sharp reprimand.

tally up *vt sep* (*count up, assess*) The clerks tallied up the numbers. It is difficult to tally up the exact amount of damage suffered.

tamp down *vt sep* (*press firmly down*) He tamped down the tobacco in his pipe.

tangle up *vt sep* (*tangle completely, mix, confuse*) The wires are all tangled up. The dog has tangled up my wool.

tank up *vi* (*a*) (*Fam: refuel*) We tanked up at the next petrol station. (*b*) (*Sl usu pass: drunk*) He's completely tanked up.

tap back 1 *vi* (*tap in return*) We tapped on the wall and the people on the other side tapped back. 2 *vt sep* (*fix back into place by tapping*) He tapped the nail back.

tap down   *vt sep*   (*fix down by tapping*) She tapped the edges of the rug down with her heel.

tap in   *vt sep*   (*fix in by tapping*) He tapped the nails in.

tap out   *vt sep*   (*a*) (*knock out by tapping*) She tapped the tablets out of the packet on to the table.   He tapped out his pipe on the fireplace.   (*b*) (*send by tapping*) The operator tapped out the morse signals.

tape down   *vt sep*   (*fix down with tape*) The carpet is firmly taped down.

tape on   *vt sep*   (*fix on with tape*) She taped the extra material on.

tape together   *vt sep* (*join together with tape*) The two pieces had been taped together.

tape up   *vt sep*   '(*tape as firmly as possible*) He taped up the split in the boards.   The kidnappers had taped up their victim's mouth.

taper off   (*decrease steadily in size*)   1 *vi*   The sides of the plane taper off beautifully.   Casualties are now tapering off.   2 *vt sep*   The carpenter tapered off the edges.

tart up   *vt sep*   (*a*) (*Sl: make oneself like a tart, make up heavily*) She has tarted herself up for her new boy-friend's benefit.   (*b*) (*Sl: brighten*) Let's tart the design up a bit and surprise everybody.

tax away   *vt sep*   (*reduce by taxing*) His income is being taxed away. The government seem intent on taxing everything away.

team up   1 *vi*   (*a*) (*co-operate*) They have teamed up for the project. He has teamed up with an odd bunch of people.   (*b*) (*match, harmonize*) These colours don't team up.   2 *vt sep*   (*bring together as a team or into harmony*) He has teamed them up in the hope of getting some good results.   It is hard to team these colours up.

*tear + particle   1 *vi*   (*Fam: move rapidly, with direction*) The car tore away.   The speedboats tore off towards the bay.   The sports car tore in from a side road.   2 *vt sep*   (*tear, with direction*) The workmen tore the building down.   Some animals had torn the branches off.   He had torn away a gap in the hedge.   The victim lay with its throat torn out.

tear away   1 *vi   see* ***tear**.   *n* a **tearaway**=a wild (young) person.   2 *vt sep*   (*a*) *see* ***tear**.   (*b*) (*Fam: force to move*) I couldn't tear him away from that book.

tear into   *vt fus*   (*Fam: attack*) The little boy tore into his tormentors.

tear up   1 *vi   see* ***tear**.   2 *vt sep*   (*a*) *see* ***tear**.   (*b*) (*Fig: reject*) The workers have torn up the agreement with the management.

He has decided to tear the contract up. (*c*) (*break surface of*) The tanks have torn up the ground.

tease out *vt sep* (*a*) (*Lit: disentangle*) She teased out the wool gently. (*b*) (*Fig: obtain by gentle persistence*) He has teased the information out of her. We must try to tease out all the significant factors in the problem.

tee off *vi* (*Golf: begin playing by driving a ball from the tee*) The players teed off at one o'clock.

tee up *vi* (*Golf: put the ball on its tee, preparatory to hitting it*) The golfer teed up carefully.

telegraph off *vi* (*send a message by telegraph, cable*) She telegraphed off for more money.

telephone in (*also* **phone in**) (*communicate with one's home or base by telephone*) 1 *vi* She telephoned in to find out what was happening. 2 *vt sep* They telephoned the news in to head office.

telephone off 1 *vi* (*intensive of* **telephone**) She telephoned off to make the reservations. 2 *vt sep* (*send off by telephone*) They telephoned the figures off to head office.

tell off *vt sep* (*a*) (*Old: count off*) He told off the sheep. (*b*) (*Mil: assign*) The men were told off for guard duty. (*c*) (*Fam: reprimand*) He told them off severely. *n* **a telling-off.**

tell on *vt fus* (*a*) (*have a bad effect on*) This work is telling on his health. (*b*) (*inform on*) Someone has told on him and the authorities are beginning to ask questions.

tense up 1 *vi* (*become tense or rigid*) The animal tensed up and listened. 2 *vt sep* (*make tense or nervous*) This kind of situation really tenses you up. All the participants were very tensed up.

test out *vt sep* (*test as fully as possible*) You must test out this theory of yours and get some practical confirmation.

tether up *vt sep* (*tie up*) The men tethered up their horses and entered the inn.

thaw off = **thaw out.**

thaw out (*melt, unfreeze*) 1 *vi* The ice on the fields has thawed out. 2 *vt sep* The sun has begun to thaw the place out.

thin down 1 *vi* (*become thin*) This liquid appears to have thinned down. 2 *vt sep* (*make thin*) The painter thinned the paint down with white spirit.

thin out (*disperse, scatter*) 1 *vi* The crowds began to thin out The trees thinned out. 2 *vt sep* The gardener thinned out the lettuces. The barber thinned out his customer's thick hair. Emigration has considerably thinned out the population.

think about *vt fus* (*a*) (*reflect on*) Think about what you are doing! What are you thinking about? (*b*) (*consider*) It's worth thinking about. I'm thinking about a holiday in Spain this year. She has been morbidly thinking about suicide.

think back *vi* (*cast the mind back, reminisce*) The photographs made me think back to my schooldays. She thought back and tried to recollect the exact wording of the letter.

think of *vt fus* (*a*) (*consider, give attention to*) He has his family to think of. I've too many things to think of at the moment. You should think of their feelings in this matter. (*b*) (*contemplate*) Whatever were you thinking of when you did that? (*c*) (*remember*) Will you think of me sometimes? I can't think of his name. (*d*) (*imagine*) Just think of the cost of that car! Now think of something nice to do. (*e*) (*consider as a possibility*) She just won't think of such a thing. They just wouldn't think of going without you. She won't think of getting married just yet. (*f*) (*have as an opinion about*) What do you think of his behaviour last night? (*g*) *Idioms:* (*i*) Think nothing of it=do not consider it important. (*ii*) Think better of doing=decide that something is not worth doing after all.

think out *vt sep* (*reason out*) I shall have to think this matter out to the end. *Idiom:* Well thought-out=well-planned.

think over *vt sep* (*consider carefully*) I hope you will think matters over before doing anything hasty. Please think it over and let me know.

think through=**think out.**

think up *vt sep* (*invent*) He has thought up some astonishingly original schemes. Whatever will you think up next?

*thrash + particle *vi* (*move with violent lashing actions, with direction*) The dying fish thrashed about on the beach. The combine harvester thrashed past, cutting and binding the wheat.

thrash out 1 *vi* *see* ***thrash.** 2 *vt sep* (*a*) (*beat out violently*) I shall thrash the truth out of that boy. (*b*) (*discuss as fully as possible*) The two sides came together to thrash the matter out once and for all.

thread in *vt sep* (*introduce as or like a thread*) (*a*) (*Lit*) The machine threads the fibres in. (*b*) (*Fig*) The crowd was thick, and he had to thread his way in carefully.

thread through 1 *vi* (*Fig: pass carefully through a crowd*) He threaded through to the door. 2 *vt sep* (*a*)=**thread in** (*a*). (*Fig*) The crowd was thick, and he had to thread his way through carefully.

throb away *vi* (*continue throbbing or vibrating*) The boat's engine throbbed away in the background while they talked. My tooth has been throbbing away for hours.

*throng + particle *vi* (*move in a crowd, with direction*) The people thronged out to see him. The visitors thronged in. We all thronged along to see the fun.

throttle back 1 *vi* (*decrease power*) The driver throttled back as he came to the dangerous bend. 2 *vt sep* (*reduce the power of*) He throttled back the engine.

throttle down=**throttle back.**

*throw + particle *vt sep* (*throw, with direction*) She threw the paper away. He threw the ball up. They threw the books down. He asked them to throw the ball back. The boys were throwing a ball about.

throw about *vt sep* (a) *see* ***throw.** (b) (*Fig: waste, dispense liberally*) He likes throwing his money about. (c) *Idiom:* To throw one's weight about=to use one's strength or power to bully someone.

throw away *vt sep* (a) *see* ***throw.** (b) (*Fig: waste, usu thoughtlessly*) You are throwing away your chance of becoming a success. She is simply throwing herself away on a person like that. (c) (*Theatre: say casually*) He threw away a line with great effect.

throw back *vt sep* (a) *see* ***throw.** (b) (*straighten*) He threw back his shoulders and decided to accept the challenge. (c) (*Fig: push back*) The crisis threw them back on their own resources. She has been thrown back on her savings. (d) *n* **a throwback** =(i) a quality or physical attribute which reappears after several generations. (ii) a person, animal etc possessing that quality.

throw down *vt sep* (a) *see* ***throw.** (b) (*Mil: surrender*) The men threw down their weapons. The general expected the enemy to throw down their arms soon. (c) *Idiom:* To throw down the gauntlet=to issue a challenge.

throw in *vt sep* (a) *see* ***throw.** (b) (*interject*) He threw in a remark about money. (c) (*Sport: return to play from the sidelines*) The footballer threw the ball in. *n* **a throw-in.** (d) (*provide as a gratuitous extra*) When we bought the bedroom suite, the manager of the shop threw in some sheets as well. (e) *Idioms:* (i) To throw in one's hand/to throw in the sponge=to surrender, give up, accept defeat. (ii) To throw in one's lot with=to join, for better or for worse.

throw off *vt sep* (a) *see* ***throw.** (b) (*escape*) The men threw off their pursuers. (c) (*get rid of*) The downtrodden people have at last thrown off the yoke of imperialism. He has thrown off his old habits.

throw on *vt sep* (*a*) *see* ***throw.*** (*b*) (*put on hurriedly*) She just threw her clothes on.

throw out *vt sep* (*a*) *see* ***throw.*** (*b*) (*dispose of*) They threw the rubbish out. (*c*) (*eject, expel*) They threw the fellow out because of his bad behaviour. He was thrown out of his first school. (*d*) (*offer*) He threw out some ideas at the meeting. (*e*) (*reject*) Parliament has thrown that bill out. They will just throw your ideas out. (*f*) (*build on*) The workmen have thrown out an extension to the house. The castle governor threw out some extra fortifications. (*g*) (*disconcert*) That reply really threw her out, didn't it?

throw over *vt sep* (*a*) *see* ***throw.*** (*b*) (*reject, give up*) She has thrown him over for someone else. They have thrown that plan over.

throw together *vt sep* (*a*) *see* ***throw.*** (*b*) (*bring together in close contact for some length of time*) The emergency situation has thrown them together again. It was funny to be thrown together in that way after such a long separation. (*c*) (*assemble hastily*) They have simply thrown that machine together.

throw up 1 *vi* (*vomit*) He threw up violently 2 *vt sep* (*a*) *see* ***throw.*** (*b*) (*resign from, eject*) He has thrown up a perfectly good job and gone off somewhere. She threw up every opportunity they ever offered her. (*c*) *Idiom:* To throw up one's hands in despair=to despair completely.

***thrust* + particle** *vt sep* (*push with some force, with direction*) They thrust me aside and went in. The guards thrust him in and closed the door. He thrust a paper out of the window. She thrust the letter down into her bag.

thrust up 1 *vi* (*grow upwards vigorously*) The young plants are thrusting up everywhere. 2 *vt sep* *see* ***thrust.***

***thud* + particle** *vi* (*move with a thudding noise, with direction*) The horses thudded along. I heard him thudding about upstairs. Heavy feet were thudding back and forward.

***thunder* + particle** *vi* (*move with a sound like thunder, with direction*) The great herd thundered along. Horsemen thundered up to the gate. A column of tanks went thundering past.

thunder out 1 *vi* (*a*) *see* ***thunder.*** (*b*) (*sound out like thunder*) A great roar of anger thundered out. 2 *vt sep* (*announce or shout like thunder*) The crowd thundered out its approval.

tick away *vi* (*continue ticking*) The clock ticked away on the shelf.

tick off *vt sep* (*a*) (*mark off with a tick*) He ticked off the names on his list. (*b*) (*Fam: reprimand, scold*) The boss ticked us off about leaving work early. *n* a **ticking-off.** *Idiom:* To get a good ticking-off = to receive a sharp reprimand.

tick over *vi* (*a*) (*Aut: idle*) The engine was ticking over. (*b*) (*function*) That machine ticks over very well. (*Fig*) Everything in the office is ticking over very smoothly.

tide over *vt sep* (*assist temporarily*) This money should tide you over until you receive your cheque. He needs some work to tide him over till his regular job starts.

tidy away *vt sep* (*clear away tidily or neatly*) She tidied away the children's toys. My husband always complains that I tidy everything away so that he can never find what he wants.

tidy out *vt sep* (*clean or clear out, in order to make tidy or neat*) She decided to tidy out the upstairs rooms. He tidied out his drawers and letter trays.

tidy up (*clear up tidily*) 1 *vi* She asked the children to tidy up. 2 *vt sep* (*a*) She tidied up the room. (*b*) (*have a wash, comb one's hair etc*) I'll just run upstairs and tidy myself up.

tie down *vt sep* (*a*) (*Lit: fix down by tying*) He tied the crate down firmly. They tied their prisoner down to pegs fixed in the floor. (*b*) (*Fig: restrict*) I am tied down to what is stated in the regulations. He is tied down to his duties. I don't want to tie you down in any way.

tie in 1 *vi* (*fit neatly*) This information all ties in. Your story ties in with what they have been telling me. 2 *vt sep* (*a*) (*fix in by tying*) He tied the ends of the ropes in through the holes. (*b*) (*blend, fit in*) I want you to try and tie your story in with his.

tie off *vt sep* (*seal off by tying or knotting*) The midwife cut and tied off the baby's umbilical cord. The men tied off the loose ends of the ropes.

tie together 1 *vi* (*match*) Their stories don't appear to tie together. 2 *vt sep* (*link by tying*) (*a*) (*Lit*) He tied the ends of the ropes together. (*b*) (*Fig*) You'll have difficulty tying those loose ends together. He never did manage to tie the bits of the story together.

tie up 1 *vi* (*a*) (*amalgamate*) The two companies have finally tied up. *n* a **tie-up** = a link, an amalgamation. (*b*) (*agree*) Your information and his certainly tie up. 2 *vt sep* (*a*) (*tie firmly*) The men tied up their prisoners. He tied up the parcel. (*b*) (*tether*) The cowboys tied up their horses. (*c*) (*bind*) The doctor tied up the wound. (*d*) (*Fig Fam: bind up, lock up*) All his capital is tied up in that firm. (*e*) (*Fam usu pass: busy*) I'm afraid the manager is tied up at the moment and can't see you.

tighten up 1 *vi* (*become tight or more strict*) We shall have to tighten up on security in this department. 2 *vt sep* (*make tight*) He tightened up the screws.   The government has tightened up the regulations considerably since last year.

*tilt + particle   *vt sep*   (*move by tilting or toppling, with direction*) The workmen tilted the huge box back.   He tilted the frame forward in an effort to move it.   They tilted the cabinet over, to see what was behind it.

tinker about/around   *vi*   (*play or work amateurishly*) He likes tinkering about with watches.   He is always tinkering around with his motorbike.

*tiptoe + particle   *vi*   (*move on tiptoe, with direction*) The children tiptoed about upstairs.   She tiptoed down to see who had come in.   The eavesdropper tiptoed quietly away.

tire out   *vt sep*   (*exhaust, tire completely*) The children have really tired me out today.   She's tired out, poor soul.   I'm quite tired out.

*toddle + particle   *vi*   (*walk like a small child, with direction*) The little boy toddled up to us.   (*Fam*) Well, I'll toddle off now. They toddled away and left us to do the washing-up.

tog up   (*Sl: dress up*)   1 *vi*   They togged up and went out.   2 *vt sep* He togged himself up and went out.

*toil + particle   *vi*   (*move laboriously, with direction*) The column of wounded soldiers toiled along.   He toiled up wearily to the gates of the monastery.   She toiled back to the town, half-dead with fatigue.

toil away   *vi*   (*a*) see ***toil**.   (*b*) (*work very hard*) The men have been toiling away all day.   She has toiled away at that machine for too long.

toil on   *vi*   (*a*) see ***toil**.   (*b*) (*work on laboriously*) The labourers toiled on to complete the work.   We must just toil on and hope for better days.

tone down   *vt sep*   (*a*) (*reduce in tone or volume*) Tone that radio down, please.   He decided to tone the colours down considerably.   (*b*) (*Fig: reduce, moderate*) The rebels have toned down most of their demands.   (*c*) (*Fam: quieten*) Tone that noise down, kids!   Tone it down, for goodness' sake!

tone in   *vi*   (*harmonize*) The various notes toned in.   This colour tones in nicely with the general décor.

tone up   *vt sep*   (*improve in health*) These exercises certainly tone you up.

tool up   *vi*   (*Industry: prepare the necessary tools*) The factory is beginning to tool up for the new models.   Every time there is a change in design, we have to tool up again.

top off 1 *vi* (*reach a peak*) The production figures have topped off. 2 *vt sep* (*a*) (*trim at the top*) He topped off the hedge. (*b*) (*Fam: finish off*) He topped the evening off with some excellent songs. Let's top things off with champagne!

top up *vt sep* (*Fam: add in order to make full*) I'll just top up the water level in the car battery.

topple down *vi* (*fall slowly down*) The ancient building began to topple down, under the impact of the explosions.

topple over *vi* (*fall slowly over sideways*) The tree toppled over. The high-sided truck hit the wall and toppled over.

*toss + particle *vt sep* (*throw nonchalantly, with direction*) He tossed the box away. She tossed the ball up in the air. They tossed the papers out of the window.

toss off *vt sep* (*a*) see ***toss.** (*b*) (*swallow quickly*) He tossed off the whisky. (*c*) (*write quickly or casually*) He tossed off a sonnet. She tossed the article off in half an hour.

toss out *vt sep* (*a*) see ***toss.** (*b*) (*get rid of*) She tossed out all the old clothes.

toss up 1 *vi* (*choose by tossing a coin*) Let's toss up for who goes. They tossed up. *n* **a toss-up** It was a toss-up whether he would get there in time or not. 2 *vt sep* see ***toss.**

tot up *vt sep* (*add up*) He totted up the score. Just tot up how much I owe you.

total up=**tot up.**

*totter + particle *vi* (*walk shakily, with direction*) The injured man tottered along. An old man tottered up to us, asking for help. He tottered away, exhausted.

touch at *vt fus* (*usu Naut: call in at, visit*) The ship touches at Bombay and Singapore.

touch down 1 *vi* (*a*) (*Aviat: land*) The aeroplane touches down at Bombay and Singapore. **a touchdown**=a landing. (*b*) (*Sport: score by putting the ball down at a special point*) *n* **a touchdown.**

touch off *vt sep* (*a*) (*Lit: ignite, usu by lighting a fuse*) They touched off the booby-trap. His foot touched off the explosion. (*b*) (*Fig: cause, ignite*) His action has touched off a crisis.

touch up *vt sep* (*improve, usu by touches of paint*) He has touched the car up quite a lot.

touch (up)on *vt fus* (*mention briefly*) I feel we should just touch upon some of these interesting points. He only touched on the matter for a few minutes.

toughen up   1 *vi*   (*become tougher or worse*) His attitude has toughened up since you last saw him. The situation has toughened up. 2 *vt sep*   (*make tougher*) They have toughened things up (a lot) recently at the school. The sergeant said that army life would toughen the recruits up.

tour about/around   *vi*   (*travel about as part of a tour*) The visitors have been touring about.

tousle up   *vt sep*   (*rumple or disturb*) His father affectionately tousled up his hair. She had a rather tousled-up look, as though she had just got out of bed.

tout about/around   *vt sep*   (*Fam: try to sell anywhere*) He has been touting that stuff about for weeks. Stop touting your wares about.

*tow + particle   *vt sep*   (*pull with a tow-rope, with direction*) The tug towed the big ship in. They towed the boat out. A lorry came and towed the car away.

towel down   *vt sep*   (*dry down with a towel*) He towelled himself down.

trace out   *vt sep*   (a) (*mark out gently or lightly*) She traced out the shapes carefully. (b) (*delineate*) They traced out the design in the sand.

track back   *vi*   (*go back the same way*) They tracked back to their base camp.

track down   *vt sep*   (*find by hunting*) The police have tracked down the escaped convict. We must try to track these people down. They hope to track down the source of the infection.

*trail + particle   1 *vi*   (*wander or move slowly, with direction*) The child trailed along behind. The vagabonds trailed up into the hills. Lines of men trailed away into the distance. 2 *vt sep* (a) (*pull or drag, with direction*) The child trailed his teddy bear along behind him. The boys trailed out all their toys. The children always come trailing in dirt. (b) (*follow, with direction*) The Indians trailed him down to the river.

train up   *vt sep*   (*train as fully as possible, educate*) We must train up a new generation of teachers. They want to train up capable people as quickly as possible.

*traipse + particle   *vi*   (*Fam: move gaily or thoughtlessly, with direction*) She enjoys traipsing about. They all traipsed along to the party. They have traipsed off somewhere.

*tramp + particle   *vi*   (*walk heavily and steadily, with direction*) The soldiers tramped along. They tramped about in the garden, spoiling the flower beds. I'm tired of the sound of feet tramping up and down.

tramp down 1 *vi* *see* *tramp.* 2 *vt sep* (*press down with the foot*) He tramped the earth down.

tramp in 1 *vi* *see* *tramp.* 2 *vt sep* (*press in with the foot*) He tramped the stones in.

trample down *vt sep* (*tread down violently or with an effort*) The cows got in and trampled down the standing wheat.

trample in *vt sep* (*tread in violently or with an effort*) All the flowers and fruit canes have been trampled in.

*transfer + particle *vt sep* (*move, with direction*) His offices have been transferred up to the fourth floor. She has been transferred across to the other department.

*travel + particle *vi* (*travel, with direction*) The gypsies just travel along as they please. He travelled up to Iceland. They slowly travelled down towards the coast.

tread down=tramp down 2 *vt sep*.

treasure up *vt sep* (*prize, cherish*) He has treasured up a large collection of valuable coins. I shall treasure up these memories.

treat of *vt fus* (*discuss, cover*) This book treats of Napoleonic history.

*trek + particle *vi* (*travel steadily and purposefully, with direction*) The settlers trekked across to the virgin lands beyond the mountains. Families have been trekking up from the south all this summer. The boys enjoy trekking about, pretending to be explorers.

trick out *vt sep* (*deck, decorate, clothe*) Her mother has tricked her out in a very gay costume. They have tricked themselves out as sailors for the fancy dress party. The boat has been tricked out very brightly.

*trickle + particle *vi* (*flow or move in small slow streams, with direction*) The water has trickled away. The stream trickles down into that hollow. Water is trickling out of the bath.

trifle away *vt sep* (*waste*) She has trifled away all the money she inherited. They just trifle away their time.

trigger off *vt sep* (*release, by means of a trigger*) (*a*) (*Lit*) Someone's foot will trigger off the booby-trap under the floor, when he steps on that board. (*b*) (*Fig*) His action has triggered off a crisis.

trill out *vi* (*sing out, usu of birds*) The birds trilled out in the nearby bushes. She trilled out something about inviting us all in for dinner.

trim away *vt sep* (*cut away neatly*) He has trimmed away all the rough edges on that hedge.

trim down *vt sep* (*reduce in size by cutting neatly*) (*a*) (*Lit*) He trimmed the hedge down. (*b*) (*Fig*) The government has trimmed down its expenditure.

trim off *vt sep* (*remove by cutting neatly*) He has trimmed off all the jagged pieces in the hedge.

trim up *vt sep* (*tidy up by cutting neatly*) He has trimmed up his beard.

*****trip + particle** *vi* (*move lightly and happily, with direction*) She tripped about, collecting flowers. She tripped in and sat down.

trip over 1 *vi* (*fall over by catching one's foot*) She tripped over and landed in a puddle. The running boy tripped over and fell headlong. 2 *vt fus* (*catch one's foot on and fall*) She tripped over a log.

trip up *vi* (*catch the foot while walking*) (*a*) (*Lit*) He tripped up and nearly fell. She tripped up on a stone. (*b*) (*Fig: make a mistake*) He tripped up over that bank account. Be careful you don't trip up in your dealings with those people.

*****troop + particle** *vi* (*move in a group, with direction*) The children got up and trooped out. More people were trooping in all the time. They have all trooped off somewhere.

*****trot + particle** 1 *vi* (*move at the pace of a horse, between walking and cantering, with direction*) The horse trotted along. The horsemen trotted up. The pony trotted away. (*Fig Fam*) I'd better just trot along now. The children will trot in sometime. 2 *vt sep* (*lead at a trot, with direction*) The trainer trotted the horse along. She trotted the ponies out. (*Fig Fam*) I'll trot the children off now.

trot out 1 *vi* *see* *****trot**. 2 *vt sep* (*a*) *see* *****trot**. (*b*) (*Fig Fam: produce*) He trots the same old stories out every time we see him. I expect them to trot out some statistics to support their case.

*****truck + particle** *vt sep* (*transport in a truck or lorry with direction*) They trucked the goods over immediately. You must truck the stuff out by five o'clock at the latest.

*****trudge + particle** *vi* (*walk heavily and slowly, with direction*) The workmen trudged along. He trudged wearily up. I watched them trudge away.

true up *vt sep* (*Carpentry etc: align, bring into line*) The various pieces of wood must be trued up before you begin.

trump up *vt sep* (*produce by faking*) They have trumped up some ridiculous charges against you. This is a trumped-up charge and I refuse to take it seriously.

*****trundle + particle** (*move heavily but steadily, usu on wheels, with direction*) 1 *vi* The tram trundled along. Small wagons were trundling past on the narrow gauge line. 2 *vt sep* They trundled the trolleys in. He trundled one of the patients out on a movable bed.

truss up *vt sep* (*tie up tightly*) They trussed their captives up and left them in a shed. He trussed the chicken's feet up.

try on *vt sep* (*a*) (*put on experimentally*) I'll try this suit on. She tried on the hat. (*b*) (*Fam: attempt*) The policeman warned the man not to try anything on (with him). Don't try it on with us. He knew better than to try anything on. *n* **a try-on**=an attempt worthy of contempt.

try over *vt sep* (*test out*) I'll try the car over for you.

try out *vt sep* (*test by using*) Let us try out this suggestion. They tried out various approaches to the problem, but none worked. *n* **a try-out**=a test.

tuck away *vt sep* (*Fam: consume*) He tucked away a huge breakfast. It's amazing the amount of food she can tuck away.

tuck in *vt sep* (*Fam: start eating*) Right, children, tuck in! He tucked in without waiting to be told. He tucks in with a will. She tucked in to that cake. *n* **a tuck-in**=a feast.

tuck up *vt sep* (*make comfortable or cosy*) She tucked the children up in bed.

*tug + particle *vt sep* (*pull persistently, with direction*) She tugged him along behind her. A man tried to tug me aside. The animal was tugging something out.

*tumble + particle *vi* (*move in a tumble or tangle, with direction*) The children tumbled down for their breakfast. The door opened and they all tumbled in. He opened the cupboard and a lot of old junk tumbled out.

tumble to *vt fus* (*Fam: realize, become aware of*) I have only just tumbled to what these people have been doing. It's time you tumbled to his tricks.

tune in 1 *vi* (*switch on a radio*) Don't forget—tune in again this time tomorrow! We always tune in to that programme. 2 *vt sep* (*Radio: prepare for reception*) He tuned the radio in. The wireless is tuned in.

tune up *vt sep* (*improve the performance of*) The engine needs tuning up.

turf in *vt sep* (*enclose with turf*) This whole space will be turfed in.

turf out *vt sep* (*Sl: eject, expel*) They have decided to turf these people out. He was turfed out (of the club) because he did not pay his debts.

turf over *vt sep* (*cover over with turf*) We intend to turf this space over.

*turn + particle (*turn, with direction*) 1 *vi* The car turned back. The road turns off at the next farmhouse. The path turned down from the hills towards the river. 2 *vt sep* She turned the bedclothes down. He turned his coat collar up because of the wind. He turned back the corner of the page. She turned her head away so that they could not see her tears.

turn away 1 *vi see* ***turn.** 2 *vt sep* (*a*) *see* ***turn.** (*b*) (*reject*) They have turned several people away because they have no more accommodation. It is unfortunate that we have to turn these beggars away.

turn down 1 *vi see* ***turn.** 2 *vt sep* (*a*) *see* ***turn.** (*b*) (*refuse, reject*) The committee has turned down his application. I'm afraid we must turn down your kind offer of help. He was turned down by several publishers. (*c*) (*reduce in quantity or force*) She turned the gas down.

turn in 1 *vi* (*a*) *see* ***turn.** (*b*) (*Fam: go to bed*) We usually turn in about midnight. 2 *vt sep* (*a*) *see* ***turn** (*b*) (*hand over to the police*) Please, don't turn me in! (*c*) (*Sl usu with 'it': stop*) Oh, turn it in, will you!

turn inside out/outside in *vt sep* (*a*) (*Lit: reverse*) He turned his coat inside out. (*b*) (*Fig: search thoroughly*) The detectives turned the place inside out.

turn off 1 *vi see* ***turn.** 2 *vt sep* (*a*) *see* ***turn.** (*b*) (*seal, stop*) She turned the tap off. They turned off the water supply. Turn off the gas, please. (*c*) (*Fig: stop*) They have turned off the supply of arms and ammunition. (*d*) (*Fig Fam: cause to lose interest*) This kind of treatment really turns me off.

turn on 1 *vi see* ***turn.** 2 *vt sep* (*a*) *see* ***turn.** (*b*) (*switch on*) Turn on the water, please. They have turned the supply on. (*c*) (*Fig: start*) They have turned on the supply of arms and ammunition. (*d*) (*Fig Fam: switch on, allow to operate*) He has turned on all his charm. (*e*) (*Sl: affect strongly and favourably*) That music turns me on, man. 2 *vt fus* (*a*) (*Fig: depend on, hinge on*) The whole project turns on one man. The deal turns on a matter of timing. (*b*) (*attack*) He turned on me with a filthy oath. The dog turned on its master.

turn out 1 *vi* (*a*) *see* ***turn.** (*b*) (*assemble*) The people turned out to see him. The soldiers turned out at 7.30 a.m. for muster parade. *n phr* (*i*) **a good turnout**=a good attendance. (*ii*) **a smart turnout**=a tidy appearance, usu in uniform. (*c*) (*transpire, end*) Things have turned out well. It turned out that she had known him for years. 2 *vt sep* (*a*) *see* ***turn.** (*b*) (*switch off*) Turn out the lights when you leave. (*c*) (*produce*) The factory turns out cars. (*d*) (*expel*) They turned him out (of the club).   He has been turned out by his father.   (*e*) (*clean out*) She turned the room out completely.   (*f*) (*release*) They have turned out the horses to grass.   (*g*) (*Mil: call out, summon out*) The duty officer turned out the guard.

turn over   1 *vi*   (*a*) *see* ***turn.**   (*b*) (*become inverted*) The car turned over in the crash.   (*c*) (*idle*) The car engine is turning over nicely.   (*d*) *n* **turnover**=(*i*) production.   *Example:* The factory's turnover has been excellent this year.   (*ii*) change. *Example:* The turnover in staff in this school has been very high in the last few months.   2 *vt sep*   (*a*) *see* ***turn.**   (*b*) (*upset, invert*) They turned the cart over.   (*c*) (*dig over*) The gardener turned over the soil.   (*d*) (*hand over, surrender*) She turned him over to the police.   They have decided to turn the documents over to the authorities.   (*e*) *Idioms:* (*i*) To turn something over in one's mind=to think something over carefully.   (*ii*) To turn over a new leaf=to start afresh, to begin again.

turn to   *vt fus*   (*ask for help*) You can always turn to us.   I have no one to turn to.

turn up   1 *vi*   (*a*) *see* ***turn.**   (*b*) (*arrive, usu casually*) They turned up at midnight with their suitcases.   She will turn up some-time.   (*c*) (*appear, be found*) Oh, that lost paper will turn up somewhere.   These things always turn up eventually, don't worry.   2 *vt sep*   (*a*) *see* ***turn.**   (*b*) (*find*) We have turned up some interesting new information.   (*c*) (*raise in force or strength*) She turned up the gas.   He turned up the oil lamp.   (*d*) (*Sl: make sick*) That kind of thing turns me up.   (*e*) *n* **turn-up**= turned-up bottom of certain kinds of trouser leg.   *n cpd* **trouser turn-ups.**   (*f*) *Fam Idiom:* That's a turn-up for the book= that's a real surprise.

turn upside down   *vt sep*   (*a*) (*Lit: invert*) He turned the box upside down.   (*b*) (*Fig: search thoroughly*) The police have turned the place upside down in the effort to find him.   (*c*) (*reduce to a shambles*) The thieves have really turned this room upside down.

tweak off   *vt sep*   (*pull or snip off, usu between finger and thumb*) He tweaked the bud off.

tweak out   *vt sep*   (*pull or snip out, with fingers or a pair of tweezers*) She tweaked the hairs out one by one.

***twirl + particle**   *vt sep*   (*rotate, with direction*) She twirled her hat about on the end of a stick.   The wind twirled the leaves along.

***twist + particle**   *vt sep*   (*move by twisting, with direction*) He twisted the cork out.   She twisted the top off.   He twisted the screw in with his fingers.

twitch away   1 *vi*   (*make involuntary muscular movements continuously*)

The dying rat was twitching away. A nerve in his face kept twitching away. 2 *vt sep* (*remove by a quick twitch*) She twitched the cloth away.

twitch off=**twitch away** 2 *vt sep.*

twitter away *vi* (*twitter continuously, keep making small noises*) (*a*) (*Lit*) The birds were happily twittering away. (*b*) (*Fig*) She twittered away about her family and friends.

*urge + particle *vt sep* (*encourage to move or do, with direction*) They urged the horses on with whips. The guide urged the tourists out of the cathedral and into the shops.

use out *vt sep* (*a*) (*use until finished*) I intend to use this jacket out before I buy another one. (*b*) (*usu pass: exhausted*) The resources of the area are used out.

use up *vt sep* (*use completely, consume*) I expect to use up quite a lot of paper during the next few months. The supply of coal has been used up, and we need more.

*usher + particle *vt sep* (*guide or escort, with direction*) We were ushered in by a polite orderly. The guards ushered the visitors out when the ceremony was over.

vamp up *vt sep* (*a*) (*Fam: concoct, invent*) He vamped up some ugly stories about them. (*b*) (*improvise*) They vamped up the music.

vanish away *vi* (*vanish or disappear completely*) The colour just vanished away. The men appear to have vanished away.

*vault + particle *vi* (*move in a single leap, with direction*) He vaulted over into the garden and ran to meet her. He looked at the fence, then ran to it and vaulted across.

*veer + particle *vi* (*move rapidly in a curve, with direction*) The little yacht suddenly veered away, caught by a gust of wind. The car veered off to the left.

*venture + particle *vi* (*move tentatively or adventurously, with direction*) She hasn't dared to venture out since the riots. The hero ventured in, in search of the monster. The men ventured forth to meet the new danger.

verge (up)on *vt fus* (*come close to*) This action verges upon aggression. I'm afraid that his behaviour verges on madness.

visit with *vt fus* (*US: visit*) We hope you will visit with us sometime. He went out to visit with some friends.

vomit forth (*Old*)=**vomit out.**

vomit out *vt sep* (*a*) (*Lit: vomit, spew out*) He vomited out the contents of his stomach. (*b*) (*Fig: pour out as if vomiting*) The enemy have begun to vomit out their evil propaganda.

vomit up *vt sep* (*spew up, regurgitate*) He was so sick he vomited up everything he had eaten.

vote down *vt sep* (*defeat by voting against*) The people have voted him down. Parliament voted down the proposals.

vote in *vt sep* (*elect by vote*) The people have voted in a new government. They voted him in as president.

vote out *vt sep* (*reject through voting*) The people have voted out the old government. They voted him out by a majority of 15.

vote through *vt sep* (*pass by voting*) The assembly has voted the new reforms through.

vouch for *vt fus* (*provide attestation for, guarantee*) I can vouch for his integrity. He asked me to vouch for him, so that he could get the job. I wouldn't like to vouch for the truth of his story.

*voyage + particle *vi* (*travel for a long time, usually by sea, with direction*) The ship voyaged on into unknown seas. The explorers voyaged down the coast to West Africa.

wad up *vt sep* (*form into a wad or pad*) He wadded up the paper into a ball. She wadded up her handkerchief nervously.

*waddle + particle *vi* (*walk like a duck, with direction*) The ducks waddled up. The rotund gentleman waddled over and introduced himself. They waddled about, looking at the sights.

*wade + particle *vi* (*walk in shallow water, with direction*) The men waded about in the stream. He waded in as we waded out. He waded back to the riverbank.

wade in 1 *vi* (*a*) *see* ***wade**. (*b*) (*Sl: join in a fight*) The soldiers and sailors waded in.

wade through *vt fus* (*Fig Fam: work steadily and slowly through*) He waded through a lot of work last night. This is a lot to wade through.

*waft + particle 1 *vi* (*move gently on the wind, with direction*) The scents wafted past. A beautiful odour wafted up from below. A delicious smell wafted out from the kitchen. 2 *vt sep* (*carry gently, with direction*) The wind wafted the boat along. The breeze wafted the scents back to us.

wag about/around 1 *vi* (*shake about*) The long poles were wagging about in the breeze. 2 *vt sep* (*wave about in an unsteady manner*) The children were wagging flags about.

wait about/around *vi* (*wait rather aimlessly*) They waited about for another bus, but none came. The people seemed to be waiting about for something to happen.

wait behind *vi* (*remain behind*) She said she would wait behind for them

wait in   *vi*   (*stay in a place*) She will wait in till you telephone.

wait on   1 *vi*   (*remain waiting*) They waited on at the scene of the accident until an ambulance arrived.   2 *vt fus*   (*serve at a meal*) He waited on us at dinner.   *Idiom:* To wait on someone hand and foot=to serve someone in every possible way, to be someone's slave.

wait out   1 *vi*   (*remain outside*) Please don't wait out in the rain.   2 *vt sep*   (*defeat by waiting*) We shall wait the enemy out, and watch them starve.

wait up   *vi*   (*Fam: remain out of bed*) I'll wait up till midnight. Please don't wait up for me.

wait upon=**wait on**   2 *vt fus*

wake up   1 *vi*   (*a*) (*waken*) He woke up at seven o'clock.   Don't wake the children up.   (*b*) (*Fig Fam: realize what is happening*) I wish you would wake up!   He woke up too late to his predicament.   2 *vt sep*   (*Fig Fam: make realize what is happening*) I wish I could wake them up to the danger they are in.

*walk + particle   (*walk, with direction*)   1 *vi*   The man walked back and forward.   I opened the door and he walked in. They walked away.   She walked out into the garden.   2 *vt sep* He walked the dog around for ten minutes.   They walked the prisoners over.   He walked the horse along.   He walked his girl-friend back to her flat.

walk off   1 *vi*   *see* ***walk**.   2 *vt sep*   (*a*) *see* ***walk**.   (*b*) (*reduce by energetic walking*) We tried to walk off the effects of the heavy meal.

walk off with   *vt fus*   (*a*) (*Sl: steal*) He walked off with several watches.   (*b*) (*win easily*) She walked off with all the prizes. (*c*) *Idiom:* Don't walk off with the idea that (I like them)=don't assume so easily that (I like them).

walk on   *vi*   (*a*) *see* ***walk**.   (*b*) (*continue to walk*) The man walked on until nightfall.   (*c*) (*Theatre: enter the play*) The leading actor now walked on.   *n cpd*   **a walking-on part**   (*in a play*)

walk out   1 *vi*   (*a*) *see* ***walk**.   (*b*) (*Industry: strike*) The men walked out.   *n* **a walkout**.   (*c*) (*Old Euph: court*) Mary and John are walking out together.

walk out on   *vt fus*   (*Fig Fam: abandon*) You can't just walk out on us like this.   They just walked out on the deal.   Don't walk out on me!

wall in   *vt sep*   (*enclose with a wall*) The garden has been walled in.

wall round   *vl sep*   (*enclose or encircle with a wall*) They walled the estate round.

wall off *vt sep* *(mark or delimit with a wall)* The garden has been walled off from its neighbours.

wall up *vt sep* *(seal with a wall)* The entrance has been walled up.

***wallop + particle** 1 *vi* *(Sl: move quickly but heavily, with direction)* The old truck walloped along.   The car was walloping about dangerously. 2 *vt sep* *(strike violently, with direction)* The cricketer walloped the ball away to the boundary.   He walloped it out.

wallow about/around *vi* *(wade about heavily)* The hippopotamus wallowed about in the mud.   They love wallowing about in the baths.

***waltz + particle** *(move in, or as if in, a waltz, with direction)* 1 *vi* She took no notice of my protests but just waltzed off. They waltzed in, laughing.   I watched them waltz away. 2 *vt sep* He waltzed her across.   He was waltzing her out into the garden.

***wander + particle** *vi* *(wander, roam with direction)* The tribe wandered off into the hills.   The boys wandered away among the trees.   She wandered in, looking rather lost.   Some refugees are still wandering about in the area.

***wangle + particle** *vt sep* *(Fam: contrive, with direction)* I'm sure you can wangle the information out of him.   He wangled the visitors in for a whole hour.   They said they would wangle the business through to a successful conclusion.

warble away *vi* *(warble or sing continuously, usu of birds)* The thrush warbled away on a branch.

warble out *vt sep* *(a)* *(Lit: sing out)* The birds warbled out happily. *(b)* *(Fig Fam: shout out)* She warbled out something about having a party.

ward off *vt sep* *(deflect)* *(a)* *(Lit)* He warded off the blow with a raised arm. *(b)* *(Fig)* The general warded off the enemy attack as best he could.   This amulet is said to ward off evil spirits.

warm up 1 *vi* *(a)* *(Lit: get or become warm)* The food has warmed up. *(b)* *(Fig: become livelier)* The party has begun to warm up. 2 *vt sep* *(a)* *(Lit: heat)* She warmed up the food. *(b)* *(Fig: enliven)* They warmed up the party. *(c)* *(Lit: re-heat)* She warmed up the leftovers of last night's dinner. *(d)* *(Fig: refurbish)* They have just warmed up the same old plan.   It's a warmed-up version of the old scheme.

warn off *vt sep* *(threaten; tell to keep away)* When we tried to enter the place, some men warned us off.   He warns everybody off who tries to be friendly with his girl-friend.

wash away 1 *vi* (*wash continuously*) That machine washes away
without you having to do anything. 2 *vt sep* (*a*) (*remove by
washing*) She washed away the stains. (*b*) (*Fig: purge*) The
preacher said that the Lord would wash away their sins. (*c*)
(*remove or displace through the action of waves*) The sea has washed
away all trace of the wreck.

wash down 1 *vi* (*come down in streams*) The soil has washed down
into the valley. 2 *vt sep* (*a*) (*clean thoroughly, in a downward
direction*) He washed the car down. (*b*) (*bring down in streams*)
The rains have washed down the mountainsides. Soil has been
washed down into the gully.

wash in 1 *vi* (*come in, in waves*) The tide washed in. 2 *vt sep*
(*bring in by the action of waves*) The tide washed the bodies in.

wash off 1 *vi* (*vanish through washing*) These stains should wash
off all right. The dye washed off. 2 *vt sep* (*a*) (*clean off by
washing*) She washed her make-up off. He washed the mud off.
(*b*) (*remove by the action of waves or streams*) The topsoil has been
completely washed off.

wash out 1 *vi*＝**wash off**. 2 *vt sep* (*a*) (*remove by washing*) They
washed all the stains out. (*b*) (*clean thoroughly by washing*) She
washed the hall out. (*c*) (*Lit: spoil by the action of rain etc*) The
rain has washed the game out. Bad weather has washed out
our hopes of winning. (*d*) (*Fig: spoil thoroughly*) This trouble
washed out any hope of getting a holiday this year. His plans
have been washed out. *Idiomatic n* **a washout**＝a complete
failure. (*e*) *Idiom:* to look (really) washed-out＝to look really
ill, exhausted.

wash up 1 *vi* (*a*) (*Brit: clean the dishes after a meal*) Let's wash up
now. (*b*) (*US: have a wash*) She washed up before lunch.
2 *vt sep* (*a*) (*Brit: clean*) Let's wash up the tea things. *n* **the
washing-up.** (*b*) (*Fam usu pass: exhausted, finished*) I feel all
washed up. (*c*) (*spoil, finish*) It's all washed up anyway.
They're all washed up now, whatever happens.

waste away *vi* (*grow weak, decline*) He's just wasting away, and
the doctors seem unable to help him.

watch out *vi* (*a*) (*observe, watch carefully*) The scouts were watching
out for enemy patrols. (*b*) (*take care*) I hope you will watch out.

water down *vt sep* (*a*) (*Lit: thin or dilute with water*) The whisky
has been watered down. (*b*) (*Fig: dilute*) You have watered
down your argument considerably since we last met. This
story is a rather watered-down version of the one I heard in
London.

*wave + particle *vt sep* (*cause to move by waving, with direction*)
He waved the waiter away. She waved us over to meet her

friends. She waved the children out (of the house).

wear away 1 *vi* (*a*) (*Lit: erode*) The inscriptions on the stones have worn away. (*b*) (*Fig*) My patience has worn away. 2 *vt sep* (*reduce by rubbing, erode*) (*a*) (*Lit*) Water has worn the banks away. The steps have been worn away by many feet. (*b*) (*Fig*) My patience has long since been worn away.

wear down 1 *vi* (*erode*) The stone has worn down. 2 *vt sep* (*rub down or erode*) (*a*) (*Lit*) Wind and rain have worn the monument down. (*b*) (*Fig*) Inaction has worn down his resolution. His strength has been worn down by illness. (*c*) (*Fig: reduce by attrition*) The general has decided to wear down the enemy's strength by a long slow campaign.

wear off *vi* (*lose power*) The effects of the medicine have worn off. The novelty has worn off (=something new has lost its special attraction).

wear on *vi* (*a*) (*pass*) The day wore on. Time wore on. (*b*) (*continue*) The discussion wore on interminably. The battle wore on through the night.

wear out 1 *vi* (*become useless*) (*a*) (*Lit*) The machinery has worn out. This material wears out quickly. (*b*) (*Fig*) His enthusiasm has worn out. 2 *vt sep* (*a*) (*wear until no longer useful*) He has worn out several suits. Most of their clothes are worn out. (*b*) (*render defunct*) They have worn that horse out. He has worn the machine out. (*c*) (*Fig: tire out exhaust,*) This situation has worn him out. She felt quite worn out after a day's shopping. *adj* **wornout**=exhausted, finished.

wear through *vt sep*=**wear out** 2 *vt sep* (*a*).

weather through *vi* (*Fam: manage along somehow; survive*) Oh, we'll weather through.

*weave + particle *vi* (*move with a winding motion, with direction*) The boys were weaving in and out among the trees. Snakes weave along. *Idiom:* To weave one's way along=to progress.

wedge in *vt sep* (*hold in with a wedge*) (*a*) (*Lit*) They wedged the post in. The plank was wedged in with a bar. (*b*) (*Fig*) The man wedged us in, and we couldn't get past him. My car was completely wedged in.

weed out *vt sep* (*Fig: remove, as if weeds*) I want you to weed out the trouble-makers. The exam helps to weed out unsatisfactory candidates.

weigh down *vt sep* (*press down*) (*a*) (*Lit*) They weighed the box down with stones and dropped it into the sea. (*b*) (*Fig*) She is weighed down with grief over her father's death.

weigh in *vi* (*a*) (*Boxing: be weighed as part of the preparation for a* *fight*) The boxers weighed in. (*b*) (*Fam: join in vigorously*) He weighed in with a strong argument against the policy.

weigh out *vt sep* (*measure out by weight*) He weighed out three kilos of sugar.

weight down *vt sep* (*hold down with a weight*) They weighted the canvas down with bricks.

welcome back *vt sep* (*welcome home, or back to a particular place*) Although he had left in anger, we all welcomed him back. The travellers were welcomed back with joy by their fellow villagers.

welcome in *vt sep* (*give hospitality to*) The farmer welcomed the people in.

well out *vi* (*rise and flow out*) Water was welling out of the ground. Blood began to well out (of the wound).

well up *vi* (*flow up*) Oil welled up out of the ground. Tears welled up in her eyes. The floodwaters welled up menacingly.

wet through *vt sep* (*wet completely*) The rain has wet us through. He's wet through.

wheedle out *vt sep* (*obtain by wheedling or teasing*) She wheedled the information out of him. You won't wheedle any more money out of me.

*wheel + particle *vt sep* (*move on wheels, with direction*) The men wheeled the aeroplane out. The patient was wheeled in and the surgeon prepared to operate. They wheeled the food away on a trolley. The crippled man wheeled himself along.

wheel about/around 1 *vi* (*turn in wide circles*) The aeroplanes were wheeling about in the sky. The hawks wheeled around overhead. 2 *vt sep* *see* ***wheel.**

wheeze out *vt sep* (*say in a wheezing voice*) The dying man wheezed out someone's name.

while away *vt sep* (*pass aimlessly*) I'll while away the time somehow, till you come back.

whine out 1 *vi* (*speak out in a whining manner*) The frightened man whined out in panic. 2 *vt sep* (*cry out in a whining manner*) He whined out something about not wanting to be left alone.

whip round *vi* (*a*) (*turn round suddenly*) He whipped round when he heard the noise. (*b*) (*Fam: make a shared contribution*) The men whipped round (among themselves) to give the guide a tip. *Idiom:* To have a **whip-round** = to collect money for a tip or a present.

whip in 1 *vi* (*Fam: move in suddenly or quickly*) He opened the door and the cat whipped in. 2 *vt sep* (*a*) (*Lit: bring in by whipping*) The overseer whipped the slaves in. (*b*) (*Fig: compel to attend* *or to perform in some way*) The party bosses whipped their followers in for the big vote. *n* a **whipper-in**=someone who whips people in to vote or take part.

whip up 1 *vi* (*Fam: go up suddenly or quickly*) He whipped up to his bedroom to put on a clean shirt. 2 *vt sep* (*a*) (*urge on with a whip*) The rider whipped up his horse. (*b*) (*Fig: stir violently*) The speakers whipped up the emotions of the crowd. (*c*) (*mix by whipping or rapid stirring*) She whipped up the eggs.

*whirl + particle (*move in whirls or circles, with direction*) 1 *vi* The leaves whirled about in the air. She whirled along to the party. Sand was whirling up from the windswept plains. 2 *vt sep* (*a*) (*Lit*) The wind whirled the leaves about. Strong gusts of wind were whirling the sand up from the barren plains. (*b*) (*Fig*) He whirled her off to the party. They whirled me away in their big car.

*whisk + particle *vt sep* (*move or lift lightly, with direction*) A light breeze whisked the papers away. He whisked us off to see the play. We were whisked out to sea in a fast launch.

*whistle + particle *vt sep* (*move or summon by whistling, with direction*) He whistled up the dogs. The policeman whistled his colleagues over to see what he had found.

whistle up *vt sep* (*a*) see ***whistle.** (*b*) (*Fam: make quickly*) She whistled up an excellent snack for us all. (*c*) (*Mil: summon quickly*) The general whistled up reinforcements. He tried to whistle up some help.

whittle away *vt sep* (*reduce gradually by cutting*) (*a*) (*Lit*) He whittled the wood away. (*b*) (*Fig*) They are slowly whittling away our power.

whittle down=**whittle away.**

*whizz + particle *vi* (*Fam: move quickly, with direction*) The fast car just whizzed along. He whizzed past on his new motorbike. The aeroplanes whizzed away. The boys whizzed out to play.

whoop up *vt sep* (*Sl usu with 'it': have parties, get drunk etc*) They enjoy whooping it up.

*whoosh + particle *vi* (*move with a whooshing or rushing noise, with direction*) The train whooshed past. The waves came whooshing up to where we stood. The churning waters whooshed in and out.

widen out 1 *vi* (*become wide*) The peninsula widens out at this point. 2 *vt sep* (*intensive of* **widen**) They have widened out the shop. The design has been considerably widened out. The general wants to widen out the campaign.

*wiggle + particle *vi* (*move with wriggling actions, with direction*)

The worms were wiggling about. She wiggled up to us.

will away *vt sep* (*give away in a will and testament*) He has willed away the whole estate to strangers. She willed the money away to a home for dogs and cats.

win back *vt sep* (*regain*) He has won back their favour. She has managed to win him back. The team has won back the trophy.

win out *vi* (*win in the end, finally triumph*) Good will win out. They will win out in the long run.

win over *vt sep* (*convert, bring over to one's own side*) They have won over a number of opponents. He wins over souls for God. She has won him over completely.

win through *vi* (*survive, reach the end successfully*) The candidates all won through. The soldiers have won through.

*wind + particle 1 *vi* (*twist or meander, with direction*) The river wound along. The road winds about for miles. An old path wound up through the hills. 2 *vt sep* (*turn on a reel, with direction*) The fisherman wound in his line. The engineers wound out more and more cable. The electrician wound the wires off.

wind down 1 *vi* (*a*) *see* ***wind.** (*b*) (*become slack*) The watch wound down and stopped. (*c*) (*come to an end slowly*) The proceedings began to wind down. (*d*) (*relax*) I felt tense, but now I'm beginning to wind down a bit. 2 *vt sep* *see* ***wind.**

wind up 1 *vi* (*a*) *see* ***wind.** (*b*) (*end, finish*) The business has wound up. You will wind up in hospital if you aren't more careful. 2 *vt sep* (*a*) *see* ***wind.** (*b*) (*make the spring tight in*) He wound up his watch. He wound up the toy car. (*c*) (*Fig Fam: brief, get ready*) He knows what to do, so all we have to do is wind him up and let him go. (*d*) (*Fig usu pass: excited*) She's all wound up. (*e*) (*close, bring to an end*) He wound up the meeting. He must wind up his affairs soon. She decided to wind up her account with that bank.

wink at *vt fus* (*overlook, ignore, condone*) I would like you to wink at their activities. Can't you wink at what they are doing? Do you expect me just to wink at something like this?

wipe away *vt sep* (*clear away by wiping*) He wiped away the grease from the windscreen of the car. She wiped away her tears.

wipe down *vt sep* (*clean down by wiping*) She wiped the car down. He wiped the windows down.

wipe off *vt sep* (*remove by wiping*) She wiped the dirty marks off.

wipe out *vt sep* (*a*) (*obliterate*) He wiped out the names on the board. (*b*) (*kill*) Thousands of men were wiped out in that battle.

wipe up *vt sep* (*clear up by wiping*) Who is going to wipe up this mess?

wire in *vt sep* (a) (*enclose with a wire fence*) The chickens are safely wired in. (b) (*Elec: connect to a circuit*) We have been wired in to the main system now.

wire up *vt sep* (a) (*Elec: connect up by means of wires*) The area has now been wired up (to the mains). (b) (*Elec: fit with all necessary wiring*) The house has now been wired up.

wither away *vi* (*decline, fade or die*) (a) (*Lit*) The flowers have all withered away. (b) (*Fig*) Her hopes withered away long ago.

wither up *vi* (*wither completely*) The plants have all withered up because of the drought.

*****wobble + particle** *vi* (*move unsteadily, with direction*) The spinning top wobbled about on the floor. The drunk man wobbled out. After his fainting spell, he wobbled in and sat down.

wolf down *vt sep* (*swallow down hungrily like a wolf*) He wolfed his food down.

work away *vi* (*work continuously*) He works away in his own room.

work in 1 *vi* (*co-operate, collaborate*) She works in with them as much as possible. 2 *vt sep* (*include*) When he wrote his essay, he worked in several quotations. She always works in some reference to her father's money.

work off 1 *vi* (*become detached or separated*) The nut has worked off. 2 *vt sep* (*discharge by working*) He has worked off all his debts. He went into the garden and worked off his bad temper on the potato patch.

work on 1 *vi* (*continue to work*) They worked on into the night. 2 *vt sep* (*fix on by gentle steady action*) He managed to work the screw on. 3 *vt fus* (a) (*be engaged in*) He is working on a new book. The child was working on a jigsaw puzzle. (b) (*Fam: seek to influence by constant attention*) If I work on him, he may decide to help you. I'll have to work on her!

work out 1 *vi* (*come right, succeed*) The plan worked out. The crossword puzzle does work out after all. 2 *vt sep* (a) (*solve*) I can't work this puzzle out. He worked out all the equations. (b) (*find by performing the proper actions*) He worked out all the answers. I just can't work out on the map where we are. (c) (*exhaust through exploitation*) The old mine is completely worked out. They worked out that seam long ago.

work out at *vt fus* (*amount to*) The bill works out at £20 each. What does that work out at?

work up *vt sep* (a) (*move up by stages*) The engineers worked the equipment up slowly. (*b*) (*develop*) He has worked the firm up from almost nothing. (*c*) (*cause, stir up*) They are trying to work up a rebellion in the provinces. (*d*) (*stimulate*) He went out for a walk to work up an appetite. I wish I could work up some enthusiasm. (*e*) (*make overwrought, nervous, excited*) Please don't work yourself up about this. I feel all worked up.

work up to *vt fus* (*a*) (*reach*) The story works up to a splendid climax. (*b*) *Fam: prepare to say*) What is he working up to?

worm in (*get in, by wriggling like a worm*) 1 *vi* (*a*) (*Lit*) The soldiers wormed in under the wire. (*b*) (*Fig*) We must be careful not to let spies worm in. 2 *vt sep* (*a*) (*Lit*) He wormed his way in under the wire. (*b*) (*Fig*) They have wormed themselves in to his affections.

worm out 1 *vi* (*wriggle out like a worm*) (*a*) (*Lit*) The prisoners wormed out through a hole in the fence. (*b*) (*Fig*) He has managed to worm out of his responsibilities again. 2 *vt sep* (*elicit by cunning or patience*) They have wormed all the information out of him. I'll worm it out of her.

worry out *vt sep* (*a*) (*work out with patience and effort*) We shall worry out the answer eventually. (*b*) (*obtain by worrying or distressing*) They intend to worry the money out of you.

wrap up 1 *vi* (*a*) (*wear warm clothes*) Make sure you wrap up in this cold wind. (*b*) (*Sl: shut up, be quiet*) I wish he would wrap up. Why don't you wrap up? Oh, wrap up! 2 *vt sep* (*a*) (*wrap completely, cover*) He wrapped up the parcel. They wrapped the child up snugly. (*b*) (*Fig Fam: seal, finalize*) They wrapped up the agreement on Friday. The whole thing has been wrapped up. He thinks he's got it all wrapped up. (*c*) (*Fig Fam usu pass: engrossed, absorbed*) He is wrapped up in that book. She is completely wrapped up in that fellow.

*wrench + particle *vt sep* (*pull violently or with some effort, with direction*) The door had been wrenched out by the hinges. The car door had been wrenched off. Much of the superstructure of the ship had been wrenched away in the storm.

wrest away *vt sep* (*pull away forcibly, usu Fig*) Power has been wrested away from the imperialists.

wrest off *vt sep* (*Old: pull off violently*) The arms of the statue had been wrested off.

wrestle about/around *vi* (*wrestle in an area*) The boys were wrestling about on the lawn.

*wriggle + particle *vi* (*wriggle, twist with direction*) The snake wriggled away. A wormlike creature was wriggling along.

wriggle out *vi* (*a*) *see* ***wriggle.** (*b*) (*escape*) He is frightened and wants to wriggle out before he gets caught.

wriggle out of *vt fus* (*escape, dodge*) They want to wriggle out of their responsibilities. You can't wriggle out of this so easily.

wring out *vt sep* (*wring as fully as possible*) (*a*) (*Lit*) She wrung out her swimsuit and hung it to dry. (*b*) (*Fig*) They hope to wring the truth out of him. She wrung a promise out of him. They may manage to wring some money out of the old man. (*c*) (*usu pass: wilted, prostrated*) I feel wrung out with anxiety.

wrinkle up (*wrinkle or crease completely*) 1 *vi* Her face wrinkled up and she began to weep. 2 *vt sep* The material is all wrinkled up.

write away *vi* (*write to a special address*) He wrote away for some catalogues. She wrote away for more information.

write back *vi* (*reply by letter*) The company wrote back, denying responsibility for the accident.

write down *vt sep* (*a*) (*commit to paper*) He wrote his ideas down in order to clarify them. She wrote the information down. (*b*) (*Fig Fam: classify*) They seem to have written him down as a fool.

write in 1 *vi* (*write to a special address, usu opp. to* **write away**) Many people have written in to us asking for samples. She wrote in as requested. 2 *vt sep* (*insert in a text*) He wrote in an extra piece at the editor's request.

write off 1 *vi*=**write away**. 2 *vt sep* (*a*) (*write quickly*) She wrote the letter off on the spur of the moment. He wrote off three letters in ten minutes. (*b*) (*clear from the records*) The debt has been written off. They wrote off $10 million. (*c*) (*Fig Fam: reckon*) He has been written off as a failure. They wrote all the passengers off as dead. (*d*) (*Fam: reject as beyond repair*) They wrote the car off. The insurance company has written it off. *n* (*phr*) **a (complete) write-off**=a (total) wreck. (*e*) (*destroy*) He wrote off three cars in a year because of his dreadful driving.

write out *vt sep* (*a*) (*write in full*) He wrote out his notes. The teacher asked her to write the whole thing out. (*b*) (*prepare in writing*) The doctor wrote out a prescription for the medicine. He wrote out a testimonial for me. She wrote out a cheque for £50.

write up *vt sep* (*a*) (*write as fully as possible*) He wrote up his notes. She wrote up the story of the young lovers. He wrote up his diary. (*b*) (*describe, review*) He wrote the play up in the next edition of the paper. *n* **a write-up**. *n phr* **a bad write-up** =a bad review.

*writhe + particle *vi* (*move with thrashing actions, with direction*) The injured snake writhed along. The poisoned cat writhed about on the floor.

*yank + particle *vt sep* (*pull violently or with a sudden effort, with direction*) The dentist yanked his tooth out. The men yanked him in from the street. The police yanked the offenders off to the police station.

yap away *vi* (*yap or bark continuously in snappish manner*) (*a*) (*Lit*) The little dog yapped away at us through the fence. (*b*) (*Fig Pej*) She was yapping away about her new clothes.

yarn away *vi* (*yarn or tell stories continuously*) The men yarned away happily in the bar of the hotel.

yell out 1 *vi* (*shout loudly*) The man yelled out in pain. 2 *vt sep* (*shout loudly*) The captain yelled out his commands.

yield up *vt sep* (*yield or surrender completely*) They have yielded up the bulk of their supplies to the enemy.

yoke together *vt sep* (*put together under the same yoke*) (*a*) (*Lit*) The oxen were yoked together. (*b*) (*Fig*) We didn't expect to be yoked together in the same office.

yoke up *vt sep* (*put into harness or under a yoke*) The oxen were yoked up.

zero in *vi* (*come in on the centre or zero of a target*) The bombers zeroed in (on the enemy positions).

*zip + particle *vi* (*Fam: move very quickly, with direction*) The little car zipped along. When the gates opened they zipped through. The little boy zipped out when the door was left open.

zip on 1 *vi* (*a*) see ***zip.** (*b*) (*fit into place with a zip fastener*) The dress zips on. 2 *vt sep* (*fit on by pulling a zip fastener*) She zipped the dress on.

zip up 1 *vi* (*a*) see ***zip.** (*b*) (*close with a zip fastener*) The dress zips up. 2 *vt sep* (*fit into position by pulling up a zip fastener*) She zipped up her dress.

*zoom + particle *vi* (*move in a long sweep, with direction*) The aeroplane zoomed down. The sports car was zooming along beautifully. They zoomed off in their new car. The TV camera zoomed in for a close-up of the lovers.